Fundamentals of Research in Criminology and Criminal Justice

Fundamentals of Research in Criminology and Criminal Justice

Ronet Bachman
University of Delaware

Russell K. Schutt
University of Massachusetts, Boston

Los Angeles • London • New Delhi • Singapore

For information:

Sage Publications, Inc.
2455 Teller Road
Thousand Oaks, California 91320
E-mail: order@sagepub.com

Sage Publications India Pvt. Ltd.
B 1/I 1 Mohan Cooperative Industrial Area
Mathura Road, New Delhi 110 044
India

Sage Publications Ltd.
1 Oliver's Yard
55 City Road
London EC1Y 1SP
United Kingdom

Sage Publications Asia-Pacific Pte. Ltd.
33 Pekin Street #02–01
Far East Square
Singapore 048763

Printed in the United States of America.

Library of Congress Cataloging-in-Publication Data

Bachman, Ronet.
Fundamentals of research in criminology and criminal justice / Ronet Bachman, Russell K. Schutt.
    p. cm.
Includes bibliographical references and index.
ISBN 978-1-4129-6052-6 (pbk. : alk. paper)
    1. Criminology—Research. 2. Criminal justice, Administration of—Research.
I. Schutt, Russell K. II. Title.

HV6024.5.B32 2008
364.072—dc22   2007037956

This book is printed on acid-free paper.

09 10 11 12   10 9 8 7 6 5 4 3 2

Acquisitions Editor:	Jerry Westby
Associate Editor:	Elise Smith
Editorial Assistant:	Eve Oettinger
Production Editor:	Karen Wiley
Copy Editor:	Susan Jarvis
Typesetter:	C&M Digitals (P) Ltd.
Proofreader:	Tracy Marcynzsyn
Indexer:	Gloria Tierney
Cover Designer:	Gail Buschman
Marketing Manager:	Jennifer Reed Banando

Brief Contents

Student Study Site

The companion Student Study Website for *The Fundamentals of Research in Criminology and Criminal Justice* can be found at www.sagepub.com/frccjstudy.

Visit the Student Study Site to enhance your understanding of the chapter content and to discover additional resources that will take your learning one step further. You can enhance your understanding of the chapters by using the comprehensive study material, which includes interactive exercises, e-flashcards, web exercises, practice self-tests, and more. You will also find special features, such as Learning from Journal Articles, which incorporates SAGE's online journal collection.

Detailed Contents

4 Sampling   81

10 Quantitative Data Analysis   271

About the Authors

Ronet Bachman, Ph.D., is Professor and Chair of the Department of Sociology and Criminal Justice at the University of Delaware. She is coauthor of *Statistical Methods for Crime and Criminal Justice,* 2nd ed., and coeditor of *Explaining Crime and Criminology: Essays in Contemporary Criminal Theory.* In addition, she is author of *Death and Violence on the Reservation;* coauthor of *Stress, Culture, and Aggression in the United States;* coauthor of *Murder American Style;* and coauthor of *Violence: The Enduring Problem* as well as numerous articles and papers that examine the epidemiology and etiology of violence, with a particular emphasis on women, the elderly, and minority populations.

Russell K. Schutt, Ph.D., is Professor of Sociology at the University of Massachusetts, Boston, and Lecturer in Sociology in the Department of Psychiatry (Beth Israel-Deaconess Medical Center) at the Harvard Medical School. In addition to *Investigating the Social World: The Process and Practice of Research,* now in its 5th edition, *Making Sense of the Social World,* now in its 2nd edition (with Dan Chambliss), and a specialized version for the field of social work (with Ray Engel), he is the author of *Organization in a Changing Environment,* coeditor of *The Organizational Response to Social Problems,* and coauthor of *Responding to the Homeless: Policy and Practice.* He has authored and coauthored numerous journal articles, book chapters, and research reports on homelessness, service preferences and satisfaction, mental health organizations, law, and teaching research methods.

Preface

If you are looking for a comprehensive yet accessible introduction to research methods, this is the book for you. After years of teaching courses in research methods, we have found that the best forum for learning is to link the teaching of key topics to contemporary research in the discipline. We have avoided the "recipe book" approach to research methods by combining discussions of research techniques along with practical research examples from the field. In this way, students not only learn how to conduct research, they also learn why it is important to do so. In *Fundamentals of Research in Criminology and Criminal Justice,* we have retained our unique method of "instruction by example" that is used in our more comprehensive text, *The Practice of Research in Criminology and Criminal Justice.* We believe this approach not only increases students' understanding of complex research methods, but also conveys to students the vital role that research plays in our discipline.

The purpose of this book is to introduce students to the basics of scientific methods of research and show how they are actually used. Each chapter in this book combines instruction in research methods with investigations of key research questions in our field: What are the causes of violent crime? What is the best police response to intimate partner violence? How do gang members perceive their world? Are boot camps effective in reducing recidivism? Do community police officers perceive their roles as different from regular patrol officers? These and many other research questions are explored through the text in tandem with a discussion of research methods. These substantive examples will help you see how research methods are used in practice.

By the end of the course, students will not only have the ability to conduct research, but will also be more adept consumers of knowledge claims about "truth" that bombard us on a daily basis. We are careful to describe the benefits and liabilities of each major approach to research and emphasize why employing a combination of them is often preferable to a single-method approach. Students will come to appreciate why the results of particular research studies must always be interpreted within the context of prior research and through the lens of social and criminological theory. Extensive exercises are provided at the end of each chapter that allow students to engage in different research tasks both individually and within groups.

ORGANIZATION OF THE BOOK

The way this book is organized reflects our beliefs in making research methods interesting, teaching students how to think critically about research, and viewing specific research techniques as parts of an integrated research strategy. Our concern with ethical issues in all types of research is underscored by the fact that we have a section on "Ethics" in every methodology chapter as well as exercises titled "Making Research Ethical" at the end of every chapter. The first two chapters introduce the why and how of research in general. Chapter 1 shows how research has helped us understand the magnitude of and the factors related to youth violence. Chapter 2 illustrates the basic stages of research with a series of experiments on the police response to intimate partner violence. Chapters 3 and 4 discuss how to evaluate the way researchers design their measures and draw their samples. Chapter 5 explores issues related to making causal connections and introduces experimental and quasi-experimental designs.

Chapter 6 presents survey research with illustrations from victimization surveys in the field. Chapter 7 focuses on qualitative methods and qualitative data analysis (including participant observation, intensive interviews, and focus groups) and uses several innovative qualitative studies from the field including studies of gangs and community policing. With illustrations from several different research projects, Chapter 8 examines methodologies that rely on existing content and includes a discussion of secondary data analysis, historical and comparative research, content analysis, and crime mapping, along with a discussion of triangulating methods. Chapter 9 covers policy and evaluation research and highlights the different alternatives to evaluation, along with a discussion of the most appropriate methods to use for each evaluation question (e.g., process versus impact). In this chapter, you will see how various methods have been used to investigate the effects of several programs and policies, including problem-oriented policing and boot camps.

Chapter 10 presents the basic statistical methods used to analyze the results of quantitative studies in a descriptive manner. We work through an analysis of survey data on self-reported delinquency to see how these statistics are used to answer actual research questions. Chapter 11 provides an overview of the main types of written reports used in criminology and criminal justice. You will learn the required sections of a research proposal and a research article along with the peer review process that accompanies such endeavors.

The substantive studies in each of these chapters show how each methodology has been used to improve our understanding of criminal justice–related issues, including the factors related to violence, how question wording affects estimates of victimization in surveys, how gang members perceive their world, how community police officers describe their role in comparison to regular patrol officers, the perceptions of jurors who have participated in a death penalty case, crime mapping in cities, the effects of war on violence in a cross-national comparison, and the effects of a prison classification system on inmate behavior, to name just a few of the examples provided.

DISTINCTIVE FEATURES OF THE BOOK

The most distinctive feature of this text compared with others in the field is the integration into each chapter of in-depth substantive examples from real criminal justice–related research. Examples from the literature are not simply dropped here and there to keep students' attention. Rather, each chapter presents a particular research method in the context of a substantive research story. As such, this book's success is due in no small measure to the availability in the research literature of so many excellent examples. The following points are additional strengths of this text:

An integrated treatment of qualitative and quantitative methods. Qualitative and quantitative methods are contrasted in Chapter 1, and most other chapters include a special section on combining qualitative and quantitative approaches. The value of multiple methods of investigation is illustrated with examples and procedural discussions in many chapters.

Ethical concerns and ethical decision making. Every step in the research process raises ethical concerns, so ethics should be treated in tandem with the study of specific methods. While you will find ethics introduced in Chapter 2, every chapter reviews the relevant ethical issues in the context of each method of data collection, data analysis, and reporting. End-of-chapter exercises also include a section on "Making Research Ethical," which allow students to debate the many ethical dilemmas faced by researchers in the field.

Examples of criminological research as they occur in real-world settings. We include interesting studies taken from the literature on a variety of topics, including the causes and correlates of violates, the efficacy of arrest for intimate partner assault, the perceptions of police officers regarding community policing, and an investigation into the lives of gang members, to name just a few. These real-world research examples illustrate the exigencies and complexities that shape the application of research methods.

End-of-chapter exercises. Several sets of exercises are provided at the end of each chapter: Discussing Research, Finding Research, Critiquing Research, Making Research Ethical, Writing a Research Proposal, and Performing Data Analysis Using SPSS. In addition to individual and group projects, real data sets are provided on the book's website (www.sagepub.com/frccjstudy) to facilitate students' experience in data analysis using SPSS, the statistical software for the social sciences. Data set examples include subsets of the National Crime Victimization Survey (NCVS), and a state-level file containing crime rates and other variables that measure structural characteristics of each state like the poverty rate, the divorce rate, etc.

Aids to effective study. Lists of main points and key terms provide quick summaries at the end of each chapter. In addition, key terms are highlighted in boldface type when first introduced and defined in the text. Definitions for them can also be found in the glossary/index at the end of the book. The instructor's manual includes more exercises that have been specially designed for collaborative group work inside and outside the classroom. Appendix A, "Conducting Literature Reviews and Finding Information," provides up-to-date information about using the internet and provides step-by-step procedures for conducting literature reviews. A case study of a literature review on the deterrence value of arrest in cases of intimate partner assault is used to illustrate guidelines for effective literature searches.

We are excited to introduce our unique approach to learning research methods in this *Fundamentals* book. If we have communicated the excitement of research and the importance of evaluating carefully the methods we use in research, then we have succeeded in representing what social scientists interested in issues related to criminal justice and criminology do. We think it conveys the latest developments in research methodology in a comprehensive yet very accessible manner.

We hope you enjoy learning how to investigate research questions related to criminal justice and criminology and will perhaps be inspired to do some research of your own along the way. We guarantee that the knowledge you develop about research methods will serve you well throughout your education, in your career, and in your community.

SUPPLEMENTS

Instructor's Resources CD-ROM
Student Study Site: www.sagepub.com/frccjstudy

A NOTE ABOUT USING SPSS AND HYPERRESEARCH

To carry out the SPSS exercises at the end of each chapter and in Appendix D, you must have SPSS installed on your computer. The student study site includes several subsets of data, including data from the National Crime Victimization Survey and the Uniform Crime Reports. Appendix D on the study site will also get you up and running with SPSS for Windows; you can then spend as much time as you like exploring the data sets provided, or even use your own data. You can also carry out analyses of the General Social Survey (GSS) at the University of California Berkeley website: http://sda.berkeley.edu:7502/archive.htm.

Appendix F on the study site contains a detailed discussion of what it is like to do qualitative research with the statistical software package HyperRESEARCH. In this appendix, you will learn how to begin a simple project in HyperRESEARCH by creating and managing data and ideas, coding, linking, modeling, and asking questions about your narrative data.

ACKNOWLEDGMENTS

We must first acknowledge our gratitude to Jerry Westby, whose hard work and guidance on this project are unrivaled. He has been more than an editor; he is an ideas man, a tenacious fact finder, a motivator, a therapist, and most important, a friend. We are also indebted to Karen Wiley for her attention to detail in marshalling the text through production, Melissa Spor for preparing the text for production, and Susan Jarvis for her meticulous copy editing.

Gratitude also goes to all the reviewers of our *Research Methods* books who have helped make this *Fundamentals* version what it is, including Ira Sommers, California State University—Los Angeles; Kristy Holtfreter, Florida State University; Amy Craddock, Indiana State University; James R. Maupin, New Mexico State University; William Wells, Southern

Illinois University—Carbondale; Gennifer Furst, The College of New Jersey; Lori Guevara, Fayetteville State University; Frank Cormier, University of Manitoba; Michael J. DeValve, Fayetteville State University; Brian Colwell, Stanford University; Susan B. Haire, University of Georgia; Lisa Anne Zilney, Montclair State University; and Stephen M. Haas, Marshall University. Reviewers of previous editions included Cathy Couglan, Texas Christian University; Lucy Hochstein, Radford University; Mark Winton, University of Central Florida; Stephen Haas, Marshall University; Hank J. Brightman, Saint Peter's College; Eric Metchick, Salem State College; Kristen Kuehnle, Salem State College; Wilson R. Palacios, University of South Florida; and Phyllis B. Gerstenfeld, California State University-Stanislaus. Andre Rosay also provided an extensive and invaluable review of the first edition of this text. We also thank Lindsay R. Reed and Hanna S. Scott for their diligence and hard work in writing the instructor's manual, Ann Dupuis and Sharlene Hesse-Biber for the appendix on HyperRESEARCH software, Lisa M. Gilman for the appendix on SPSS, and Kathryn Stoeckert as well as Heather Albertson and Peggy Plass for additional interactive exercises.

We continue to be indebted to the many students we have had an opportunity to teach and mentor, at both the undergraduate and graduate levels. In many respects, this book could not have been written without these ongoing reciprocal teaching and learning experiences. You inspire us to become better teachers!

Ronet is indebted to her colleagues in the Department of Sociology and Criminal Justice at the University of Delaware who are unwavering sources of support and inspire her by their exemplary dedication to mentorship, teaching, and the research process. A special thanks to Linda Keen, whose meticulous proofreading allowed her to make the book deadline and confirmed her suspicion that gremlins sneak into a document and place misspelled words in the text even after it was thought to be error-free! Ronet is also indebted to an amazing circle of friends who endured graduate school together and continue to be there for guidance, support, therapy, and laughter: Dianne Carmody, Gerry King, Peggy Plass, and Barbara Wauchope. You are the most amazing women in the world, and I am so blessed to have you in my life. To Alex Alvarez and Michelle Meloy, my other kindred spirits, for their support, guidance, and especially their humor; to my mother, Jan, who remains my hero; and to my father, Ron, for his steadfast critical eye in all matters of life.

And most important, we both wish to thank our spouses, Raymond Paternoster and Elizabeth Schneider Schutt, for their love and support (and editorship!), and our children, John and Julia, for all the remarkable joy they have brought to our lives.

Science, Society, and Criminological Research

In this chapter, you will learn how the methods of social science research go beyond stories in the popular media to help us answer questions like "What are the causes of youth violence?" We will examine the motivations for research using youth violence as a theme. We will also explore the differences between quantitative and qualitative research methods and the philosophies of science behind each. By the chapter's end, you should know what is scientific in criminal justice and criminology and appreciate how the methods of social science can help us understand and answer research questions in this discipline.

WHAT DO WE HAVE IN MIND?

By now the scenario is burned into the minds of the world. On April 16, 2007, Cho Seung Hui killed 32 students, faculty, and staff and left about 30 others injured on the campus of Virginia Tech in Blacksburg, Virginia. Cho was armed with two semiautomatic handguns that he had legally purchased and had a vest-full of ammunitions. As the police were closing in on the scene, he killed himself. The shooting rampage is now the deadliest in U.S. history. Prior to this incident of mass murder, on April 20, 1999, Eric Harris and Dylan Klebold turned Columbine High School, in suburban Colorado, into the scene of the deadliest high school shooting in American history. After killing 12 students and a teacher, the youths apparently shot themselves in the head. In the end, 15 people were left dead and 28 injured. After the bloodbath, police found the school in Littleton littered with bombs and other booby traps. Harris and Klebold were not typical terrorists. They were apparently bright young men who became social outcasts at their school, affiliated with a group known as the Trenchcoat Mafia, whose outward symbols included dark trenchcoats, dark sunglasses, and berets, part of a larger group described as "Goths." But signs of trouble were evident to many before the killings. Harris's web pages were filled with images of fire, skulls, devils, and weapons, and included recipes for and sketches of pipe bombs. The two young men also wrote poetry about death for their English class and made a video about guns for a video class.

Whenever such a tragedy occurs, it causes a media frenzy. Headlines such as "The School Violence Crisis" and "School Crime Epidemic" were plastered across national newspapers and weekly news journals. From a statistical standpoint, these headlines seemed a little late, particularly because the juvenile arrest rate for murder had been declining. In addition, the thousands of other shootings that occurred in less privileged communities during the same time rarely made the national news. For example, there were no such declarations when an 11-year-old boy was shot and killed in Chicago because he had allegedly shorted an 18-year-old on drug money. And where were such declarations the night two teenagers were shot outside a Baltimore nightclub when guns turned an argument into the final solution?

Many factors influence our beliefs about social phenomena, but the media play a large role in how we perceive both problems and solutions. What are your perceptions of violence committed by youth, and how did you acquire such perceptions? What do you believe are the causes of youth violence? Many factors have been blamed for youth violence in American society, including the easy availability of guns, the use of weapons in movies and television, the moral decay of our nation, poor parenting, unaware teachers, school and class size, racial prejudice, teenage alienation, the internet and the World Wide Web, anti-Semitism, rap and rock music, and the Goth culture. When trying to make sense out of the Littleton incident, President Bill Clinton talked about hate, prejudice, community policing, conflict resolution, parental responsibility, and violence in the culture. Charlton Heston, spokesman for the National Rifle Association, blamed the absence of armed security guards in schools, even though one was present in Littleton. Heston also blamed the parents and the school for allowing kids to wear black.

You probably have your own ideas about what factors may be related to violence in general and youth violence in particular. However, the factors you believe are important in explaining a phenomenon may not always be the ones supported by empirical research.

REASONING ABOUT THE SOCIAL WORLD

Case Study: Exploring Youth Violence

The story of just one murderous youth raises many questions. Take a few minutes to read each of the following questions and jot down your answers. Don't ruminate about the questions or worry about your responses. This is not a test; there are no wrong answers.

- How would you describe Eric Harris?
- Why do you think Eric Harris wanted to kill other students?
- Was Eric Harris typical of other murderers under 18 years of age?
- In general, why do people become murderers?
- How have you learned about youth violence?

Now let us consider the possible answers to some of these questions. The information about Eric Harris is somewhat inconsistent (Duggan, Shear, & Fisher 1999). He was the 18-year-old son of middle-class professionals. He had an older brother who attended the University of Colorado. Harris apparently thought of himself as a white supremacist, but he also loved music by antiracist rock bands. On his web page, he quoted from KMFDM, a German rock band whose song "Waste" includes these lyrics: "What I don't say I don't do. What I don't do I don't like. What I don't like I waste." Online, Harris referred to himself as "Darkness."

Do you have enough information now to understand why Eric went on a shooting rampage in his school?

A year before the shootings at Columbine High School, Harris was arrested on a felony count of breaking into a car. A juvenile court put him on probation, required him to perform community service and take criminal justice classes, and sent him to a school counseling program. He was described by one of his probation officers as a "very bright young man who is likely to succeed in life."

Now can you construct an adequate description of Eric Harris? Can you explain the reason for his murderous rampage? Or do you feel you need to know more about Eric Harris, about his friends and the family in which he grew up? And how about his experiences in school and with the criminal justice system? We have attempted to investigate just one person's experiences, and already our investigation is spawning more and more questions.

Questions and Answers

When the questions concern not just one person but many people or general social processes, the possible questions and the alternative answers multiply. For example, consider the question of why incidents of school violence occur. Responses to a 1997 survey of mothers with children between the ages of 12 and 15 found that the majority of mothers considered the most important factors that contributed to school violence to be parents who did not teach children morals (84%), parents who supported aggressive behavior (78%), and gang or peer pressure (70%) (Kandakai et al. 1999). Compare these answers with the opinion you recorded earlier. Was your idea about the causes of youth violence one of the more popular ones held by this sample of mothers?

We cannot avoid asking questions about the actions and attitudes of others. We all try to make sense of the social world, which is a very complex place, and to make sense of our position in it, in which we have quite a personal stake. In fact, the more that you begin to "think like a social scientist," the more questions will come to mind.

But why does each question have so many possible answers? Surely our perspective plays a role. One person may see a homicide offender as a victim of circumstance, and another person may see the same individual as inherently evil. Answers to questions we ask in the criminological sciences also vary because individual life experiences and circumstances vary. The study of mothers' perceptions conducted by Kandakai et al. (1999), summarized in Exhibit 1.1, gives some idea of how opinions about the causes and cures for school violence vary. Even though previous research has found that the general public believes school violence is worse in urban schools than in suburban and rural schools, only 14% of the mothers who had children in urban schools believed their child's school was more violent than other schools. However, a higher percentage of urban mothers (37%) than suburban mothers (17%) reported that their child had been involved in one or more fights at school. Somewhat surprisingly, even though these mothers perceived parental support for violence as a major contributor to school violence, 4 in 10 of them believed it was acceptable for their child to fight in certain situations.

EXHIBIT 1.1 Mothers' Perceptions of the Factors Related to School Violence	
	Percentage Who Said Factor Contributed a Great Deal
Parents who do not teach their kids right from wrong	87
Parent support for aggressive behavior	78
Gang or peer pressure	70
Lack of family involvement	67
Sale of alcohol or cigarettes to children	61
Poor parent-teacher communication	60
Seeing violence in the community	53
Violent messages in rap music	47
Seeing violence in the media	44
Lack of a dress code	30

Everyday Errors in Reasoning

People give different answers to research questions for yet another reason: it is simply too easy to make errors in logic, particularly when we are analyzing the social world in which we ourselves are conscious participants. We can call some of these everyday errors, because they occur so frequently in the nonscientific, unreflective discourse about the social world that we hear on a daily basis.

For evidence of everyday errors, just listen to your conversations or the conversations of others for one day. At some point in the day, it is inevitable that you or someone you are talking with will say something like, "Well, I knew a person who did X and then Y happened." From this one piece of information, you therefore draw a conclusion about the likelihood of Y. Four general errors in everyday reasoning can be made: overgeneralization, selective or inaccurate observation, illogical reasoning, and resistance to change.

Overgeneralization

Overgeneralization, an error in reasoning, occurs when we conclude that what we have observed or what we know to be true for some cases is true for all cases. We are always drawing conclusions about people and social processes from our own interactions with them, but sometimes we forget that our experiences are limited. The social (and natural) world is, after all, a complex place. We have the ability (and inclination) to interact with just a small fraction of the individuals who inhabit the social world, especially in a limited span of time.

Selective or Inaccurate Observation

Selective observation is choosing to look only at things that are in accordance with our preferences or beliefs. When we are inclined to criticize individuals or institutions, it is all too easy to notice their every failing. For example, if we are convinced in advance that all kids who are violent are unlikely to be rehabilitated and will go on to commit violent offenses in adulthood, we will probably find many confirming instances. But what about other youths who have become productive and stable citizens after engaging in violence as adolescents? Or the child who was physically or sexually abused and joined a gang to satisfy the need for a family surrogate? If we acknowledge only the instances that confirm our predispositions, we are victims of our own selective observation. Exhibit 1.2 depicts the difference between selective observation and overgeneralization.

Our observations also can simply be inaccurate. If a woman says she is *hungry* and we think she said she is *hunted,* we have made **an inaccurate observation**. If we think five people are standing on a street corner when there are actually seven, we have made an inaccurate observation. Such errors occur often in casual conversation and in everyday observation of the world around us. In fact, our perceptions do not provide a direct window to the world around us, for what we think we have sensed is not necessarily what we have seen (or heard, smelled, felt, or tasted). Even when our senses are functioning fully, our minds have to interpret what we have sensed (Humphrey 1992).

EXHIBIT 1.2   The Difference Between Overgeneralization and Selective Observation

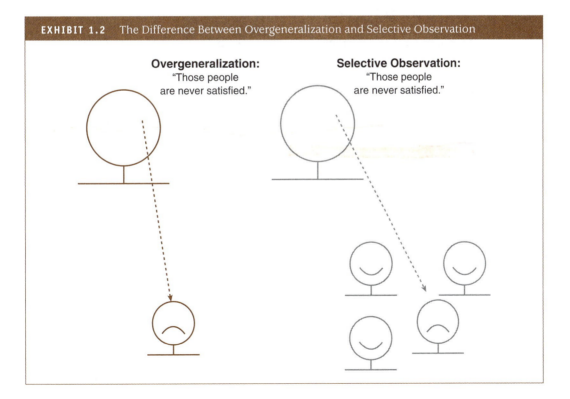

Overgeneralization:
"Those people
are never satisfied."

Selective Observation:
"Those people
are never satisfied."

Illogical Reasoning

When we prematurely jump to conclusions or argue on the basis of invalid assumptions, we are using **illogical reasoning**. For example, it is not reasonable to propose that depictions of violence in media such as television and movies cause violence if evidence indicates that the majority of those who watch such programs do not become violent. However, it is also illogical to assume that media depictions of gratuitous violence have no effect on individuals. Of course, logic that seems impeccable to one person can seem twisted to another; the problem usually is reasoning from different assumptions rather than failing to "think straight."

Resistance to Change

Resistance to change, the reluctance to change our ideas in light of new information, may occur for several reasons:

- *Ego-based commitments*. We all learn to greet with some skepticism the claims by leaders of companies, schools, agencies, and so on that people in their organization are happy, that revenues are growing, that services are being delivered in the best possible way, and so forth. We know how tempting it is to make statements about the social world that conform to our own needs rather than to the observable facts. It also can be difficult to admit that we were wrong once we have staked out a position on an issue.
- *Excessive devotion to tradition*. Some degree of devotion to tradition is necessary for the predictable functioning of society. Social life can be richer and more meaningful if it is allowed to flow along the paths charted by those who have preceded us. But too much devotion to tradition can stifle adaptation to changing circumstances. When we distort our observations or alter our reasoning so that we can maintain beliefs that "were good enough for my grandfather, so they're good enough for me," we hinder our ability to accept new findings and develop new knowledge.
- *Uncritical agreement with authority*. If we do not have the courage to evaluate critically the ideas of those in positions of authority, we will have little basis for complaint if they exercise their authority over us in ways we do not like. And if we do not allow new discoveries to call our beliefs into question, our understanding of the social world will remain limited. People often accept the beliefs of those in positions of authority without question.

Now take just a minute to reexamine the beliefs about youth violence that you recorded earlier. Did you grasp at a simple explanation even though the reality was far more complex? Were your beliefs influenced by your own ego and feelings about your similarities to or differences from individuals prone to violence? Are your beliefs perhaps based on depictions of violence in the media or fiction? Did you weigh carefully the opinions of authority figures, including politicians, teachers, and even your parents, or just accept or reject those opinions out of hand? Could knowledge of research methods help to improve your own understanding of the factors related to violent behavior? By now you can see some of the challenges faced by social scientists studying issues related to crime and the criminal justice system.

You do not have to be a scientist or use sophisticated research techniques to recognize and avoid these four errors in reasoning. If you recognize these errors for what they are and make a conscious effort to avoid them, you can improve your own reasoning. In the process, you will also be heeding the admonishments of your parents (or minister, teacher, or other adviser) to refrain from stereotyping people, to avoid jumping to conclusions, and to look at the big picture. These are the same errors that the methods of social science are designed to help criminologists avoid.

HOW THE SCIENTIFIC APPROACH IS DIFFERENT

The social science approach to answering questions about the social world is designed to greatly reduce these potential sources of error in everyday reasoning. **Science** relies on logical and systematic methods to answer questions, and it does so in a way that allows others to inspect and evaluate its methods. In the realm of social research, these methods are not so unusual. After all, they involve asking questions, observing social groups, and counting people, which we often do in our everyday lives. However, social scientists develop, refine, apply, and report their understanding of the social world more systematically, or specifically, than Joanna Q. Public.

- **Social science** research methods can reduce the likelihood of overgeneralization by using systematic procedures for selecting individuals or groups to study that are representative of the individuals or groups that we wish to generalize.
- Social science methods can reduce the risk of selective or inaccurate observation by requiring that we measure and sample phenomena systematically.
- To avoid illogical reasoning, social researchers use explicit criteria for identifying causes and for determining if these criteria are met in a particular instance.
- Scientific methods lessen the tendency to develop answers about the social world from ego-based commitments, excessive devotion to tradition, and/or unquestioning respect for authority.

Science A set of logical, systematic, documented methods for investigating nature and natural processes; the knowledge produced by these investigations.

Social science The use of scientific methods to investigate individuals, societies, and social processes, including questions related to criminology and criminal justice; the knowledge produced by these investigations.

Why We Do Criminological Research

Like you, social scientists read stories about incidents of violence committed by youth, observe this violence occasionally in their lives, and try to make sense of what they see. For most, that is the end of it. But for some social scientists, the problem of youth violence has become a major research focus. The motivations for selecting this particular research focus, as with any social science topic, can be any one or some combination of the following:

Policy motivations. Many social service agencies and elected officials seek better assessments and descriptions of youth violence so they can identify needs and allocate responsibility among agencies that could meet these needs. For example, federal agencies such as the U.S. Department of Justice and the Centers for Disease Control and Prevention want to identify the magnitude of youth violence, and many state and local officials use social research to guide development of their social service budgets. Programs designed to rehabilitate young offenders often use research to learn more about the needs of their clientele. These policy guidance and program management needs have resulted in numerous research projects.

Academic motivations. Young offenders have been a logical focus for researchers interested in a number of questions, ranging from how an individual's connection to parents and peers influences their behavior to how the social conditions under which they live, such as poverty, affect their behavior. For example, social scientists have long been concerned with the impact that social disorganization has on individual behavior. Early in this century, researchers at the University of Chicago were interested in the effects that residential mobility and immigration had on levels of crime and delinquency in urban neighborhoods. Today, researchers are exploring similar questions concerning the impact of disintegrating economic bases in central cities and their relationship to crime and violence. Other researchers have focused on individual-level explanations such as neurological damage. Those who study social policy also have sought to determine whether correctional programs such as boot camps and other forms of shock incarceration serve to decrease the probability of juveniles reoffending in the future.

Personal motivations. Many who conduct research on youth violence feel that by doing so they can help to prevent it and/or ameliorate the consequences of this violence when it occurs. Some social scientists first volunteered with at-risk youth in such organizations as Big Sisters and Big Brothers, and only later began to develop a research agenda based on their experiences.

Social Criminological Research in Action

Of course, youth violence did not first appear in the United States in the 1980s. In fact, youth violence always has been a popular topic of social science research. However, the sharp increase in this violence in the United States that began in the late 1980s was unprecedented. Predictably, whenever a phenomenon is perceived as an epidemic, numerous explanations emerge to explain it. Unfortunately, most of these explanations are based on the media and popular culture, not on empirical research. Despite the anecdotal information floating around in the mass media about the factors that may have contributed to increases in youth violence, social scientists interested in this phenomenon have amassed a substantial body of findings that have refined knowledge about the problem and shaped social policy (Tonry & Moore 1998). These studies fall into the four categories of purposes for social scientific research:

Descriptive research. Defining and describing social phenomena of interest are part of almost any research investigation, but **descriptive research** is the primary focus of many studies of youth crime and violence. Some of the central questions used in these studies were "How many people are victims of youth violence?" "How many youth are offenders?"

"What are the most common crimes committed by youthful offenders?" and "How many of the different youth are arrested and incarcerated each year for crime?" Measurement (see chapter 3) and sampling (see chapter 4) are central concerns in descriptive research.

Exploratory research. **Exploratory research** seeks to find out how people get along in the setting under question, what meanings they give to their actions, and what issues concern them. The goal is to answer the question, "What is going on here?" and to investigate social phenomena without expectations. This purpose is associated with the use of methods that capture large amounts of relatively unstructured information. For example, researchers investigating the emergence of youth gangs in the 1980s were encountering a phenomenon of which they had no direct experience. Thus an early goal was to find out what it was like to be a gang member and how gang members made sense of their situation. Exploratory research like this frequently involves qualitative methods (see chapter 7).

Explanatory research. Many people consider explanation to be the premier goal of any science. **Explanatory research** seeks to identify causes and effects of social phenomena, to predict how one phenomenon will change or vary in response to variation in some other phenomenon. Researchers adopted explanation as a goal when they began to ask such questions as "Why do people become offenders?" and "Does the unemployment rate influence the frequency of youth crime?" Methods with which to identify causes and effects are the focus of chapter 5.

Evaluation research. **Evaluation research** seeks to determine the effects of a social program or other types of intervention. It is a type of explanatory research, because it deals with cause and effect. However, evaluation research differs from other forms of explanatory research because evaluation research considers the implementation and effects of social policies and programs. These issues may not be relevant in other types of explanatory research. The increase of youth violence in the 1980s spawned many new government programs and, with them, evaluation research to assess the impact of these programs. Some of these studies are reviewed in chapter 9, which covers evaluation research.

We will now summarize one study in each of these four areas to give you a feel for the projects motivated by those different concerns.

Description: What Is the Magnitude of Youth Violence?

One large research project undertaken to examine the magnitude of youth violence (along with other risk-taking behavior such as taking drugs and smoking) is called the Youth Risk Behavior Survey, which has been conducted every two years in the United States since 1990. Respondents to this survey are a national sample of approximately 16,000 high school students in Grades 9 through 12. To determine trends and patterns in violence-related behavior, Brener et al. (1999) examined the data for the years 1991 and 1997 and published their findings in the prestigious *Journal of the American Medical Association*.

To measure the extent of youth violence, students were asked the following questions: "During the past 30 days, on how many days did you carry a weapon such as a gun, knife, or club?" "During the past 12 months, how many times were you in a physical fight?" "During the past 12 months, how many times were you in a physical fight in which you were injured and had to be seen by a doctor or nurse?" "During the past 30 days, how many times did you carry a weapon such as a gun, knife, or club on school property?" "During the past 12 months, how many times were you in a physical fight on school property?" and "During the past 12 months, how many times has someone threatened or injured you with a gun, knife, or club on school property?"

Brener et al. (1999) found that the number of all students who carried a weapon within the 30 days preceding the survey actually decreased by 30% from 1991 to 1997. Similarly, the number of students who engaged in a physical fight one or more times during the 12 months preceding the survey decreased by 14%, and the number injured in a physical fight decreased by 20%. Trends in violence occurring on school property also decreased during this time period. The number of students who carried a gun on school property on one or more of the 30 days preceding the survey decreased by 28%, and the number of students who engaged in a physical fight on school property one or more times during the 12 months preceding the survey decreased by 9%.

This research is consistent with other studies that have found that official rates of youth violence, and youth homicide in particular, peaked in the early 1990s and declined thereafter (Cook & Laub 1998). What accounted for this unprecedented rise in youth violence during the late 1980s and early 1990s? To answer this question, explanatory research is necessary. After their in-depth descriptive analysis of youth violence during this time, Cook and Laub (1998) contended that the increasing homicide rates began with the introduction of crack cocaine and the conflict that surrounded its marketing. However, the primary factor postulated by Cook and Laub was the increased easy availability of firepower: "All of the increase in homicide rates was with guns, and it appears to be changing access [to] and use of guns, rather than a change in the character of the youths, that best accounts for their increased involvement in lethal violence" (1998: 60).

Exploration: How Do Schools Respond to Gun Violence?

Research that is exploratory in nature is generally concerned with uncovering detailed information about a given phenomenon, learning as much as possible about particular people and/or events. Asmussen and Creswell (1995) were interested in the responses to school shooting incidents. Because school shootings are relatively rare and there was virtually no empirical literature that addressed the topic, Asmussen and Creswell performed an in-depth qualitative case study of a shooting incident that occurred at a large public university. The incident occurred in a senior-level actuarial science class when a male graduate student arrived early for the class one Monday morning armed with a vintage Korean War semiautomatic military rifle loaded with a 30-round clip of .30-caliber ammunition. He carried another 30-round clip in his pocket. Twenty of the 34 students in the class were already there, and most of them were quietly reading the students' newspaper. The instructor was en route to class. The gunman pointed the rifle at the students, swept it across the room, and pulled the trigger. The gun jammed. Trying to unlock the rifle, he hit the butt of it on the desk and quickly tried firing it again. Again it did not fire. By this time, most students had realized what was happening and dropped to the floor, overturned their desks, and tried to hide behind them. After about 20 seconds, one of the students shoved a desk into the gunman, students ran past him out into the hall and out of the building. The gunman hastily left the room and went out of the building to his parked car, which he had left running. He was captured by police within the hour.

Asmussen and Creswell (1995) were surprised to find that, instead of seeking safety after leaving the classroom, all the students had stood together just outside the building. Although a few were openly emotional and crying, many were kidding about the incident, as if it had posed no real danger. This denial response is noted by the mental health literature, which finds that feelings of fear and anger usually follow an initial response of denial and disbelief. The researchers found that many other people, in addition to the students who witnessed the incident, were traumatized by the incident. In fact, three distinct groups of people sought counseling services during the weeks following the event. The first group had some direct involvement with the assailant, either by seeing him the day of the gun incident or because they had known him personally. The second group comprised the "silent connection," individuals who were indirectly involved and yet emotionally traumatized. Many members of this group were parents. The third group included people who had previously experienced a trauma and whose fears were reactivated by this incident.

Because the assailant's future was in the hands of the criminal justice system, the importance of information from this system became critical to feelings of safety. Two combined debriefing sessions by mental health counselors, the campus police chief, and two county attorneys were held for all those interested.

Another phenomenon observed on the campus was an increase in the number of professors and staff members who were concerned with disruptive students or students who exhibited aberrant behavior in class. To deal with this, the Student Judiciary Office advised departments on various methods of dealing with students who exhibited abnormal behavior in class. In addition, plainclothes police officers were sent to sit outside classrooms and offices whenever faculty and staff indicated concerns.

To their surprise, Asmussen and Creswell (1995) found that the campus did not establish a special unit to manage future incidents. The only structural change made was the installation of emergency phones throughout the campus. In addition, no discussion was reported about formal linkages with community agencies that might assist in the event of a future tragedy. In the end, Asmussen and Creswell's exploratory research illustrates the complexity involved in responding to a campus shooting.

Explanation: What Factors Are Related to Youth Delinquency and Violence?

Felson et al. (1994) sought to determine whether individual and group differences in beliefs and attitudes about violence were related to committing acts of delinquency and interpersonal violence. The theoretical argument they were attempting to test is actually termed the "subculture of violence" thesis (Wolfgang & Ferracuti 1967). According to this thesis, some groups are more violent than others because they have a distinctive set of values that either support or tolerate violence.

Felson et al. (1994) used a data set called the Youth in Transition data, which was a panel study of high school boys. The first interviews were conducted with sophomore boys attending 87 randomly selected public high schools. The second interview was collected 18 months later at the end of the boys' junior year in high school. The researchers measured each boy's adherence to a subculture of violence by asking him about situations in which he would approve of aggression as a legitimate expression of grievances and as an appropriate response to personal attack. For example, each boy was presented with a series of personal values and asked whether each was a "good thing for people to do": (1) turning the other cheek and forgiving others when they harm you, (2) replying to anger with gentleness, and (3) being kind to people even if they do things against one's own beliefs. These items each focus on the approval of nonaggressive responses to some type of provocation. Agreement with these statements therefore suggests that respondents disapprove of aggressive responses to personal attacks and wrongdoing. Disagreement with these statements would result in a high score on the subculture of violence. Each boy was asked about the frequency with which he engaged in eight activities: got into a serious fight with a student in school; obtained something by telling a person something bad would happen to the person if he did not get what he wanted; hurt someone badly enough to need bandages or a doctor; hit a teacher; hit his father; hit his mother; took part in a group brawl in which his friends fought with another group; and used a knife or gun or some other thing to get something from a person. The respondents were also asked about other delinquent acts such as engaging in theft and vandalism.

The students' scores on the subculture of violence index were then used to predict scores on the interpersonal violence index, after controlling for the effects of other important variables such as socioeconomic status, race, attitudes toward academic achievement, and family stability. Felson et al. (1994) performed analyses using both individual and school-level data and found that an aggressive response to a provocation was likely to meet with more peer approval in some schools than in others. They found that individuals who approved of aggressive responses to provocation were more likely to commit acts of interpersonal violence. In addition, individuals who went to schools where there was an atmosphere permissive of violence were more likely to act violently, a discovery that remained true even after controlling for individual attitudes. Felson and his colleagues attribute this to a social control process and explain: "If boys are expected to retaliate when provoked, it appears that they are more likely to engage in violence and other delinquent behavior, no matter what their personal values may be" (1994: 164).

Evaluation: Do Violence Prevention Programs in Schools Work?

To reduce violence and create a safer atmosphere at schools across the country, literally thousands of schools have adopted some form of violence prevention training (Powell, Muir-McClain, & Halasyamani 1995). These programs generally provide cognitive-behavioral and social skills training on various topics using a variety of methods. Such programs are commonly referred to as *conflict resolution* and *peer mediation training*. Many of these prevention programs are designed to improve interpersonal problem-solving skills among children and adolescents by training children in cognitive processing, such as identifying the interpersonal problem and generating nonaggressive solutions. However, there is limited evidence that such programs are actually effective in reducing violence.

Grossman et al. (1997) assessed the efficacy of one such program for children in elementary school called "The Second Step: A Violence Prevention Curriculum." The program involved 30 lessons, each lasting about 35 minutes, taught once or twice a week. Each lesson consisted of a photograph accompanied by a social scenario that formed the basis for discussion, role playing, and conceptual activities. Lessons were arranged in three units:

1. empathy training, in which students identified their own feelings and those of others;

2. impulse control, in which students were presented with a problem-solving strategy and behavioral skills for affecting solutions (e.g., apologizing or dealing with peer pressure); and

3. anger management, in which students were presented with a coping strategy and behavioral skills for tense situations.

Twelve elementary schools in King County, Washington, were paired according to three criteria: the school district, the proportion of students receiving free or reduced-cost lunch, and the proportion of minority enrollment. After pairing, schools in each pair were randomly assigned either to receive the Second Step program (experimental groups) or to receive no violence prevention curriculum (control groups). Random assignment was necessary so the researchers could be more confident that any differences observed in aggression and violent behavior between the two groups after the program could be attributed to the program alone and not to some other factor. Violent and aggressive behavior was measured in three ways: teacher ratings of each child's behavior; parent ratings; and direct observation of students by trained observers in the classroom, playground, and cafeteria. Measures of aggression were taken at three time periods: before the start of the curriculum (baseline); two weeks after the conclusion of the curriculum; and six months after the curriculum.

To determine the effectiveness of the Second Step program, researchers examined the change in aggression between scores measured at baseline and those from the second and third periods of data collection. Grossman et al. (1997) found encouraging results: Observed physically aggressive behavior decreased significantly more among children who engaged in the curriculum than among children in the control group who were not exposed to the Second Step program. Moreover, prosocial behavior increased significantly among children in the Second Step program compared with the control group. Grossman and colleagues concluded, "This violence prevention curriculum appears to lead to modest reductions in levels of aggressive behavior and increases in neutral/prosocial behavior in school among second and third graders" (1997: 1608).

STRENGTHS AND LIMITATIONS OF SOCIAL RESEARCH

These case studies are only four of the hundreds of studies investigating youth violence, but they illustrate some of the questions criminological research can address, several different methods social scientists studying these issues can use, and ways criminological research can inform public policy. Notice how each of the four studies was designed to reduce the errors common in everyday reasoning:

- The clear definition of the population of interest in each study and the selection of a broad, representative sample of that population in two studies increased the researchers' ability to draw conclusions without overgeneralizing findings to groups to which they did not apply.
- The use of surveys in which each respondent was asked the same set of questions reduced the risk of selective or inaccurate observation.
- The risk of illogical reasoning was reduced by carefully describing each stage of the research, clearly presenting the findings, and carefully testing the basis for cause-and-effect conclusions.
- Resistance to change was reduced by using an experimental design that randomly assigned classes to an experimental treatment (the Second Step program) and a control group to fairly evaluate the efficacy of the program.

Nevertheless, we would be less than honest if we implied that you enter the realm of beauty, truth, and light whenever you engage in research or whenever you base your opinions only on the best available social research. Research always has some limitations and some flaws (as does any human endeavor), and findings are always subject to differing interpretations. Social research permits you to see more, to observe with fewer distortions, and to describe more clearly to others the basis for your opinions, but it will not settle all arguments. Other people will always have differing opinions, and some of those others will be social scientists who have conducted their own studies and drawn different conclusions. Do other programs similar to Second Step reduce levels of aggression among students? Only a handful of studies have used randomized controlled designs to examine these programs, and the results of these studies have been mixed. Like the Grossman et al. (1997) study, some researchers have found a reduction in aggressive behavior by children exposed to such social skills training programs, whereas others have not. Until more scientific research is conducted to evaluate these programs, it is difficult to determine whether the money poured into such programs by school districts is well spent.

But even in areas of research that are fraught with controversy, where social scientists differ in their interpretations of the evidence, the quest for new and more sophisticated research has value. What is most important for improving understanding of the social world and issues in criminology is not the results of any particular study but the accumulation of evidence from different studies of related issues. By designing new studies that focus on the weak points or controversial conclusions of prior research, social scientists contribute to a body of findings that gradually expands our knowledge about the social world and resolves some of the disagreements about it.

Whether you plan to conduct your own research projects, read others' research reports, or just think about and act in the social world, knowing about research methods has many benefits. This knowledge will give you greater confidence in your own opinions, improve your ability to evaluate others' opinions, and encourage you to refine your questions, answers, and methods of inquiry about the social world.

Of course, the methods of social science, as careful as they may be, cannot answer all questions of interest to criminologists. Should we do unto others what we would have them do unto us? That is a very important question that has been asked throughout history, but we must turn to religion or philosophy to answer questions about values. Social research on the consequences of forgiveness or the sources of interpersonal conflict may help us understand and implement our values, but even the best research cannot tell us which values should guide our lives.

TYPES OF RESEARCH METHODS

As you will see in this book, the data we utilize in criminological research are derived from many different sources, and the research methods we employ in criminology and criminal justice are very diverse.

An **experimental approach** is used in criminological research, particularly when the efficacy of a program or policy is being evaluated. As we will see in chapter 5, true experiments must have three aspects: two groups (one receiving the treatment or intervention and the other receiving no treatment or another form thereof), random assignment to these two groups, and an assessment of change in the outcome variable after the treatment or policy has been received. Quasi-experimental designs, experiments that lack one of these three ingredients, also are used in our discipline. Chapter 9 focuses exclusively on research designs used in evaluation research.

Asking people questions on **surveys** or **questionnaires** is another popular method used by criminological researchers and is probably the most versatile. Most concepts about individuals can be defined in such a way that measurement with one or more questions becomes an option. These surveys can be self-administered by respondents (e.g., through the mail) or can be read by an interviewer (e.g., through a telephone survey).

Although in principle survey questions can be a straightforward and efficient means to measure individual characteristics, facts about events, level of knowledge, and opinions of any sort, in practice, survey questions can result in misleading or inappropriate answers. All questions proposed for a survey must be screened carefully for their adherence to basic guidelines and then tested and revised until the researcher feels some confidence that they will be clear to the intended respondents (Fowler 1995). Some variables may prove to be inappropriate for measurement with any type of question. We have to recognize that memories and perceptions of the events about which we might like to ask can be limited. Specific guidelines for writing questions and developing surveys are presented in chapter 6.

In other cases, a researcher may want to make their presence known and directly participate in the activity being observed. Included in this type of research design is **participant observation**, which involves developing a sustained relationship with people while they go about their normal activities. In other instances, the subject matter of interest may not be amenable to a survey, or perhaps we want more detailed and in-depth information than questions with fixed formats can answer. In these cases, we turn to research techniques such as participant observation and **intensive interviewing**. These methods are preferred when we seek in-depth information on an individual's feelings, experiences, and perceptions. Chapter 7 shows how these methods and other field research techniques can uncover aspects of the social world that we are likely to miss in experiments and surveys.

Secondary data analysis (Riedel 2000), which is the reanalysis of already existing data, is another method used by researchers. These data usually come from one of two places: from official sources such as local or federal agencies (e.g., rates of crime reported to police, information on incarcerated offenders from state correctional authorities, adjudication data from the courts), or from surveys sponsored by government agencies or conducted by other researchers. Virtually all the data collected by government agencies and a great deal of survey data collected by independent researchers are made available to the public through the Inter-University Consortium for Political and Social Research (ICPSR), which is located at the University of Michigan. When documents from the past, such as correspondence, newspaper accounts, and trial transcripts, are analyzed, the research is generally termed *historical events research*. Another type of indirect measurement is called **content analysis**. In this type of study, a researcher studies representations of the research topic in such media forms as news articles, TV shows, and radio talk shows. An investigation of the drinking climate on campuses might include a count of the amount of space devoted to ads for alcoholic beverages in a sample of issues of the student newspaper. Campus publications also might be coded to indicate the number of times that statements discouraging substance abuse appear. Content analysis techniques also can be applied to legal opinions, historical documents, novels, songs, or other cultural productions. With the advent of computer technology, **crime mapping** also has become a popular method for examining the relationship between criminal behavior and other social indicators. Combining methodologies to answer a research question, called **triangulation**, is also increasingly used by research. Chapter 8 covers each of these methodologies and illustrates the importance of these unobtrusive research techniques in describing criminology and criminal justice.

Quantitative and Qualitative Methods

In general, research methods can be divided into two somewhat different domains called quantitative research methods and qualitative research methods. Did you notice the difference between the types of data the case studies discussed at the beginning of the chapter used? The data collected in the Youth Risk Behavior Survey were counts of the responses students gave on the survey. These data were numerical, so we say that this study used **quantitative methods**. Felson et al. (1994) looked at the extent to which changes in attitudes toward violence also changed violent behavior; they examined this relationship with statistical methods like correlations and regression coefficients. These, too, are quantitative methods. In contrast, Asmussen and Creswell's (1995) exploratory study used in-depth interviews with people who had experienced the attempted school shooting. This methodology was designed to capture the social reality of the participants as they experienced it, in their own words rather than in predetermined categories. Because they focused on the participants' words rather than counts and numbers, we say that this study used quantitative and qualitative methods.

Quantitative methods Methods such as surveys and experiments that record variation in social life in terms of categories that vary in amount. Data that are treated as quantitative are either numbers or attributes that can be ordered in terms of magnitude.

Qualitative methods Methods such as participant observation, intensive interviewing, and focus groups that are designed to capture social life as participants experience it, rather than in categories predetermined by the researcher. Data that are treated as qualitative are mostly written or spoken words, or observations that do not have a direct numerical interpretation.

The distinction between quantitative and qualitative methods involves more than just the type of data collected. Quantitative methods are most often used when the motives for research are explanation, description, or evaluation. Exploration is the most common motive for using qualitative methods, although researchers also use these methods for descriptive and evaluative purposes. The goals of quantitative and qualitative researchers also may differ. Whereas quantitative researchers generally accept the goal of developing an understanding that correctly reflects what is actually happening in the real world, some qualitative researchers instead emphasize the goal of developing an "authentic" understanding of a social process or social setting (Gubrium & Holstein 1997). An authentic understanding is one that reflects *fairly* the various perspectives of participants in that setting.

As important as it is, we do not want to place too much emphasis on the distinction between qualitative and quantitative methods because social scientists often combine these methods to enrich their research. For example, "qualitative knowing" about social settings can be essential for understanding patterns in quantitative data (Campbell & Russo 1999: 141). Qualitative data can be converted to quantitative data—for example, when we count the frequency of particular words or phrases in a text or measure the time elapsed between different behaviors that we have observed. Surveys that collect primarily quantitative data also may include questions asking for written responses, and these responses may be used in a qualitative, textual analysis. Researchers using quantitative methods may engage in some exploration in order to find unexpected patterns in their data. Qualitative researchers may test explicit explanations of social phenomena using textual or observational data. We will discuss qualitative methods in greater detail in chapter 7, but we will highlight these "mixed method" approaches throughout the text. Despite the use of mixed methods in criminological research, it is important to understand the different research philosophies that underlie the two categories of methods.

SOCIAL RESEARCH PHILOSOPHIES

What influences the choice of a research strategy? The motive for conducting research is critical: an explanatory or evaluative motive generally leads a researcher to use quantitative methods, whereas an exploratory motive often results in the use of qualitative methods. Of course, a descriptive motive means choosing a descriptive research strategy.

Positivism and Postpositivism

A researcher's philosophical perspective on reality and on the appropriate role of the researcher also will shape their choice of methodological preferences. Researchers with a **positivist** philosophy believe that there is an objective reality that exists apart from the perceptions of those who observe it; the goal of science is to better understand this reality.

Whatever nature "really" is, we assume that it presents itself in precisely the same way to the same human observer standing at different points in time and space . . . We assume that it also presents itself in precisely the same way across different human observers standing at the same point in time and space. (Wallace 1983: 461)

This philosophy is traditionally associated with science (Weber 1949: 72), with the expectation that there are universal laws of human behavior, and with the belief that scientists must be objective and unbiased to see reality clearly.

Postpositivism is a philosophy of reality that is closely related to positivism. Postpositivists believe that there is an external, objective reality, but are very sensitive to the complexity of this reality and the limitations of the scientists who study it—and, for social scientists, the biases they bring to the study of social beings like themselves (Guba & Lincoln 1994: 109–111). As a result, they do not think scientists can ever be sure that their methods allow them to perceive objective reality; the goal of science can only be to achieve **intersubjective agreement** among scientists about the nature of reality (Wallace 1983: 461). For example, postpositivists may worry that researchers' predispositions may bias them in favor of deterrence theory. Therefore, they will remain somewhat skeptical of results that support predictions based on deterrence until a number of researchers feel that they have found supportive evidence. The postpositivist retains much more confidence in the ability of the community of social researchers to develop an unbiased account of reality than in the ability of any individual social scientist to do so (Campbell & Russo 1999: 144).

Positivist Research Guidelines

To achieve an accurate, or valid, understanding of the social world, a researcher operating within the positivist or postpositivist tradition must adhere to some basic guidelines about how to conduct research:

1. *Test ideas against empirical reality without becoming too personally invested in a particular outcome.* This guideline requires a commitment to "testing," as opposed to just reacting to events as they happen or looking for what we want to see (Kincaid 1996: 51–54).

2. *Plan and carry out investigations systematically.* Social researchers have little hope of conducting a careful test of their ideas if they do not think through in advance how they should go about the test and then proceed accordingly.

3. *Document all procedures and disclose them publicly.* Social researchers should disclose the methods on which their conclusions are based so that others can evaluate for themselves the likely soundness of these conclusions (Kincaid 1996).

4. *Clarify assumptions.* No investigation is complete in itself; whatever the researcher's method, the research rests on some background assumptions. For example, research to determine whether arrest has a deterrent effect assumes that potential law violators think rationally, and that they calculate potential costs and benefits prior to committing crimes.

5. *Specify the meaning of all terms.* Words often have multiple or unclear meanings. "Recidivism," "self-control," "poverty," "overcrowded," and so on can mean different things to different people. In scientific research, all terms must be defined explicitly and used consistently.

6. *Maintain a skeptical stance toward current knowledge.* The results of any particular investigation must be examined critically, although confidence about interpretations of the social or natural world increases after repeated investigations yield similar results.

7. *Replicate research and build social theory.* No one study is definitive by itself. We cannot fully understand a single study's results apart from the larger body of knowledge to which it is related, and we cannot place much confidence in these results until the study has been replicated.

8. *Search for regularities or patterns.* Positivist and postpositivist scientists assume that the natural world has some underlying order of relationships, so that unique events and individuals can be understood at least in part in terms of general principles (Grinnell 1992: 27–29).

Real investigations by social scientists do not always include much attention to theory, specific definitions of all terms, and so forth. But it behooves any social researcher to study these guidelines and to consider the consequences of not following any with which they do not agree.

A Positivist Research Goal: Advancing Knowledge

The goal of the traditional positivist scientific approach is to advance scientific knowledge. This goal is achieved when research results are published in academic journals or presented at academic conferences.

The positivist approach regards value considerations to be beyond the scope of science: "An empirical science cannot tell anyone what he should do—but rather what he can do— and under certain circumstances—what he wishes to do" (Weber 1949: 54). The idea is that developing valid knowledge about how society *is* organized, or how we live our lives, does not tell us how society *should* be organized or how we *should* live our lives. The determination of empirical facts should be a separate process from the evaluation of these facts as satisfactory or unsatisfactory (Weber 1949: 11).

Positivism The belief, shared by most scientists, that there is a reality that exists quite apart from our own perception of it, although our knowledge of this reality may never be complete.

Intersubjective agreement An agreement by different observers on what is happening in the natural or social world.

Postpositivism The belief that there is an empirical reality but that our understanding of it is limited by its complexity and by the biases and other limitations of researchers.

Interpretivism and Constructivism

Qualitative research is often guided by a different, **interpretivist** philosophy. Interpretive social scientists believe that social reality is socially constructed and that the goal of social scientists is to understand what meanings people give to reality, not to determine how reality works apart from these interpretations. This philosophy rejects the positivist belief that there is a concrete, objective reality that scientific methods help us to understand (Lynch & Bogen 1997); instead, interpretivists believe that scientists construct an image of reality based on their own preferences and prejudices and their interactions with others.

Here is the basic argument: The empirical data we collect all come to us through our own senses and must be interpreted with our own minds. This suggests that we can never be sure that we have understood reality properly, or that we ever can, or that our own understandings can really be judged more valid than someone else's.

> Searching for universally applicable social laws can distract from learning what people know and how they understand their lives. The interpretive social researcher examines meanings that have been socially constructed . . . There is not one reality out there to be measured; objects and events are understood by different people differently, and those perceptions are the reality—or realities— that social science should focus on. (Rubin & Rubin 1995: 35)

The **constructivist paradigm** extends interpretivist philosophy by emphasizing the importance of exploring how different stakeholders in a social setting construct their beliefs (Guba & Lincoln 1989: 44–45). It gives particular attention to the different goals of researchers and other participants in a research setting and seeks to develop a consensus among participants about how to understand the focus of inquiry. The constructivist research report will highlight different views of the social program or other issue and explain how a consensus can be reached among participants.

Interpretivism The belief that reality is socially constructed and that the goal of social scientists is to understand what meanings people give to that reality. Max Weber termed the goal of interpretivist research *verstehen*, or "understanding."

Constructivist paradigm A perspective that emphasizes how different stakeholders in social settings construct their beliefs.

Constructivist inquiry uses an interactive research process, in which a researcher begins an evaluation in some social setting by identifying the different interest groups in that setting. The researcher goes on to learn what each group thinks, and then gradually tries to develop a shared perspective on the problem being evaluated (Guba & Lincoln 1989: 42).

Interpretivist/Constructivist Research Guidelines

Researchers guided by an interpretivist philosophy reject some of the guidelines to which positivist researchers seek to adhere. In fact, there are a wide variety of specific approaches that can be termed "interpretivist," and each has some guidelines that it highlights. For those working within the constructivist perspective, Guba and Lincoln (1989: 42) suggest four key steps for researchers, each of which may be repeated many times in a given study:

1. Identify stakeholders and solicit their "claims, concerns, and issues."

2. Introduce the claims, concerns, and issues of each stakeholder group to the other stakeholder groups and ask for their reactions.

3. Focus further information collection on claims, concerns, and issues about which there is disagreement among stakeholder groups.

4. Negotiate with stakeholder groups about the information collected and attempt to reach consensus on the issues about which there is disagreement.

An Interpretivist Research Goal: Creating Change

Some social researchers with an interpretivist or constructivist orientation often reject explicitly the traditional positivist distinction between facts and values (Sjoberg & Nett 1968). Bellah et al. (1985) have instead proposed a model of "social science as public philosophy." In this model, social scientists focus explicit attention on achieving a more just society.

Whyte (1991) proposed a more activist approach to research called **participatory action research**. As the name implies, this approach encourages social researchers to get "out of the academic rut" and bring values into the research process (1991: 285).

In participatory action research, the researcher involves as active participants some members of the setting studied. Both the organizational members and the researcher are assumed to want to develop valid conclusions, to bring unique insights, and to desire change, but Whyte (1991) believes these objectives are more likely to be obtained if the researcher collaborates actively with the persons studied.

An Integrated Philosophy

It is tempting to think of positivism and postpositivism as representing an opposing research philosophy to interpretivism and constructivism. Then it seems that we should choose the one philosophy that seems closest to our own preferences and condemn the other as "unscientific," "uncaring," or perhaps just "unrealistic." But there are good reasons to prefer a research philosophy that integrates some of the differences between these philosophies (Smith 1991).

And what about the important positivist distinction between facts and values in social research? Here, too, there is evidence that neither the "value-free" presumption of positivists nor the constructivist critique of this position is entirely correct. For example, Savelsberg, King, and Cleveland (2002) examined influences on the focus and findings of published criminal justice scholarship. They found that criminal justice research was more likely to be oriented to topics and theories suggested by the state when it was funded by government agencies. This reflects a political influence on scholarship. However, government funding did not have any bearing on the researchers' conclusions about the criminal justice processes they examined. This suggests that scientific procedures can insulate the research process itself from political pressure.

VALIDITY: THE GOAL OF SOCIAL RESEARCH

A scientist seeks to develop an accurate understanding of empirical reality—the reality we encounter firsthand—by conducting research that leads to valid knowledge about the world. But when is knowledge valid? In general, we have reached the goal of validity when our statements or conclusions about empirical reality are correct. If you look out your window and observe that it is raining, this is probably a valid observation if your eyes and ears are to be trusted. However, if you pick up the newspaper and read that the majority of Americans favor the death penalty, this conclusion is of questionable validity because it is probably based on an interpretation of a social survey. As you will see in chapter 6, attitudes toward the death penalty vary substantially depending on the wording of the questions asked.

This book is about validity more than anything else: about how to conduct research that leads to valid interpretations of the social world. We will refer to validity repeatedly, and we ask you to register it in your brain now as the central goal of all the research conducted in our field. The goal of research conducted by social scientists investigating issues related to criminology and criminal justice is not to come up with conclusions that people will like or conclusions that suit their personal preferences. The goal is to determine the most valid answers through empirical research methods.

We must be concerned with three aspects of validity: **measurement validity**, **generalizability**, and **causal validity** (also known as internal validity). Each of these three aspects of validity is essential: Conclusions based on invalid measures, invalid generalizations, or invalid causal inferences will themselves be invalid.

Imagine that we survey a sample of 250 high school seniors and ask them two questions: "Do you have friends who have taken illegal drugs in the past six months?" (the measure of peer behavior) and "Have you taken illegal drugs in the past six months?" (individual use measure). We then compare the frequency of illegal drug use between students who have friends who have used illegal drugs and those whose friends have not used illegal drugs. We find that students who have friends who have used illegal drugs in the past six months are more likely to have used drugs themselves, and we conclude that drug use is, in part, due to the influence of peers.

But did our questions indeed tell us the frequency with which the students and their peers took illegal drugs? If they did, we achieved measurement validity. Do our results hold true of the larger adolescent population to which our conclusion referred? If so, our conclusion would satisfy the criterion for generalizability. Did the likelihood of students taking drugs actually increase if they had friends who also took drugs? If so, our conclusion is causally valid.

Measurement validity Exists when a measure measures what we think it measures.

Generalizability Exists when a conclusion holds true for the population, group, setting, or event that we say it does, given the conditions that we specify.

Causal validity (internal validity) Exists when a conclusion that A leads to or results in B is correct.

The goal in research is to achieve valid understandings of the social world by coming to conclusions that rest on valid measures and valid causal assertions and that are generalizable to the population of interest. Once we have learned how to develop studies that give us reasonably valid results and how to evaluate studies according to how well they meet this criterion, we will be well along on the road to becoming expert researchers. Chapters 3, 4, and 5 discuss these three aspects of validity and the specific techniques used to maximize the validity of our measures, our generalizations, and our causal assertions in greater detail.

CONCLUSION

We hope this first chapter has given you an idea of what to expect in the rest of this book. Our aim is to introduce you to social research methods by describing what social scientists have learned about issues in criminology and criminal justice as well as how they learned it. The substance of social science inevitably is more interesting than its methods, but the methods also become more interesting when they are not taught as isolated techniques. We have focused attention on research on youth violence and delinquency in this chapter; in subsequent chapters, we will introduce research examples from other areas.

Chapter 2 continues to build the foundation for our study of social research by reviewing the types of problems that criminologists study, the role of theory, the major steps in the research process, and other sources of information that may be used in social research.

We stress the importance of considering scientific standards in social research and review generally accepted ethical guidelines. Throughout the chapter, we use several studies of domestic violence to illustrate the research process.

KEY TERMS

Causal validity (internal validity)	Measurement validity
Constructivist paradigm	Overgeneralization
Content analysis	Participant observation
Crime mapping	Participatory action research
Descriptive research	Positivism
Evaluation research	Postpositivism
Experimental approach	Qualitative methods
Explanatory research	Quantitative methods
Exploratory research	Questionnaire
External validity	Resistance to change
Generalizability	Science
Hermeneutic circle	Secondary data analysis
Illogical reasoning	Selective observation
Inaccurate observation	Social science
Intensive interviewing	Survey
Interpretivism	Unobtrusive measures
Intersubjective agreement	Validity

HIGHLIGHTS

- Criminological research cannot resolve value questions or provide answers that will convince everyone and remain settled for all time.

- All empirically based methods of investigation are based on either direct experience or others' statements.

- Four common errors in reasoning are overgeneralization, selective or inaccurate observation, illogical reasoning, and resistance to change. Illogical reasoning is due to the complexity of the social world, self-interest, and human subjectivity. Resistance to change may be due to unquestioning acceptance of tradition or of those in positions of authority, or to self-interested resistance to admitting the need to change one's beliefs.

- Social science is the use of logical, systematic, documented methods to investigate individuals, societies, and social processes, as well as the knowledge produced by these investigations.

- Criminological research can be motivated by policy guidance and program management needs, academic concerns, and charitable impulses.

- Criminological research can be descriptive, exploratory, explanatory, or evaluative, or some combination of these.

- Quantitative methods record variation in social life in terms of categories that vary in amount. Qualitative methods are designed to capture social life as participants experience it, rather than in categories predetermined by the researcher.

- Positivism is the belief that there is a reality that exists quite apart from one's own perception of it that is amenable to observation.

- Intersubjective agreement is an agreement by different observers on what is happening in the natural or social world.

- Postpositivism is the belief that there is an empirical reality but that our understanding of it is limited by its complexity and by the biases and other limitations of researchers.

- Interpretivism is the belief that reality is socially constructed and the goal of social science should be to understand what meanings people give to that reality.

- The constructivist paradigm emphasizes the importance of exploring and representing the ways in which different stakeholders in a social setting construct their beliefs. Constructivists interact with research subjects to gradually develop a shared perspective on the issue being studied.

- Valid knowledge is the central concern of scientific research. The three components of validity are measurement validity, generalizability (both from the sample to the population from which it was selected and from the sample to other populations), and causal (internal) validity.

EXERCISES

Discussing Research

1. What criminological topic or issue would you focus on if you could design a research project without any concern for costs? What are your motives for studying this topic? List at least four of your beliefs about this phenomenon. Try to identify the sources of each belief—for example, television, newspaper, parental influence.

2. Develop four research questions related to a topic or issue, one for each of the four types of research (descriptive, exploratory, explanatory, and evaluative). Be specific.

3. Outline your own research philosophy. You can base your outline primarily on your reactions to the points you have read in this chapter, but try also to think seriously about which perspective seems more reasonable to you.

Finding Research on the Web

1. You have been asked to prepare a brief presentation on a criminological topic or issue of interest to you. Go to the Bureau of Justice Statistics (BJS) website at www.ojp.usdoj.gov/bjs. Browse the BJS publications for a topic that interests you. Write a short outline for a 5- to 10-minute presentation regarding your topic, including statistics and other relevant information.

2. Go to the Federal Bureau of Investigation (FBI) website at www.fbi.gov. Explore the types of programs and initiatives sponsored by the FBI. Discuss at least three of these programs or initiatives in terms of their purposes and goals. For each program or initiative examined, do you believe the program or initiative is effective? What are the major weaknesses? What changes would you propose the FBI make to more effectively meet the goals of the program or initiative?

3. There are many interesting websites that discuss philosophy of science issues. Read the summaries of positivism and interpretivism at www.ruthssociology.com/research-methods (under the "Background" heading). What do these summaries add to your understanding of these philosophical alternatives?

Critiquing Research

1. Continue the debate between positivism and interpretivism with an in-class debate. Be sure to review the guidelines for these research philosophies and the associated goals. You might also consider whether an integrated philosophy is preferable.

2. Read an article in a recent issue of a major criminological journal or on the study site for this book (www.sagepub.com/frccjstudy). Identify the type of research conducted for each study. Are the research questions clearly stated? Can you identify the purpose of the research (e.g., description, explanation, exploration, evaluation)?

Making Research Ethical

Throughout the book, we will be discussing the ethical challenges that arise in research on crime and criminal justice. At the end of each chapter, we will ask you to consider some questions about ethical issues related to that chapter's focus. We introduce this critical topic formally in chapter 2, but we will begin here with some questions for you to ponder.

1. You have now learned about Asmussen and Creswell's (1995) qualitative study of a school shooting incident. We think it provided important information for policy makers about the social dynamics in these tragedies. But what would *you* do if you were conducting a similar study in a high school and you learned that another student was planning to bring a gun to school to kill some other students? What if he was only thinking about it? Or just talking with his friends about how "neat" it would be? Can you suggest some guidelines for researchers?

2. Grossman et al. (1997) found that the Second Step program reduced aggressive behavior in schools and increased prosocial behavior. If you were David Grossman, would you announce your findings in a press conference and encourage schools to adopt this program? If you were a school principal who heard about this research, would you agree to let another researcher replicate (repeat) the Grossman et al. study in your school, with some classrooms assigned to receive the Second Step program randomly (on the basis of the toss of a coin) and others not allowed to receive the program for the duration of the study?

Developing a Research Proposal

1. What topic would you focus on if you could design a social research project without any concern for costs? What are your motives for studying this topic?

2. Develop four questions that you might investigate about the topic you just selected. Each question should reflect a different research motive: description, exploration, explanation, or evaluation. Be specific.

3. Which question most interests you? Would you prefer to attempt to answer that question using quantitative or qualitative methods? Why?

Performing Data Analysis in SPSS

The SPSS exercises at the end of each chapter use the data sets included on the companion website. In NCS.POR, a sample of 503 robbery incidents from the National Crime Victimization Survey, variable V2089 identifies the metropolitan statistical area (MSA) status (urban, suburban, or rural) of each robbery incident included in the data set.

1. Create a bar chart of V2089 using the graph procedure to show the percentage of robbery incidents occurring in urban, suburban, and rural areas. Be sure to select "options" and indicate that you want to leave out the missing values.

2. Do a frequency distribution of V3010, which is the age of the victim in years. In the Statistics box, ask for the mean and the median. How would you describe the typical robbery victim? What accounts for the difference between the mean and the median?

3. Do a frequency distribution for the victim and offender relationship in robbery victimizations using the two variables, V4239 and V4243. Do the results surprise you?

Student Study Site

The companion Student Study Website for *The Fundamentals of Research in Criminology and Criminal Justice* can be found at www.sagepub.com/frccjstudy.

Visit the Student Study Site to enhance your understanding of the chapter content and to discover additional resources that will take your learning one step further. You can enhance your understanding of the chapters by using the comprehensive study material, which includes interactive exercises, e-flashcards, web exercises, practice self-tests, and more. You will also find special features, such as Learning from Journal Articles, which incorporates SAGE's online journal collection.

The Process and Problems of Criminological Research

In this chapter, you will learn that one source of the motivation to do research is criminological theory. In criminology, as in any other science, theory plays an important role as a basis for formulating research questions and later understanding the larger implications of one's research results. Another motivation for research is one's personal interests. There are other motivational sources for research that we will explore in this chapter, including helping to answer questions illuminated by earlier research. We use the Minneapolis experiment and the SARP replication research to illustrate the three main research strategies: deductive, inductive, and descriptive research. In all three, theory and data are inextricably linked. The chapter ends with scientific and ethical guidelines that should be adhered to no matter what research strategy is used, and shows how the Minneapolis experiment followed these guidelines. By the chapter's end, you should be ready to formulate a criminological research question, design a general strategy for answering this question, and critique previous studies that have addressed this question.

WHAT DO WE HAVE IN MIND?

Consider the impact of criminological research on the crime of domestic violence. Intimate partner violence (violence between spouses or intimates), sometimes referred to as domestic violence, is a major problem in our society, with police responding to between 2 million and 8 million complaints of assault by a spouse or lover yearly (Sherman 1992: 6). Moreover, it is estimated from victimization surveys that many of these assaults are never reported to police (Bachman & Saltzman 1995; Tjaden & Thoennes 2000). Domestic violence is not just a frequent crime, it is also costly both in terms of the injuries suffered by the parties involved and the shattered families it leaves in its wake. What to do about this major social problem is an important policy question. Perhaps the police could respond to incidents of domestic violence in such a way that the offender would be less likely to be violent in the future—that is, proper police response could possibly prevent some acts of domestic violence. But what is the proper police response?

In 1981, the Police Foundation and the Minneapolis Police Department began an experiment to determine whether arresting accused spouse abusers on the spot would deter future offending incidents. In responding to police calls for service in misdemeanor domestic cases, the responding officer randomly assigned the case to be resolved by either arresting or not arresting the suspect on the scene. The experimental treatment, then, was whether the suspect was arrested, and the researchers wanted to know whether arrest was better than not arresting the suspect in reducing recidivism (subsequent assaults against the same victim). The study's results, which were widely publicized, indicated that arrest did have a deterrent effect. Partly as a result of the reported results of this experiment, the percentage of urban police departments that made arrest the preferred response to complaints of domestic violence rose from 10% in 1984 to 90% in 1988 (Sherman 1992: 14). Six other cities then hosted studies like the Minneapolis experiment (collectively, this was called the Spouse Assault Replication Program [SARP]), but the results were not always so clear-cut as in the original study (Buzawa & Buzawa 1996; Hirschel, Hutchison, & Dean 1992; Pate & Hamilton 1992; Sherman 1992; Sherman & Berk 1984). In some cities (and for some people), arrest did seem to prevent future incidents of domestic assault; in other cities, it seemed only to make matters worse, contributing to additional assault; and in still other cities, arrest seemed to have no discernable effect. After these replications of the original Minneapolis experiment, people still wondered, "Just what is the effect of arrest in reducing domestic violence cases, and how should the police respond to such cases?" The answer was not clear. The Minneapolis Domestic Violence Experiment, the studies modeled after it, and the related controversies provide many examples for a systematic overview of the social research process.

The first concern in criminological research (indeed, in any research) is deciding what to study. That is, how does one go about selecting an issue, problem, or question to address with research?

CRIMINOLOGICAL RESEARCH QUESTIONS

A **criminological research question** is a question about some aspect of crime or criminals that you seek to answer through the collection and analysis of firsthand, verifiable, empirical data. The types of questions that can be asked are virtually limitless. For example, "Are children who are violent more likely than nonviolent children to use violence as adults?" "Does the race of victim who is killed influence whether someone is sentenced to death rather than life imprisonment?" "Why do some kinds of neighborhoods have more crime than others? Is it due to the kinds of people who live there or characteristics of the neighborhood itself?" "Does community policing reduce the crime rate?" "Has the U.S. government's war on drugs done anything to reduce the use of illegal drugs?" So many research questions are possible in criminology that it is more of a challenge to specify what does not qualify as a social research question than to specify what does.

But that does not mean it is easy to specify a research question. In fact, formulating a good research question can be surprisingly difficult. We can break the process into three stages: identifying one or more questions for study, refining the questions, and then evaluating the questions.

Identifying Criminological Research Questions

Formulating a research question is often an intensely personal process in addition to being a scientific or professional one. Research questions may emerge from your "personal troubles," as Mills (1959) put it, or your personal experiences. These troubles or experiences could range from how you felt when you were picked up by the police and perhaps arrested when you were a teenager for something you did not do to the awareness you may have that crime is not randomly distributed within a city but that there seem to be "good" or safe parts of town and "bad" or unsafe areas. Can you think of other possible research questions that flow from your own experience in the world?

The experience of others is another fruitful source of research questions. Knowing a relative who was abused by a spouse, seeing a TV special about violence, or reading a gang member's autobiography can stimulate questions about general criminological processes. Can you draft a research question based on a relative's experiences, a TV show, or a book?

Other researchers may also pose interesting questions for you to study. Most research articles end with some suggestions for additional research that highlight unresolved issues. Any issue of a journal in your field is likely to have comments that point toward unresolved issues.

The primary source of research questions for many criminologists is criminological theory. As you will soon learn, criminological theory provides an explanation as to why crime occurs, or why it occurs in some places and under some conditions but not others. Theory, then, is a very rich source of research ideas. Some researchers spend much of their careers conducting research intended to refine an answer to one central question. For example, you may find rational choice theory to be a useful approach to understanding diverse forms of social behavior, like crime, because you think people do seem to make decisions on the basis of personal cost–benefit calculations. So you may ask whether rational choice theory can explain why some people commit crimes and others do not, or why some people decide to quit committing crimes while others continue their criminal ways.

Finally, some research questions have very pragmatic sources. You may focus on a research question posed by someone else because doing so seems to be to your professional or financial advantage. Some criminologists conduct research on specific questions posed by a funding source in what is termed a request for proposals (RFP). (Sometimes the acronym RFA is used, meaning request for applications.) Or you may learn that the public defenders in your city are curious as to whether they are more successful in getting their clients acquitted of a criminal charge than private lawyers.

Refining Criminological Research Questions

As you have perhaps surmised by now, the problem is not so much coming up with interesting criminological questions for research as focusing on a problem of manageable size. We are often interested in much more than we can reasonably investigate with our limited time and resources (or the limited resources of a funding agency). Researchers may worry about staking a research project (and thereby a grant) on a particular problem and so address several research questions at once, often in a jumbled fashion. It may also seem risky to focus on a research question that may lead to results discrepant with our own cherished assumptions about the social world.

The best way to avoid these problems is to develop the research question one bit at a time with a step-by-step strategy. Do not keep hoping that the perfect research question will just spring forth from your pen. Instead, develop a list of possible research questions as you go along. Narrow your list to the most interesting, most workable candidates. Repeat this process as long as it helps to improve your research questions. Keep in mind that the research on which you are currently working will likely generate additional research questions for you to answer.

Evaluating Criminological Research Questions

In the third stage of selecting a criminological research question, you evaluate the best candidate against the criteria for good social research questions: feasibility given the time and resources available, social importance, and scientific relevance (King, Keohane, & Verba 1994).

The research question in the Minneapolis Domestic Violence Experiment, "Does the formal sanction of police arrest versus nonarrest inhibit domestic violence?" certainly meets the criteria of social importance and scientific relevance, but it would not be a feasible question for a student project because it would require you to try to get the cooperation of a police department.

Feasibility

You must be able to conduct any study within the timeframe and resources you have. If time is short, questions that involve long-term change—for example, "If a state has recently changed its law so that it now permits capital punishment for those convicted of murder, does it eventually see a reduction in the homicide rate over time?"—may not be feasible. This is an interesting and important question, but one that requires years of data collection and research. Another issue is the people or groups to whom you can expect to gain access. Although well-experienced researchers may be granted access to police or correctional department files to do their research, less seasoned and less well-known researchers or students may not be granted such access.

Social Importance

Criminological research is not a simple undertaking, so you must focus on a substantive area that you feel is important and that is either important to the discipline or important for public policy. You also need to feel personally motivated to carry out the study; there is little point in trying to answer a question that does not interest you.

In addition, you should consider whether the research question is important to other people. Will an answer to the research question make a difference for society? Again, the Minneapolis Domestic Violence Experiment is an exemplary case. If that study showed that a certain type of police response to domestic violence reduced the risk of subsequent victimization, a great deal of future violence could be prevented. But clearly, criminology and criminal justice are not wanting for important research questions.

Scientific Relevance

Every research question in criminology should be grounded in the existing empirical literature. By *grounded* we mean the research we do must be informed by what others before us have done on the topic. Whether you formulate a research question because you have been stimulated by an academic article or because you want to investigate a current public policy problem, you must turn to the criminological literature to find out what has already been learned about this question. (Appendix A explains how to find information about previous research, using both printed and computer-based resources.)

For example, the Minneapolis experiment was built on a substantial body of contradictory theorizing about the impact of punishment on criminality (Sherman & Berk 1984). Deterrence theory predicted that, because it was a more severe penalty, arresting people would better deter them from repeat offenses than not arresting them. Labeling theory, on the other hand, predicted that arrest would make repeat offenses more likely because it would stigmatize offenders. Studies among adults and nonexperimental research had not yielded consistent findings about the effects of arrest on recidivism in domestic violence cases. Clearly, the Minneapolis researchers had good reason for another study. Prior research and theory also helped them develop the most effective research design.

THE ROLE OF CRIMINOLOGICAL THEORY

We have already pointed out that criminological **theory** can be a rich source of research questions. What deserves more attention at this point is the larger role of theory in research. Criminological theories do many things:

- They help us explain or understand things like why some people commit crimes or more crimes than others, why some people quit and others continue, and what the expected effect of good families, harsh punishment, or other factors might be on crime.
- They help us make predictions about the criminological world: "What would be the expected effect on the homicide rate if we employed capital punishment rather than life imprisonment?" "What would be the effect on the rate of property crimes if unemployment were to substantially increase?"
- They help us organize and make sense of empirical findings in a discipline.
- They help guide research.
- They help guide public policy: "What should we do to reduce the level of domestic violence?"

Social scientists, such as criminologists, who connect their work to theories in their discipline can generate better ideas about what to look for in a study and develop conclusions with more implications for other research. Building and evaluating theory are therefore among the most important objectives of a social science like criminology.

Theory A logically interrelated set of propositions about empirical reality. Examples of criminological theories are social learning, routine activities, labeling, general strain, and social disorganization theory.

For centuries, scholars have been interested in developing theories about crime and criminals. Sometimes these theories involve very fanciful ideas that are not well developed or organized, whereas at other times they strike us as being very compelling and well organized. Theories usually contain what are called **theoretical constructs**. In criminology, these theoretical constructs describe what is important to look at to understand, explain, predict, and "do something about" crime. Some criminological theories reflect a substantial body of research and the thinking of many social scientists; others are formulated in the course of one investigation. A few have been widely accepted, at least for a time; others are the subject of vigorous controversy, with frequent changes and refinements in response to criticism and new research.

We can use the studies of the police response to domestic assault to illustrate the value of theory for social research. Even in this very concrete and practical matter, we must draw on social theories to understand how people act and what should be done about those actions. Consider the three action options that police officers have when they confront a domestic assault suspect (Sherman & Berk 1984: 263). Fellow officers might urge forced separation to achieve short-term peace; police trainers might prefer mediation to resolve the underlying dispute; feminist groups might urge arrest to protect the victim. None of these recommendations is really a theory, but each suggests a different perspective on crime and legal sanctions. The traditional police perspective sees domestic violence as a family matter that should not be the object of formal legal action. The preference for mediation reflects the view that domestic violence involves a family crisis that can be solved with special counseling. The pro-arrest position views domestic violence as a crime as serious as that between strangers and favors arrest for its presumed deterrent effect.

You will encounter these different perspectives if you read much of the literature on domestic violence, or even if you talk with your friends about it. Each perspective reflects different assumptions about gender roles, about the sources of crime, and about the impact of punishment. In turn, these assumptions reflect different experiences with family conflict, police actions, and the legal system. What we believe about one crime and the appropriate response to it relates to a great many other ideas we have about the social world. Recognizing these relationships is a first step toward becoming a theoretically guided social researcher and a theoretically informed consumer of social research.

Remember, however, that social theories do not provide the answers to the questions we confront as we formulate topics for research. Instead, social theories suggest the areas on which we should focus and the propositions that we should consider for a test. That is, theories suggest testable hypotheses about things and research verifies whether those hypotheses are true. In fact, one of the most important requirements of theory is that it be testable, or what philosophers of science call **falsifiable**; theoretical statements must be capable of being proven wrong. If a body of thought cannot be empirically tested, it is more likely philosophy than theory.

Sherman and Berk's (1984) domestic violence research was actually a test of predictions derived from two alternative theories of the impact of punishment on crime, deterrence theory, and labeling theory:

Deterrence theory presumes that human beings are at least marginally rational beings who are responsive to the expected costs and benefits of their actions. Committing a crime nets certain benefits for offenders; therefore, if we want to inhibit crime, there must be a compensating cost. One cost is the criminal sanction (arrest, conviction, punishment). Deterrence theory expects punishment to inhibit crime in two ways. General deterrence occurs when people see that crime results in undesirable punishments for others, that "crime doesn't pay." The persons who are punished serve as examples for those who have not yet committed an offense but might be thinking of what awaits them should they engage in proscribed acts. Specific deterrence occurs when persons who are punished decide not to commit another offense so they can avoid further punishment (Lempert & Sanders 1986: 86–87). Deterrence theory leads to the prediction that arresting spouse abusers will reduce the likelihood of their reoffending when compared with a less serious sanction (not being arrested but being warned or counseled).

Labeling theory distinguishes between primary deviance—the acts of individuals that lead to public sanctions—and secondary deviance—the deviance that occurs in response to public sanction (Hagan 1994: 33). Arrest or some other public sanction for misdeeds labels the offender as deviant in the eyes of others. Once the offender is labeled, others will treat the offender as a deviant, and he or she is then more likely to act in a way that is consistent with the deviant label. Ironically, the act of punishment stimulates more of the very behavior that it was intended to eliminate (Tannenbaum 1938). This theory suggests that persons arrested for intimate partner violence are more likely to reoffend than those who are caught but not punished because the formal sanction of arrest is more stigmatizing than being warned or counseled. This prediction about the effect of formal legal sanctions is the reverse of the deterrence theory prediction.

Exhibit 2.1 summarizes how these general theories relate to the question of whether to arrest spouse abusers.

EXHIBIT 2.1	Two Social Theories and Their Predictions About the Effect of Arrest for Intimate Partner Assault	
	Rational Choice Theory	*Symbolic Interactionism*
Theoretical assumption	People's behavior is shaped by calculations of the costs and benefits of their actions.	People give symbolic meanings to objects, behaviors, and other people
Criminological component	Deterrence theory: People break the law if the benefits of doing so outweigh the costs.	Labeling theory: People label offenders as deviant, promoting further deviance.
Prediction (effect of arrest for domestic assault)	Abusing spouse, having seen the costs of abuse (namely, arrest), decides not to abuse again.	Abusing spouse, having been labeled as "an abuser," abuses more often.

Does either deterrence theory or labeling theory make sense to you as an explanation for the impact of punishment? Do they seem consistent with your observations of social life? More than a decade after Sherman and Berk's (1984) study, Paternoster et al. (1997) decided to study punishment of domestic violence from a different perspective. They turned to a social psychological theory called procedural justice theory, which explains law-abidingness as resulting from a sense of duty or morality (Tyler 1990). People obey the law from a sense of obligation that flows from seeing legal authorities as moral and legitimate. From this perspective, individuals who are arrested seem less likely to reoffend if they are treated fairly, irrespective of the outcome of their case, because fair treatment will enhance their view of legal authorities as moral and legitimate. Procedural justice theory expands our view of the punishment process by focusing attention on how police act and how authorities treat subjects, rather than just on the legal decisions they make. Thus it gives us a sense of the larger importance of the research question.

Are you now less certain about the likely effect of arrest for intimate partner violence? Will arrest decrease abuse because abusers do not wish to suffer from legal sanctions again? Will it increase abuse because abusers feel stigmatized by being arrested and thus are more likely to act like criminals? Or will arrest reduce abuse only if the abusers feel they have been treated fairly by the legal authorities? By suggesting such questions, social theory makes us much more sensitive to the possibilities and so helps us to design better research. Before, during, and after a research investigation, we need to keep thinking theoretically.

SOCIAL RESEARCH STRATEGIES

All social research, including criminological research, is the effort to connect theory and empirical data, the evidence we find in the real world. As Exhibit 2.2 shows, theory and data have a two-way, mutually reinforcing relationship. Research that begins with a theory implying that certain data should be found involves **deductive reasoning**, which moves from general ideas (theory) to specific reality (data). In contrast, **inductive reasoning** moves from the specific to the general.

Both deductive reasoning and inductive reasoning are essential to criminologists. We cannot test an idea fairly unless we use deductive reasoning, stating our expectations in advance and setting up a test in which our idea could be shown to be wrong (falsified). A theory that has not survived these kinds of tests can be regarded only as very tentative. Yet theories, no matter how cherished, cannot make useful predictions for every social situation or research problem that we seek to investigate. Moreover, we may find unexpected patterns in the data we collect, called **serendipitous findings** or **anomalous findings**. In either situation, we should reason inductively, making whatever theoretical sense we can of our unanticipated findings. Then, if the new findings seem sufficiently important, we can return to deductive reasoning and plan a new study to formally test our new ideas.

EXHIBIT 2.2   The Links Between Theory and Data

The Research Circle

This process of conducting research, moving from theory to data and back again, or from data to theory and back again, can be characterized as a **research circle**. Exhibit 2.3 depicts this circle. Note that it mirrors the relationship between theory and data shown in Exhibit 2.2 and that it comprises three main research strategies: deductive research, inductive research, and descriptive research.

Deductive Research

As Exhibit 2.3 shows, **deductive research** proceeds from theorizing to data collection and then back to theorizing. In essence, a specific expectation is deduced from a general premise and then tested.

Notice that a theory leads first to a **hypothesis**, which is a specific implication deduced from the more general theory. Researchers actually test a hypothesis, not the complete theory itself, because theories usually contain many hypotheses. A hypothesis proposes a relationship between two or more theoretical constructs or **variables**. A variable is a characteristic or property that can vary. A **constant** is a characteristic or a property that cannot vary. For example, if we were to conduct some research in a male adult penitentiary, the theoretical construct "type of crime committed" would be a variable because persons will have been incarcerated for different offenses (one person for armed robbery, another for rape, etc.). However, the theoretical construct "gender" would be a constant because every inmate in the penitentiary would be male.

EXHIBIT 2.3   The Research Circle

Hypothesis A tentative statement about empirical reality, involving a relationship between two or more variables.

> *Example of a hypothesis:* The higher the level of residential mobility in a community, the higher its rate of crime will be.

Variable A characteristic or property that can vary (take on different values or attributes).

Constant A characteristic or property that does not vary but takes on only one value.

Variables are of critical importance in research because, in a hypothesis, variation in one variable is proposed to predict, influence, or cause variation in the other variable. The proposed influence is the **independent variable**; its effect or consequence is the **dependent variable**. After the researchers formulate one or more hypotheses and develop research procedures, they collect data with which to test the hypothesis.

Independent variable A variable that is hypothesized to cause, or lead to, variation in the dependent variable.

> *Example of an independent variable:* Residential mobility (residents moving in and out of the community).

Dependent variable A variable that is hypothesized to vary depending on or under the influence of the independent variable.

> *Example of a dependent variable:* The rate of crime in a community per 1,000 residents.

Hypotheses can be worded in several different ways, and identifying the independent and dependent variables is sometimes difficult. When in doubt, try to rephrase the hypothesis as an if–then statement: "If the independent variable increases (or decreases), then the dependent variable increases (or decreases)." Exhibit 2.4 presents several hypotheses with their independent and dependent variables and their if–then equivalents.

EXHIBIT 2.4   Examples of Hypotheses

Original Hypothesis	Independent Variable	Dependent Variable	If-Then Hypothesis
1. The greater the social disorganization in a community, the higher the rate of crime.	Social disorganization	Crime rate	If social disorganization is higher, then the crime rate is higher.
2. As one's self-control gets stronger, the fewer delinquent acts one commits.	Self-control	Self-reported delinquency	If self-control is higher, then the number of delinquent acts is lower.
3. As the unemployment rate in a community decreases, the community rate of property crime decreases.	Unemployment rate	Rate of property crime	If the unemployment rate is lower, then the rate of property crime is lower.
4. As the discrepancy between one's aspirations and expectations increases, one's level of strain increases.	Discrepancy between one's aspirations and expectations	Strain	If the discrepancy between one's aspirations and expectations is high, then the level of strain is high.
5. Crime is lower in those communities where the police patrol on foot.	Presence of foot patrols	Crime	If a community has police foot patrols, then the level of crime is lower.

Exhibit 2.4 demonstrates another feature of hypotheses: **direction of association**. When researchers hypothesize that one variable increases as the other variable increases, the direction of the association is positive (Hypotheses 1 and 4 in the exhibit); when one variable decreases as the other variable decreases, the direction of association is also positive (Hypothesis 3). In positive relationships, then, the independent and dependent variables move in the same direction (as one increases, the other increases; or as one decreases, the other decreases). But when one variable increases as the other decreases, or vice versa, the direction of association is negative, or inverse (Hypothesis 2). In a negative relationship, then, the independent and dependent variables move in opposite directions (as one increases, the other decreases; or as one decreases, the other increases). Hypothesis 5 is a special case in which the independent variable is categorical. The independent variable cannot be said to increase or decrease. In this case, the concept of direction of association does not apply, and the hypothesis simply states that one category of the independent variable is associated with higher values on the dependent variable.

You can get a better sense of what the direction of a relationship means by looking at Exhibits 2.5 through 2.9, which correspond to the five hypotheses shown in Exhibit 2.4. In these graphs, the independent variable is displayed as the x or horizontal axis and the dependent variable is displayed as the y or vertical axis. Exhibit 2.5 illustrates the hypothesis that social disorganization and a community's crime rate are positively related. The positive association implies that as social disorganization (the independent variable) increases (moves from being low to being high), the expected change is that the dependent variable will also increase (move from being low to high). This is the same thing as saying that, as the level of social disorganization in a community moves from low to high, the level of crime also moves from low to high. In other words, the more social disorganization, the more crime there is. Notice that in a positive relationship, the independent and dependent variables are moving in the same direction; as social disorganization increases, so does crime.

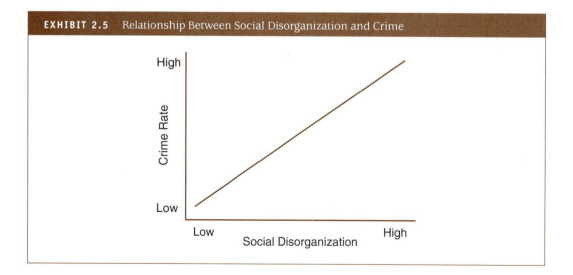

EXHIBIT 2.5   Relationship Between Social Disorganization and Crime

Exhibit 2.6 illustrates a graph for a negative association. This graph shows that, as one's self-control becomes high (where more self-control means greater restraint over one's impulses), then the number of delinquent acts one commits declines or moves to low. This means that as self-control increases or strengthens, the frequency of delinquent behavior declines or decreases in number. Notice two things about this negative relationship. First, the independent and dependent variables move in opposite directions; as the independent variable (self-control) increases, the dependent variable (delinquency) decreases. Notice also that this negative relationship is shown as a downward-sloping line on the graph.

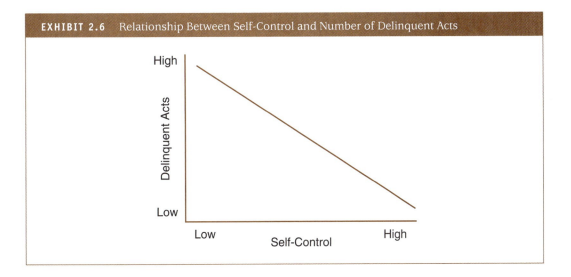

EXHIBIT 2.6   Relationship Between Self-Control and Number of Delinquent Acts

Finally, Exhibit 2.7 illustrates a relationship with a graph that is slightly different. Here, the hypothesis (Hypothesis 5 in Exhibit 2.4) states that we expect to see lower crime in communities that have foot patrols compared with communities that do not have foot patrols. Unlike the other independent variables, the independent variable "foot patrol" does not vary from low to high: Either there are foot patrols in the community or there are not. If the hypothesis is true, what we should expect to see is that most of the communities that do not have foot patrols should have high rates of crime, whereas most of those communities that do have foot patrols should have lower rates of crime. This expectation is shown in Exhibit 2.7 with the clump of points (representing communities) for the "no foot patrol" communities at the high range of crime and the clump of points for the "yes foot patrol" communities at the low range of crime.

The motives for deductive research include both explanation and evaluation (as described in chapter 1). An example of explanatory deductive research is the Minneapolis Domestic Violence Experiment, in which Sherman and Berk (1984) sought to explain what sort of response by the authorities might keep a spouse abuser from repeating the offense. The researchers deduced from deterrence theory the expectation that arrest would deter domestic violence. They then collected data to test this expectation.

EXHIBIT 2.7   Relationship Between Foot Patrols and Crime

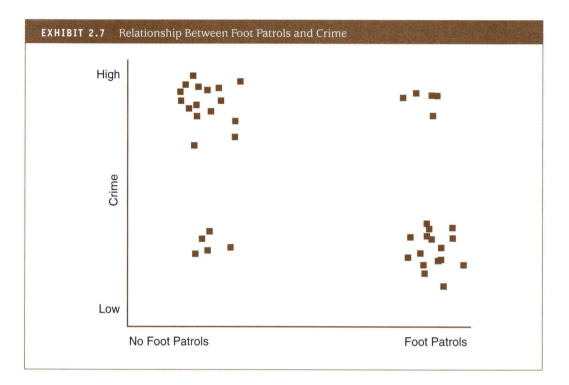

An example of evaluative deductive research is the study of the Second Step violence prevention curriculum, by Grossman et al. (1997), that was discussed in chapter 1. The developers of the Second Step program had deduced from previous research in the violence prevention literature that violence in children could be inhibited if they learned and had practice with empathy, impulse control, and anger management. Based on this trinity of approaches, Second Step was devised to reduce the expressed violence among those children in the program. Grossman and colleagues collected data to test this expectation.

In both explanatory and evaluative research, the statement of expectations for the findings and the design of the research to test these expectations strengthens the confidence we can place in the test. Deductive researchers show their hand or state their expectations in advance and then design a fair test of those expectations. Then "the chips fall where they may"—in other words, the researcher accepts the resulting data as a more or less objective picture of reality.

Inductive Research

In contrast to deductive research, **inductive research** begins at the bottom of the research circle and then works upward (see Exhibit 2.3). The inductive researcher begins with specific data, which are then used to develop (induce) a general explanation (a theory) to account for the data. The patterns in the data are then summarized in one or more **empirical generalizations**.

The motive for inductive research is exploration. In chapter 1, you read about an exploratory study of individuals' responses to an incident involving a school shooting (Asmussen & Creswell 1995). The incident took place at a public university where a gunman tried to shoot the students in his class. Fortunately, the gun jammed and all the students escaped uninjured. Because there was very little previous work in this area, Asmussen and Creswell (1995) conducted in-depth interviews with the students and tried to classify typical responses to the situation. Although the researchers did not develop a theory from their work, they did develop a classification scheme or taxonomy of different responses to traumatic events.

In strictly inductive research, researchers already know what they have found when they start theorizing, or attempting to explain what accounts for these findings. The result can be new insights and provocative questions. But the adequacy of an explanation formulated after the fact is necessarily less certain than an explanation presented prior to the collection of data. Every phenomenon can always be explained in some way. Inductive explanations are thus more trustworthy if they are tested subsequently with deductive research.

A Qualitative Exploration of the Response to Domestic Violence

Qualitative research is often inductive: Researchers begin by observing social interaction or interviewing social actors in depth and then developing an explanation for what has been found. The researchers often ask questions like "What is going on here?" or "How do people interpret these experiences?" Rather than testing a hypothesis, the researchers are trying to make sense of some social phenomenon. Bennet, Goodman, and Dutton (1999) used this approach to investigate one of the problems that emerge when police arrest domestic batterers: The victims often decide not to press charges. Bennett and colleagues did not set out to test hypotheses with qualitative interviews (there was another, hypothesis-testing, component in their research), but sought, inductively, to "add the voice of the victim to the discussion" and present "themes that emerged from [the] interviews" (1999: 762).

Research assistants interviewed 49 victims of domestic violence in one court; Lauren Bennett also worked in the same court as a victim advocate. The researchers were able to cull from their qualitative data four reasons why victims became reluctant to press charges: Some were confused by the court procedures, while others were frustrated by the delay; some were paralyzed by fear of retribution; and still others did not want to send the batterer to jail.

Explanations developed inductively from qualitative research can feel authentic because we have heard what people have to say "in their own words" and we have tried to see the social world "as they see it." One victim interviewed by Bennett, Goodman, and Dutton (1999) felt that she "was doing time instead of the defendant;" another expressed her fear by saying that she would like "to keep him out of jail if that's what it takes to keep my kids safe" (1999: 768–769). Explanations derived from qualitative research will be richer and more finely textured than those resulting from quantitative research, but they are likely to be based on fewer cases from a limited area. We cannot assume that the people studied in this setting are like others or that other researchers would develop explanations similar to ours to make sense of what was observed or heard.

DOMESTIC VIOLENCE AND THE RESEARCH CIRCLE

The Sherman and Berk (1984) study of domestic violence that we have been discussing in this chapter is a good example of how the research circle works. In an attempt to determine ways to prevent the recurrence of intimate partner violence, the researchers repeatedly linked theory and data, developing both hypotheses and empirical generalizations.

Phase 1: Deductive Research

The first phase of Sherman and Berk's (1984) study was designed to test a hypothesis. According to deterrence theory, punishment will reduce recidivism, or the propensity to commit further crimes. From this theory, Sherman and Berk deduced a specific hypothesis: "Arrest for spouse abuse reduces the risk of repeat offenses." In this hypothesis, arrest is the independent variable, and variation in the risk of repeat offenses is the dependent variable (it is hypothesized to depend on arrest).

Sherman and Berk (1984) tested their hypothesis by setting up an experiment in which the police responded to complaints of spouse abuse in one of three ways, one of which was to arrest the offender. When the researchers examined their data (police records for the persons in their experiment), they found that of those arrested for assaulting their spouse, only 13% repeated the offense, compared with a 26% recidivism rate for those who were separated from their spouse by the police without any arrest. This pattern in the data, or empirical generalization, was consistent with the hypothesis that the researchers deduced from deterrence theory. The theory thus received support from the experiment (see Exhibit 2.8).

EXHIBIT 2.8   The Research Circle: Minneapolis Domestic Violence Experiment

Theory
Deterrence theory

Empirical generalizations

Action	Recidivism
Arrest	13%
Separation	26%

Hypothesis
More arrests, less recidivism

Data
Measures for 330 domestic assault cases

In designing their study, Sherman and Berk (1984) anticipated an important question: "How valid was the connection they [the researchers] were trying to make between theory and data?" The three dimensions of validity—measurement validity, generalizability, and causal validity—were at issue.

Determining whether spouses were assaulted after the initial police intervention was the key measurement concern. Official records of subsequent assaults by the suspect would provide one measure. But most spousal assaults are not reported to the police, so research assistants also sought out the victims for interviews every two weeks during a six-month follow-up period. Although fewer than half the victims completed all the follow-up interviews, the availability of the self-report measure allowed the researchers to shed some light on the validity of the official data. In general, the two measures yielded comparable results, although some discrepancies troubled critics.

The generalizability of the study's results was the researchers' greatest concern. Minneapolis is no more a typical U.S. city than any other, and we cannot assume that police policies which are effective in Minneapolis will be equally effective in cities with very different political histories, criminal justice agencies, and population characteristics. Sherman and Berk (1984) warned readers, "External validity will have to wait for replications" (1984: 269)—that is, for repetitions of the study using the same research methods to answer the same research question.

Finally, Sherman and Berk's (1984) claims about the causal validity of their results rested primarily on the experimental design they used. The 330 domestic assault cases in the study were handled by the police in one of three ways: an arrest, an order that the offending spouse leave the house for eight hours, or some type of verbal advice by the police officers. The officers were not allowed to choose which treatment to apply (except in extreme cases, such as when severe injury had occurred or when the spouse had demanded that an arrest be made). Instead, the treatments were carried out by police in random order, according to the color of the next report form on a pad that had been prepared by the researchers.

By insisting on the random assignment of cases to treatments, the researchers tried to ensure that police officers would not arrest just the toughest spouses or the spouses who seemed most obnoxious or the spouses they encountered late in the day. In other words, the random assignment procedure made it unlikely that arrested spouse abusers would differ, on average, from the other spouse abusers except for the fact that they were arrested (although, because of chance factors, the possibility of other differences cannot completely be ruled out). The researchers' conclusion that arrest caused a lower incidence of repeat offenses therefore seems valid.

Phase 2: Deductive Research

Because of their doubts about the generalizability of their results, Sherman, Berk, and new collaborators began to journey around the research circle again, with funding from the National Institute of Justice for **replications** (repetitions) of the experiment in six more cities. These replications used the same basic research approach but with some improvements. The random assignment process was tightened up in most of the cities so that police officers would be less likely to replace the assigned treatment with a treatment of their own choice. In addition, data were collected about repeat violence against other victims as well as against the original complainant. Some replications also examined different aspects of the arrest process, to see whether professional counseling helped and whether the length of time spent in jail after arrest mattered at all.

By the time results were reported from five of the cities in the new study, a problem was apparent. In three cities—Omaha, Nebraska; Charlotte, North Carolina; and Milwaukee, Wisconsin—researchers were finding long-term increases in domestic violence incidents among arrestees. But in Colorado Springs, Colorado; and Dade County, Florida; the predicted deterrent effects seemed to be occurring (Sherman et al. 1992).

Researchers had now traversed the research circle twice in an attempt to answer the original research question, first in Minneapolis and then in six other cities. But, rather than leading to more confidence in deterrence theory, the research results were calling it into question. Deterrence theory now seemed inadequate to explain empirical reality, at least as the researchers had measured this reality. So the researchers began to reanalyze the follow-up data from several cities to try to explain the discrepant results, thereby starting the research circle once again (Berk et al. 1992; Pate & Hamilton 1992; Sherman et al. 1992).

Phase 3: Inductive Research

At this point, the researchers' approach became more inductive, and they began trying to make sense of the differing patterns in the data collected in the different cities. Could systematic differences in the samples or in the implementation of arrest policies explain the differing outcomes? Or was the problem an inadequacy in the theoretical basis of their research? Was deterrence theory really the best way to explain the patterns in the data they were collecting?

Sherman et al. (1992) now turned to control theory (Toby 1957), yet another broad explanation for social behavior. It predicts that having a stake in conformity (resulting from inclusion in social networks at work or in the community) decreases a person's likelihood of committing crimes. The implication is that people who are employed and married are more likely to be deterred by the threat of arrest than those without such stakes in conformity. This is because an arrest for domestic violence could jeopardize one's job and one's marriage, thus making arrest more costly for the employed and married. This, indeed, is what a reexamination of the data revealed: Individuals who were married and employed were deterred from repeat offenses by arrest, but individuals who were unmarried and unemployed were actually more likely to commit repeat offenses if they were arrested. This was an important theoretical insight. It suggested that one powerful way that formal sanctions work is that they can potentially trigger informal sanctions or costs (e.g., loss of respect from friends and family).

Now the researchers had traversed the research circle almost three times, a process perhaps better described as a spiral (see Exhibit 2.9). The first two times the researchers had traversed the research circle in a deductive, hypothesis-testing way: They started with theory and then deduced and tested hypotheses. The third time they traversed the research circle in a more inductive, exploratory way: They started with empirical generalizations from the data they had already obtained and then turned to a new theory to account for the unexpected patterns in the data. At this point, their belief was that deterrence theory makes correct predictions given certain conditions and that another theory, control theory, may specify what these conditions are.

After two and one-half cycles through the research circle, the picture became more complex but also conceptually richer. The researchers came closer to understanding how to inhibit domestic violence, but they cautioned us that their initial question, the research problem, was still not completely answered. Employment status and marital status alone do not measure the strength of social attachments; they also are related to how much people earn and the social standing of victims in court. So perhaps social ties are not really what makes arrest an effective deterrent to domestic violence. More research was still needed (Berk et al. 1992).

EXHIBIT 2.9   The Research Spiral: Minneapolis Domestic Violence Experiment

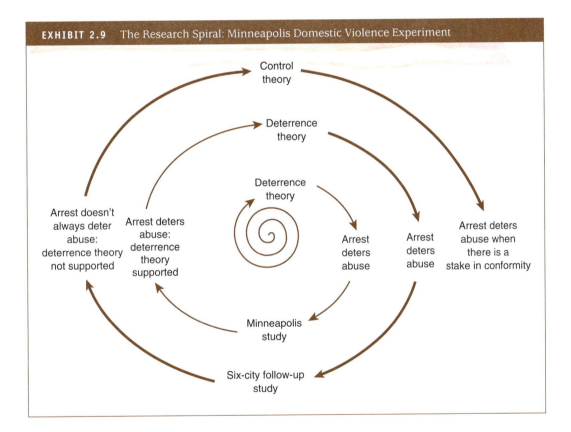

Phase 4: Deductive Research

In 1997, Paternoster et al. reexamined data from the Milwaukee Domestic Violence Experiment to test hypotheses derived from yet another theory, procedural justice theory. As explained earlier, procedural justice theory predicts that people will comply with the law out of a sense of duty and obligation if they are treated fairly by legal authorities. In the Milwaukee sample, arrest had a criminogenic effect: Those who were arrested were subsequently more likely to abuse their spouses than those who were simply warned. Paternoster et al. (1997) thought that this effect might have been due to the way subjects were treated when they were arrested rather than simply to the fact that they were arrested. One of their hypotheses spells out the reasoning:

> Among those persons arrested for spouse assault, those who perceive themselves as being treated in a procedurally unfair manner will be more likely to commit acts of spouse assault in the future than those arrested persons who perceive themselves as being treated in a procedurally fair manner, net of other determinants of violence. (1997: 173)

To carry out this study, Paternoster et al. (1997) reexamined data collected earlier in Milwaukee, where the findings had seemed anomalous. However, this reanalysis of the data qualifies as deductive research, because the hypotheses were derived from theory and then tested with the data, rather than being induced by the data.

The procedural justice hypotheses were supported: Persons who were arrested in the Milwaukee experiment became more likely to reoffend only if they perceived that they had been treated unfairly by the police. Otherwise, their rate of rearrest was similar to that for the persons who were not arrested. Thus another element was added to our understanding of the effects of the police response to domestic violence.

Clearly our understanding of effective responses to domestic violence will never truly be complete, but research to date has greatly improved our understanding of this social problem. The future should yield an even better understanding, even though at times it may be hard to make sense out of conflicting findings from different studies. Science is an ongoing enterprise in which findings cumulate and eventually yield greater understanding, or even radical revisions in our understanding. Needless to say, researchers do not need to worry about running out of work to do.

GUIDELINES FOR CRIMINOLOGISTS

The guidelines followed by social researchers fall into two categories: those that help keep research scientific and those that help keep research ethical. Both types of guidelines are essential for a field of inquiry that seeks empirical generalizations about human society. To point out their value, we use examples from the domestic violence research.

Scientific Guidelines

The following nine guidelines are applicable to any type of scientific research, but they are particularly useful to criminologists and to those who read about criminology and criminal justice. Adherence to these guidelines will reduce the temptation "to project on what is observed whatever [they] want the world to be for [their] own private purposes" (Hoover 1980: 131).

1. *Test ideas against empirical reality without becoming too personally invested in a particular outcome.* This testing approach is reflected in the research process and is implicit in the goal of validity. Empirical testing requires a neutral and open-minded

approach: Scientists are personally disinterested in the outcome and not swayed by the popularity or the social status of those who would prefer other outcomes. This does not mean that the researchers are not personally involved or interested in the research—they must be; rather, the point is that they cannot have so much invested in a research project personally or professionally that they try in subtle or not-so-subtle ways to affect the outcome.

2. *Plan and carry out investigations systematically.* Social researchers have little hope of conducting a careful test of their ideas if they do not think through in advance how they should go about the test and then proceed accordingly. But a systematic approach is not always easy. For example, Sherman and Berk (1984) needed to ensure that spouse abusers were assigned to be either arrested or not on a random basis, rather than on the basis of the police officers' personal preferences. So the researchers devised an elaborate procedure using randomly sequenced report sheets in different colors. But the researchers found that police officers did not always follow this systematic procedure. Subsequently, in some replications of the study, the researchers ensured compliance with their research procedures by requiring police officers to call in to a central number to receive the experimentally determined treatment.

3. *Document all procedures, and disclose them publicly.* Social researchers who disclose the methods on which their conclusions rest allow others to evaluate for themselves the likely soundness of these conclusions. Such disclosure is a key feature of science. Again, Sherman and Berk (1984) provide a compelling example. In their research report, after describing the formal research plan, they described at length the apparent slippage from this plan, which occurred primarily because some police officers avoided implementing the random assignment procedure.

4. *Clarify assumptions.* No investigation is complete unto itself; whatever the researcher's method, the research rests on some background assumptions. Research to determine whether arrest has a deterrent effect assumes that potential law violators think rationally, that they calculate potential costs and benefits prior to committing crimes. When a researcher conducts an election poll, the assumption is that people actually vote for the candidate they say they will vote for. By definition, research assumptions are not tested, so we do not know whether they are correct. By taking the time to think about and to disclose their assumptions, researchers provide important information for those who seek to evaluate the validity of their conclusions.

5. *Specify the meaning of all terms.* Words often have multiple or unclear meanings. Strain, differential association, social disorganization, subculture of violence, problem-oriented policing, and so on can mean different things to different people. Thus the terms used in scientific research must be defined explicitly and used consistently.

6. *Maintain a skeptical stance toward current knowledge.* Scientists may feel very confident about interpretations of the social or natural world that have been supported by repeated investigations, but the results of any particular

investigation must be examined critically. A general skepticism about current knowledge stimulates researchers to improve the validity of current research results and expand the frontier of knowledge.

7. *Replicate research and accumulate knowledge.* No one study can be viewed as definitive in itself; usually at least some plausible threats to the validity of the conclusions exist. And no conclusion can be understood adequately apart from the larger body of knowledge to which the study is related. Scientific investigations may begin with a half-baked or off-the-wall idea, but a search of the literature for other relevant work must be conducted in short order. The other side of the coin is that the results of scientific research must be published, to serve as a foundation for others who seek to replicate or extend the research.

8. *Maintain an interest in theory.* Theories organize the knowledge accumulated by numerous investigations into a coherent whole and serve as a guide to future inquiries. Even though much research is purely descriptive, this research can still serve as a basis for others to evaluate different theories. The Minneapolis Domestic Violence Experiment was devised initially as a test of the competing predictions of deterrence and labeling theory, but the researchers extended their attention to control theory to help them explain unanticipated findings. These theoretical connections make the research much more relevant to other criminologists working to understand different types of crime and social control.

9. *Search for regularities or patterns.* Science is concerned with classes rather than with individuals (except inasmuch as individuals are representatives of a class). Scientists assume that the natural world has some underlying order of relationships, and that every event and individual is not so unique that general principles cannot be discerned (Grinnell 1992: 27–29). The goal of elaborating individual cases is to understand social patterns that characterize many individuals.

These general guidelines are only ideals for social research. No particular investigation will follow every guideline exactly. Real investigations by criminologists do not always include much attention to theory, specific definitions of all terms, and so forth. Any study that strays far from these guidelines cannot be considered scientific.

Ethical Guidelines

Every methodology (e.g., surveys, experiments, participant observation) has its own unique ethical considerations. As such, we will discuss ethics in all methodology chapters in this text. However, there are some general ethical guidelines that we would like to present here. Every scientific investigation has an ethical dimension. First and foremost, the scientific concern with validity requires that scientists be honest and reveal their methods. (How else could we determine whether the requirement of honesty has been met?) Scientists also have to consider the uses to which their findings will be put. In addition, because criminological research deals with people such as criminals, criminal suspects, and incarcerated inmates, and controversial topics (involvement in crime), criminologists have some unique ethical concerns.

Honesty and Openness

Research distorted by political or personal pressures to find particular outcomes or to achieve the most marketable results is unlikely to be carried out in an honest and open fashion or to achieve valid results.

Being open about one's research is particularly important when the research is used or influential in public policy matters. For example, an economist who was interested in the study of crime, Professor Isaac Ehrlich (1975), conducted a study that examined whether capital punishment deters murder. Using national data for the time period 1933–1969, Ehrlich concluded that each execution prevented or deterred seven to eight homicides—in other words, Ehrlich claimed that executions saved seven to eight innocent crime victims. This was one of a very few studies at the time to find a deterrent effect for capital punishment. In fact, his results were cited in a U.S. Supreme Court case (*Gregg v. Georgia,* 1976) as evidence in support of deterrence. His reported findings caused both a stir among proponents of capital punishment and skeptical hostility among its critics. The controversy surrounding his findings grew when other researchers tried to duplicate his findings with data they collected and found that, when they analyzed slightly different years, with slightly different variables and sometimes slightly different statistical strategies, the effect of executions changed. In some analyses, executions seemed to deter murder; in some others, it seemed to increase murders (what was called a brutalization effect); and in others, it had no discernable effect at all. The controversy about Ehrlich's findings bubbled for years and might have been resolved much sooner had Ehrlich been more open and forthcoming about his data.

Openness about research procedures and results goes hand in hand with honesty in research design. Openness is also essential if researchers are to learn from the work of others. In spite of this need for openness, some researchers may hesitate to disclose their procedures or results to prevent others from building on their ideas and taking some of the credit. You may have heard of the long legal battle between a U.S. researcher and a French researcher about how credit should be allocated for discovering the AIDS virus. Although such public disputes are unusual, concerns with priority of discovery are common. Scientists are like other people in their desire to be first. Enforcing standards of honesty and encouraging openness about research is the best solution to these problems.

The Uses of Science

Scientists must also consider the extent to which they should publicize their research and the uses to which it is put. Although many scientists believe that personal values should be left outside the laboratory, some argue that it is proper, even desirable, for scientists in their role as citizens to attempt to influence public policy. In other words, if their research has something to say about how things *should be* done, some scientists feel that they should actively promote their work.

Throughout this chapter, we have been talking about one criminological experiment, the Minneapolis Domestic Violence Experiment, which found that arresting domestic violence suspects was more effective in reducing subsequent violence than not arresting them. Although Sherman and Berk (1984) were generally cautious about the kinds of conclusions that should be drawn from their work, they were both active and passive in promoting their findings. Not only was their work published in scientific journals, but it also received widespread publicity in the national media: one of the authors and the Minneapolis chief of police wrote an editorial in the *Wall Street Journal* recommending that other jurisdictions pass laws similar to those of Minneapolis, and one of the authors contracted with a Minneapolis television station to film a documentary on the research. In their published findings, they concluded,

> We favor a *presumption* of arrest: an arrest should be made unless there are good, clear reasons why an arrest would be counterproductive. We do not, however, favor *requiring* arrests in all misdemeanor domestic assault cases. (1984: 270)

Sherman and Berk (1984) were criticized by other scholars on the basis that the findings of one study are not a sufficient empirical basis from which to draw such an important public policy recommendation. In fact, Sherman and Berk did caution that their findings might not be replicated in other locations, and that their position is that police should be able to arrest domestic violence suspects, not that they should be required to. Nevertheless, because Sherman publicized the results of the research in the mass media, he was criticized by some social scientists for implicitly encouraging police departments to change their policies on the basis of preliminary evidence (the results of just one study in one city) (Binder & Meeker 1993; Lempert 1989). In part, the question was whether basing policy on partial information was preferable to waiting until the information was more complete (more studies conducted in different locations). Sherman argued that public policy is better guided by partial knowledge than no knowledge at all.

Research on People

In physics or chemistry, research subjects (objects and substances) may be treated to extreme conditions and then discarded when they are no longer useful. However, social (and medical) scientists must concern themselves with the way their human subjects are treated in the course of research. This treatment may involve manipulations and deceptions in laboratory experiments, sensitive questions in survey research, observations in field studies, or analyses of personal data. Here we will briefly review current ethical standards for the treatment of human subjects and dilemmas in their application. In the chapters on data collection, chapters 5 through 8, we will examine the specific ethical problems that may arise in the course of using particular research methods.

Contemporary standards for the treatment of human subjects are set by the federal government, by professional associations, by special university review boards, and in some cases by ethics committees in other organizations. Federal regulations require that the proposals of researchers seeking federal funds for research on human subjects be reviewed by an **institutional review board (IRB)** before they are submitted for federal review. IRBs at universities and other agencies in turn apply ethics standards set by government agencies, like the National Institutes of Health, and may develop more specific guidelines of their own. The American Society of Criminology (ASC), one of criminology's professional organizations, is in the process of redrafting its code of ethics, but advises members to seek guidance from similar organizations, including the American Sociological Association (ASA). The ASA's standards (ASA 1997) concerning the treatment of human subjects include federal regulations and ethics guidelines emphasized by most professional social science organizations:

- Research should cause no harm to subjects.
- Participation in research should be voluntary, and therefore subjects must give their informed consent to participate in the research.
- Researchers should fully disclose their identity.
- Anonymity or confidentiality must be maintained for individual research participants, unless it is voluntarily and explicitly waived.
- The benefits of a research project should outweigh any foreseeable risks.

As simple as these guidelines may seem, they are difficult to interpret in specific cases and harder yet to define in a way agreeable to all criminologists. For example, how should we interpret the admonition that no harm should be done to subjects? Consider the question of possible harm to the subjects of a well-known prison simulation study (Haney, Banks, & Zimbardo 1973). The study was designed to investigate the impact of social position on behavior—specifically, the impact of being either a guard or a prisoner in a prison, a total institution. The researchers selected 20 young men whom they judged to be the most stable and mature, and the least antisocial, of 75 applicants. The participants signed a contract agreeing to be either a guard or a prisoner in a simulated prison for two weeks, during which time they would be paid and receive food, clothing, housing, and medical care. Some were randomly selected to be guards and were told to maintain order among the prisoners, who were then incarcerated in a makeshift basement prison. Within the first two days, marked differences in behavior emerged between the two groups. The prisoners acted in a passive and disorganized manner, and the guards became verbally and physically aggressive (although physical abuse was not allowed) and arbitrary. Five prisoners were soon released for depression, uncontrollable crying, fits of rage, and in one case a psychosomatic rash; on the sixth day the researchers terminated the experiment. However, follow-up during the next year indicated no lasting negative effects on the participants and some benefits in the form of greater insight.

Would you ban such experiments because of the potential for harm to subjects? Does the fact that the experiment yielded significant insights into the effect of a situation on human behavior, insights that could be used to improve prisons, make any difference (Reynolds 1979: 133–139)? Do you believe that this benefit outweighed the foreseeable risks?

The requirement of informed consent is also more difficult to define than is at first apparent. To be informed, consent must be given by persons who are competent to consent, have consented voluntarily, are fully informed about the research, and have comprehended what they have been told (Reynolds 1979). Can prisoners give informed consent? Can children or juveniles give their own consent? Can parents or guardians give consent on behalf of their children? Can students who are asked to participate in research by their professor give consent? Can participants in covert experiments do so?

Fully informed consent may alter participation in research and, because signing consent forms prior to participation may change participants' responses, produce biased results (Larson 1993: 114). In addition, there is always the problem that those persons who give their support in a research project may be quite different from those who do not. This differential selection of participants has implications for both the validity of the reported results and the generalizability of the study. Experimental researchers whose research design requires some type of subject deception try to get around this problem by withholding some information before the experiment begins but then debriefing subjects at the end. In the **debriefing**, the researcher explains to the subject what happened in the experiment and why.

Maintaining confidentiality is another key ethical obligation. This standard, however, should be overridden if a health- or life-threatening situation arises and participants need to be alerted. Also, the standard of confidentiality does not apply to observation in public places and information available in public records.

The potential of withholding a beneficial treatment from some subjects is also cause for ethical concern. The Sherman and Berk (1984) experiment required the random assignment of subjects to treatment conditions and thus had the potential of causing harm to the victims of domestic violence whose batterers were not arrested. The justification for the study design, however, is quite persuasive: The researchers did not know prior to the experiment which response to a domestic violence complaint would be most likely to deter future incidents (Sherman 1992). The experiment provided clear evidence about the value of arrest, so it can be argued that the benefits outweighed the risks.

The evaluation of ethical issues in a research project should be based on a realistic assessment of the overall potential for harm to research subjects rather than an apparent inconsistency between any particular aspect of a research plan and a specific ethical guideline. For example, full disclosure of what is really going on in an experimental study is unnecessary if subjects are unlikely to be harmed. Nevertheless, researchers should make every effort to foresee all possible risks and to weigh the possible benefits of the research against these risks.

CONCLUSION

Criminological researchers can find many questions to study, but not all questions are equally worthy. Those that warrant the expense and effort of social research are feasible, socially important, and scientifically relevant.

The simplicity of the research circle presented in this chapter belies the complexity of the social research process. In the following chapters, we will focus on particular aspects of that process.

As you encounter the specifics of research methods in the following chapters, do not lose sight of the basic guidelines that researchers need to follow to overcome the most common impediments to social research. Owning a large social science toolkit is no guarantee of making the right decisions about which tools to use and how to use them in the investigation of particular research problems. More importantly, our answers to research questions will never be complete or entirely certain. Thus, when we complete a research project, we should point out how the research could be extended and evaluate the confidence we have in our conclusions. Recall how the gradual elaboration of knowledge about the deterrence of domestic violence required sensitivity to research difficulties, careful weighing of the evidence, and identification of unanswered questions by several research teams.

Ethical issues should be considered when evaluating research proposals and completed research studies. As the preceding examples show, ethical issues in social research are no less complex than the other issues that researchers confront. It is inexcusable to jump into research on people without any attention to ethical considerations.

KEY TERMS

Anomalous finding
Constant
Criminological research question
Debriefing
Deductive reasoning
Deductive research
Dependent variable
Direction of association
Empirical generalization
Falsifiable statement
Hypothesis

Independent variable
Inductive reasoning
Inductive research
Institutional review
    board (IRB)
Replication
Research circle
Serendipitous finding
Theoretical construct
Theory
Variable

HIGHLIGHTS

- Research questions should be feasible (within the time and resources available), socially important, and scientifically relevant.

- Building criminological theory is a major objective of criminological research. Investigate relevant theories before starting criminological projects, and draw out the theoretical implications of research findings.

- The type of reasoning in most criminological research can be described as primarily deductive or inductive. Research based on deductive reasoning proceeds from general ideas, deduces specific expectations from these ideas, and then tests the ideas with empirical data. Research based on inductive reasoning begins with specific data and then develops general ideas or theories to explain patterns in the data.

- It may be possible to explain unanticipated research findings after the fact, but such explanations have less credibility than those that have been tested with data collected for the purpose of the study.

- The scientific process can be represented as circular, with connections from theory to hypotheses to data to empirical generalizations. Research investigations may begin at different points along the research circle and traverse different portions of it. Deductive research begins at the point of theory; inductive research begins with data but ends with theory. Descriptive research begins with data and ends with empirical generalizations.

- Replications of a study are essential to establish its generalizability in other situations. An ongoing line of research stemming from a particular question should include a series of studies that, collectively, traverse the research circle multiple times.

- Criminologists, like all social scientists, should structure their research so that their own ideas can be proved wrong, should disclose their methods for others to critique, and should recognize the possibility of error. Nine specific guidelines are recommended.

- Scientific research should be conducted and reported in an honest and open fashion. Contemporary ethical standards also require that social research not place subjects in any jeopardy, that research subjects be forewarned of any risk to them, that participation be voluntary as expressed in informed consent, that researchers fully disclose their identity, and that researchers fully and honestly report their research findings and sources of financial support.

EXERCISES

Discussing Research

1. State a problem for research related to a criminological topic or issue of interest to you. Write down as many questions as you can about this topic.
   a. Considering your interest, opportunities, and the work for others, which of your research questions does not seem feasible or interesting?
   b. Pick out one question that seems feasible and that your other coursework suggests has been the focus of prior research or theorizing. Write this research question in one sentence. Elaborate on your question in a single paragraph. List at least three reasons why it is a good research question to investigate.

Finding Research

1. Search the scholarly literature on your topic of interest. Refer to Appendix A for guidance on conducting the search if necessary.
   a. Copy at least 10 citations to recent articles reporting research relevant to your research question.
   b. Look up at least three of these articles. Write a brief description of each article, and evaluate its relevance to your research question. What additions or changes to your thoughts about the research question are suggested by these sources?
   c. Would you characterize the findings of these articles as largely consistent or inconsistent? How would you explain discrepant findings?
   d. How well did the authors summarize their work in their abstracts for the articles you consulted? What important points would you have missed if you had relied on only the abstracts?

2. You have been assigned to write a paper on domestic violence and the law. To start, you would like to find out what the American Bar Association's stance is on the issue. Go to the American Bar Association Commission on Domestic Violence's website at www.abanet .org/domviol/mrdv/identify.html. What is the American Bar Association's definition of domestic violence? How does it suggest one can identify a person as a victim of domestic violence?

3. Go to the Bureau of Justice Statistics (BJS) website at www.ojp.usdoj.gov/bjs. Go to "Publications." Browse the list of publications for topics related to domestic violence. List the titles of all publications focusing on violence between intimate partners. Choose the most recent publication. How does the BJS define "intimate partners?" What are some of the characteristics of intimate partner violence? What trends are identified in the report?

Critiquing Research

1. Using one of the research articles you consulted in the last section, identify and look up one of the cited articles or websites. Compare the cited source to what was said about it in the original article or website. Was the discussion in the cited source accurate?

2. Using the same research article you focused on for the last exercise, identify the stages of the research project corresponding to the points on the research circle. Did the research cover all four stages? Identify the theories and hypotheses underlying the study. What data were collected or utilized for the study? What were the findings (empirical generalizations)?

Making Research Ethical

1. Review the ethical guidelines adopted by the American Sociological Association (1997: 63). Indicate whether you think each guideline was followed in the Sherman and Berk (1984) research on the policy response to domestic violence. If you find it hard to give a simple "yes" or "no" answer for each guideline, indicate the issues that make this evaluation difficult.

2. Concern with how research results are used is one of the hallmarks of ethical researchers, but deciding what form that concern should take is often difficult. You learned in this chapter about the controversy that occurred after Sherman and Berk (1984) encouraged police departments to adopt a pro-arrest policy in domestic abuse cases, based on findings from their Minneapolis study. Do you agree with the researchers' decision to suggest policy changes to police departments based on their study, in an effort to minimize domestic abuse? Several replication studies failed to confirm the Minneapolis findings. Does this influence your evaluation of what the researchers should have done after the Minneapolis study was completed? What about Larry Sherman's argument that failure to publicize the Omaha study finding of the effectiveness of arrest warrants resulted in some cases of abuse that could have been prevented? In one paragraph, propose a policy that researchers should follow about how much publicity is warranted and at what point in the research it should occur.

Developing a Research Proposal

The next exercises are very critical first steps in writing a research proposal.

1. State a problem for research. If you have not already identified a problem for study, or if you need to evaluate whether your research problem is doable, a few suggestions should help to get the ball rolling and keep it on course:
   a. Jot down a few questions you have had about some issue. Now take stock of your interests and your opportunities. Which of your research questions no longer seem feasible or interesting?
   b. Write out your research question in one sentence, and elaborate on it in one paragraph. List at least three reasons why it is a good research question for you to investigate.

2. Search the literature (and the web) on the research question you identified. Refer to Appendix A for guidance on conducting the search. Copy down at least 10 citations to articles and five websites reporting research that seems highly relevant to your research question. Inspect the article bibliographies and the links in the website and identify at least one more relevant article and website from each source. What additions or changes to your thoughts about the research question are suggested by the sources?

3. Propose at least two hypotheses that pertain to your research question. Justify these hypotheses in terms of the literature you have read.

4. Which standards for the protection of human subjects might pose the most difficulty for researchers on your proposed topic? Explain your answers and suggest appropriate protection procedures for human subjects.

Performing Data Analysis in SPSS

Browse the variables in YOUTH.POR, a survey of high school youth regarding attitudes toward delinquency and delinquent behavior.

1. From these variables (excluding sex of respondent), write two hypotheses about levels of delinquency (DELINQ1) among high school youth.

2. Create a bar chart for at least one of the variables you hypothesize to be associated with levels of delinquency.

3. Compare the distribution of your chosen variable across gender groups. Select all males (SEX = 1) and request a bar chart of your chosen variable; then select all females (SEX = 2) and generate the bar chart again.

4. Compare the distributions between the two bar charts and formulate a hypothesis as to the relationship between the two variables. Is there a relationship between SEX and your chosen variable?

5. From these results, what do you hypothesize is the relationship between gender and level of delinquency?

Student Study Site

The companion Student Study Website for *The Fundamentals of Research in Criminology and Criminal Justice* can be found at www.sagepub.com/frccjstudy.

Visit the Student Study Site to enhance your understanding of the chapter content and to discover additional resources that will take your learning one step further. You can enhance your understanding of the chapters by using the comprehensive study material, which includes interactive exercises, e-flashcards, web exercises, practice self-tests, and more. You will also find special features, such as Learning from Journal Articles, which incorporates SAGE's online journal collection.

CHAPTER 3

Conceptualization and Measurement

Every time you begin to review or design research, you will have to answer two questions: (1) What do the main concepts mean in this research? and (2) How are the main concepts measured? Both questions must be answered to evaluate the validity of any research. For example, to investigate the impact of community policing on the crime rate, you may conceptualize "community policing" strategies as those which involve active, ongoing contact between police and community members. You might measure the presence of community policing with the use of foot patrols, police–community crime-prevention meetings, and support for resident-initiated crime control (such as Neighborhood Watch programs). We cannot make sense of a research study until we know how the concepts were defined and measured. Nor can we begin our own research until we have defined our concepts clearly and constructed valid measures of them.

In this chapter, we first address the issue of conceptualization, or defining your main terms. We then describe measurement sources, such as available data, questions, observations, and less direct and obtrusive measures. Next we discuss the level of measurement reflected in different measures. The final topic is how to assess the validity and reliability of these measures. By chapter's end, you should have a good understanding of measurement, the first of the three legs on which a research project's validity rests.

WHAT DO WE HAVE IN MIND?

A May 1997 *New York Times* article (Johnson 1997) reported that five U.S. colleges were participating in a pilot program to ban alcohol in their fraternities. Moreover, the article claimed that substance-free housing would soon become the norm on U.S. campuses. Do you know what the article means? Some of these **concepts**—*alcohol, colleges, campuses,* and *pilot program*—are widely understood and commonly used. However, do we all have the same thing in mind when we hear these terms? For example, are junior colleges subsumed within the term *college?* Does the concept of *on campus* extend to fraternity houses that are not physically on college property? Does *substance-free housing* mean banning tobacco products as well as alcohol?

Concept A mental image that summarizes a set of similar observations, feelings, or ideas.

CONCEPTS

Concepts such as *substance-free housing* require an explicit definition before they are used in research because we cannot be certain that all readers will share the same definition. It is even more important to define concepts that are somewhat abstract or unfamiliar. When we refer to concepts such as *poverty,* or *social control,* or *strain,* we cannot be certain that others know exactly what we mean.

Clarifying the meaning of such concepts does not just benefit those unfamiliar with them; even experts often disagree about their meaning. But we need not avoid using these concepts; we just have to specify clearly what we mean when we use them, and we must expect others to do the same.

Conceptualization The process of specifying what we mean by a term. In deductive research, conceptualization helps to translate portions of an abstract theory into testable hypotheses involving specific variables. In inductive research, conceptualization is an important part of the process used to make sense of related observations.

Defining Youth Gangs

Do you have a clear image in mind when you hear the term *youth gangs?* Although this is a very ordinary term, social scientists' attempts to define precisely the concept "youth gang" have not yet succeeded: "Neither gang researchers nor law enforcement agencies can agree on a common definition . . . and a concerted national effort . . . failed to reach a consensus" (Howell 2003: 75). Exhibit 3.1 lists a few of the many alternative definitions of youth gangs.

What is the basis of this conceptual difficulty? Howell (2003: 27–28) suggests that defining the term *youth gangs* has been difficult for four reasons:

- Youth gangs are not particularly cohesive.
- Individual gangs change their focus over time.
- Many have a "hodgepodge of features," with diverse members and unclear rules.
- There are many incorrect but popular "myths" about youth gangs.

In addition, youth gangs are only one type of social group, and it is important to define youth gangs in a way that distinguishes them from these other types of groups—for example, childhood play groups, youth subculture groups, delinquent groups, and adult criminal organizations. You can think of "social group" as a broader concept that has multiple dimensions, one of which is youth gangs. In the same way, you can think of substance abuse as a concept with three dimensions: alcohol abuse, drug abuse, and polysubstance abuse. Whenever you define a concept, you need to consider whether the concept is unidimensional or multidimensional. If it is multidimensional, your job of conceptualization is not complete until you have specified the related subconcepts that belong under the umbrella of the larger concept.

CONCEPTS AND VARIABLES

After we define the concepts in a theory, we can identify variables corresponding to the concepts and develop procedures to measure them. This is an important step. Consider the concept of social control, which Donald Black (1984) defines as "all of the processes by which people define and respond to deviant behavior." What variables can represent this conceptualization of social control? Proportion of persons arrested in a community? Average length of sentences for crimes? Types of bystander reactions to public intoxication? Some combination of these?

EXHIBIT 3.1   Alternative Definitions of Youth Gangs

The term "gang" tends to designate collectivities that are marginal members of mainstream society, loosely organized, and without a clear, social purpose. (Ball & Curry 1995: 227)

The gang is an interstitial group (between childhood and maturity) originally formed spontaneously, and then integrated through conflict. (Thrasher 1927: 18)

[A gang is] any denotable adolescent group of youngsters who a) are generally perceived as a distinct aggregation by others in the neighborhood, b) recognize themselves as a denotable group (almost invariably with a group name), and c) have been involved in a sufficient number of delinquent incidents to call forth a consistently negative response from neighborhood residents and/or law enforcement agencies. (Klein 1971: 13)

A youth gang is a self-formed association of peers united by mutual interests with identifiable leadership and internal organization who act collectively or as individuals to achieve specific purposes, including the conduct of illegal activity and control of a particular territory, facility, or enterprise. (Miller 1991: 21)

[A gang is] an age-graded peer group that exhibits some permanence, engages in criminal activity, and has some symbolic representation of membership. (Decker & Van Winkle 1996: 31)

[A gang is] a self-identified group of kids who act corporately, at least sometimes, and violently, at least sometimes. (Kennedy, Piehl, & Braga 1996: 158)

A Criminal Street Gang is any ongoing organization, association, or group of three or more persons, whether formal or informal, having as one of its primary activities the commission of criminal acts. (Street Terrorism Enforcement and Prevention Act, 1988, California Penal Code sec. 186.22[f])

Source: Based on Howell (2003: 76).

Although we must proceed carefully to specify what we mean by a concept like social control, some concepts are represented well by the specific variables in the study and need not be defined so carefully. We may define binge drinking as heavy episodic drinking and measure it, as a variable, by asking people how many drinks they consumed in succession during some period (see Wechsler et al. 1994). That is pretty straightforward.

Be aware that not every concept in a study is represented by a variable. For example, if the term *tolerance of drinking* is defined as the absence of rules against drinking in a fraternity, it brings to mind a phenomenon that varies across different fraternities at different colleges. But if we study social life at only those fraternities that prohibit drinking, tolerance of drinking would not be a variable: All the fraternities studied have the same level of tolerance, and thus tolerance of drinking is a constant and not a variable. Of course, the concept of tolerance of drinking would still be important for understanding social life in the "dry" fraternities.

HOW WILL WE KNOW WHEN WE'VE FOUND IT?

After we have defined our concepts in the abstract—that is, after conceptualizing—and after we have specified the specific variables we want to measure, we must develop our measurement procedures. The goal is to devise **operations** that actually measure the concepts we intend to measure—in other words, to achieve measurement validity.

Operationalization The process of specifying the operations that will indicate the value of a variable for each case.

Exhibit 3.2 represents the **operationalization** process in three studies. The first researcher defines her concept (binge drinking) and chooses one variable (frequency of heavy episodic drinking) to represent it. This variable is then measured with responses to a single question, or indicator: "How often within the past two weeks did you consume five or more drinks containing alcohol in a row?" The second researcher defines her concept, poverty, as having two aspects or dimensions, subjective poverty and absolute poverty. Subjective poverty is measured with responses to a survey question: "Do you consider yourself poor?" Absolute poverty is measured by comparing family income to the poverty threshold. The third researcher decides that her concept, social class, can be indicated with three measured variables: income, education, and occupational prestige.

Good conceptualization and operationalization can prevent confusion later in the research process. For example, a researcher may find that substance abusers who join a self-help group are less likely to drink again than those who receive hospital-based substance abuse treatment. But what is it about these treatment alternatives that is associated with successful abstinence? Level of peer support? Beliefs about the causes of alcoholism? Financial investment in the treatment? If the researcher had considered such aspects of the concept of substance abuse treatment before collecting her data, she might have been able to measure different aspects of treatment and so figure out which, if any, were associated with differences in abstinence rates. Because she did not measure these variables, she will not contribute as much as she might have to our understanding of substance abuse treatment.

EXHIBIT 3.2   Concepts, Variables, and Indicators

Concept	Variable	Indicator
Binge drinking	Frequency of heavy episodic drinking	"How often within the past two weeks did you consume five or more drinks containing alcohol in a row?"
Poverty	Subjective poverty	"Would you say you are poor?"
	Absolute poverty	Family income ÷ poverty
Social class	Income	
	Education	Income + education + prestige
	Occupational prestige	

Social researchers have many options for operationalizing their concepts. Measures can be based on activities as diverse as asking people questions, reading judicial opinions, observing social interactions, coding words in books, checking census data, enumerating the contents of trash receptacles, or drawing urine and blood samples. We focus here on the operations of using published data, asking questions, observing behavior, and using unobtrusive means of measuring people's behavior and attitudes.

Using Available Data

Government reports are rich and readily accessible sources of criminal justice data, as are data sets available from nonprofit advocacy groups, university researchers, and some private businesses. For example, law-enforcement and health statistics provide several community-level indicators of substance abuse (Gruenewald et al. 1997). Statistics on arrests for the sale and possession of drugs, drunk driving arrests, and liquor law violations (such as sales to minors) can usually be obtained on an annual basis, and often quarterly, from local police departments or state crime information centers.

Indicators like these cannot be compared across communities or over time without reviewing carefully how they were constructed (Gruenewald et al. 1997: 14). We also cannot assume that available data are accurate, even when they appear to measure the concept in which we are interested in a way that is consistent across communities.

Government statistics that are generated through a central agency like the U.S. Bureau of the Census are generally of high quality, but caution is still warranted when using official data. The problem is even more severe for data collected by local levels of government. For example, the Uniform Crime Reports (UCR) program administered by the Federal Bureau of Investigation imposes standard classification criteria, with explicit guidelines and regular training at the local level, but data are still inconsistent for many crimes. Different jurisdictions vary in their definition of terms such as "more than necessary force" and even in the classification of offenses as aggravated or simple assaults (Mosher, Miethe, & Phillips 2002: 66). A new National Incident-Based Reporting System (NIBRS) corrects some of the problems with the UCR, but it requires much more training and documentation and has not yet been widely used (Mosher, Miethe, & Phillips 2002: 70).

Constructing Questions

Asking people questions is the most common and probably the most versatile operation for measuring social variables. "Overall, how satisfied are you with the police in your community?" "How would you rate your current level of safety?" Most concepts about individuals are measured with such questions.

Questions can be designed with or without explicit response choices. The question that follows is a **closed-ended (fixed-choice) question** because respondents are offered explicit responses to choose from. It has been selected from the Core Alcohol and Drug Survey distributed by the Core Institute (Presley, Meilman, & Lyerla 1994), Southern Illinois University, for the Fund for the Improvement of Postsecondary Education (FIPSE) (Core Analysis Grantee Group; Presley, Meilman, & Lyerla 1994).

Compared with other campuses with which you are familiar, this campus's use of alcohol is . . . (*Mark one*)

_____ Greater than for other campuses

_____ Less than for other campuses

_____ About the same as for other campuses

Response choices should be mutually exclusive and exhaustive, so that every respondent can find one, and only one, choice that applies to him or her (unless the question is of the "Check all that apply" format). To make response choices exhaustive, researchers may need to offer at least one option with room for ambiguity. For example, a questionnaire asking college students to indicate their school status should not use freshman, sophomore, junior, senior, and graduate student as the only response choices. Most campuses also have students in a "special" category, so you might add "Other (please specify)" to the five fixed responses to this question. If respondents do not find a response option that corresponds to their answer to the question, they may skip the question entirely or choose a response option that does not indicate what they are really thinking.

Most surveys of a large number of people primarily contain fixed-choice questions, which are easy to process with computers and analyze with statistics. With fixed-choice questions, respondents are also more likely to answer the question that the researcher really wants them to answer. Including response choices reduces ambiguity and makes it easier for respondents to answer. However, fixed-response choices can obscure what people really think if the choices do not match the range of possible responses to the question; many studies show that some respondents will choose response choices that do not apply to them simply to give some sort of answer (Peterson 2000: 39).

Open-ended questions—questions without explicit response choices, to which respondents write in their answers—are preferable when the range of responses cannot adequately be anticipated. By this we mean questions that have not previously been used in surveys and questions that are asked of new groups. Open-ended questions can also lessen confusion about the meaning of responses involving complex concepts. The next question is an open-ended version of the earlier fixed-choice question:

How would you say alcohol use on this campus compares to that on other campuses?

Making Observations

Observations can be used to measure characteristics of individuals, events, and places. The observations may be the primary form of measurement in a study, or they may supplement measures obtained through questioning.

Robert J. Sampson and Stephen W. Raudenbush (1999) used direct observation (and other techniques) in their study of neighborhood disorder and crime. Teams drove in "a sport utility vehicle at a rate of five miles per hour down every street" in a sample of Chicago neighborhoods. Two video cameras recorded people and activities on both sides of the vehicle, while a trained observer completed a log for each block—a very careful method of observing phenomena termed **systematic social observation (SSO)** (Reiss 1971). The resulting 23,816 observer logs contained information about building conditions and land use, while the videotapes were coded to measure features of streets, buildings, businesses, and social interaction on 15,141 blocks. Direct observation is often the method of choice for measuring behavior in natural settings, as long as it is possible to make the requisite observations.

Collecting Unobtrusive Measures

Unobtrusive measures allow us to collect data about individuals or groups without their direct knowledge or participation. In their classic book (now revised), Webb et al. (2000 [1966]) identified four types of unobtrusive measures: physical trace evidence, archives (available data), simple observation, and contrived observation (using hidden recording hardware or manipulation to elicit a response). We will focus attention in this section on physical trace evidence and archives.

The physical traces of past behavior are one type of unobtrusive measure that is most useful when the behavior of interest cannot directly be observed (perhaps because it is hidden or occurred in the past) and has not been recorded in a source of available data. To measure the prevalence of drinking in college dorms or fraternity houses, we might count the number of empty bottles of alcoholic beverages in the surrounding dumpsters. However, you can probably see that care must be taken to develop trace measures that are useful for comparative purposes. For instance, comparison of the number of empty bottles in dumpsters outside different dorms can be misleading; at the very least, you would need to take into account the number of residents in the dorms, the time since the last trash collection, and the accessibility of each dumpster to passers by.

Unobtrusive measures can also be created from such diverse forms of media as newspaper archives or magazine articles, TV or radio talk shows, legal opinions, historical documents, personal letters, or e-mail messages. An investigation of the drinking climate on campuses might include a count of the amount of space devoted to ads for alcoholic beverages in a sample of issues of the student newspaper. Campus publications also might be coded to indicate the number of times that statements discouraging substance abuse appear. With this tool, you could measure the frequency of articles reporting substance abuse–related crimes, the degree of approval of drinking expressed in TV shows or songs, or the relationship between region of the country and amount of space devoted in the print media to drug usage.

Combining Measurement Operations

Using available data, asking questions, making observations, and using unobtrusive indicators are interrelated measurement tools, each of which may include or be supplemented by the others. From people's answers to survey questions, the U.S. Bureau of the Census develops widely consulted census reports containing available data on people, firms, and geographic units in the United States. Data from employee surveys may be supplemented by information available in company records. Interviewers may record observations about those whom they question. Researchers may use insights gleaned from questioning participants to make sense of the social interaction they have observed. Unobtrusive indicators can be used to evaluate the honesty of survey responses.

Questioning can be a particularly poor approach for measuring behaviors that are very socially desirable, such as voting or attending church, or that are socially stigmatized or illegal, such as abusing alcohol or drugs. **Triangulation**, the use of two or more different measures of the same variable, can strengthen measurement considerably (Brewer & Hunter 1989: 17). When we achieve similar results with different measures of the same variable, particularly when they are based on such different methods as survey questions and field-based observations, we can be more confident in the validity of each measure. If results diverge with different measures, it may indicate that one or more of these measures are influenced by more measurement error than we can tolerate. Divergence between measures could also indicate that they actually operationalize different concepts. An interesting example of this interpretation of divergent results comes from research on crime. Official crime statistics only indicate those crimes that are reported to and recorded by the police; when surveys are used to measure crimes with self-reports of victims, many "personal annoyances" are included as if they were crimes (Levine 1976).

HOW MUCH INFORMATION DO WE REALLY HAVE?

Whether we collect information through observations, questions, available data or using unobtrusive measures, the data that result from our particular procedures may be more or less mathematically precise. We express this level of mathematical precision as the variable's **level of measurement**. Level of measurement also has important implications for the types of statistics that can be used with the variable, as you will learn in chapter 10. There are four levels of measurement: nominal, ordinal, interval, and ratio. Exhibit 3.3 depicts the differences among these four levels.

EXHIBIT 3.3   Levels of Measurement

Level of measurement The mathematical precision with which the values of a variable can be expressed. The nominal level of measurement, which is qualitative, has no mathematical interpretation; the quantitative levels of measurement (ordinal, interval, and ratio) are progressively more precise mathematically.

Nominal Level of Measurement

The **nominal level of measurement** (also called the categorical or qualitative level) identifies variables whose values have no mathematical interpretation; they vary in kind or quality but not in amount. In fact, it is conventional to refer to the values of nominal variables as "attributes" instead of values. Gender is one example. The variable "gender" has two attributes (or categories or qualities): male and female. We might indicate male with the value 1 and female with the value 2, but these numbers do not tell us anything about the difference between male and female except that they are different. Female is not one unit more of "gender" than male, nor is it twice as much "gender." Ethnicity, occupation, religious affiliation, and region of the country are also measured at the nominal level. A person may be Spanish or Portuguese, but one ethnic group does not represent more ethnicity than another, just a different ethnicity. A person may be a doctor or a truck driver, but one does not represent three units more occupation than the other.

Although the attributes of categorical variables do not have a mathematical meaning, they must be assigned to cases with great care. The attributes we use to measure, or categorize, cases must be mutually exclusive and exhaustive:

- A variable's attributes or values are **mutually exclusive attributes** if every case can have only one attribute.
- A variable's attributes or values are **exhaustive attributes** when every case can be classified into one of the categories.

When a variable's attributes are mutually exclusive and exhaustive, every case corresponds to one, and only one, attribute.

Ordinal Level of Measurement

The first of the three quantitative levels is the **ordinal level of measurement**. At this level, the numbers assigned to cases specify only the order of the cases, permitting greater-than and less-than distinctions. For example, the Core Alcohol and Drug Survey (Presley, Meilman, & Lyerla 1994) measures substance abuse with a series of questions that permit ordinal distinctions (see Exhibit 3.4). You can determine with these categories whether one respondent consumes approximately the same amount of alcohol, or more or less than another respondent, but you don't know exactly how much more or less.

The properties of variables measured at the ordinal level are illustrated in Exhibit 3.3 by the contrast between the level of conflict in two groups. The first group, symbolized by two people shaking hands, has a low level of conflict. The second group, symbolized by two persons pointing guns at each other, has a higher level of conflict. To measure conflict, we could put the groups "in order" by assigning the number 1 to the low-conflict group and the number 2 to the group using guns. The numbers thus indicate the relative position or order of the cases. Although low level of conflict is represented by the number 1, it is not mathematically two less units of conflict than the high level of conflict, which is represented by the number 3.

As with nominal variables, the different values of a variable measured at the ordinal level must be mutually exclusive and exhaustive. They must cover the range of observed values and allow each case to be assigned no more than one value.

Interval Level of Measurement

The numbers indicating the values of a variable at the **interval level of measurement** represent fixed measurement units but have no absolute, or fixed, zero point. This level of measurement is represented in Exhibit 3.3 by the difference between two Fahrenheit temperatures. Although 60 degrees is 30 degrees hotter than 30 degrees, 60 in this case is

EXHIBIT 3.4 Example of Ordinal Measures: Core Alcohol and Drug Survey

Within the last year, about how often have you used . . . . (mark one for each line)	Did Not Use	Once a Year	6 Times a Year	Once a Month	Twice a Month	Once a Week	3 Times a Week	5 Times a Week	Every Day
a. Tobacco (smoke, chew, snuff)									
b. Alcohol (beer, wine, liquor)									
c. Marijuana (pot, hash, hash oil)									
d. Cocaine (crack, rock, freebase)									
e. Amphetamines (diet pills, speed)									
f. Sedatives (downers, ludes)									
g. Hallucinogens (LSD, PCP)									
h. Opiates (heroin, smack, horse)									
i. Inhalants (glue, solvents, gas)									
j. Designer drugs (ecstasy, MDMA)									
k. Steroids									
1. Other illegal drugs									

Source: Core Institute. 1994. "Core Alcohol and Drug Survey: Long Form." Carbondale: FIPSE Core Analysis Grantee Group. Core Institute, Student Health Programs. Southern Illinois University not twice as hot as 30. Why not? Because heat does not "begin" at 0 degrees on the Fahrenheit scale. The numbers can therefore be added and subtracted, but ratios between them (2 to 1, or "twice as much") are not meaningful.

Sometimes social scientists create **indexes** by combining responses to a series of questions measured at the ordinal level. An index of this sort could be created with responses to the Core Institute's (Presley, Meilman, & Lyerla 1994) questions about friends' disapproval of substance use (see Exhibit 3.5). The survey has 13 questions on the topic, each of which has the same three response choices. If "Don't disapprove" is valued at 1, "Disapprove" is valued at 2, and "Strongly disapprove" is valued at 3, the summed index of disapproval would range from 12 to 36. Many social scientists would consider scores on an index like this to reflect an interval-level measure. So a score of 20 could be treated as if it were four more units than a score of 16.

EXHIBIT 3.5   Ordinal Level Variables Can be Added to Create an Index With Interval-Level Properties: Core Alcohol and Drug Survey

How do you think your close friends feel (or would feel) about you . . . (mark one for each line)	Do Not Disapprove	Disapprove	Strongly Disapprove
a. Trying marijuana once or twice			
b. Smoking marijuana occasionally			
c. Smoking marijuana regularly			
d. Trying cocaine once or twice			
e. Taking cocaine regularly			
f. Trying LSD once or twice			
g. Taking LSD regularly			
h. Trying amphetamines once or twice			
i. Taking amphetamines regularly			
j. Taking one or two drinks of an alcoholic beverage (beer, wine, liquor) nearly every day			
k. Taking four or five drinks nearly every day			
l. Having five or more drinks in one sitting			
m. Taking steroids for bodybuilding or improved athletic performance			

Source: Core Institute. 1994. "Core Alcohol and Drug Survey: Long Form." Carbondale: FIPSE Core Analysis Grantee Group, Core Institute, Student Health Programs, Southern Illinois University

Ratio Level of Measurement

The numbers indicating the values of a variable at the **ratio level of measurement** represent fixed measuring units and an absolute zero point (zero means absolutely no amount of whatever the variable indicates). On a ratio scale, 10 is two points higher than 8 and is also two times greater than 5. Ratio numbers can be added and subtracted, and because the numbers begin at an absolute zero point, they can be multiplied and divided (so ratios can be formed between the numbers).

For example, people's ages can be represented by values ranging from 0 years (or some fraction of a year) to 120 or more. A person who is 30 years old is 15 years older than someone who is 15 years old (30 − 15 = 15) and is twice as old as that person (30/15 = 2). Of course, the numbers also are mutually exclusive and exhaustive, so that every case can be assigned one and only one value.

Exhibit 3.3 displays an example of a variable measured at the ratio level. The number of people in the first group is 5, and the number in the second group is 7. The ratio of the two groups' sizes is then 1.4, a number that mirrors the relationship between the sizes of the groups. Note that there does not actually have to be any group with a size of 0; what is important is that the numbering scheme begins at an absolute zero—in this case, the absence of any people.

Comparison of Levels of Measurement

Exhibit 3.6 summarizes the types of comparisons that can be made with different levels of measurement, as well as the mathematical operations that are legitimate. All four levels of measurement allow researchers to assign different values to different cases. All three quantitative measures allow researchers to rank cases in order.

Researchers *choose* levels of measurement in the process of operationalizing the variables; the level of measurement is not inherent in the variable itself. Many variables can be measured at different levels, with different procedures.

EXHIBIT 3.6   Properties of Measurement Levels

Examples of Comparison Statements	Appropriate Math Operations	Nominal	Ordinal	Interval	Ratio
A is equal to (not equal to) *B*	= (≠)	✓	✓	✓	✓
A is greater than (less than) *B*	> (<)		✓	✓	✓
A is three more than (less than) *B*	+ (−)			✓	✓
A is twice (half) as large as *B*					✓

Relevant Level of Measurement

For example, The Core Alcohol and Drug Survey (Presley, Meilman, & Lyerla 1994) identifies binge drinking by asking students, "Think back over the last two weeks. How many times have you had five or more drinks at a sitting?" You might be ready to classify this as a ratio-level measure, but you must first examine the fixed-response options given to respondents. This is a **closed-ended question**, and students are asked to indicate their answer by checking None, Once, Twice, 3 to 5 times, 6 to 9 times, or 10 or more times. Use of these categories makes the level of measurement ordinal. The distance between any two cases cannot be clearly determined. A student with a response in the "6 to 9 times" category could have binged just one more time than a student who responded 3 to 5 times, or they could have binged four more times. With these response categories, you cannot mathematically distinguish the number of times a student binged, only the relative amount of binging behavior.

Usually, it is a good idea to measure variables at the highest level of measurement possible, if doing so does not distort the meaning of the concept that is to be measured. For example, measure age in years, if possible, rather than in categories. You can always combine the responses into categories that compare teenagers to young adults, but it is impossible to obtain the actual age in years when the question is asked in the first place using just an ordinal response format.

Be aware, however, that other considerations may preclude measurement at a high level. For example, many people are very reluctant to report their exact incomes, even in anonymous questionnaires. So asking respondents to report their income in categories (such as under $10,000, $10,000–19,999, $20,000–29,999, etc.) will result in more responses, and thus more valid data, than asking respondents for their income in dollars.

DID WE MEASURE WHAT WE WANTED TO MEASURE?

Do the operations developed to measure our concepts actually do so—are they valid? If we have weighed our measurement options, carefully constructed our questions and observational procedures, and carefully selected indicators from the available data, we should be on the right track. But we cannot have much confidence in a measure until we have empirically evaluated its validity. We must also evaluate its reliability (consistency).

Measurement Validity

We can consider **measurement validity** the first concern in establishing the validity of research results, because without having measured what we think we measured, we really do not know what we are talking about.

Measurement validity The extent to which measures indicate what they are intended to measure.

As an example of the importance of measurement validity, consider the United States' "War on Drugs," which heated up in the 1980s. During this time, arrest rates for drug offenses soared, according to the *Uniform Crime Reports (UCR)* produced by the Federal Bureau of Investigation (FBI). This change gave the impression that drug use was increasing at an epidemic pace, but self-report surveys that asked citizens directly about their drug use behavior during this time period found that use of most illicit drugs was actually declining (Regoli & Hewitt 1994). In your opinion, which measure of drug use, the UCR or self-report surveys, was more valid? Before you answer this question, let us continue with the delinquency example.

The extent to which measures indicate what they are intended to measure can be assessed with one or more of four basic approaches: face validation, content validation, criterion validation, and construct validation.

Face Validity

Researchers apply the term **face validity** to the confidence gained from careful inspection of a concept to see if it is appropriate "on its face." More precisely, we can say that a measure has face validity if it obviously pertains to the concept being measured more than to other concepts (Brewer and Hunter 1989: 131). For example, measuring people's favorite color seems unlikely on its face to tell us much about their alcohol consumption patterns. A measure with greater face validity would be a count of how many drinks they had consumed in the past week.

Although every measure should be inspected in this way, face validation in itself does not provide very convincing evidence of measurement validity. The question "How much beer or wine did you have to drink last week?" may look valid on its face as a measure of frequency of drinking, but people who drink heavily tend to underreport the amount they drink. So the question would be an invalid measure in a study that includes heavy drinkers.

Content Validity

Content validity establishes that the measure covers the full range of the concept's meaning. To determine that range of meaning, the researcher may solicit the opinions of experts and review literature that identifies the different aspects of the concept.

Criterion Validity

When people drink an alcoholic beverage, the alcohol is absorbed into their bloodstream and then gradually metabolized (broken down into other chemicals) in their liver (National Institute of Alcohol Abuse and Alcoholism [NIAAA] 1997). The alcohol that remains in their blood at any point, unmetabolized, impairs both thinking and behavior (NIAAA 1994). As more alcohol is ingested, cognitive and behavioral consequences multiply. These biological processes can be identified with direct measures of alcohol concentration in the blood, urine, or breath. Questions about drinking behavior, on the other hand, can be viewed as attempts to measure indirectly what biochemical tests measure directly.

Criterion validity is established when the scores obtained on one measure can accurately be compared to those obtained with a more direct or already validated measure of the same phenomenon (the criterion). A measure of blood-alcohol concentration or a urine test could serve as the criterion for validating a self-report measure of drinking, as long as the questions we ask about drinking refer to the same period. Observations of substance use by friends or relatives could also, in some circumstances, serve as a criterion for validating self-report substance use measures.

An attempt at criterion validation is well worth the effort because it greatly increases confidence that the measure is measuring what was intended. However, often no other variable might reasonably be considered a criterion for feelings or beliefs or other subjective states. Even with variables for which a reasonable criterion exists, the researcher may not be able to gain access to the criterion, as would be the case with a tax return or employer document as criterion for self-reported income.

Construct Validity

Measurement validity also can be established by showing that a measure is related to a variety of other measures as specified in a theory. This validation approach, known as **construct validity**, is commonly used in social research when no clear criterion exists for validation purposes. For example, in one study of the validity of the Addiction Severity Index (ASI), A. Thomas McLellan et al. (1985) compared subject scores on the ASI to a number of indicators that they felt from prior research should be related to substance abuse: medical problems, employment problems, legal problems, family problems, and psychiatric problems. They could not use a criterion validation approach because they did not have a more direct measure of abuse, such as laboratory test scores or observer reports. However, their extensive research on the subject had given them confidence that these sorts of problems were all related to substance abuse, and thus their measures seemed to be valid from the standpoint of construct validity. Indeed, the researchers found that individuals with higher ASI ratings tended to have more problems in each of these areas, giving us more confidence in the ASI's validity as a measure.

The distinction between criterion and construct validation is not always clear. Opinions can differ about whether a particular indicator is indeed a criterion for the concept that is to be measured. For example, if you need to validate a question-based measure of sales ability for applicants to a sales position, few would object to using actual sales performance as a criterion. But what if you want to validate a question-based measure of the amount of social support that people receive from their friends? Should you just ask people about the social support they have received? Could friends' reports of the amount of support they provided serve as a criterion? Even if you could observe people in the act of counseling or otherwise supporting their friends, can an observer be sure that the interaction is indeed supportive? There isn't really a criterion here, just related concepts that could be used in a construct validation strategy.

What construct and criterion validation have in common is the comparison of scores on one measure to scores on other measures that are predicted to be related. It is not so important that researchers agree that a particular comparison measure is a criterion rather than a related construct. But it is very important to think critically about the quality of the comparison measure and whether it actually represents a different measure of the same phenomenon. For example, it is only a weak indication of measurement validity to find that scores on a new self-report measure of alcohol use are associated with scores on a previously used self-report measure of alcohol use.

Reliability

Reliability means that a measurement procedure yields consistent scores when the phenomenon being measured is not changing (or that the measured scores change in direct correspondence to actual changes in the phenomenon). If a measure is reliable, it is affected less by random error, or chance variation, than if it is unreliable. Reliability is a prerequisite for measurement validity; we cannot really measure a phenomenon if the measure we are using gives inconsistent results.

Reliability A measure is reliable when it yields consistent scores or observations of a given phenomenon on different occasions. Reliability is a prerequisite for measurement validity.

There are four possible methods for measuring the reliability of a measure: test–retest reliability, interitem reliability, alternate-forms reliability, and interobserver reliability.

Test–Retest Reliability

When researchers measure a phenomenon that does not change between two points separated by an interval of time, the degree to which the two measurements yield comparable, if not identical, values is the **test–retest reliability** of the measure. If you take a test of your math ability and then retake the test two months later, the test is performing reliably if you receive a similar score both times, presuming that nothing happened during the two months to change your math ability. Of course, if events between the test and the retest have changed the variable being measured, then the difference between the test and retest scores should reflect that change.

When ratings by an observer, rather than ratings by the subjects themselves, are being assessed at two or more points in time, test–retest reliability is termed **intraobserver reliability** or **intrarater reliability**.

Interitem Reliability (Internal Consistency)

When researchers use multiple items to measure a single concept, they are concerned with **interim reliability** (or internal consistency). For example, if we are to have confidence that a set of questions (such as those in Exhibit 3.7) reliably measures attitudes toward violence, the answers to the questions should be highly associated with one another. The stronger the association among the individual items, and the more items that are included, the higher the reliability of the index.

Alternate-Forms Reliability

Researchers are testing **alternate-forms reliability** when they compare subjects' answers to slightly different versions of survey questions (Litwin 1995: 13–21). A researcher may reverse the order of the response choices in an index or modify the question wording in minor ways and then readminister that index to subjects. If the two sets of responses are not too different, alternate-forms reliability is established.

A related test of reliability is the **split-halves reliability** approach. A survey sample is divided in two by flipping a coin or using some other random assignment method. These two halves of the sample are then administered the two forms of the questions. If the responses of the two halves of the sample are about the same, the measure's reliability is established.

EXHIBIT 3.7   Questions Used in the Violent Defensive Values Index

Would you approve of a man punching a stranger who had hit the man's child after the child accidentally damaged the stranger's car?

_____ No (0)

_____ I don't know or not sure (1)

_____ Yes (2)

Would you approve of a man punching a stranger who was beating up a woman and the man saw it?

_____ No (0)

_____ I don't know or not sure (1)

_____ Yes (2)

Would you approve of a man punching a stranger who had broken into the man's house?

_____ No (0)

_____ I don't know or not sure (1)

_____ Yes (2)

Source: Cao, L., Adams, A. and V. J. Jensen (1997) "A Test of the Black Subculture of Violence Thesis: A Research Note." *Criminology* 35(2): 367–79. Reprinted with permission.

Interobserver Reliability

When researchers use more than one observer to rate the same persons, events, or places, **interobserver reliability** is their goal. If observers are using the same instrument to rate the same thing, their ratings should be very similar. If they are similar, we can have much more confidence that the ratings reflect the phenomenon being assessed rather than the orientations of the observers.

Can We Achieve Both Reliability and Validity?

The reliability and validity of measures in any study must be tested after the fact to assess the quality of the information obtained. But then if it turns out that a measure cannot be considered reliable and valid, little can be done to save the study. Hence it is supremely important to select in the first place measures that are likely to be reliable and valid. In studies that use interviewers or observers, careful training is often essential to achieving a consistent approach. In most cases, however, the best strategy is to use measures that have been used before and whose reliability and validity have been established in other contexts. But the selection of "tried and true" measures still does not absolve researchers from the responsibility of testing the reliability and validity of the measure in their own studies.

It may be possible to improve the reliability and validity of measures in a study that already has been conducted if multiple measures were used. For example, in our study of housing for homeless mentally ill persons, funded by the National Institute of Mental Health, we assessed substance abuse with several different sets of direct questions as well as with reports from subjects' case managers and others (Goldfinger et al. 1996). We found that the observational reports were often inconsistent with self-reports, and that different self-report measures were not always in agreement and were thus unreliable. A more reliable measure of substance abuse was initial reports of lifetime substance abuse problems. This measure was extremely accurate in identifying all those who subsequently abused substances during the project. We concluded that the lifetime measure was a valid way to identify persons at risk for substance abuse problems.

EXHIBIT 3.8   The Difference Between Reliability and Validity: Drinking Behavior

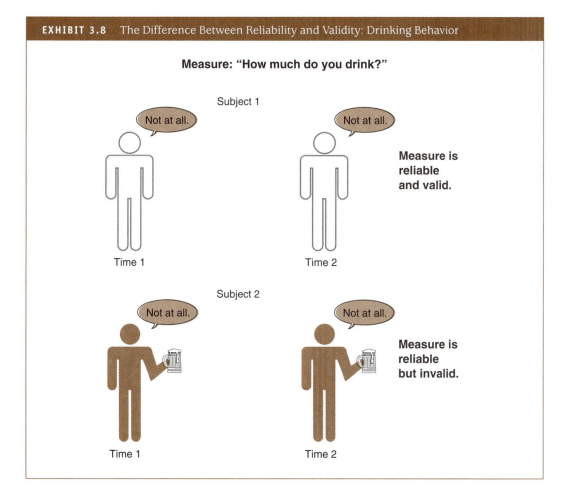

CONCLUSION

Remember always that measurement validity is a necessity for social research. Gathering data without careful conceptualization or conscientious efforts to operationalize key concepts often is a wasted effort.

The difficulties of achieving valid measurement vary with the concept being operationalized and the circumstances of the particular study. The examples in this chapter of difficulties in achieving valid measures of substance abuse should sensitize you to the need for caution, particularly when the concepts you wish to measure are socially stigmatized and/or illegal.

Planning ahead is the key to achieving valid measurement in your own research; careful evaluation is the key to sound decisions about the validity of measures in others' research. Statistical tests can help to determine whether a given measure is valid after data have been collected, but if it appears after the fact that a measure is invalid, little can be done to correct the situation. If you cannot tell how key concepts were operationalized when you read a research report, do not trust the findings. And if a researcher does not indicate the results of tests used to establish the reliability and validity of key measures, remain skeptical.

KEY TERMS

Alternate-forms reliability
Closed-ended question
Concept
Conceptualization
Construct validity
Content validity
Criterion validity
Dichotomy
Discriminant validity
Exhaustive attributes
Face validity
Indicator
Interitem reliability
Interobserver reliability
Interval level of measurement
Intraobserver reliability (intrarater reliability)

Level of measurement
Measurement validity
Mutually exclusive attributes
Nominal level of measurement
Open-ended questions
Operation
Operationalization
Ordinal level of measurement
Ratio level of measurement
Reliability
Split-halves reliability
Systematic social observation
Test–retest reliability
Triangulation
Unobtrusive measures

HIGHLIGHTS

- Conceptualization plays a critical role in research. In deductive research, conceptualization guides the operationalization of specific variables; in inductive research, it guides efforts to make sense of related observations.

- Concepts are operationalized in research by one or more indicators, or measures, which may derive from observation, self-report, available records or statistics, books and other written documents, clinical indicators, discarded materials, or some combination of these.

- The validity of measures should always be tested. There are four basic approaches: face validation, content validation, criterion validation, and construct validation. Criterion validation provides the strongest evidence of measurement validity, but there often is no criterion to use in validating social science measures.

- Measurement reliability is a prerequisite for measurement validity, although reliable measures are not necessarily valid. Reliability can be assessed through test–retest procedures, in terms of interitem consistency, through a comparison of responses to alternate forms of the test, or in terms of consistency among observers.

- Level of measurement indicates the type of information obtained about a variable and the type of statistics that can be used to describe its variation. The four levels of measurement can be ordered by complexity of the mathematical operations they permit: nominal (least complex), ordinal, interval, and ratio (most complex). The measurement level of a variable is determined by how the variable is operationalized. Dichotomies are a special case of measurement.

EXERCISES

Discussing Research

1. Pick one important, frequently used concept such as "crime," "juries," "community policing," "racism," or some other concept suggested by your instructor. Then find five uses of it in newspapers, magazines, or journals. Is the concept defined clearly in each article? How similar are the definitions? Write up what you have found in a short report.

2. How would you define "rape?" Write a brief definition. Based on this conceptualization, what circumstances constitute rape? Describe a method of measurement that would be valid for a study of rape (as you define it). Now go to the Rape Victim Advocates' website at www.RapeVictimAdvocates.org. Go to "Myths & Facts." Discuss some facts about rape that you were previously unaware of or some myths you believed. Rewrite your definition of rape based on your new knowledge. What additional circumstances constitute rape based on your new conceptualization?

3. Do you and your classmates share the same beliefs about the meanings of important concepts? First, divide your class into several groups, with each group having at least six students. Then assign each group a concept from the following list: violence, stress, social support, mental illness, social norms. In each group, each student should independently write a brief definition of his or her concept and some different examples supporting it. Finally, all students who have worked on the same concept should meet together, compare their definitions and examples, and try to reach agreement on the meaning of the concept. Discuss what you learned from this effort.

4. Propose an open-ended question to measure one of the concepts you discussed in the preceding exercises. Compare your approach to those adopted by other students.

Finding Research

1. Are important concepts in criminological research always defined clearly? Are they defined consistently? Search the literature for six articles that focus on "violent crime," "domestic violence," or some other concept suggested by your instructor. Is the concept defined clearly in each article? How similar are the definitions? Write what you have found in a short report.

2. How would you define "alcoholism?" Write a brief definition. Based on this conceptualization, describe a method of measurement that would be valid for a study of alcoholism (as you define it). Now go to the National Council on Alcohol and Drug Dependence (NCADD) website (www.ncadd.org/facts/defalc.html) and read its official "Definition of Alcoholism." What is the definition of alcoholism used by NCADD? How is alcoholism conceptualized? How does this compare to your definition?

3. What are some of the research questions you could attempt to answer with available statistical data? Visit your library and ask for an introduction to the government documents collection. Inspect the volumes from the Federal Bureau of Investigation (FBI) Uniform Crime Report (UCR) or the *Sourcebook for Criminal Justice Statistics*, both of which report statistics on crimes committed by offender characteristics. List 10 questions you could explore with such data.

Critiquing Research

1. Develop a plan for evaluating the validity of a measure. Your instructor will give you a copy of a questionnaire actually used in a study. Choose one question and define the concept that you believe it is intended to measure. Then develop a construct validation strategy involving other measures in the questionnaire that you think should be related to the question of interest—that is, it measures what you think it does.

2. Compare two different measures of substance abuse. A site maintained by the National Institute on Alcoholism and Alcohol Abuse (http://silk.nih.gov/silk/niaaa1/publication/instable.htm) provides many of the most popular measures. Pick two of them. What concept of substance abuse is reflected in each measure? Is either measure multidimensional? What do you think the relative advantages of each measure might be? What evidence is provided about their reliability and validity? What other test of validity would you suggest?

Making Research Ethical

1. In order to measure disorder in Chicago neighborhoods, Sampson and Raudenbush (1999) recorded the street scene with video cameras in a van with darkened windows. Do you judge this measurement procedure to be ethical? Refer to each of the guidelines in chapter 2. How could the guideline about "informed consent" be interpreted to permit this type of observational procedure?

2. Both some Homeland Security practices and inadvertent releases of web-searching records have raised new concerns about the use of unobtrusive measures of behavior and attitudes. If all identifying information is removed, do you think criminologists should be able to study who is stopped by police for traffic violations? What types of books are checked out in libraries in different communities? The extent of use of pornography in different cities by analyzing store purchases? How much alcohol different types of people use by linking credit card records to store purchases?

Developing a Research Proposal

At this point, you can begin the processes of conceptualization and operationalization. You will need to assume that your primary research method will be conducting a survey.

1. List at least 10 variables that will be measured in your research. No more than two of these should be sociodemographic indicators like race or age. The inclusion of each variable should be justified in terms of theory or prior research that suggests it would be an appropriate independent or dependent variable, or will have some relation to either of these.

2. Write a conceptual definition for each variable. Whenever possible, this definition should come from the existing literature, either a book you have read for a course or the research literature that you have been searching. Ask two class members for feedback on your definitions.

3. Develop measurement operations for each variable. Several measures should be single questions and indexes that were used in prior research (search the web and the journal literature in *Criminal Justice Abstracts, Soc Abstracts,* or *Pscyh Abstracts*). Make up a few questions and one index yourself. Ask classmates to answer these questions and give you feedback on their clarity.

4. Propose tests of reliability and validity for four of the measures.

Performing Data Analysis in SPSS

HOMICIDE.POR contains a sample of homicide defendants from a sample of 33 U.S. counties for the year 1988.

1. Obtain a frequency distribution for the variables INTIMATE, NUMVICT, and PRIMTIME. At what levels (nominal or categorical, ordinal, interval, ratio) are each of these variables measured?

2. What conclusions do you make about the victim–offender relationship, number of victims, and length of sentence received based on these frequency distributions?

Student Study Site

The companion Student Study Website for *The Fundamentals of Research in Criminology and Criminal Justice* can be found at www.sagepub.com/frccjstudy.

   Visit the Student Study Site to enhance your understanding of the chapter content and to discover additional resources that will take your learning one step further. You can enhance your understanding of the chapters by using the comprehensive study material, which includes interactive exercises, e-flashcards, web exercises, practice self-tests, and more. You will also find special features, such as Learning from Journal Articles, which incorporates SAGE's online journal collection.

CHAPTER 4

Sampling

In this chapter, we first review the rationale for using sampling in social research and consider two alternatives to sampling. We then turn to the topic of specific sampling methods and when they are most appropriate, using a variety of examples from the criminological research literature. We also briefly introduce the concept of a sampling distribution and explain how it helps in estimating our degree of confidence in statistical generalizations. By the chapter's end, you should know which questions you need to ask to evaluate the generalizability of a study as well as what choices you need to make to design a sampling strategy.

WHAT DO WE HAVE IN MIND?

When a jury in Albany, New York, acquitted the four Caucasian police officers who had fired 41 bullets and killed a young African immigrant named Amadou Diallo, reporters went to the streets to uncover the public sentiment about the verdict. Reporters from the Associated Press went to the people gathered outside Diallo's Bronx home; reporters were also gathered to hear reaction from the rally at Reverend Al Sharpton's National Action Network headquarters in Harlem. Speakers at both rallies were not just average citizens but also politicians running for office or seeking reelection. For example, the Associated Press paraphrased U.S. Representative Charles Rangel's contention that officers never would have shot Diallo if he had been Caucasian. Other citizens' anger and frustration were revealed by these statements: "Murderers!" they shouted, "Racist cops!" "We want justice!" Providing quotations from individuals within news stories is a common technique in journalism. These quotes help to create a human face to go with the story.

The problem with these journalistic methods, however, is that we do not know whether the opinions selected to be printed by journalists represent the opinions of the larger population. For example, is the sentiment of Representative Rangel similar to that of all U.S. representatives from New York? All Democratic U.S. representatives? Do the quotes from citizens represent the opinion of everyone living in Harlem? How about the Bronx, or New York City as a whole? In other words, we do not know how generalizable these comments are, and if we do not have confidence in their generalizability, their validity is suspect. In reality, of course, we have no idea whether these opinions are widely shared or unique.

SAMPLE PLANNING

You have encountered the problem of generalizability in each of the studies you have read about in this book. For example, Felson et al. (1994) generalized their sample-based explanation of adolescent aggression and violence to the population of high school students in the United States; Powell, Muir-McClain, and Halasyamani (1995) generalized their evaluation findings of violence prevention programs from an elementary school in King County, Washington, to all public elementary schools; and Lawrence Sherman, Richard Berk (1984) and others (Berk et al. 1992; Dunford, Huizinga, & Elliott 1990; Garner, Fagan, & Maxwell 1995; Hirschel, Hutchison, & Dean 1992; Pate & Hamilton 1992; Sherman et al. 1992) tried to determine the generalizability of findings from the original study of domestic violence in Minneapolis. Whether we, like these other researchers, are designing a sampling strategy or evaluating the generalizability of someone else's findings, we have to understand how and why researchers decide to sample. Sampling is very common in social research, but sometimes it is not necessary.

Define Sample Components and the Population

Let us say that we are designing a study of a topic that involves a lot of people (or other entities such as cities or countries), which are the elements in our study. We do not have the time or resources to study the entire **population**—all the elements in which we are interested—and so we resolve to study a **sample** or subset of this population.

Population The entire set of elements (e.g., individuals, cities, states, countries, prisons, schools) in which we are interested.

Sample A subset of elements from the larger population.

We may collect our data directly from the elements in our sample. Some studies are not so simple, however. The entities we can easily reach to gather information are not the same as the entities about whom we really want information. So we may collect information about the elements from another set of entities called the **sampling units**. For example, if we interview mothers to learn about their families, the families are the elements and the mothers are the sampling units. If we survey prison wardens to learn about prisons, the prisons are the elements and the wardens are the sampling units.

A single-stage sample is a study in which individual people are sampled and are the focus of the study; the sampling units are the same as the elements. However, if a sample is selected in two or more stages, the units selected—let's say groups and individuals—at each stage within the groups are sampling units, but it may be that only one sampling unit is the study's element (see Exhibit 4.1). For example, a researcher might sample families for a survey about household theft victimizations and then interview only one adult representative of the family, such as a parent (a sample), to obtain information about any victimizations. The families are the primary sampling units (and are the elements in the study), and the parents are secondary sampling units (but they are not elements, because they provide information about the family).

EXHIBIT 4.1   Sample Components in a Two-Stage Study

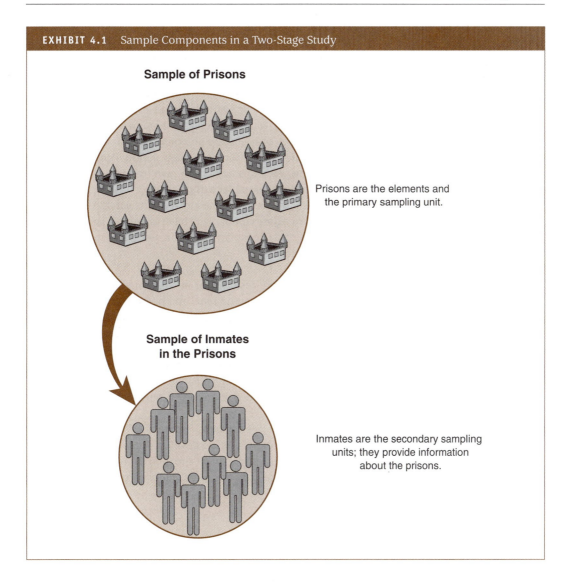

Sample of Prisons

Prisons are the elements and the primary sampling unit.

Sample of Inmates in the Prisons

Inmates are the secondary sampling units; they provide information about the prisons.

One key issue with selecting or evaluating sample components is understanding exactly what population they represent. In a survey of adult Americans, the general population may be reasonably construed as all residents of the United States who are at least 21 years old. But always be alert to ways in which the population may have been narrowed by the sample-selection procedures. Perhaps only English-speaking adult residents of the continental United States were actually sampled. The population for a study is the aggregation of elements that we actually focus on and sample from, not a larger aggregation that we really wish we could have studied.

Some populations cannot easily be identified by a simple criterion such as a geographic boundary or an organizational membership. Let us say you were interested in victimizations experienced by the homeless population. In this case, a clear definition of the homeless population is difficult, but quite necessary. In research, anyone should be able to determine what population was actually studied. However, studies of homeless persons in the early 1980s "did not propose definitions, did not use screening questions to be sure that the people they interviewed were indeed homeless, and did not make major efforts to cover the universe of homeless people" (Burt 1996: 15). For example, some studies relied on homeless persons in only one shelter. The result was "a collection of studies that could not be compared" (Burt 1996: 15). Several studies of homeless persons in urban areas addressed the problem by employing a more explicit definition of the population: People are homeless if they have no home or permanent place to stay of their own (renting or owning) and no regular arrangement to stay at someone else's place (Burt 1996).

Even this more explicit definition still leaves some questions unanswered: What is a regular arrangement? How permanent does a permanent place have to be? In a study of homeless persons in Chicago, Sosin, Colson, and Grossman (1988) answered these questions in their definition of the population of interest:

> We define the homeless as those currently residing for at least one day but for less than fourteen with a friend or relative, not paying rent, and not sure that the length of stay will surpass fourteen days; those currently residing in a shelter, whether overnight or transitional; those currently without normal, acceptable shelter arrangements and thus sleeping on the street, in doorways, in abandoned buildings, in cars, in subway or bus stations, in alleys, and so forth; those residing in a treatment center for the indigent who have lived at the facility for less than 90 days and who claim that they have no place to go, when released. (1988: 22)

This definition accurately reflects these researchers' concept of homelessness and allows researchers in other locations or at other times to develop procedures for studying a comparable population. The more complete and explicit the definition of the population from which a sample is selected, the more precise our generalizations from a sample to that population can be.

Evaluate Generalizability

After we have clearly defined the population we will sample, we need to determine the scope of the generalizations we will seek to make from our sample. Let us say we were interested in the extent to which high school youth are fearful of being attacked or harmed at school or going to and from their schools. It would be easy to go down to the local high school and hand out a survey asking students to report their level of fear in these situations. But what if my local high school were located in a remote and rural area of Alaska? Would this sample reflect levels of fear perceived by suburban youth in California or urban youth in New York City? Obviously not. Oftentimes, regardless of the sample utilized, researchers will go on to talk about "this percentage of high school students are fearful" or "freshman students are more fearful than seniors," as if their study results represented all high school students. Many social researchers and criminologists (and most everyone else, for that matter) are eager to draw conclusions about all individuals they are interested in, not just their samples. Generalizations make their work (and opinions) sound more important. If every high school student were like every other one, generalizations based on observations of one high school student would be valid. But of course that is not the case.

Generalizability has two aspects. **Sample generalizability** refers to the ability to generalize from a sample, or subset, of a larger population to that population itself. This is the most common meaning of generalizability. **Cross-population generalizability** refers to the ability to generalize from findings about one group, population, or setting to other groups, populations, or settings (see Exhibit 4.2). In this book, we use the term **external validity** to refer only to cross-population generalizability, not to sample generalizability.

Sample generalizability Exists when a conclusion based on a sample, or subset, of a larger population holds true for that population.

Cross-population generalizability Exists when findings about one group, population, or setting hold true for other groups, populations, or settings. This is also called *external validity*.

Sample generalizability is a key concern in survey research, whether you are interested in measuring the extent of violent victimization, perceived levels of fear, or any other issue. A good example of the importance of sample generalizability comes from legitimate pollsters such as Gallup and Roper. Say we were interested in the likely winner of the next presidential election. To determine this, these pollsters might study a sample of likely voters, and then generalize their findings to the entire population of likely voters. No one would be interested in the results of political polls if they represented only the tiny sample that actually was surveyed rather than the entire population.

Cross-population generalizability occurs to the extent that the results of a study hold true for multiple populations; these populations may not all have been sampled, or they may be represented as subgroups within the sample studies. For example, our cross-population generalizability would be called into question if we said all high school students perceived low levels of fear while going to and from school and we only had our rural Alaskan sample.

Generalizability is a key concern in research design. We rarely have the resources to study the entire population that is of interest to us, so we have to select cases to study that will allow our findings to be generalized to the population of interest. We can never be sure that our propositions will hold under all conditions, so we should be cautious in generalizing to populations that we did not actually sample.

This chapter primarily focuses on the problem of sample generalizability: Can findings from a sample be generalized to the population from which the sample was drawn? This is the most basic question to ask about a sample, and social research methods provide many tools to address it.

Sample generalizability depends on sample quality, which is determined by the amount of **sampling error**. Sampling error can generally be defined as the difference between the characteristics of a sample and the characteristics of the population from which it was selected. The larger the sampling error, the less representative the sample, and thus the less generalizable the findings. To assess sample quality when you are planning or evaluating a study, ask yourself these questions:

EXHIBIT 4.2 Sample and Cross-Population Generalizability

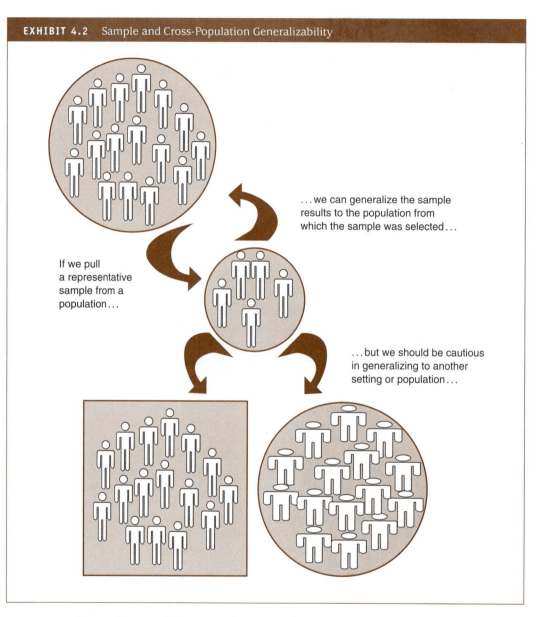

If we pull a representative sample from a population...

...we can generalize the sample results to the population from which the sample was selected...

...but we should be cautious in generalizing to another setting or population...

- From what population were the cases selected?
- What method was used to select cases from this population?
- Do the cases that were studied represent, in the aggregate, the population from which they were selected?

Sampling error Any difference between the characteristics of a sample and the characteristics of the population from which it was drawn. The larger the sampling error, the less representative the sample is of the population.

In reality, researchers often project their theories on to groups or populations much larger than, or simply different from, those they have actually studied. The **target population** is a set of elements larger than or different from the population that was sampled, and to which the researcher would like to generalize any study findings. When we generalize findings to target populations, we must be somewhat speculative. We must carefully consider the claim that the findings can be applied to other groups, geographic areas, cultures, or times.

Because the validity of cross-population generalizations cannot be tested empirically, except by conducting more research in other settings, we do not focus much attention on this problem here. We will return to the problem of cross-population generalizability in chapter 5, which addresses experimental research.

Assess Population Diversity

Sampling is unnecessary if all the units in the population are identical. Physicists do not need to select a representative sample of atomic particles to learn about basic physical processes. They can study a single atomic particle, because it is identical to every other particle of its type. Similarly, biologists do not need to sample a particular type of plant to determine whether a given chemical has toxic effects on it. The idea is, "If you've seen one, you've seen 'em all."

What about people? Certainly all people are not identical—nor are animals in many respects. Nonetheless, if we are studying physical or psychological processes that are the same among all people, sampling is not needed to achieve generalizable findings. Psychologists and social psychologists often conduct experiments on college students to learn about processes that they think are identical for all individuals. They believe that most people will have the same reactions as the college students if they experience the same experimental conditions. Field researchers who observe group processes in a small community sometimes make the same assumption.

There is a potential problem with this assumption, however. There is no way to know whether the processes being studied are identical for all people. In fact, experiments can give different results depending on the type of people studied or the conditions for the experiment. Milgram's (1965) classic experiments on obedience to authority, among the most replicated experiments in the history of social psychological research, illustrate this point very well. The Milgram experiments tested the willingness of male volunteers in New Haven, Connecticut, to comply with instructions from an authority figure to give electric shocks to someone else, even when these shocks seemed to harm the person receiving them. In most cases, the volunteers complied. Milgram concluded that people are very obedient to authority.

Were these results generalizable to all men, to men in the United States, or to men in New Haven? Similar results were obtained in many replications of the Milgram experiments when the experimental conditions and subjects were similar to those studied by Milgram. Other studies, however, showed that some groups were less likely to react so obediently. Given certain conditions, such as another subject in the room who refused to administer the shocks, subjects were likely to resist authority.

Generalizing the results of experiments and of participant observation is risky, because such research often studies a small number of people who do not represent a particular population. Researchers may put aside concerns about generalizability when they observe the social dynamics of specific clubs, or college dorms, or a controlled experiment that tests the effect of, say, a violent movie on feelings for others. But we should be cautious about generalizing the results of such studies.

The important point is that social scientists rarely can skirt the problem of demonstrating the generalizability of their findings. If a small sample has been studied in an experiment or field research project, the study should be replicated in different settings or, preferably, with a **representative sample** of the population for which the generalizations are sought (see Exhibit 4.3).

EXHIBIT 4.3   Representative and Unrepresentative Samples

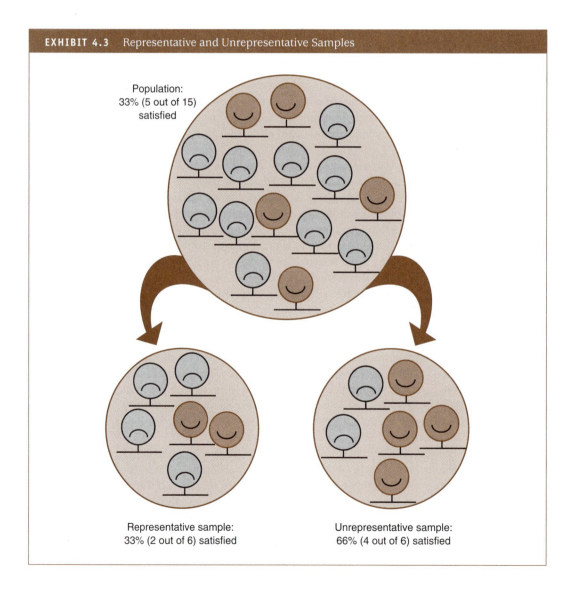

Population:
33% (5 out of 15)
satisfied

Representative sample:
33% (2 out of 6) satisfied

Unrepresentative sample:
66% (4 out of 6) satisfied

The social world and the people in it are just too diverse to be considered identical units. Social psychological experiments and small field studies have produced good social science, but they need to be replicated in other settings, with other subjects, to claim any generalizability. Even when we believe that we have uncovered basic social processes in a laboratory experiment or field observation, we should be very concerned with seeking confirmation in other samples and other research.

Representative sample A sample that looks like the population from which it was selected in all respects that are potentially relevant to the study. The distribution of characteristics among the elements of a representative sample is the same as the distribution of those characteristics among the total population. In an unrepresentative sample, some characteristics are overrepresented or underrepresented.

Consider a Census

In some circumstances, it may be feasible to skirt the issue of generalizability by conducting a **census** studying the entire population of interest rather than drawing a sample. The federal government tries to do this every 10 years with the U.S. Census. A census can also include studies of all the employees (or students) in small organizations (or universities), studies comparing all 50 states, and studies of the entire population of a particular type of organization in a particular area. However, in all these instances—except for the U.S. Census—the population studied is relatively small.

Social scientists do not often attempt to collect data from all the members of some large population simply because doing so would be too expensive and time-consuming. Some social scientists do conduct research with data from the U.S. Census, but it is the government that collects the data and your tax dollars that pay for the effort. For the 2000 census, the Bureau of the Census used half a million temporary workers just to follow up on the 34% of households that did not return their census form in the mail.

Even if the population of interest for a survey is a small town of 20,000 or students in a university of 10,000, researchers will have to sample. The costs of surveying just thousands of individuals far exceed the budgets for most research projects.

SAMPLING METHODS

As you can probably guess, the most important feature to know about a sample is whether it is truly representative of the population from which it was selected. The most important distinction made about samples is whether they are based on a probability or a nonprobability sampling method. Sampling methods that allow us to know in advance how likely it is that any element of a population will be selected for the sample are **probability sampling methods**. Sampling methods that do not let us know the likelihood in advance are **nonprobability sampling methods**.

Probability sampling methods rely on a random selection procedure. In principle, this is the same as flipping a coin to decide which person wins and which one loses. Heads and tails are equally likely to turn up in a coin toss, so both persons have an equal chance to win. That chance, their **probability of selection** is 1 out of 2, or .5.

Probability of selection The likelihood that an element will be selected from the population for inclusion in the sample. In a census of all the elements of a population, the probability that any particular element will be selected is 1.0 because everyone will be selected. If half the elements in the population are sampled on the basis of chance (say, by tossing a coin), the probability of selection for each element is one-half, or 0.5. When the size of the sample as a proportion of the population decreases, so does the probability of selection.

Flipping a coin is a fair way to select one of two people, because the selection process harbors no systematic bias. You might win or lose the coin toss, but you know that the outcome was due simply to chance, not to bias (unless your opponent tossed a two-headed coin!). For the same reason, rolling a six-sided die is a fair way to choose one of six possible outcomes (the odds of selection are 1 out of 6, or .17). Similarly, state lotteries use a random process to select winning numbers. Thus the odds of winning a lottery, the probability of selection, are known even though they are very small (perhaps one out of 1 million) compared with the odds of winning a coin toss. As you can see, the fundamental strategy in probability sampling is the **random selection** of elements into the sample. When a sample is randomly selected from the population, every element has a known and independent chance of being selected into the sample.

Random selection The fundamental element of probability samples. The essential characteristic of random selection is that every element of the population has a known and independent chance of being selected into the sample.

There is a natural tendency to confuse the concept of probability, in which cases are selected only on the basis of chance, with a haphazard method of sampling. On first impression, leaving things up to chance seems to imply not exerting control over the sampling method. But to ensure that nothing but chance influences the selection of cases, the researcher must proceed very methodically, leaving nothing to chance except the selection of the cases themselves. The researcher must carefully follow controlled procedures if a purely random process is to occur. In fact, when reading about sampling methods, do not assume that a random sample was obtained just because the researcher used a random selection method at some point in the sampling process. Look for these two particular problems: selecting elements from an incomplete list of the total population and failing to obtain an adequate response rate (say, only 45% of the people who were asked to participate actually agreed).

The list from which the elements of the population are selected is the **sampling frame**. If this list is incomplete, a sample selected randomly from the list will obviously not be a random sample of the population because not everyone in the population was represented on the list. Thus you should always consider the adequacy of the sampling frame. Even for a simple population like a university's student body, the registrar's list is likely to be at least a bit out of date at any given time. For example, some students will have dropped out, but their status will not yet be officially recorded. Although you may judge the amount of error introduced in this particular situation to be negligible, the problems are greatly compounded for a larger population. The sampling frame for a city, state, or nation is always likely to be incomplete because of constant migration into and out of the area. Even unavoidable omissions from the sampling frame can bias a sample against particular groups within the population.

A very inclusive sampling frame may still yield systematic bias if many sample members cannot be contacted or refuse to participate. **Nonresponse** is a major hazard in survey research because individuals who do not respond to a survey are likely to differ systematically from those who take the time to participate. You should not assume that findings from a randomly selected sample will be generalizable to the population from which the sample was selected if the rate of nonresponse is considerable (certainly not if it is much above 30%).

Probability Sampling Methods

Probability sampling methods are those in which the probability of selection is known and is not zero (so there is some chance of selecting each element). These methods randomly select elements and therefore have no systematic bias; nothing but chance determines which elements are included in the sample. This feature of probability samples, sometimes referred to as random samples, makes them much more desirable than nonprobability samples when the goal is to generalize your findings to a larger population.

Even though a random sample has no systematic bias, it certainly will have some sampling error due to chance. The probability of selecting a head is .5 in a single toss of a coin, and in 20, 30, or however many tosses of a coin you like. But it is perfectly possible to toss a coin twice and get a head both times. The random sample of the two sides of the coin is selected in an unbiased fashion, but it still is unrepresentative. Imagine randomly selecting a sample of 10 people from a population comprising 50 men and 50 women. Just by chance it is possible that your sample of 10 people will include seven women and only three men. Fortunately, we can determine mathematically the likely degree of sampling error in an estimate based on a random sample (as you will see later in this chapter), assuming that the sample's randomness has not been destroyed by a high rate of nonresponse or by poor control over the selection process.

In general, both the size of the sample and the homogeneity (sameness) of the population affect the degree of error due to chance; the proportion of the population that the sample represents does not. To elaborate:

The larger the sample, the more confidence we can have in the sample's representativeness of the population from which it was drawn. If we randomly pick five people to represent the entire population of our city, our sample is unlikely to be very representative of the entire population in terms of age, gender, race, attitudes, and so on. But if we randomly pick 100 people, the odds of having a representative sample are much better; with a random sample of 1,000, the odds become very good indeed.

The more homogeneous the population, the more confidence we can have in the representativeness of a sample of any particular size. Let us say we plan to draw samples of 50 from each of two communities to estimate mean family income. One community is very diverse, with family incomes ranging from $12,000 to $85,000. In the more homogeneous community, family incomes are concentrated in a narrower range, from $41,000 to $64,000. The estimated average family income based on the sample from the homogeneous community is more likely to be representative than is the estimate based on the sample from the more heterogeneous community. With less variation, fewer cases are needed to represent the homogeneous community.

The fraction of the total population that a sample contains does not affect the sample's representativeness, unless that fraction is large. We can regard any sampling fraction under 2% with about the same degree of confidence (Sudman 1976: 184). In fact, sample representativeness is not likely to increase much until the sampling fraction is quite a bit higher. Other things being equal, a sample of 1,000 from a population of 1 million (with a sampling fraction of 0.001, or 0.1%) is much better than a sample of 100 from a population of 10,000 (although the sampling fraction is 0.01, or 1%, which is 10 times higher). The size of a sample is what makes representativeness more likely, not the proportion of the whole that the sample represents.

The Gallup poll did quite well in predicting the result of the remarkable 2000 presidential election. The final Gallup prediction was that George W. Bush would win with 48% (Al Gore was predicted to receive only 46%, and Green Party nominee Ralph Nader was predicted to secure 4%). Although the race turned out to be much closer, with Gore actually winning the popular vote (before losing in the electoral college), Gallup accurately noted that there appeared to have been a late-breaking trend in favor of Gore (Newport 2000). In 2004, the final Gallup prediction of 49% for Bush was within two percentage points of his winning total of 51%.

Because they do not disproportionately exclude or include particular groups within the population, random samples that are successfully implemented avoid systematic bias. Random sampling error can still be considerable, however, and different types of random samples vary in their ability to minimize it. The four most common methods for drawing random samples are simple random sampling, systematic random sampling, stratified random sampling, and cluster sampling.

Simple Random Sampling

Simple random sampling requires a procedure that generates numbers or identifies cases strictly on the basis of chance. As you know, flipping a coin and rolling a die can be used to identify cases strictly on the basis of chance, but these procedures are not very efficient tools for drawing a sample. A **random number table**, such as the one in Appendix D, simplifies the process considerably. The researcher numbers all the elements in the sampling frame and then uses a systematic procedure for picking corresponding numbers from the random number table. Alternatively, a researcher may use a lottery procedure. Each case number is written on a small card, and then the cards are mixed up and the sample selected from the cards.

When a large sample must be generated, these procedures are very cumbersome. Fortunately, a computer program can easily generate a random sample of any size. The researcher must first number all the elements to be sampled (the sampling frame) and then run the computer program to generate a random selection of the numbers within the desired range. The elements represented by these numbers are the sample.

Organizations that conduct phone surveys often draw random samples with another automated procedure called **random digit dialing**. A machine dials random numbers within the phone prefixes corresponding to the area in which the survey is to be conducted. Random digit dialing is particularly useful when a sampling frame is not available. The researcher simply replaces any inappropriate numbers (e.g., those no longer in service or for businesses) with the next randomly generated phone number.

The probability of selection in a true simple random sample is equal for each element. If a sample of 500 is selected from a population of 17,000 (i.e., a sampling frame of 17,000), then the probability of selection for each element is 500/17,000, or .03. Every element has an equal and independent chance of being selected, just like the odds in a toss of a coin (1/2) or a roll of a die (1/6). Thus, sample random sampling is an equal probability of selection method (EPSEM).

Simple random sampling can be done either with or without replacement sampling. In **replacement sampling**, each element is returned to the sampling frame from which it is selected so that it may be sampled again. In sampling without replacement, each element selected for the sample is then excluded from the sampling frame. In practice it makes no difference whether sampled elements are replaced after selection, as long as the population is large and the sample is to contain only a small fraction of the population.

Systematic Random Sampling

Systematic random sampling is a variant of simple random sampling and is a little less time-consuming. When you systematically select a random sample, the first element is selected randomly from a list or from sequential files, and then every nth element is systematically selected thereafter. This is a convenient method for drawing a random sample when the population elements are arranged sequentially. It is particularly efficient when the elements are not actually printed (i.e., there is no sampling frame) but instead are represented by folders in filing cabinets.

Systematic random sampling requires three steps:

1. The total number of cases in the population is divided by the number of cases required for the sample. This division yields the **sampling interval**, the number of cases from one sampled case to another. If 50 cases are to be selected out of 1,000, the sampling interval is 20 (1,000/50 = 20); every 20th case is selected.

2. A number from 1 to 20 (the sampling interval) is selected randomly. This number identifies the first case to be sampled, counting from the first case on the list or in the files.

3. After the first case is selected, every nth case is selected for the sample, where n is the sampling interval. If the sampling interval is not a whole number, the size of the sampling interval is systematically varied to yield the proper number of cases for the sample. For example, if the sampling interval is 30.5, the sampling interval alternates between 30 and 31.

In almost all sampling situations, systematic random sampling yields what is essentially a simple random sample. The exception is a situation in which the sequence of elements is affected by **periodicity**—that is, the sequence varies in some regular, periodic pattern. Thus the list or folder device from which the elements are selected must be truly random. For example, we could not have a list of convicted felons sorted by offense type, age, or some other characteristic of the population. If the list is sorted in any meaningful way, this will introduce bias to the sampling process and the resulting sample is not likely to be representative of the population.

Stratified Random Sampling

Although all probability sampling methods use random sampling, some add steps to the sampling process to make sampling more efficient or easier. One sample is more efficient than another when it is easier to obtain without sacrificing confidence that the sample statistics are representative of the population. Samples are easier to collect when they require less time, money, or prior information.

Stratified random sampling uses information known about the total population prior to sampling to make the sampling process more efficient. First, all elements in the population (i.e., in the sampling frame) are distinguished according to their value on some relevant characteristic, which forms the sampling strata. Next, elements are sampled randomly from within these strata. For example, race may be the basis for distinguishing individuals in some population of interest. Within each racial category selected for the strata, individuals are then sampled randomly.

Why is this method more efficient than drawing a simple random sample? Well, imagine that you plan to draw a sample of 500 from an ethnically diverse neighborhood. The neighborhood population is 15% African American, 10% Hispanic, 5% Asian, and 70% Caucasian. If you drew a simple random sample, you might end up with disproportionate numbers of each group. But if you created sampling strata based on race and ethnicity, you could randomly select cases from each stratum: 75 African Americans (15% of the sample), 50 Hispanics (10%), 25 Asians (5%), and 350 Caucasians (70%). By using **proportionate stratified sampling** you would eliminate any possibility of error in the sample's distribution of ethnicity. Each stratum would be represented exactly in proportion to its size in the population from which the sample was drawn (see Exhibit 4.4).

In **disproportionate stratified sampling**, the proportion of each stratum that is included in the sample is intentionally varied from what it is in the population. In the case of the sample stratified by ethnicity, you might select equal numbers of cases from each racial or ethnic group: 125 African Americans (25% of the sample), 125 Hispanics (25%), 125 Asians (25%), and 125 Caucasians (25%). In this type of sample, the probability of selection of every case is known but unequal between strata. You know what the proportions are in the population, and so you can easily adjust your combined sample statistics to reflect these true proportions. For instance, if you want to combine the ethnic groups and estimate the average income of the total population, you would have to weight each case in the sample. The weight is a number you multiply by the value of each case based on the stratum it is in. For example, you would multiply the incomes of all African Americans in the sample by 0.6 (75/125), the incomes of all Hispanics by 0.4 (50/125), and so on. Weighting in this way reduces the influence of the oversampled strata and increases the influence of the undersampled strata to just what they would have been if pure probability sampling had been used.

Why would anyone select a sample that is so unrepresentative in the first place? The most common reason is to ensure that cases from smaller strata are included in the sample in sufficient numbers. Only then can separate statistical estimates and comparisons be made between strata (e.g., between African Americans and Caucasians). Remember that one determinant of sample quality is sample size. If few members of a particular group are in the population, they need to be oversampled. Such disproportionate sampling may also result in a more efficient sampling design if the costs of data collection differ markedly between strata or if the variability (heterogeneity) of the strata differs.

EXHIBIT 4.4   Stratified Random Sampling

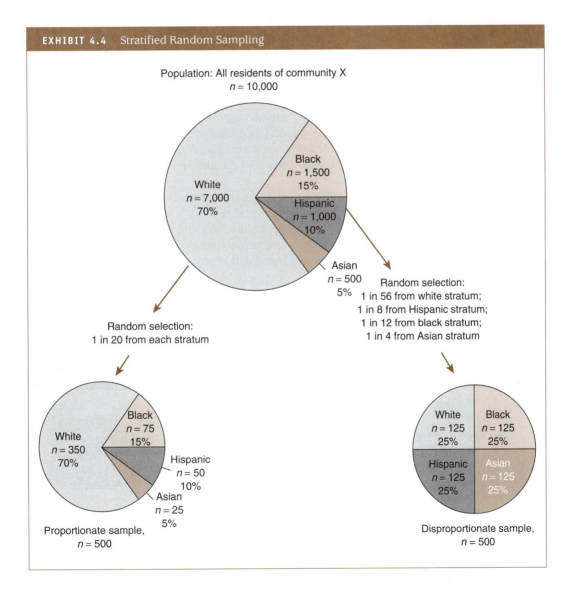

Cluster Sampling

Although stratified sampling requires more information than usual prior to sampling (about the size of strata in the population), **cluster sampling** requires less prior information. Specifically, cluster sampling can be useful when a sampling frame is not available, as often is the case for large populations spread across a wide geographic area or among many different organizations. In fact, if we wanted to obtain a sample from the entire U.S. population, there would be no list available. Yes, there are lists in telephone books of residents in various places who have telephones, lists of those who have registered to vote, lists of those who hold driver's licenses, and so on. However, all these lists are incomplete: some people do not list their phone number or do not have a telephone; some people are not registered to vote, and so on. Using incomplete lists such as these introduces bias into a sample.

In such cases, the sampling procedures become a little more complex. We usually end up working toward the sample we want through a series of steps, first by extracting a random sample of groups or clusters of elements that are available and then by randomly sampling the individual elements of interest from within these selected clusters. So what is a cluster? A **cluster** is a naturally occurring, mixed aggregate of elements of the population, with each element appearing in one and only one cluster. Schools could serve as clusters for sampling students, blocks could serve as clusters for sampling city residents, counties could serve as clusters for sampling the general population, and businesses could serve as clusters for sampling employees.

Drawing a cluster sample is at least a two-stage procedure. First, the researcher draws a random sample of clusters. A list of clusters should be much easier to obtain than a list of all the individuals in each cluster in the population. Next, the researcher draws a random sample of elements within each selected cluster. Because only a fraction of the total clusters are involved, obtaining the sampling frame at this stage should be much easier.

In a cluster sample of city residents, for example, blocks could be the first-stage clusters. A research assistant could walk around each selected block and record the addresses of all occupied dwelling units. Or, in a cluster sample of students, a researcher could contact the schools selected in the first stage and make arrangements with the registrars to obtain lists of students at each school. Cluster samples often involve multiple stages (see Exhibit 4.5).

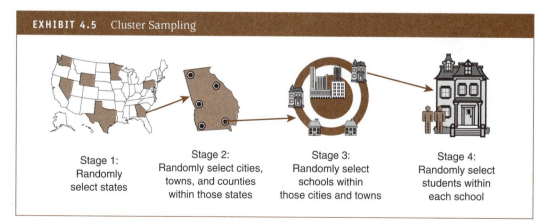

EXHIBIT 4.5   Cluster Sampling

| Stage 1: | Stage 2: | Stage 3: | Stage 4: |
| Randomly select states | Randomly select cities, towns, and counties within those states | Randomly select schools within those cities and towns | Randomly select students within each school |

Many professionally designed surveys use multistage cluster samples or even combinations of cluster and stratified probability sampling methods. For example, the U.S. Justice Department's National Crime Victimization Survey (NCVS) is an excellent example of a cluster sample. In the NCVS, the first stage of clusters selected are referred to as primary sampling units (PSUs) and represent a sample of rural counties and large metropolitan areas. From these PSUs, another stage of sampling involves the selection of geographic districts within each of the PSUs that have been listed by the U.S. Bureau of the Census population census. Finally, a probability sample of residential dwelling units is selected from these geographic districts. These dwelling units, or addresses, represent the final stage of the multistage sampling. Anyone who resides at a selected address who is 12 years of age or older and is a U.S. citizen is eligible for the NCVS sample. Approximately 50,500 housing units or other living quarters are designated for the NCVS each year and are selected in this manner.

How would we evaluate the NCVS sample, using the sample evaluation questions?

- *From what population were the cases selected?* The population was clearly defined for each cluster.
- *What method was used to select cases from this population?* The random selection method was carefully described.
- *Do the cases that were studied represent, in the aggregate, the population from which they were selected?* The unbiased selection procedures make us reasonably confident in the representativeness of the sample.

Nonprobability Sampling Methods

Unlike probability samples, when collecting a sample using nonprobability sampling techniques, elements within the population do not have a known probability of being selected into the sample. Thus, because the chance of any element being selected is unknown, we cannot be certain the selected sample actually represents our population. Why, you may be asking yourself right now, would we want to use such a sample if we cannot generalize our results to a larger population? Well, because these methods are useful for several purposes, including those situations in which we do not have a population list, when we are exploring a research question that does not concern a large population, or when we are doing a preliminary or exploratory study. Suppose, for example, that we were interested in the crime of shoplifting and wanted to investigate the rationalization used by shoplifters. It would be hard to define a population in this case because we do not have a list of shoplifters from which to randomly select. There may be lists of convicted shoplifters, but of course they only represent those shoplifters who were actually caught.

There are four nonprobability sampling methods frequently used in criminological research: availability sampling, quota sampling, purposive sampling, and snowball sampling.

Availability Sampling

The definition of **availability sampling** is straightforward: Elements are selected because they are available or easy to find. Consequently, this sampling method is also known as haphazard, accidental, or convenience sampling. News reporters often use person-on-the-street interviews—availability samples—to inject a personal perspective into a news story and show what ordinary people may think of a given topic. Availability samples are also used by university professors and researchers all the time. Have you ever been asked to complete a questionnaire in one of your classes? If so, you have been selected for inclusion in an availability sample.

Even though they are not generalizable, availability samples are often appropriate in research—for example, when a field researcher is exploring a new setting and trying to get some sense of prevailing attitudes or when a survey researcher conducts a preliminary test of a questionnaire. There are a variety of ways to select elements for an availability sample: standing on street corners and talking to anyone walking by, asking questions of employees who come to pick up their paychecks at a personnel office, or distributing questionnaires to an available and captive audience such as a class or a group meeting. Availability samples are also frequently used in fieldwork studies interested in obtaining detailed information about a particular group.

How do the answers to the sample evaluation questions differ for an availability sample compared with those obtained for probability samples? Well, there is no clearly definable population sampling from which the respondents were drawn, and no systematic technique was used to select the respondents. Consequently, there is not much likelihood that the sample is representative of any target population; the problem is that we can never be sure.

Quota Sampling

Quota sampling is intended to overcome the most obvious flaw of availability sampling: that the sample will just consist of who or what is available, without any concern for its similarity to the population of interest. The distinguishing feature of a quota sample is that quotas are set to ensure that the sample represents certain characteristics in proportion to their prevalence in the population.

Quota samples are similar to stratified probability samples, but they are generally less rigorous and precise in their selection procedures. Quota sampling simply involves designating the population into proportions of some group that you want to be represented in your sample. Similar to stratified samples, in some cases these proportions may actually represent the true proportions observed in the population. At other times, these quotas may represent predetermined proportions of subsets of people you deliberately want to oversample.

The problem is that even when we know that a quota sample is representative of the particular characteristics for which quotas have been set, we have no way of knowing if the sample is representative in terms of any other characteristics. In Exhibit 4.6, for example, quotas have been set for gender only. Under the circumstances, it's no surprise that the sample is representative of the population only in terms of gender, not in terms of race. Interviewers are only human; they may avoid potential respondents with menacing dogs in the front yard, or they could seek out respondents who are physically attractive or who look like they would be easy to interview. Realistically, researchers can set quotas for only a small fraction of the characteristics relevant to a study, so a quota sample is really not much better than an availability sample (although following careful, consistent procedures for selecting cases within the quota limits always helps).

EXHIBIT 4.6   Quota Sampling

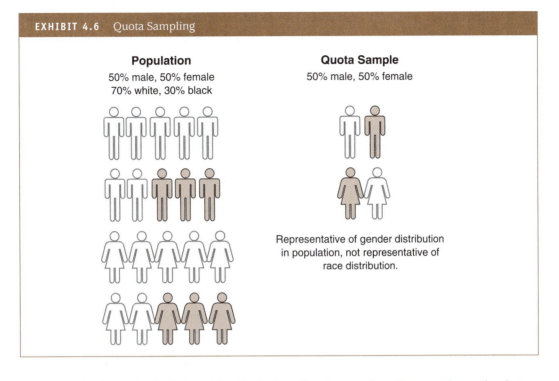

Population
50% male, 50% female
70% white, 30% black

Quota Sample
50% male, 50% female

Representative of gender distribution
in population, not representative of
race distribution.

This last point leads to another limitation of quota sampling: You must know the characteristics of the entire population to set the right quotas. In most cases, researchers know what the population looks like in terms of no more than a few of the characteristics relevant to their concerns, and in some cases they have no such information on the entire population.

Purposive or Judgment Sampling

In **purposive sampling**, each sample element is selected for a purpose, usually because of the unique position of the sample elements. It is sometimes referred to as *judgment sampling*, because the researcher uses his or her own judgment about whom to select into the sample, rather than drawing sample elements randomly. Purposive sampling may involve studying the entire population of some limited group (members of a street gang) or a subset of a population (juvenile parolees). Or a purposive sample may be a key informant survey, which targets individuals who are particularly knowledgeable about the issues under investigation.

Rubin and Rubin (1995: 66) suggest three guidelines for selecting informants when designing any purposive sampling strategy. Informants should be

- knowledgeable about the cultural arena or situation or experience being studied;
- willing to talk; and
- representative of the range of points of view.

Purposive sampling does not produce a sample that represents some larger population, but it can be exactly what is needed in a case study of an organization, community, or some other clearly defined and relatively limited group. For example, in their book *Crimes of the Middle Class*, Weisburd et al. (1991) examined a sample of white-collar criminal offenders convicted in seven federal judicial districts. These judicial districts were not randomly selected from an exhaustive list of all federal districts, but were instead deliberately selected by the researchers because the seven districts were judged by them to provide a suitable amount of geographical diversity. They were also selected because they were believed to have a substantial proportion of white-collar crime cases. The cost of such nonprobability sampling, you should realize by now, is generalizability; we do not know if their findings hold true for white-collar crime in other areas of the country.

Snowball Sampling

For **snowball sampling**, you identify one member of the population and speak to him or her, then ask that person to identify others in the population and speak to them, then ask them to identify others, and so on. The sample thus snowballs in size. This technique is useful for hard-to-reach or hard-to-identify, interconnected populations where at least some members of the population know each other, such as drug dealers, prostitutes, practicing criminals, gang leaders, and informal organizational leaders.

In their study of juvenile gangs in St. Louis, Decker and Van Winkle (1996) utilized the technique of snowball sampling. Specifically, the snowball began with an earlier fieldwork project involving active residential burglars (Wright & Decker 1994). The young members from this sample, along with contacts a field ethnographer had with several active street criminals, started the referral process. The initial interviewees then nominated other gang members as potential interview subjects.

One problem with this technique is that the initial contacts may shape the entire sample and foreclose access to some members of the population of interest. Because Decker and Van Winkle (1996) wanted to interview members from several gangs, they had to restart the snowball sampling procedure many times to gain access to a large number of gangs. One problem, of course, was validating whether individuals claiming to be gang members—so-called wannabes—actually were legitimate members. Over 500 contacts were made before the final sample of 99 was complete.

More systematic versions of snowball sampling can also reduce the potential for bias. The most sophisticated version, *respondent-driven sampling*, gives financial incentives, also called gratuities, to respondents to recruit peers (Heckathorn 1997). Limitations on the number of incentives that any one respondent can receive increase the sample's diversity. Targeted incentives can steer the sample to include specific subgroups. When the sampling is repeated through several waves, with new respondents bringing in more peers, the composition of the sample converges on a more representative mix of characteristics. Exhibit 4.7 shows how the sample spreads out through successive recruitment waves to an increasingly diverse pool (Heckathorn 1997: 178). As with all nonprobability sampling techniques, however, researchers using even the most systematic versions of snowball sampling cannot be confident that their sample is representative of the population of interest.

EXHIBIT 4.7   Respondent-Driven Sampling—A Version of Snowball Sampling

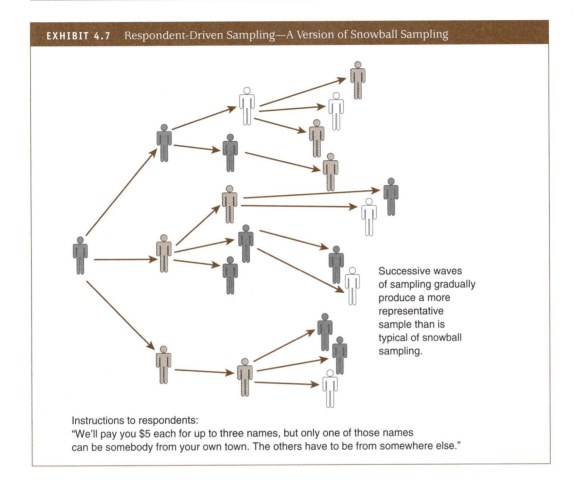

Successive waves of sampling gradually produce a more representative sample than is typical of snowball sampling.

Instructions to respondents:
"We'll pay you $5 each for up to three names, but only one of those names can be somebody from your own town. The others have to be from somewhere else."

Lessons About Sample Quality

Some lessons are implicit in our evaluations of the samples in this chapter:

- We cannot evaluate the quality of a sample if we do not know what population it is supposed to represent. If the population is unspecified because the researchers were never clear about just what population they were trying to sample, then we can safely conclude that the sample itself is no good.
- We cannot evaluate the quality of a sample if we do not know exactly how cases in the sample were selected from the population. If the method was specified, we then need to know whether cases were selected in a systematic fashion or on the basis of chance. In any case, we know that a haphazard method of sampling (as in person-on-the-street interviews) undermines generalizability.
- Sample quality is determined by the sample actually obtained, not just by the sampling method itself. If many of the people (or other elements) selected for our

sample do not respond or participate in the study, even though they have been selected for the sample, the quality of our sample is undermined even if we chose the sample in the best possible way.

- We need to be aware that even researchers who obtain very good samples may talk about the implications of their findings for some group that is larger than or just different from the population they actually sampled. For example, findings from a representative sample of students in one university often are discussed as if they tell us about university students in general. And maybe they do; the problem is, we just don't know.

SAMPLING DISTRIBUTIONS

A well-designed probability sample is one that is likely to be representative of the population from which it was selected. But, as you have seen, random samples still are subject to sampling error due only to chance. To deal with that problem, social researchers take into account the properties of a **sampling distribution**, a hypothetical distribution of a statistic across an infinite number of random samples that could be drawn from a population. Any single random sample can be thought of as just one of an infinite number of random samples that, in theory, could have been selected from the population. If we had the finances of Bill Gates and the patience of Job, and were able to draw an infinite number of samples, and we calculated the same type of statistic (e.g., percentage of those in favor of the three strikes laws) for each of these samples, we would then have a sampling distribution. Understanding sampling distributions is the foundation for understanding how researchers can estimate sampling error.

Sampling distribution A hypothetical distribution of a statistic (e.g., proportion, mean) across an infinite number of random samples that could be drawn from a population.

What does a sampling distribution look like? Because a sampling distribution is based on some statistic calculated for different samples, we need to choose a statistic. Let us focus on the arithmetic average, or mean. We will explain the calculation of the mean in chapter 10, but you may already be familiar with it: It is simply the arithmetic average of a variable distribution and is obtained by adding up the values of all the cases and then dividing this sum by the total number of cases. Let us say you draw a random sample of 500 families and find that their average (mean) family income is $36,239. This $36,239 would be the sample statistic for this one sample. But imagine that you then drew another random sample, and another, and another, and so on, and calculated the mean from each of these samples. Then imagine marking these means on graph paper. The resulting graph would be a sampling distribution of the mean.

Estimating Sampling Error

In reality, we do not actually observe sampling distributions in real research: It would take too much time and money. Instead, researchers just draw the best sample they can. (Now you understand why it is important to have a sample that is representative of the population.) A sampling distribution usually remains hypothetical or a theoretical distribution. We can use the properties of sampling distributions, however, to calculate the amount of sampling error that was likely with the random sample used in a study. The tools for calculating sampling error are called **inferential statistics**.

Inferential statistics Mathematical tools for estimating how likely it is that a statistical result based on data from a random sample is representative of the population from which the sample was selected.

Sampling distributions for many statistics, including the mean, have a normal shape. A graph of a **normal distribution** looks like a bell, with one hump in the middle, centered around the population mean, and a number of cases tapering off on both sides of the mean. Note that a normal distribution is symmetrical: if you fold it in half at its center (at the population mean), the two halves will match perfectly. This shape is produced by **random sampling error**. The value of the statistic varies from sample to sample because of chance, so higher and lower values are equally likely. A good example of a normally shaped distribution is the grades that will be received in the class for which you are reading this text. The majority of students in the class will receive C's, fewer will receive B's and D's, and fewer still will receive A's and F's.

Exhibit 4.8 shows what the sampling distribution of family incomes would look like if it formed a perfectly normal distribution—this would occur if, rather than 50 random samples, we had selected thousands of random samples.

Systematic sampling error Overrepresentation or underrepresentation of some population characteristics in a sample due to the method used to select the sample. A sample shaped by systematic sampling error is a biased sample.

Random sampling error Differences between the population and the sample that are due only to chance factors (random error), not to systematic sampling error. Random sampling error may or may not result in an unrepresentative sample. The magnitude of sampling error due to chance factors can be estimated statistically.

As we have stated earlier, in research our goal is to generalize what we observe in our sample to the population of interest. In statistical terminology, a **sample statistic** is an estimate of the population parameter we want to estimate. The properties of a sampling distribution facilitate this process of statistical inference. In the sampling distribution, the most frequent value of the sample statistic (such as the mean) computed from sample data is identical to the **population parameter**, the statistic computed for the entire population. In other words, we can have a lot of confidence that the value at the peak of the bell curve represents the norm for the entire population.

Sample statistic An estimated statistic (e.g., proportion, mean) from the one sample we actually selected from a population.

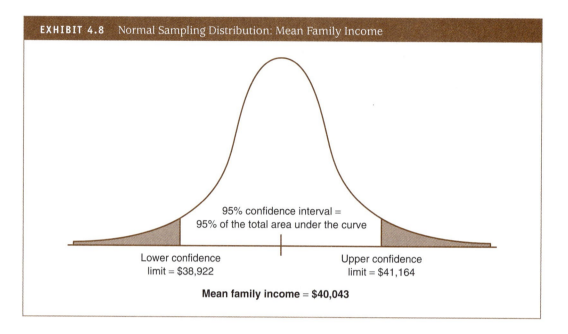

EXHIBIT 4.8   Normal Sampling Distribution: Mean Family Income

95% confidence interval =
95% of the total area under the curve

Lower confidence
limit = $38,922

Upper confidence
limit = $41,164

Mean family income = $40,043

In a normal distribution, a predictable proportion of cases also falls within certain ranges under the curve. Inferential statistics take advantage of this feature and allow us to estimate how likely it is that, given a particular sample, the true population value will be within some range around the statistic. For example, a statistician might conclude from a sample of 30 families that we can be 95% confident that the true mean family income in the total population is between $23,012 and $38,120. The interval from $23,012 to $38,120 would then be called the **confidence interval** for the mean. The upper ($38,120) and lower ($23,012) bounds of this interval are the **confidence limits**.

Although all normal distributions have these same basic features, they differ in the extent to which they cluster around the mean. A sampling distribution is more compact when it is based on larger samples. Stated another way, we can be more confident in estimates based on large random samples because we know that a larger sample creates a more compact sampling distribution. This should make intuitive sense. If you want to estimate the average family income of residents in New York City and you only select a sample of 30 families, the mean you estimate from this sample of 30 is less likely to reflect New York City residents' annual family income than a sample of, say, 3,000.

In most social science disciplines, including ours, researchers typically rely on 95% or 99% confidence intervals. In fact, every time you read the results of an opinion poll in the newspaper or hear about one on a news broadcast, you are really being given a confidence interval. For example, when a newspaper reports that 30% of high school seniors have used marijuana in the past six months, the reporter will also usually add the phrase "plus or minus four percentage points." This is a confidence interval. These conventional confidence limits reflect the conservatism inherent in classical statistical inference. As researchers, we cannot make an inferential statement (e.g., the population does or believes such and such) unless we are very confident (at least 95% confident) that it is correct.

UNITS OF ANALYSIS AND ERRORS IN CAUSAL REASONING

In criminological research, we obtain samples from many different units, including individuals, groups, cities, prisons, countries, and so on. When we make generalizations from a sample to the population, it is very important to keep in mind the units under study, which are referred to as the **units of analysis**. These units of analysis are the level of social life on which the research question is focused, such as individuals, groups, towns, or nations.

Individual and Group Units of Analysis

In most social science research, including criminological studies, the units of analysis are individuals. The researcher may collect survey data from individuals, analyze the data, and then report on how many individuals felt socially isolated and whether recidivism by individuals related to their feelings of social isolation. Data are collected from individuals, and the focus of analysis is on the individual.

In other instances, however, the units of analysis may instead be groups, such as families, schools, prisons, towns, states, or countries. For example, a researcher may collect data from town and police records on the number of accidents in which drivers were intoxicated, and the presence or absence of a server liability law, which makes those who serve liquor liable for accidents caused by those they served. The researcher can then analyze the relationship between server liability laws and the frequency of accidents due to drunk driving (perhaps also taking into account town population). Because the data describe the towns, towns are the units of analysis.

In some studies, groups are the units of analysis but data are collected from individuals. For example, Sampson, Raudenbush, and Earls (1997) studied influences on violent crime in Chicago neighborhoods. Collective efficacy was one variable they hypothesized as an influence on the neighborhood crime rate. This variable was a characteristic of the neighborhood residents who were likely to help other residents and were trusted by other residents. However, they measured this variable in a survey of individuals. The responses of individual residents about their perceptions of their neighbors' helpfulness and trustworthiness were averaged to create a collective efficacy score for each neighborhood. It was this neighborhood measure of collective efficacy that was used to explain variation in the rate of violent crime between neighborhoods. The data were collected from individuals and were about individuals, but they were combined (aggregated) so as to describe neighborhoods. The units of analysis were thus groups (neighborhoods).

In a study such as that of Sampson and colleagues', we can distinguish the concept of units of analysis from the units of observation. Data were collected from individuals, the **units of observation**, and then the data were aggregated and analyzed at the group level. In some studies, the units of observation and the units of analysis are the same. The important point is to know when this is true. A conclusion that crime increases with joblessness could imply that individuals who lose their jobs are more likely to commit a crime, that a community with a high unemployment rate is likely to have a high crime rate, or both. Whether we are drawing conclusions from data or interpreting others' conclusions, we have to be clear about which relationship is referenced.

To interpret statistics appropriately, we also have to know the units of analysis. Measures of association tend to be stronger for group-level than for individual-level data because measurement errors at the individual level tend to cancel out at the group level (Bridges & Weis 1989: 29–31).

The Ecological Fallacy and Reductionism

Researchers should make sure that their conclusions reflect the units of analysis in their study. Conclusions about processes at the individual level should be based on individual-level data; conclusions about group-level processes should be based on data collected about groups. In most cases, violation of this rule creates one more reason to suspect the validity of the causal conclusions.

A researcher who draws conclusions about individual-level processes from group-level data is making an **ecological fallacy** (see Exhibit 4.9). The conclusions may or may not be correct, but we must recognize that group-level data do not describe individual-level processes. For example, a researcher may examine prison employee records and find that the higher the percentage of correctional workers without college education in prisons, the higher the rate of inmate complaints of brutality by officers in prisons. But the researcher would commit an ecological fallacy if they then concluded that individual correctional officers without a college education were more likely to engage in acts of brutality against inmates. This conclusion is about an individual-level causal process (the relationship between the education and criminal propensities of individuals), even though the data describe groups (prisons). It could actually be that college-educated officers are the ones more likely to commit acts of brutality. If more officers in prison are not college educated, perhaps the college-educated officers feel they would not be suspected.

Bear in mind that conclusions about individual processes based on group-level data are not necessarily wrong. The data simply do not provide information about processes at the individual level. Suppose we find that communities with higher average incomes have lower crime rates. The only thing special about these communities may be that they have more individuals with higher incomes, who tend to commit fewer crimes. Even though we collected data at the group level and analyzed them at the group level, they reflect a causal process at the individual level (Sampson & Lauritsen 1994: 80–83).

When data about individuals are used to make inferences about group-level processes, a problem occurs that can be thought of as the mirror image of the ecological fallacy: the **reductionist fallacy** or **reductionism** (see Exhibit 4.9).

The solution to these problems is to know what the units of analysis and units of observation were in a study, and to take these into account when weighing the credibility of the researcher's conclusions. The goal is not to reject conclusions that refer to a level of analysis different from what was actually studied. Instead, the goal is to consider the likelihood that an ecological fallacy or a reductionist fallacy has been made when estimating the causal validity of the conclusions.

EXHIBIT 4.9   Errors in Causal Conclusions

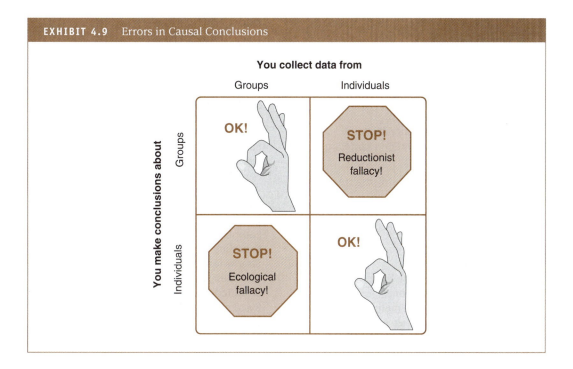

CONCLUSION

Sampling is the fundamental starting point in criminological research. Probability sampling methods allow a researcher to use the laws of chance, or probability, to draw samples from population parameters that can be estimated with a high degree of confidence. A sample of just 1,000 or 1,500 individuals can be used to reliably estimate the characteristics of the population of a nation comprising millions of individuals.

The alternatives to random, or probability-based, sampling methods are almost always much less palatable, even though they typically are much cheaper. Without a method of selecting cases likely to represent the population in which the researcher is interested, research findings will have to be carefully qualified. Unrepresentative samples may help researchers understand which aspects of a social phenomenon are important, but questions about the generalizability of this understanding are left unanswered.

Social scientists often seek to generalize their conclusions from the population that they studied to some larger target population. The validity of generalizations of this type is necessarily uncertain, for having a representative sample of a particular population does not at all ensure that what we find will hold true in other populations. Nonetheless, the accumulation of findings from studies based on local or otherwise unrepresentative populations can provide important information about broader populations.

KEY TERMS

Availability sampling
Census
Cluster
Cluster sampling
Confidence interval
Confidence limits
Cross-population generalizability
Disproportionate stratified sampling
Ecological fallacy
External validity
Inferential statistics
Nonprobability sampling method
Nonresponse
Normal distribution
Periodicity
Population
Population parameter
Probability of selection
Probability sampling method
Proportionate stratified sampling
Purposive sampling
Quota sampling
Random digit dialing

Random number table
Random sampling error
Random selection
Reductionist fallacy
   (reductionism)
Replacement sampling
Representative sample
Sample
Sample generalizability
Sample statistic
Sampling distribution
Sampling error
Sampling frame
Sampling interval
Sampling unit
Simple random sampling
Snowball sampling
Stratified random sampling
Systematic random sampling
Systematic sampling error
Target population
Units of analysis
Units of observation

HIGHLIGHTS

- Sampling is usually necessary except in two conditions: (1) when the elements that would be sampled are identical, which is almost never the case; and (2) when you have the option of conducting a complete census of a population.

- Nonresponse undermines sample quality: It is the obtained sample, not the desired sample, that determines sample quality.

- Probability sampling methods rely on a random selection procedure to ensure there is no systematic bias in the selection of elements. In a probability sample, the odds of selecting elements are independent, equal, and known, and the method of selection is carefully controlled.

- Simple random sampling and systematic random sampling are equivalent probability sampling methods in most situations. However, systematic random sampling is inappropriate for sampling from lists of elements that have a regular, periodic structure.

- Other types of random sampling include stratified random sampling, which uses prior information about a population to make sampling more efficient, and cluster sampling.

- Nonprobability sampling methods can be useful when random sampling is not possible, when a research question does not concern a larger population, and when a preliminary exploratory study is appropriate. However, the representativeness of nonprobability samples cannot be determined.

- The likely degree of error in an estimate of a population characteristic based on a probability sample decreases as the size of the sample increases. Sampling error also decreases if the population from which the sample was selected is homogeneous.

EXERCISES

Discussing Research

1. Locate one or more newspaper articles reporting the prevalence of crime or drugs or alcohol. What information does the article provide on the sample that was selected? What additional information do you need to determine whether the sample was a representative one?

2. Select a random sample using the table of random numbers in Appendix D. Now find information on crime rates from some source such as the government documents section of your library or online at the Bureau of Justice Statistics or the FBI. Find a listing of crime rates (e.g., robbery or homicide) by some geographical units (e.g., states, cities) and number them. Now apply your selected random sample to the list and extract the sample. Compute the average crime rate from your sample. Now compute the average for the entire population list. How does the sample average compare to the corresponding figure for the entire population?

Finding Research

1. What can you learn about sampling on the web? Conduct a search on "sampling" and "population" and select a few of these sites. List a few new points that you learn about sampling.

2. Go to the INFOMINE Scholarly Internet Resource Collections website at http://lib-www.ucr.edu. Search for five resources containing information on crime or victimization. Briefly describe your sources and list the websites where they can be found. How do these sources of information differ in their approaches to collecting information? Do they report the sampling information? What statistics do they present? Do they report the sampling method used in the studies from which they obtained these statistics? What sampling methods were used? Evaluate the sampling methods in terms of representativeness and generalizability. How would you improve on the sampling methods to increase the representativeness and generalizability of the data? If no sampling methods are mentioned, propose one that would have been appropriate to obtain the statistics.

Critiquing Research

1. Select five scholarly journal articles that describe criminological research using a sample drawn from some population. Identify the type of sample used in each study, and note any strong and weak points in how the sample was actually drawn. Did the researchers have a problem due to nonresponse? Considering the sample, how confident are you in the validity of generalizations about the population based on the sample? Do you need

any additional information to evaluate the sample? Do you think a different sampling strategy would have been preferable? What larger population were the findings generalized to? Do you think these generalizations were warranted? Why or why not?

Making Research Ethical

1. Milgram's research on obedience to authority has generated much controversy about research ethics. If you were on your school's IRB (institutional review board for the protection of human subjects), would you vote to approve a study like Milgram's involving students? Would you approve a similar study involving volunteers from the general population? What about if it involved people with a psychiatric illness? More generally, who should the researchers attempt to screen out of the study?

2. Tjaden and Thoennes (2000) sampled adults with random digit dialing in order to study violent victimization. Do you believe that the researchers had any ethical obligation to take any action whatsoever when they learned that a respondent was currently being victimized? Are any of the ethical guidelines presented in chapter 2 relevant to this situation? Teachers and medical personnel are required by law to report cases they believe to represent incidents of child abuse. Should researchers have the same obligation? How would this affect large-scale surveys using random digit dialing in which you want to preserve the anonymity of respondents?

Developing a Research Proposal

Consider the possibilities for sampling:

1. Propose a sampling design that would be appropriate if you were to survey students on your campus only. Define the population, identify the sampling frame(s), and specify the elements and any other units at different stages. Indicate the exact procedure for selecting people to be included in the sample.

2. Propose a different sampling design for conducting your survey in a larger population, such as your city, state, or the entire nation.

Performing Data Analysis in SPSS

In NCS.POR, the V2089 variable measures the location (urban, suburban, rural) of each robbery incident.

1. Create a frequency distribution for this variable, and record the valid percentage for each category.

2. Select a random sample of approximately 5% of all cases. Create a second frequency distribution for the robbery location, and record the valid percentage for each category.

3. Select a random sample containing approximately 1% of all cases. Create a third frequency distribution, and record the valid percentage for each category.

4. Compare the three frequency distributions. How does sample size influence the results? Does the sample size affect the reliability or validity of where robbery is most likely to occur?

Student Study Site

The companion Student Study Website for *The Fundamentals of Research in Criminology and Criminal Justice* can be found at www.sagepub.com/frccjstudy.

Visit the Student Study Site to enhance your understanding of the chapter content and to discover additional resources that will take your learning one step further. You can enhance your understanding of the chapters by using the comprehensive study material, which includes interactive exercises, e-flashcards, web exercises, practice self-tests, and more. You will also find special features, such as Learning from Journal Articles, which incorporates SAGE's online journal collection.

Causation and Research Design

This chapter considers the meaning of causation and then reviews the criteria for achieving causally valid explanations, the ways in which experimental and quasi-experimental research designs seek to meet these criteria, and the difficulties that can sometimes result in invalid conclusions. By the end of the chapter, you should have a good grasp of the meaning of causation and the logic of experimental design—and understand why the features of experiments are so well suited to testing causal hypotheses. In subsequent chapters, we will show how causal issues are handled in other research designs.

WHAT DO WE MEAN BY CAUSATION?

Identifying causes—figuring out why things happen—is the goal of most social science research. Unfortunately, valid explanations of the causes of social phenomena do not come easily. Since the 1990s, violent crime victimization rates have been declining steadily, according to the National Crime Victimization Survey (Catalano 2006). However, in some cities, rates of violence have begun to increase tremendously. Is the recent rise in violence in some cities due to the release of hard-core convicts who had been imprisoned during the crime wave of the 1980s and early 1990s (Liptak 2004)? Is it simply a "crime-drop party is over" phenomenon (cited in Lichtblau 2000: A2)? And why has the violent crime rate continued its downward trend in some cities like New York (Dewan 2004a: A25)? Is it because of Compstat, the city's computer program that identifies to police where crimes are clustering (Dewan 2004b: A1; Kaplan 2002: A3)? Or should credit be given to New York's "Safe Streets, Safe Cities" program, which increased the numbers of police officers (Rashbaum 2002)? To determine which of these possibilities could contribute to the increase or decline of serious crime, we must design our research strategies carefully.

CAUSAL EXPLANATION

A cause is an explanation for some characteristic, attitude, or behavior of groups, individuals, or other entities (such as families, organizations, or cities) or for events. Most social scientists seek causal explanations that reflect tests of the types of hypotheses with which you are familiar (see chapter 3). The independent variable is the presumed cause, and the dependent variable is the potential effect. For example, the study by Robert Sampson and Stephen Raudenbush (2001) tested whether disorder in urban neighborhoods (the independent variable) leads to crime (the dependent variable). (As you know, they concluded that it didn't—at least not directly.)

More specifically, a causal effect is said to occur if variation in the independent variable is followed by variation in the dependent variable, when all other things are equal (***ceteris paribus***). For instance, we know that men are more likely than women to commit violent crimes. But is this because of a genetic predisposition? Different patterns of socialization to violence? Perhaps different levels of job frustration? We need to know whether men commit more crimes than women, *ceteris paribus*.

We admit that you can legitimately argue that "all" other things can't literally be equal. We can't compare the same people at the same time in exactly the same circumstances— except for the variation in the independent variable (King et al. 1994). However, you will see that we can design research to create conditions that are comparable indeed, so that we can confidently assert our conclusions *ceteris paribus*—other things being equal.

Causal effect When variation in one phenomenon, an independent variable, leads to or results, on average, in variation in another phenomenon, the dependent variable.

> ***Example of a causal effect:*** Individuals arrested for domestic assault tend to commit fewer subsequent assaults than do similar individuals who are accused in the same circumstances but not arrested.

Five criteria must be considered when deciding whether a causal connection exists. When a research design leaves one or more of the criteria unmet, we may have some important doubts about causal assertions the researcher may have made. The first three criteria are generally considered the necessary and most important bases for identifying a causal effect: empirical association, appropriate time order, and nonspuriousness. The other two criteria—identifying a causal mechanism and specifying the context in which the effect occurs—can also considerably strengthen causal explanations.

Research designs that allow us to establish these criteria require careful planning, implementation, and analysis. Many times, researchers have to leave one or more of the criteria unmet and are left with some important doubts about the validity of their causal conclusions, or they may even avoid making any causal assertions.

Association

Exhibit 5.1 displays the association that Brad Bushman found between watching a violent videotape and aggressive behavior. Students who watched a violent videotape in his lab administered more intense noise to an opponent than those who watched a nonviolent videotape. So variation in exposure to media violence is associated with a likelihood of exhibiting aggressive behavior. A change in the independent variable is associated with— correlated with—a change in the dependent variable. By contrast, if there is no association between two variables, there cannot be a causal relationship. For this reason, researchers have concluded that the popular DARE (Drug Abuse Resistance Education) elementary school program has no effect on students' subsequent drug abuse (Ringwalt et al. 1994). There is no association between participation in the program and drug use in later years, so DARE cannot be considered to be an independent variable that causes variation in drug abuse (the dependent variable).

Time Order

Association is a necessary criterion for establishing a causal effect, but it is not sufficient. We must also ensure that the variation in the independent variable came *before* variation in the dependent variable—the cause must come before the presumed effect. This is the

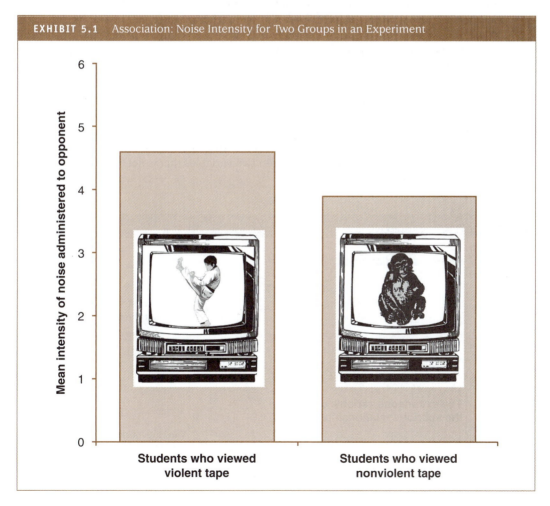

EXHIBIT 5.1   Association: Noise Intensity for Two Groups in an Experiment

Mean intensity of noise administered to opponent

Students who viewed violent tape

Students who viewed nonviolent tape

Source: Adapted from Bushman (1995).

criterion of **time order**. Bushman's experiment satisfied this criterion because he controlled the variation in the independent variable: All the students saw the videotape excerpts (which varied in violent content) before their level of aggressiveness was measured. As you can imagine, we cannot be so sure about time order when we use a cross-sectional research design to test a causal hypothesis. If we find that neighborhoods with higher levels of disorder have higher crime rates, we can't be sure that the level of disorder came first, and led to more crime. Maybe higher crime rates made residents too fearful to keep things in order. Without longitudinal data or other clues to time order, we just don't know.

Nonspuriousness

Even when research establishes that two variables are associated and that variation in the independent variable precedes variation in the dependent variable, we cannot be sure we identified a causal relationship between the two variables. Have you heard the old adage "Correlation does not prove causation?" It is meant to remind us that an association between two variables might be caused by something else. If we measure children's shoe sizes and their academic knowledge, for example, we will find a positive association. However, the association results from the fact that older children have larger feet as well as more academic knowledge. Shoe size does not cause increased knowledge or vice versa. We would say that the association between shoe size and knowledge is **spurious**.

Before we conclude that variation in an independent variable causes variation in a dependent variable, we must have reason to believe that the relationship is nonspurious. **Nonspuriousness** is a relationship between two variables that is not due to variation in a third variable (see Exhibit 5.2).

EXHIBIT 5.2   A Spurious Relationship

Spurious relationship

View the movie
Money Train → Commit
violent crime

**The extraneous variable creates
the spurious relationship**

Feel enraged
against society → View the movie
Money Train

→ Commit
violent crime

Mechanism

Confidence in a conclusion that two variables have a causal connection will be strengthened if a **mechanism**—some discernible means of creating a connection—can be identified (Cook & Campbell 1979: 35; Marini & Singer 1988). Many social scientists believe that a causal explanation is not adequate until a causal mechanism is identified. What process or mechanism actually is responsible for the relationship between the independent and dependent variables?

For instance, there seems to be an empirical association at the individual level between poverty and delinquency: Children who live in impoverished homes seem more likely to be involved in petty crime. But why? Some researchers have argued for a *mechanism* of low parent–child attachment, inadequate supervision of children, and erratic discipline as the means by which poverty and delinquency are connected (Sampson & Laub 1993). In this way, figuring out some aspects of the process by which the independent variable influenced the variation in the dependent variable can increase confidence in our conclusion that there was a causal effect (Costner 1989).

Context

In the social world, it is virtually impossible to claim that one and only one independent variable is responsible for causing or affecting a dependent variable. Stated another way, no cause can be separated from the larger **context** in which it occurs. A cause is really only one of a set of interrelated factors required for the effect (Hage & Meeker 1988; Papineau 1978). When relationships among variables differ across geographic units like counties or across other social settings, or even between different types of individuals, researchers say there is a **contextual effect**. Identification of the context in which a causal relationship occurs can help us to understand that relationship.

In a classic study of children's aggressive behavior in response to media violence, Albert Bandura, Dorothea Ross, and Sheila Ross (1963) examined several contextual factors. They found that effects varied with the children's gender and with the gender of the opponent toward whom they acted aggressively, but not with whether they saw a real (acted) or filmed violent incident. For example, children reacted more aggressively after observing men committing violent acts than after observing women committing these same acts. Bandura and colleagues strengthened their conclusions by focusing on a few likely contextual factors.

In summary, before researchers can infer a causal relationship between two variables, three criteria are essential: empirical association, appropriate time order, and nonspuriousness. After these three conditions have been met, two other criteria are also important: causal mechanism and context.

WHY EXPERIMENT?

Experimental research provides the most powerful design for testing causal hypotheses because it allows us to confidently establish the first three criteria for causality—association, time order, and nonspuriousness. **True experiments** have at least three features that help us meet these criteria:

1. Two comparison groups—one receiving the experimental condition (e.g., treatment or intervention), termed the **experimental group**, and the other receiving no treatment/intervention or another form thereof, termed the **control group**.
2. **Random assignment** to the two (or more) comparison groups.
3. Assessment of change in the dependent variable for both groups after the experimental condition has been received.

We can determine whether an association exists between the independent and dependent variables in a true experiment because two or more groups differ in terms of their value on the independent variable. One group receives some "treatment" that is a manipulation of the value of the independent variable. This group is termed the **experimental group**. In a simple experiment, there may be one other group that does not receive the treatment; it is termed the **control group.**

Experimental group In an experiment, the group of subjects that receives the treatment or experimental manipulation.

Control group A comparison group that receives no treatment.

Consider now the Bushman experiment in detail (see the simple diagram in Exhibit 5.3). Does watching a violent video lead to aggressive behavior? Imagine a simple experiment. Suppose you (like Brad Bushman) believe that watching violent movies leads people to be aggressive, commit crimes, and so on. But other people think that violent media has no effect and that it is people who are already predisposed to violence who seek out violent movies to watch. To test your hypothesis ("Watching violent movies causes aggressive behavior"), you need to compare two groups of subjects, a control group and an experimental group. First, people in the two groups will interact among themselves. Then the control group will watch a video about gardening while the experimental group will watch a video featuring a lot of violence. Next, both groups will sit and interact again among themselves. At the end, the interactions within both groups before and after the videos will be coded and you will see whether either group increased in aggressiveness. Thus you may establish *association*.

You may find an association outside the experimental setting, but it won't establish time order. Perhaps aggressive people choose to watch violent videos, while nonaggressive people do not. So there would be an association, but *not* the causal relation for which we are looking. By controlling who watches the violent video, and when, we establish *time order.*

All true experiments have a **posttest**—that is, a measurement of the outcome in both groups after the experimental group has received the treatment. Many true experiments also have **pretests** that measure the dependent variable before the experimental intervention. A pretest is exactly the same as a posttest, just administered at a different time. Strictly speaking, though, a true experiment does not require a pretest. When researchers use random assignment, the groups' initial scores on the dependent variable and on all other variables are very likely to be similar. Any difference in outcome between the experimental and

EXHIBIT 5.3   Experimental Design Used in the Bushman (1995) Research

comparison groups is therefore likely to be due to the intervention (or to other processes occurring during the experiment), and the likelihood of a difference just on the basis of chance can be calculated.

Finally, it is crucial that the two groups be more or less equal at the beginning of the study. If you let students choose which group to be in, the more violent students may pick the violent movie, hoping to have their aggressive habits reinforced. If so, your two groups won't be equivalent at the beginning of the study, and so any difference in their aggressiveness may be the result of that initial difference (a source of spuriousness), not watching the violent video.

So you randomly sort the students into the two different groups. You can do this by flipping a coin for each one of them, or by pulling names out of a hat, or by using a random number table as described in the previous chapter. In any case, the subjects themselves should not be free to choose, nor should you (the experimenter) be free to put them into whatever group you want.

Note that the random assignment of subjects to experimental and comparison groups is not the same as random sampling of individuals from some larger population (see Exhibit 5.4). In fact, **random assignment (randomization)** does not help at all to ensure that the research subjects are representative of some larger population; instead, representativeness is the goal of random sampling. What random assignment does—create two (or more) equivalent groups—is useful for ensuring internal validity, not generalizability.

Matching is another procedure sometimes used to equate experimental and comparison groups, but by itself it is a poor substitute for randomization. Matching of individuals in a treatment group with those in a comparison group might involve pairing persons on the basis of similarity of gender, age, year in school, or some other characteristic. The basic problem is that, as a practical matter, individuals can be matched on only a few

EXHIBIT 5.4 Random Sampling Versus Random Assignment

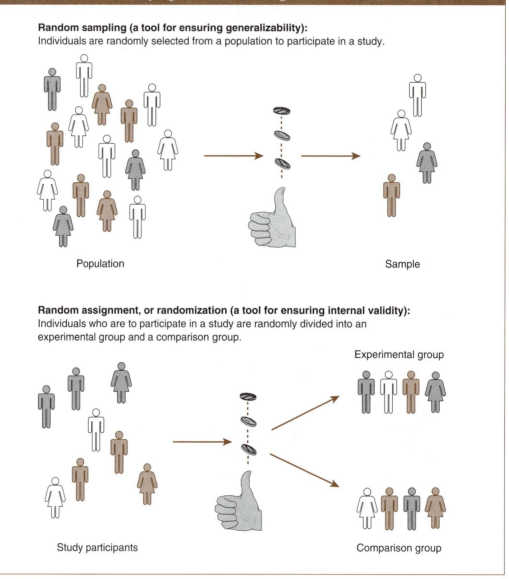

Random sampling (a tool for ensuring generalizability):
Individuals are randomly selected from a population to participate in a study.

Population

Sample

Random assignment, or randomization (a tool for ensuring internal validity):
Individuals who are to participate in a study are randomly divided into an
experimental group and a comparison group.

Experimental group

Study participants

Comparison group

characteristics; unmatched differences between the experimental and comparison groups
may still influence outcomes.

These defining features of true experimental designs give us a great deal of confidence
that we can meet the three basic criteria for identifying causes: association, time order, and
nonspuriousness. However, we can strengthen our understanding of causal connections,
and increase the likelihood of drawing causally valid conclusions, by also investigating
causal mechanism and causal context.

An Experiment in Action: Prison Classification and Inmate Behavior

There is wide variability in the criteria used to classify prisoners across states. Regardless of how these classifications are made, once these labels are assigned, they have the effect that all labels have: they attach various expectations to prisoners. Bench and Allen (2003: 371) state,

> An offender classified as maximum security instantly obtains an image of one who is hard to handle, disrespectful of authority, prone to fight with other inmates, and at a high risk for escape. In contrast, an offender classified as medium security is generally regarded as more manageable, less of an escape risk, and not requiring as much supervision as a maximum-security offender.

To examine whether prison classification actually affected inmate behavior, Bench and Allen (2003) obtained a random sample of 200 inmates admitted to the Utah State Prison who had been classified as maximum security following their initial assessment based on the following criteria: severity of current crime, expected length of incarceration, criminal violence history, escape history, prior institutional commitment, age, history of institutional adjustment, and substance abuse history.

From this group, inmates were randomly assigned to either an experimental group, in which inmates were reclassified to medium-security status, or to a control group, in which inmates retained their maximum-security status. The independent variable, then, was security classification. The dependent variable was the number of disciplinary infractions received by each group. Disciplinary infractions are generally the violation of prison rules. Infractions were weighted to control for the severity of the violations (e.g., possession of unauthorized food was weighted lower than assaulting another inmate). The primary hypothesis was that the experimental group, those reclassified as medium-security, would have a lower number of disciplinary infractions compared with the control group, the inmates who retained their maximum-security classification. A diagram depicting the experiment is provided in Exhibit 5.5. Results indicated that, although inmates reclassified to medium-security did not receive a lower number of infractions, both groups received about the same number of disciplinary infractions, regardless of security classification.

EXHIBIT 5.5   Experiment Examining the Effect of Prison Classification on Inmate Behavior (Bench & Allen 2003)

WHAT IF A TRUE EXPERIMENT ISN'T POSSIBLE?

Often, testing a hypothesis with a true experimental design is not feasible. A true experiment may be too costly or take too long to carry out; it may not be ethical to randomly assign subjects to the different conditions; or it may be too late to do so. Researchers may instead use "quasi-experimental" designs that retain several components of experimental design but differ in important details.

In a **quasi-experimental design**, a comparison group is predetermined to be comparable to the treatment group in critical ways, such as being eligible for the same services or being in the same school cohort (Rossi & Freeman 1989: 313). These research designs are only "quasi"-experimental because subjects are not randomly assigned to the comparison and experimental groups. As a result, we cannot be as confident in the comparability of the groups as in true experimental designs. Nonetheless, in order to term a research design "quasi-experimental," we have to be sure that the comparison groups meet specific criteria.

We will discuss here the two major types of quasi-experimental designs, as well as one type—ex post facto (after the fact) control group design—that is often mistakenly termed quasi-experimental (other types can be found in Cook & Campbell 1979, and Mohr 1992).

- *Nonequivalent control group designs*—**Nonequivalent control group designs** have experimental and comparison groups that are designated before the treatment occurs but are not created by random assignment.
- *Before-and-after designs*—**Before-and-after designs** have a pretest and posttest but no comparison group. In other words, the subjects exposed to the treatment serve, at an earlier time, as their own control group.
- *Ex post facto control group designs*—These designs use nonrandomized control groups designated after the fact.

These designs are weaker than true experiments in establishing the nonspuriousness of an observed association—that it does not result from the influence of some third, uncontrolled variable. On the other hand, because these quasi-experiments do not require the high degree of control necessary in order to achieve random assignment, quasi-experimental designs can be conducted using more natural procedures in more natural settings, so we may be able to achieve a more complete understanding of causal context. In identifying the mechanism of a causal effect, though, quasi-experiments are neither better nor worse than experiments.

Nonequivalent Control Group Designs

In this type of quasi-experimental design, a comparison group is selected so as to be as comparable as possible to the treatment group. Two selection methods can be used:

1. *Individual matching*—Individual cases in the treatment group are matched with similar individuals in the comparison group. This can sometimes create a comparison group that is very similar to the experimental group, such as when Head Start participants were matched with their siblings to estimate the effect of

participation in Head Start. However, in many studies it may not be possible to match on the most important variables.

2. *Aggregate matching*—In most situations when random assignment is not possible, the second method of matching makes more sense: identifying a comparison group that matches the treatment group in the aggregate rather than trying to match individual cases. This means finding a comparison group that has similar distributions on key variables: the same average age, the same percentage female, and so on. For this design to be considered quasi-experimental, however, it is important that individuals must themselves have chosen to be in the treatment group or the control group.

Roy Watson's (1986) study of the deterrent effect of police action on violations of a seatbelt law illustrates a quasi-experimental nonequivalent control group design. Watson's quasi-experimental design is shown in Exhibit 5.6. This study used aggregate matching and a pretest. It was conducted in British Columbia, Canada, where a mandatory seatbelt law had been enacted but had not elicited high rates of compliance. Watson selected two communities of comparable size where police enforcement of the seatbelt law was low. The units of analysis in the study were the drivers, and seatbelt usage was the dependent variable.

EXHIBIT 5.6 Quasi-Experimental Design

Nonequivalent control group design			
Police enforcement of seatbelt laws (Watson 1986)			
Experimental group	O_1	X	O_2
Comparison group	O_1		O_2
Experimental community	Pretest: percentage using seatbelts	Police enforcement of seatbelt law	Posttest: percentage using seatbelts
Comparison community	Pretest: percentage using seatbelts		Posttest: percentage using seatbelts

Note: O = Observation (pretest or posttest); X = Experimental treatment.

In a pretest, Watson (1986) measured seatbelt usage in both communities. Then, in the experimental community, he instituted a media campaign to increase seatbelt usage, followed by increased police enforcement of the seatbelt law. A posttest followed both the media campaign and the increased police enforcement. In the comparison community, one posttest was conducted at about the same time as a final posttest was conducted in the experimental community. Because the two communities were geographically distant and in different media markets, it seemed unlikely that the experiment in one community would have affected the other community while the study was in progress. Results indicated that the experimental program had a marked effect on seatbelt use.

Before-and-After Designs

The common feature of before-and-after designs is the absence of a comparison group: All cases are exposed to the experimental treatment. The basis for comparison is instead provided by the pretreatment measures in the experimental group. These designs are thus useful for studies of interventions that are experienced by virtually every case in some population.

The simplest type of before-and-after design is the fixed-sample panel design. In a panel design, the same individuals are studied over time; the research may entail one pretest and one posttest. However, this type of before-and-after design does not qualify as a quasi-experimental design because comparing subjects with themselves at just one earlier point in time does not provide an adequate comparison group. Many influences other than the experimental treatment may affect a subject following the pretest—for instance, basic life experiences for a young subject.

A more powerful way to ensure that the independent variable actually affected the dependent variable when using a before-and-after design is by using a **multiple group before-and-after design.** In this design, before-and-after comparisons are made of the same variables between different groups. Another type of before-and-after design involves multiple pretest and posttest observations of the same group. **Repeated measures panel designs** include several pretest and posttest observations, allowing the researcher to study the process by which an intervention or treatment has an impact over time; hence, they are better than a simple before-and-after study.

Time series designs include many (preferably 30 or more) such observations in both pretest and posttest periods. They are particularly useful for studying the impact of new laws or social programs that affect large numbers of people and that are readily assessed by some ongoing measurement. For example, we might use a time series design to study the impact of a new seatbelt law on the severity of injuries in automobile accidents, using a monthly state government report on insurance claims. Special statistics are required to analyze time series data, but the basic idea is simple: identify a trend in the dependent variable up to the date of the intervention, then project the trend into the postintervention period. This *projected* trend is then compared to the *actual* trend of the dependent variable after the intervention. A substantial disparity between the actual and projected trend is evidence that the intervention or event had an impact (Rossi & Freeman 1989: 260–261, 358–363).

How well do these before-and-after designs meet the five criteria for establishing causality? The before–after comparison enables us to determine whether an *association* exists between the intervention and the dependent variable (because we can determine whether there was a change after the intervention). They also clarify whether the change in the dependent variable occurred after the intervention, so *time order* is not a problem. However, there is no control group so we cannot rule out the influence of extraneous factors as the actual cause of the change we observe; *spuriousness* may be a problem. Some other event may have occurred during the study that resulted in a change in posttest scores. Overall, the longitudinal nature of before-and-after designs can help to identify causal mechanisms, while the loosening of randomization requirements makes it easier to conduct studies in natural settings, where we learn about the influence of contextual factors.

Ex Post Facto Control Group Designs

The **ex post facto control group design** appears to be very similar to the nonequivalent control group design and is often confused with it, but it does not meet as well the criteria for quasi-experimental designs. Like nonequivalent control group designs, this design has experimental and comparison groups that are not created by random assignment. But, unlike the groups in nonequivalent control group designs, the groups in ex post facto designs are designated after the treatment has occurred. The problem with this is that if the treatment takes any time at all, people with particular characteristics may select themselves for the treatment or avoid it. Of course, this makes it difficult to determine whether an association between group membership and outcome is spurious. However, the particulars will vary from study to study; in some circumstances, we may conclude that the treatment and control groups are so similar that causal effects can be tested (Rossi & Freeman 1989: 343–344).

David P. Farrington's (1977) classic study of the deviance amplification process is an excellent example of an ex post facto control group design (Exhibit 5.7). Farrington tested the hypothesis that juveniles who were publicly labeled as deviant through being found guilty of a delinquent act would increase their deviant behavior compared with those who were not so labeled. Using data from the Cambridge Study of Delinquent Development, involving 400 London working-class youths from ages 8 to 18, Farrington showed that youth who were labeled as delinquent (through conviction) subsequently committed more delinquent acts than similar youth who were not labeled in this way.

WHAT ARE THE THREATS TO INTERNAL VALIDITY AND GENERALIZABILITY IN EXPERIMENTS?

Like any research design, experimental designs must be evaluated for their ability to yield valid conclusions. True experiments are particularly well suited to producing valid conclusions about causality (internal validity), but they are less likely to fare well in achieving generalizability. Quasi-experiments may provide more generalizable results than true experiments, but they are more prone to problems of internal invalidity (although some allow the researcher to rule out almost as many potential sources of internal invalidity as does a true experiment). In general, nonexperimental designs (such as survey research and participant observation) permit less certainty about internal validity.

EXHIBIT 5.7   Ex Post Facto Control Group Design: Farrington's (1977) Test of Deviance Amplification

Causal (Internal) Validity

An experiment's ability to yield valid conclusions about causal effects is determined by the comparability of its experimental and comparison groups. First, of course, a comparison group must be created. Second, this comparison group must be so similar to the experimental group that it will show what the experimental group would be like if it did not receive the experimental treatment—if the independent variable was not varied. For example, the only difference between the two groups in Bushman's (1995) study was that one group watched a violent movie and the other group did not.

There are five basic sources of internal invalidity:

1. *Selection bias.* When characteristics of the experimental and comparison group subjects differ.

2. *Endogenous change.* When the subjects develop or change during the experiment as part of an ongoing process independent of the experimental treatment.

3. *External events/history effects.* When something occurs during the experiment, other than the treatment, that influences outcome scores.

4. *Contamination.* When either the experimental group or the comparison group is aware of the other group and is influenced in the posttest as a result (Mohr 1992).

5. *Treatment misidentification.* When variation in the independent variable (the treatment) is associated with variation in the observed outcome, but the change occurs through a process that the researcher has not identified.

Selection Bias

You may already realize that the composition of the experimental and comparison groups in a true experiment is unlikely to be affected by their difference. If it were affected, it would cause **selection bias**. Random assignment equates the groups' characteristics, though with some possibility for error due to chance. The likelihood of difference due to chance can be identified with appropriate statistics.

Even when the random assignment plan works, the groups can differ over time because of **differential attrition**, or what can be thought of as deselection. That is, the groups become different because for various reasons subjects are more likely to drop out of groups. This is not a likely problem for a laboratory experiment that occurs in one session, but for experiments in which subjects must be involved over time, differential attrition may become a problem.

When subjects are not randomly assigned to treatment and comparison groups, as in nonequivalent control group designs, there is a serious threat of selection bias. Even if the researcher selects a comparison group that matches the treatment group on important variables, there is no guarantee that the groups were similar initially in terms of the dependent variable or another characteristic that ultimately influences posttest scores.

Endogenous Change

The type of problem considered an **endogenous change** occurs when natural developments in the subjects, independent of the experimental treatment, account for some or all of the observed change between pretest and posttest. Endogenous change includes three specific threats to internal validity:

1. *Testing*. Taking the pretest can in itself influence posttest scores. Subjects may learn something or be sensitized to an issue by the pretest and, as a result, respond differently when they are asked the same questions in the posttest.

2. *Maturation*. Changes in outcomes scores during experiments that involve a lengthy treatment period may be due to maturation. Subjects may age or gain experience in school or grow in knowledge, all as part of a natural maturational experience, and thus respond differently on the posttest from the way they responded on the pretest.

3. *Regression*. People experience cyclical or episodic changes that result in different posttest scores, a phenomenon known as a **regression effect**. Subjects who are chosen for a study because they received very low scores on a test may show improvement in the posttest, on average, simply because some of the low scorers were having a bad day. On the other hand, individuals selected for an experiment because they are suffering from tooth decay will not show improvement in the posttest because a decaying tooth is not likely to improve in the natural course of things. It is hard, in many cases, to know whether a phenomenon is subject to naturally occurring fluctuations, so the possibility of regression effects should be considered whenever subjects are selected because of their extremely high or low values on the outcome variable (Mohr 1992: 56, 71–79).

Testing, maturation, and regression effects are generally not a problem in true experiments. Both the experimental group and the comparison group take the pretest, and they are both subject to maturation and regression effects, so even if these possibilities lead to a change in posttest scores, the comparison between the experimental and comparison groups will not be affected. Of course, in experiments with no pretest, testing effects themselves are not a problem. However, in most before-and-after designs without a comparison group, endogenous change effects could occur and lead to an invalid conclusion that there had been an effect of the independent variable.

External Events

External events, sometimes referred to as the **history effect** during the experiment—things that happen outside the experiment—can also change the subjects' outcome scores. An example of this is a newsworthy event that has to do with the focus of an experiment and the major disasters to which subjects are exposed. What if researchers were evaluating the effectiveness of a mandatory arrest policy in decreasing incidents of intimate partner assault, and an event such as the murder trial of O. J. Simpson occurred during the experiment? This would clearly be a historical event that might compromise the results. The media were obsessed with the trial of O. J. Simpson, and as a result intimate partner assault and homicide were given a tremendous amount of media attention. Because of this increased awareness, many victims of intimate partner violence reported their victimizations during this time—police agencies and women's shelters were flooded with calls. If a researcher had been using calls to police in a particular jurisdiction as an indicator of the incidence of intimate partner assault, this historical event would have seriously jeopardized the internal validity of his or her results. Why? Because the increase in police calls would have had more to do with the trial than with any recent change in arrest policies.

Causal conclusions can be invalid in true experiments because of the influence of external events, but not every experiment is affected by them. The specific features of an experiment must be considered carefully to evaluate the possibility of problems due to external events. For example, in an experiment in which subjects go to a particular location for the treatment and the control group subjects do not, something that happens at the experimental location unrelated to the treatment could influence the experimental subjects. The more carefully controlled the conditions for experimental and comparison groups are, the less likely it is that external events will invalidate the causal conclusions of an experiment.

Contamination

Contamination occurs in an experiment when the comparison group is in some way affected by, or affects, the treatment group. This problem basically arises from failure to adequately control the conditions of the experiment. When comparison group members become aware that they are being denied some advantage, they may increase their efforts to compensate, creating a problem called **compensatory rivalry**, or the **John Henry effect** (Cook & Campbell 1979: 55). On the other hand, comparison group members may become demoralized if they feel that they have been left out of some valuable treatment and may perform worse than they would have outside the experiment. The treatment may seem, in comparison, to have a more beneficial effect than it actually did. Both compensatory rivalry and demoralization can thus distort the impact of the experimental treatment.

The danger of contamination can be minimized if the experiment is conducted in a laboratory, if members of the experimental group and the comparison group have no contact while the study is in progress, and if the treatment is relatively brief. To the degree that these conditions are not met, the likelihood of contamination will increase.

Treatment Misidentification

Treatment misidentification occurs when subjects experience a "treatment" that wasn't intended by the researcher. Treatment misidentification has at least three sources:

1. *Expectancies of experimental staff.* Change among experimental subjects may be due to the positive **expectancies of the experimental staff** who are delivering the treatment rather than due to the treatment itself. This type of treatment misidentification can occur even in randomized experiments when well-trained staff convey their enthusiasm for an experimental program to the subjects in subtle ways. Such positive staff expectations create a self-fulfilling prophecy. Because social programs are delivered by human beings, such expectancy effects can be very difficult to control in field experiments. However, in some experiments on the effects of treatments such as medical drugs, **double-blind procedures** can be used. Staff will deliver the treatments without knowing which subjects are getting the treatment and which are receiving a placebo—something that looks like the treatment but has no effect. These procedures can be used in other experiments as well. In fact, the prison experiment discussed at the beginning of this chapter used a double-blind procedure to randomly assign inmates. In the experiment, only the executive director of the Corrections Department and the director of classification were aware of the research. Correctional staff, other individuals who worked with the inmates, and the inmates themselves were unaware of the study. In this way, any expectancies that the staff may have had were unlikely to affect inmate behavior.

2. *Placebo effect.* Treatment misidentification may occur when subjects receive a treatment that they consider likely to be beneficial, then improve because of that expectation rather than the treatment itself. In medical research the placebo is often a chemically inert substance that looks like the experimental drug but actually has no medical effect. Research indicates that the **placebo effect** produces positive health effects in two-thirds of patients suffering from relatively mild medical problems (Goleman 1993: C3). Placebo effects can also occur in social science research. The only way to reduce this threat to internal validity is to treat the comparison group with something similar.

3. *Hawthorne effect.* Members of the treatment group may change in terms of the dependent variable because their participation in the study makes them feel special. This problem can occur when treatment group members compare their situation to that of the control group members who are not receiving the treatment. In this case, this is a type of contamination effect. But experimental group members could feel special simply because they are in the experiment. The **Hawthorne effect** is named after a famous productivity experiment at the Hawthorne electric plant outside Chicago. Workers were moved to a special room for a study of the effects of lighting intensity and other work conditions on their productivity. After this move, the workers began to increase their output no matter what change was made in their working conditions, even when the conditions became worse. The researchers concluded that the workers felt they should work harder because they were part of a special experiment. By the time the study was over, the researchers were convinced that

it was social interaction among workers, not physical arrangements, that largely determined their output. Most management historians believe that the human relations school of management began with this insight.

In a **process analysis**, periodic measures are taken throughout the experiment to assess whether the treatment is being delivered as planned. To avoid treatment misidentification, field researchers are now using process analysis more often than in the past. Process analysis is also a necessary component of evaluation studies, when researchers need to be very confident that the effects they observe are caused by the policy or program change they are studying (Hunt 1985: 272–274).

Generalizability

The need for generalizable findings can be thought of as the Achilles heel of the true experimental design. The design components that are essential for a true experiment and minimize the threats to causal (internal) validity make it more difficult to achieve sample generalizability—the ability to apply the findings to a clearly defined, larger population.

Sample Generalizability

Subjects who can be recruited for a laboratory experiment, randomly assigned to a group, and kept under carefully controlled conditions for the study's duration are unlikely to be a representative sample of any large population of interest to social scientists. In fact, most are recruited from college populations. Can they be expected to react to the experimental treatment in the same way as members of the larger population? The more artificial the experimental arrangements, the greater the problem can be (Campbell & Stanley 1996: 20–21).

It is not only the characteristics of the subjects themselves that determine the generalizability of the experimental results. The generalizability of the treatment and of the setting for the experiment also must be considered (Cook & Campbell 1979: 73–74). However, researchers can take steps both before and after an experiment to increase a study's generalizability. Field experiments are likely to yield findings that are more generalizable to broader populations than are laboratory experiments using subjects who must volunteer. Sherman and Berk's experimental study of arrest and domestic violence and Watson's quasi-experimental study of seatbelt use were both conducted with people and police engaged in their normal activities in real communities, greatly increasing our confidence in the studies' generalizability.

When random selection is not feasible, the researchers may be able to increase generalizability by selecting several sites for conducting the experiments that offer obvious contrasts in the key variables of the population. The follow-up studies to Sherman and Berk's work, for example, were conducted in cities that differed from Minneapolis, the original site, in social class and ethnic composition. As a result, although the findings are not statistically generalizable to a larger population, they do give some indication of the study's general applicability (Cook & Campbell 1979: 76–77).

External Validity (Cross-Population Generalizability)

Researchers are often interested in determining whether the treatment effects identified in an experiment hold true for subgroups of subjects or across different populations. Of course, determining that a relationship between the treatment and the outcome variable holds true for certain subgroups does not establish that the same relationship also holds true for these subgroups in the larger population, but it does suggest that the relationship might be **externally valid**.

External validity The applicability of a treatment effect (or noneffect) across subgroups within an experiment and/or across different populations, times, or settings.

> *Example of external validity:* Sherman and Berk (1984) found that arrest reduced repeat offenses for employed subjects but not for unemployed subjects. The effect of arrest thus varied with employment status, so a conclusion that arrest deters recidivism would not be externally valid.

Interaction of Testing and Treatment

A variation of the problem of external validity occurs when the experimental treatment is effective only when particular conditions created by the experiment occur. For example, if subjects have had a pretest it may sensitize them to a particular issue, so when they are exposed to the treatment, their reaction is different from what it would have been if they had not taken the pretest. In other words, testing and treatment interact to produce the outcome.

Suppose you were interested in the effects of a diversity training film on prejudicial attitudes. After answering questions in a pretest about their attitudes on various topics related to diversity (e.g., racial or sexual prejudice), the subjects generally became more sensitive to the issue of prejudice without seeing the training film. On the posttest, then, their attitudes may be different from pretest attitudes simply because they have become sensitized to the issue of diversity through pretesting. In this situation, the treatment may actually have an effect, but it would be difficult to determine how much of the effect was attributable to the sensitizing pretest and how much was due to seeing the film.

This possibility can be tested with what is called the **Solomon four-group design**. In this version of a true experimental design, subjects are randomly assigned to at least two experimental groups and at least two comparison groups. One experimental group and one comparison group will have a pretest, and the other two groups will not have a pretest (see Exhibit 5.8). If testing and treatment do interact, the difference in outcome scores between the experimental and comparison groups will differ between the subjects who took the pretest and those who did not.

Ultimately, the external validity of experimental results will increase with the success of replications taking place at different times and places, using different forms of the treatment. As indicated by the replications of the Sherman and Berk study of arrest for domestic violence, the result may be a more detailed, nuanced understanding of the hypothesized effect.

EXHIBIT 5.8   Solomon Four-Group Design Testing the Interaction of Pretesting and Treatment

Experimental group	R	O1	X	O2
Comparison group	R	O1		O2
Experimental group	R		X	O2
Comparison group	R			O2

Note: R = random assignment; O = observation (pretest or posttest); X = experimental treatment.

The Element of Time in Research

Nonexperimental research designs can be either cross-sectional or longitudinal. In a **cross-sectional research design**, all data are collected at one point in time. Identifying the **time order** of effects—what happened first, and so on—is critical for developing a causal analysis, but can be an insurmountable problem with a cross-sectional design. In **longitudinal research designs**, data are collected at two or more points in time, and so identification of the time order of effects can be quite straightforward. An experiment, of course, is a type of longitudinal design because subjects are observed at two or more points in time.

Much of the research you have encountered so far in this text has been cross-sectional. Although each survey and interview takes some time to carry out, if they measure the actions, attitudes, and characteristics of respondents at only one time, they are considered cross-sectional. The name comes from the idea that a snapshot from a cross-section of the population is obtained at one point in time.

In contrast, longitudinal research collects data at two or more points in time and, as such, data can be ordered in time. By measuring the value of cases on an independent variable and a dependent variable at different times, the researcher can determine whether variation in the independent variable precedes variation in the dependent variable.

In some longitudinal designs, the same sample (or panel) is followed over time; in other designs, sample members are rotated or completely replaced. The population from which the sample is selected may be defined broadly, as when a longitudinal survey of the general population is conducted. Or the population may be defined narrowly, as when members of a specific age group are sampled at multiple points in time. The frequency of follow-up measurement can vary, ranging from a before-and-after design with just one follow-up to studies in which various indicators are measured every month for many years.

Certainly it is more difficult to collect data at two or more points in time than at one time. Quite frequently, researchers simply cannot, or are unwilling to, delay completion of a study for even one year in order to collect follow-up data. But think of the many research questions that really should involve a much longer follow-up period: Does community-oriented policing decrease rates of violent crime? What is the impact of job training in prison on recidivism rates? How effective are batterer-treatment programs for individuals convicted of intimate partner assault? Do parenting programs for young mothers and fathers reduce the likelihood of their children becoming delinquent? It is safe to say that we will never have enough longitudinal data to answer many important research questions. Nonetheless, the value of longitudinal data is so great that every effort should be made to develop longitudinal research designs when they are appropriate for the research question asked. The following discussion of the three major types of longitudinal designs will give you a sense of the possibilities (see Exhibit 5.9).

Repeated Cross-Sectional Designs

Studies that use a **repeated cross-sectional design**, also known as **trend studies**, have become fixtures of the political arena around election time. Particularly in presidential election years, we have all become accustomed to reading weekly, even daily, reports on the percentage of the population that supports each candidate. Similar polls are conducted to track sentiment on many other social issues. For example, a 1993 poll reported that 52% of adult Americans supported a ban on the possession of handguns, compared with 41% in a similar poll conducted in 1991. According to pollster Louis Harris, this increase indicated a "sea

EXHIBIT 5.9   Three Types of Longitudinal Design

change" in public attitudes (cited in Barringer 1993). Another researcher said, "It shows that people are responding to their experience [of an increase in handgun-related killings]" (cited in Barringer 1993: A14).

Repeated cross-sectional design (trend study) A type of longitudinal study in which data are collected at two or more points in time from different samples of the same population.

Repeated cross-sectional surveys are conducted as follows:

1. A sample is drawn from a population at Time 1, and data are collected from the sample.
2. As time passes, some people leave the population and others enter it.
3. At Time 2, a different sample is drawn from this population.

Fixed-Sample Panel Designs

Panel designs allow us to identify changes in individuals, groups, or whatever we are studying. This is the process for conducting **fixed-sample panel designs**.

1. A sample (called a panel) is drawn from a population at Time 1, and data are collected from the sample.
2. As time passes, some panel members become unavailable for follow-up, and the population changes.
3. At Time 2, data are collected from the same people as at Time 1 (the panel), except for those people who cannot be located.

Because a panel design follows the same individuals, it is better than a repeated cross-sectional design for testing causal hypotheses. For example, Sampson and Laub (1990) used a fixed-sample panel design to investigate the effect of childhood deviance on adult crime. They studied a sample of white males in Boston when the subjects were between 10 and 17 years old and then followed up when the subjects were in their adult years. Data were collected from multiple sources, including the subjects themselves and criminal justice records. Sampson and Laub (1990: 614) found that children who had been committed to a correctional school for persistent delinquency were much more likely than other children in the study to commit crimes as adults: 61% were arrested between the ages of 25 and 32, compared with 14% of those who had not been in correctional schools as juveniles. In this study, juvenile delinquency unquestionably occurred before adult criminality. If the researchers had used a cross-sectional design to study the past of adults, the juvenile delinquency measure might have been biased by memory lapses, by self-serving recollections about behavior as juveniles, or by loss of agency records.

If you now wonder why not every longitudinal study is designed as a panel study, you have understood the advantages of panel designs. However, remember that this design does not in itself establish causality. Variation in both the independent variable and the dependent variables may be due to some other variable, even to earlier variation in what is considered the dependent variable.

Panel designs are also a challenge to implement successfully, and often are not even attempted, because of two major difficulties:

1. *Expense and attrition.* It can be difficult, and very expensive, to keep track of individuals over a long period, and inevitably the proportion of panel members who can be located for follow-up will decline over time. Panel studies often lose more than one quarter of their members through attrition (Miller 1991: 170), and those who are lost are often not necessarily like those who remain in the panel.

2. *Subject fatigue.* Panel members may grow weary of repeated interviews and drop out of the study, or they may become so used to answering the standard questions in the survey that they start giving stock answers rather than actually thinking about their current feelings or actions (Campbell 1992). This is called the problem of **subject fatigue**. Fortunately, subjects do not often seem to become fatigued in this way, particularly if the research staff have maintained positive relations with them.

Event-Based Designs

In an **event-based design**, often called a *cohort study*, the follow-up samples (at one or more times) are selected from the same **cohort**, people who all have experienced a similar event or a common starting point. Examples include the following:

- *birth cohorts:* those who share a common period of birth (those born in the 1940s, 1950s, 1960s, etc.);
- *seniority cohorts:* those who have worked at the same place for about five years, about 10 years, and so on; and
- *school cohorts:* freshmen, sophomores, juniors, and seniors.

HOW DO EXPERIMENTERS PROTECT THEIR SUBJECTS?

Social science experiments often involve subject deception. Primarily due to this, some experiments have prompted contentious debates about research ethics. Experimental evaluations of social programs also pose ethical dilemmas because they require researchers to withhold possibly beneficial treatment from some subjects who are selected on the basis of chance. In this section, we weigh the ethical problems posed by experimental research and discuss the two primary ethical dilemmas: deception and selective distribution of benefits.

Deception

Deception occurs whenever subjects are misled about the procedures or treatment they will receive. Deception, of course, is necessary in many instances to determine how subjects will react to the treatment if they are not research subjects. As such, deception is a critical component of many social experiments, in part due to the difficulty of simulating real-world stresses and dilemmas in a laboratory setting. Virtually all of the experiments we have discussed in this text involve some type of deception.

Although the American Society of Criminology's (ASC) and the American Sociological Association's Codes of Ethics do not discuss experimentation explicitly, both codes highlight the ethical dilemma posed by deceptive research. But does informed consent mean that subjects must be told exactly what they will be experiencing and why? When are the risks of research greater than those of everyday life? There is no easy answer to such questions.

Some of the most well-known experiments have stimulated many questions about research ethics due to their use of deception. Stanley Milgram's (1965) experiments on obedience to authority raise most of the relevant issues. Milgram's research was stimulated by the success of Germany's Nazi regime of the 1930s and 1940s in enlisting the participation of ordinary citizens in unconscionable acts of terror and genocide. Milgram set out to identify through laboratory experiments the conditions under which ordinary citizens will be obedient to authority figures' instructions to inflict pain on others. He operationalized this obedience by asking subjects to deliver electric shocks (fake, of course) to students supposedly learning a memory task. Subjects ("teachers") were told to administer a shock to the learner each time he gave a wrong response and to move one level higher on the shock generator each time an incorrect response was given.

Can you imagine your reaction if you volunteered for such an experiment and were forced to inflict pain on another human being? Much to the surprise of Milgram and others, the great majority of subjects administered shocks beyond the danger level, even though the actor being shocked begged (fake begging, of course) the subjects to stop, complained about a heart condition, and/or banged on the wall in feigned pain. The teacher-subjects were not oblivious to the pain they were supposedly causing—they trembled, groaned, broke into nervous laughter, and generally did not seem to want to go on. But in many cases they did go on.

Milgram's research was an empirical success. He identified at least some of the conditions under which ordinary people will resist authority. But was the research ethical? Thorough **debriefing** of each participant was used to lessen the probability of harm to subjects. All subjects were told the victim did not receive dangerous electric shocks, and each subject had a friendly reconciliation with the unharmed learner and an extended discussion about the experiment's purposes and methods with the experimenter. Obedient subjects were assured that their behavior was entirely normal and that their feelings of conflict or tension were shared by other participants. To determine long-term trauma, participants were also interviewed after one year. No evidence of lingering trauma was uncovered, and almost all participants said they strongly supported the research.

Today researchers must usually follow more stringent standards set by current federal ethical guidelines and administered by institutional review boards (IRBs). It is unlikely that an experiment like Milgram's would pass the requirements of an IRB today. At minimum, the current guidelines would require informed consent to be obtained from the subjects. Informed consent, in turn, would require subjects to be told that another human being would not be harmed in the experiment. And since the experimental design required deceiving subjects about this precise point, informed consent could not have been carried out. Clearly, the need to adhere to ethical standards can conflict with the investigation of important social issues.

Selective Distribution of Benefits

Although all experiments, whether conducted in the laboratory or in the field, can involve issues of informed consent (Hunt 1985: 275–276), one ethical issue somewhat unique to field experiments is the **distribution of benefits**. How much are subjects harmed by the way benefits are distributed as part of an experiment? This issue is particularly salient for treatments that may hold some positive benefit for the experimental subjects and deny the same benefits to subjects in the control group. Although this issue poses more ethical dilemmas for medical research investigating the effectiveness of new drugs, it is also important for many social and criminological experiments. For example, Sherman and Berk's experiment, and its successors, required police to make arrests in domestic violence cases primarily on the basis of a random process. When arrests were not made, did the subjects' abused spouses suffer?

Is it ethical to give some potentially advantageous or disadvantageous treatment to people on a random basis? As a general rule, random distribution of benefits is justified when the researchers do not know whether some treatment actually is beneficial or not—and, of course, it is the goal of the experiment to find out. In this case, random assignment is the only way to assess whether one treatment is more beneficial than another or than no treatment at all. Also, if insufficient resources are available to fully fund a benefit for every eligible person, distribution of the benefit on the basis of chance to equally needy persons is ethically defensible.

Let's examine the experiment carried out by Sherman and Berk (1984). Victims who called police to report an incident of misdemeanor assault perpetrated by an intimate during the course of the experiment (and who did not insist on arrest) did not know they were in a research study and had no choice about whether their assailants were arrested or received a warning. Perhaps it seems unreasonable to let a random procedure determine how police resolve cases of domestic violence. And indeed it would be unreasonable if this procedure were regular police practice. The Sherman and Berk experiment and its successors do pass ethical muster, however, when seen for what they were—a way of learning how to increase the effectiveness of police response to this all too common crime.

CONCLUSION

True experiments play two critical roles in criminological research. First, they are the best research design for testing causal hypotheses. Even when conditions preclude the use of a true experimental design, many research designs can be improved by adding experimental components. Second, true experiments provide a comparison point for evaluating the ability of the other research designs to achieve causally valid results.

In spite of their obvious strengths, true experiments are used infrequently to study many research problems related to criminology and criminal justice. There are three basic reasons for this:

1. The experiments required to test many important hypotheses require more resources than most social scientists can access.

2. Most research problems of interest to social scientists simply are not amenable to experimental designs, for reasons ranging from ethical considerations to the limited possibilities for randomly assigning people to different conditions in the real world.

3. The requirements of experimental design usually preclude large-scale studies and so limit generalizability to a degree that is unacceptable to many social scientists.

When a true experimental design is not feasible, researchers may instead use a quasi-experimental design, including nonequivalent control group designs, before-and-after designs, and ex post facto control group designs. These research designs are termed "quasi"-experimental because the units under study are not randomly assigned to the comparison and experimental groups. As a result, we cannot be as confident in the comparability of the groups in these designs. However, there are several steps that can be taken, such as matching certain individual or group characteristics across the two groups, to allow us to have more confidence in the results of quasi-experimental research.

KEY TERMS

Association	Longitudinal research design
Before-and-after designs	Matching
Causal effect	Mechanism
Cohort study	Nonequivalent control
Compensatory rivalry	group designs
Context	Nonspuriousness
Contextual effect	Placebo effect
Control group	Posttest
Cross-sectional research design	Pretest
Debriefing	Process analysis
Differential attrition	Quasi-experimental design
Distribution of benefits	Random assignment
Double-blind procedures	Regression effect
Endogenous change	Repeated measures
Event-based design	panel design
Ex post facto control group design	Selection bias
Expectancies	Solomon four-group design
Experimental group	Spurious relationship
Extraneous variable	Subject fatigue
Fixed-sample panel design	Time order
Hawthorne effect	Time series design
History effect	Treatment misidentification
Intervening variable	True experiment

HIGHLIGHTS

- A causal explanation relies on a comparison. The value of cases on the dependent variable is measured after they have been exposed to variation in an independent variable. This measurement is compared to what the value of cases on the dependent variable would have been if they had not been exposed to the variation in the independent variable (the counterfactual). The validity of causal conclusions rests on how closely the comparison group comes to the ideal counterfactual.

- Three criteria are generally viewed as necessary for identifying a causal relationship: association between the variables, proper time order, and nonspuriousness of the association. In addition, the basis for concluding that a causal relationship exists is strengthened by identification of a causal mechanism and the context for the relationship.

- Association between two variables is in itself insufficient evidence of a causal relationship. This point is commonly made with the expression "Correlation does not prove causation."

- Experiments use random assignment to make comparison groups as similar as possible at the outset of an experiment in order to reduce the risk of spurious effects due to extraneous variables.

- Nonexperimental designs use statistical controls to reduce the risk of spuriousness. A variable is controlled when it is held constant so that the association between the independent and dependent variables can be assessed without being influenced by the control variable.

- Longitudinal designs are usually preferable to cross-sectional designs for establishing the time order of effects. Longitudinal designs vary in terms of whether the same people are measured at different times, how the population of interests is defined, and how frequently follow-up measurements are taken. Fixed-sample panel designs provide the strongest test for the time order of effects, but they can be difficult to carry out successfully because of their expense as well as subject attrition and fatigue.

- Ethical and practical constraints often preclude the use of experimental designs.

EXERCISES

Discussing Research

1. Review articles in several newspapers, copying down all causal assertions. These might range from assertions that the presence of community policing was related positively to decreasing rates of violence, that the stock market declined because of uncertainty in the Middle East, or to explanations about why a murder was committed. Inspect the articles carefully, noting all evidence used to support the causal assertions. Which criteria for establishing casualty are met? What other potentially important influences on the reported outcome have been overlooked?

2. Select several research articles in professional journals that assert, or imply, that they have identified a causal relationship between two or more variables. Is each of the criteria for establishing the existence of a causal relationship met? Find a study in which subjects were assigned randomly to experimental and comparison groups to reduce the risk of spurious influences on the supposedly causal relationship. How convinced are you by the study?

3. The web-based interactive exercises contain lessons on causation and experimental design. Try them out at this point.

4. Go to the Stanford Prison Experiment website at www.prisonexp.org. Read the information provided about the Stanford Prison Experiment.
   a. Write a brief essay on the study, including the purpose of the study, the type of experiment, the participant selection process, the problems encountered during the study, and the results.
   b. Go to the discussion questions provided on the website. Answer the questions listed. What conclusions do you make about the Stanford Prison Experiment?

Finding Research

1. Read an original article describing a social experiment. (Social psychology "readers," collections of such articles for undergraduates, are a good place to find interesting studies.) Critique the article focusing on the extent to which experimental conditions were controlled and the causal mechanism was identified. Did inadequate control over conditions or inadequate identification of the causal mechanism make you feel uncertain about the causal conclusions?

2. Go to the website of the Community Policing Consortium at www.communitypolicing.org/about2.html. What causal assertions are made? Pick one of these assertions and propose a research design with which to test this assertion. Be specific.

3. Go to Sociosite at www.pscw.uva.nl/sociosite. Select "Subject Areas." Pick a sociological subject area in which you are interested. Find an example of research that has been done using experimental methods in this subject. Explain the experiment. Choose at least five of the key terms listed at the end of this chapter that are relevant to and incorporated in the research experiment you have located on the internet Explain how each of the five key terms you have chosen plays a role in the research example you found on the web.

Critiquing Research

1. Go to this book's Study Site, www.sagepub.com/frccjstudy, and choose two research articles that include some attention to causality (as indicated by a check in that column of the article matrix). Describe the approach taken in each article to establishing causality. How do the approaches differ from each other? Which approach seems stronger to you?

2. Select a true experiment, perhaps from the *Journal of Experimental Criminology* or from sources suggested in class. Diagram the experiment using the exhibits in this chapter as a model. Discuss the extent to which experimental conditions were controlled and the causal mechanism was identified. How confident can you be in the causal conclusions from the study, based on review of the threats to internal validity discussed in this chapter: selection bias, endogenous change, external events, contamination, and treatment misidentification? How generalizable do you think the study's results are to the population from which the cases were selected? How generalizable are they to specific subgroups in the study? How thoroughly do the researchers discuss these issues?

3. Go to the Disaster Center website, www.disastercenter.com/crime. Review the crime rate nationally and, by picking out links to state reports, compare the recent crime rates in two states. Report on the prevalence of the crimes you have examined. Propose a causal explanation for variation in crime between states, over time, or both. What research design would you propose to test this explanation? Explain.

Making Research Ethical

1. Under what conditions do you think that randomized assignment of subjects to a specific treatment is ethical in criminal justice research? Was it ethical for Sherman and Berk and the researchers who conducted the replication studies to randomly assign individuals accused of domestic violence to an arrest or nonarrest treatment? What about in a laboratory study with students like yourself? Do you think it would be ethical to assign students randomly to be "prisoners" in a study like Zimbardo's?

2. Critique the ethics of one of the experiments presented in this chapter, or some other experiment you have read about. What specific rules do you think should guide researchers' decisions about subject deception and the selective distribution of benefits?

3. Bushman (1995) tested the impact of watching a violent video on students' level of aggressiveness. He found that watching the violent video increased aggressiveness. Do you consider it ethical to expose subjects to an intervention that might increase their aggressiveness? Are there any situations in which you would not approve of such research? Any types of subjects you would exclude from such research? Any limits you would draw on the type of intervention that could be tested? Would you impose any requirements for debriefing?

Developing a Research Proposal

How will you try to establish the causal effects you hypothesize?

1. Identify at least one hypothesis involving what you expect is a causal relationship.

2. Identify key variables that should be controlled in your survey design in order to increase your ability to avoid arriving at a spurious conclusion about the hypothesized causal effect. Draw on relevant research literature and social theory to identify these variables.

3. Add a longitudinal component to your research design. Explain why you decided to use this particular longitudinal design.

4. Review the criteria for establishing a nomothetic causal effect and discuss your ability to satisfy each one.

Performing Data Analysis in SPSS

We can use the GSS2004 mini data to learn how causal hypotheses can be evaluated with nonexperimental data.

1. Specify four hypotheses in which CAPPUN is the dependent variable and the independent variable is also measured with a question in the GSS2004. The independent variables should have no more than 10 valid values (check the variable list).
   a. Inspect the frequency distributions of each independent variable in your hypotheses. If it appears that any have little valid data or were coded with more than 10 categories, substitute another independent variable.
   b. Generate crosstabulations that show the association between CAPPUN and each of the independent variables. Make sure that CAPPUN is the row variable and that you select "Column Percents."
   c. Does support for capital punishment vary across the categories of any of the independent variables? By how much? Would you conclude that there is an association, as hypothesized, for any pairs of variables?

2. Do prior convictions influence the number of days to which homicide defendants are sentenced?
   a. Obtain a frequency distribution for the variable PRCONV (prior convictions). According to the data, do homicide defendants frequently have prior convictions? What do you hypothesize is the relationship between prior convictions and sentence length? Why?
   b. Compare the mean sentence length in days received by defendants against their number of prior convictions. For example, do defendants who had no prior convictions

receive a shorter sentence length compared to those with at least one prior conviction? Do the data support your hypothesis? Do any of the categories deviate from what you hypothesized? Explain.

c. Recode the PRCONV variable into a new dichotomous variable, measuring whether the homicide defendant had prior convictions or no prior convictions. If necessary, reword your hypothesis to reflect the dichotomous nature of the new variable.

d. Test your hypothesis by comparing the mean sentence length in days received by defendants with prior convictions and those with no prior convictions. What conclusions do you make about the relationship between prior convictions and sentence length of homicide defendants?

Student Study Site

The companion Student Study Website for *The Fundamentals of Research in Criminology and Criminal Justice* can be found at www.sagepub.com/frccjstudy.

Visit the Student Study Site to enhance your understanding of the chapter content and to discover additional resources that will take your learning one step further. You can enhance your understanding of the chapters by using the comprehensive study material, which includes interactive exercises, e-flashcards, web exercises, practice self-tests, and more. You will also find special features, such as Learning from Journal Articles, which incorporates SAGE's online journal collection.

CHAPTER 6

Survey Research

In this chapter we will introduce you to survey research. You will learn about the challenges of designing a survey along with some basic rules of question construction. We will also discuss the ways in which surveys can be administered. Important ethical issues surrounding surveys are discussed in the final section. By the chapter's end, you should be well on your way to becoming an informed consumer of survey reports and a knowledgeable developer of survey designs. We hope you will have an increased appreciation for the fact that designing a survey involves a great deal of thought and planning and is much more difficult than putting a few questions together. In addition, you will become a more informed student of the methodological issues surrounding the measurement of violent victimization in the United States.

SURVEY RESEARCH IN ACTION: MEASURING VICTIMIZATION

Despite more than two decades of research, the magnitude of rape and intimate-perpetrated violence against men and women is still frequently disputed. For many reasons, including the historical stigma attached to rape and intimate partner violence (IPV), fear of retaliation from their perpetrators, and other safety concerns, estimating incidence rates of this violence has always been a difficult task. The most enduring source of statistical information about violent crime in the United States is the Uniform Crime Report (UCR) Program compiled by the Federal Bureau of Investigation (FBI). The UCR collects information about criminal incidents of violence that have been reported to the police. However, using police reports to estimate incidence rates of violence between intimates and family members is problematic for several reasons. Perhaps foremost is the fact that a large percentage of these crimes are never reported to police. Based on comparisons with national survey data, it is estimated that only 40–50% of crimes become known to police, and the percentage may be much lower for crimes committed by intimates and other family members (Reiss & Roth 1993).

Due to the weaknesses of the UCR program in estimating rates of violence within families, random sample surveys of the population are now being used as a social science tool of choice for uncovering incidents of violence within families. However, as can be expected, surveys employing diverse methodologies and different definitions of violence result in tremendously diverse estimates. For example, studies show that the number of women who experience violence by an intimate partner annually range from 9.3 per 1,000 women (Bachman & Saltzman 1995) to 116 per 1,000 women (Straus & Gelles 1990).

To increase our understanding of violent victimization, in 1995 the National Institute of Justice and the Centers for Disease Control and Prevention cosponsored a national telephone survey called the National Violence Against Men and Women (NVAMW) Survey, conducted by the Center for Policy Research (Tjaden & Thoennes 2000). Respondents to the NVAMW Survey were asked about a number of health and safety issues, including physical assault they experienced as children by adult caretakers, physical assault they experienced as adults by any type of perpetrator, and forcible rape or stalking they experienced at any time in their life by any type of perpetrator. In this chapter, we will use this project along with the U.S. Justice Department's National Crime Victimization Survey (NCVS) to illustrate some key features of survey research.

WHAT IS A SURVEY?

Survey research involves the collection of information from a sample of individuals through their responses to questions. In addition to social scientists, many newspaper editors, political pundits, and marketing gurus have turned to survey research because it is an efficient method for systematically collecting data from a broad spectrum of individuals and social settings. The results of surveys are broadcast daily on most network news programs. In fact, surveys have become such a vital part of our nation's social fabric that we cannot assess much of what we read in the newspaper or see on TV without having some understanding of this method of data collection (Converse 1984).

The U.S. Bureau of the Census also began to supplement its 10-year census with more frequent surveys of population samples to monitor respondents' income and other economic variables. And in 1973, the U.S. Department of Justice implemented the National Crime Surveys to capture incidents of crime victimization not reported to police.

Since the early days of survey research, professional survey organizations have provided a base of support for social science researchers affiliated with universities. The development of electronic computers also aided the growth of survey research, allowing great increases in the speed and accuracy for processing and reporting data. Surveys soon became the most popular research method in the social sciences.

Attractive Features of Survey Research

Regardless of its scope, survey research owes its continuing popularity to three features: versatility, efficiency, and generalizability.

Versatility

The first and foremost reason for the popularity of survey methods is their versatility. Although a survey is not the ideal method for testing all hypotheses or learning about every social process, a well-designed survey can enhance our understanding of just about any social issue. In fact, there is hardly any topic of interest to social scientists that has not been studied at some time with survey methods.

Efficiency

Surveys also are popular because data can be collected from many people at relatively low cost and, depending on the survey design, relatively quickly. For the NVAMW Survey, Tjaden and Thoennes (2000) contracted with Schulman, Ronca, and Bucuvalas, Inc. (SRBI) to conduct the telephone survey, primarily because SRBI had conducted nationally representative sample surveys before on sensitive subject matter such as victimization. As you would expect, phone surveys are the quickest survey method, which accounts for their popularity in political polling.

Surveys are efficient research methods because many variables can be measured without substantially increasing the time or cost. Mailed questionnaires can include up to 10 pages of questions before respondents lose interest (and before more postage must be added). The maximum time limit for phone surveys seems to be about 45 minutes. In-person interviews can last much longer, taking more than an hour.

Generalizability

Survey methods lend themselves to probability sampling from large populations. Thus, survey research is very appealing when sample generalizability is a central research goal. In fact, survey research is often the only means available for developing a representative picture of the attitudes and characteristics of a large population.

Surveys also are the research method of choice when cross-population generalizability is a primary concern. They allow a range of social contexts and subgroups to be sampled, and the consistency of relationships can be examined across the various subgroups.

The Omnibus Survey

Most surveys are directed at a specific research question. In contrast, an **omnibus survey** covers a range of topics of interest to different social scientists. It has multiple sponsors or is designed to generate data useful to a broad segment of the social science community rather than answer one particular research question.

One of the most successful omnibus surveys is the General Social Survey (GSS) of the National Opinion Research Center at the University of Chicago. Starting in 1972, the National Science Foundation agreed to fund the GSS as an annual, publicly available national survey on topics of general interest to sociologists. In 1992, the GSS changed to a biennial schedule. Today, the GSS is administered every two years as a 90-minute interview to a probability sample of almost 3,000 Americans. It includes more than 500 questions about background characteristics and opinions, with an emphasis on social stratification, race relations, family issues, law and social control, and morale. Since 1988, most of the questions have been asked in each survey, but many of them have been asked of only a randomly selected subset of respondents. This **split-ballot design** allows the inclusion of more questions without increasing the survey's cost. The split-ballot design also allows for experiments on the effect of question wording; different phrasings of the same question are included in the split-ballot subsets.

Although the NVAMW Survey is not an omnibus survey, it was developed to obtain detailed information on a number of phenomena related to victimization. For example, because the Centers for Disease Control and Prevention were cosponsors of the survey, many questions were added to obtain detailed information on a respondent's history of health and injuries in addition to injuries resulting from victimization.

Most survey data sets sponsored by the federal government are made available for use by scholars through the Inter-University Consortium for Political and Social Research (ICPSR). For example, all the data sets produced by the Bureau of Justice Statistics, including the NCVS, the National Prison Survey, and many others, can be obtained almost instantaneously from the ICPSR website (www.icpsr.umich.edu).

The deficiency of the omnibus approach is the limited depth that can be achieved in any one substantive area. In some years, the GSS avoids this problem by going into greater depth in one particular area. But the best way to get survey data about one particular topic is still the survey developed around the topic alone. The surveys we will highlight in this chapter were all developed to measure one topic: victimization.

QUESTIONNAIRE DEVELOPMENT AND ASSESSMENT

The **questionnaire** (or **interview schedule**, as it is often called in interview-based studies) is the central feature of the survey process. Without a well-designed questionnaire tailored to the study's purposes, survey researchers have little hope of achieving their research goals.

> *Questionnaire* The survey instrument containing the questions for a self-administered survey.
>
> *Interview schedule* The survey instrument containing the questions asked by the interviewer for an in-person interview or phone survey.

The correct design of a questionnaire varies with the specific survey method used and the other particulars of a survey project. There is no precise formula for a well-designed questionnaire. Nonetheless, some key principles should guide the design of any questionnaire, and some systematic procedures should be considered for refining it.

Maintain Consistent Focus

A survey (with the exception of an omnibus survey) should be guided by a clear conception of the research problem under investigation and the population to be sampled. Does the study seek to describe some phenomenon in detail, explain some behavior, or explore some type of social relationship? Until the research objective is clearly formulated, survey design cannot begin. Throughout the process of questionnaire design, this objective should be the primary basis for making decisions about what to include and exclude, and what to emphasize or treat in a cursory fashion. Moreover, the questionnaire should be viewed as an integrated whole, in which each section and every question serves a clear purpose related to the study's objective and complements other sections or questions.

Build on Existing Instruments

When another researcher already has designed a set of questions to measure a key concept in your study, that existing set of questions can be called a survey instrument. If evidence from previous surveys indicates that these questions provide a good measure of the concept or behaviors in which you are interested, then why reinvent the wheel? To measure incidents of physical assault, Tjaden and Thoennes (2000) modified an instrument that had already been widely used in the literature: the Conflict Tactics Scale (CTS) (Straus 1979). To measure incidents of rape and sexual victimization, Tjaden and Thoennes utilized questions that had already been used by Kilpatrick et al. at the University of South Carolina in the National Women's Study (National Victim Center and the Crime Victims Research and Treatment Center 1992). As you can see from Exhibit 6.1, these questions were very specific in nature and covered all behaviors that are legally defined as rape or sexual assault in most states. In contrast, you will also see from Exhibit 6.1 that the screening questions used by the NCVS to uncover incidents of rape and sexual assault are not as specific about behavior.

Respondents to the NVAMW Survey who answered yes to any of these screening questions were asked many specific questions about the nature of the victimization, including information about the offender, injuries sustained, and reports to police. Respondents to the NCVS who answered yes to their screening questions were further queried, "Do you mean forced or coerced sexual intercourse?" Only if respondents answered yes to this question were they counted as rape victims; the others were classified as other sexual assault victims. In the end, both surveys purport to measure incidents of rape in the United States, but which methodology is most appropriate? In the next section, we will provide you with some specific guidelines for writing questions and you will see that the answer to this question is not so clear-cut.

WRITING QUESTIONS

Asking people questions is the most common operation for measuring social variables, and probably the most versatile. In principle, survey questions can be a straightforward and efficient means of measuring individual characteristics, facts about events, levels of knowledge, and opinions of any sort. In practice, however, survey questions can result in misleading or inappropriate answers. All questions proposed for a survey must be screened carefully for their adherence to basic guidelines and then tested and revised until the researcher feels confident they will be clear to the intended respondents (Fowler 1995). Some variables may prove to be inappropriate for measurement with any type of question. We have to recognize that memories and perceptions of the events we might like to ask about can be limited.

Structurally, questions on surveys generally fall into two categories: those with and those without explicit response choices. Recall from chapter 3 that **open-ended questions** are

---

EXHIBIT 6.1   Rape-Screening Questions Used by the NVAMW Survey and by the NCVS

National Violence Against Men and Women (NVAMW) Survey

[For females only] Regardless of how long ago it happened, has a man ever made you have sex by using force or threatening to harm you or someone close to you? Just so there is no mistake, by sex we mean putting a penis in your vagina.

[For males and females] Has anyone, male or female, ever made you have oral sex by using force or threat of harm? Just so there is no mistake, by oral sex we mean that a man or boy put his penis in your mouth or someone, male or female, penetrated your vagina or anus with their mouth or tongue.

[For males and females] Has anyone ever made you have anal sex by using force or threat of harm? Just so there is no mistake, by anal sex we mean that a man or boy put his penis in your anus.

[For males and females] Has anyone, male or female, ever put fingers or objects in your vagina or anus against your will by using force or threats?

[For males and females] Has anyone, male or female, ever attempted to make you have vaginal, oral, or anal sex against your will, but intercourse or penetration did not occur?

National Crime Victimization Survey (NCVS)

Incidents involving forced or unwanted sexual acts are often difficult to talk about. Have you been forced or coerced to engage in unwanted sexual activity by

a. someone you didn't know before,
b. a casual acquaintance, or
c. someone you know well?

---

those without explicit response choices. This type of question is usually used only for explorative purposes when there is little knowledge about a particular topic and you want to uncover as much about it as possible without restricting responses. For example, if you are investigating the perceptions of residents regarding a new community policing program instituted in the neighborhood, open-ended questions such as the following one could be very informative:

> In your opinion, what have been the benefits of the community policing program in your neighborhood?

The information obtained from open-ended questions such as this could then be used as the basis for questions with fixed responses in future studies that evaluate the efficacy of community policing.

Open-ended questions are also excellent tools for obtaining respondents' interpretations in greater detail and can often illuminate flaws in other questions. A survey researcher can also try to understand what respondents mean by their responses after the fact by including additional open-ended questions in the survey. Adding such **interpretive questions** after key survey questions is always a good idea, but it is of utmost importance when the questions in a survey have not been pretested. An example from a study of people with motor vehicle driving violations illustrates the importance of interpretive questions:

> When asked whether their emotional state affected their driving at all, respondents would reply that their emotions had very little effect on their driving habits. Then, when asked to describe the circumstances surrounding their last traffic violation, respondents typically replied, "I was mad at my girlfriend," or "I had a quarrel with my wife," or "We had a family quarrel," or "I was angry with my boss." (Labaw 1980: 71)

Were these respondents lying in response to the first question? Probably not. More likely, they simply did not interpret their own behavior in terms of a general concept such as "emotional state." But their responses to the first question were likely to be misinterpreted without the further detail provided by answers to the second.

In summary, one strength of open-ended questions is the wealth of information they provide. This wealth of information, however, is exactly why many researchers do not use them. The verbatim text narratives obtained from open-ended questions take a great deal of time and energy to organize and summarize. In addition, many respondents may feel overwhelmed about writing a lengthy essay. If you want to ask a large number of open-ended questions, it is perhaps best to consider an in-person interview or phone interview instead of a questionnaire (both of which are discussed later in this chapter).

When respondents are offered explicit responses to choose from, this type of question is referred to as a **closed-ended question** or a **fixed-choice questions**. For example, in the NVAMW Survey, respondents were asked:

> Overall, would you say that personal safety in this country has improved since you were a child, gotten worse since you were a child, or stayed about the same?

> Improved

> Gotten worse

> Stayed about the same

Most surveys of a large number of people primarily contain fixed-choice questions, which are easy to process with computers and analyze with statistics. With fixed-choice questions, respondents are also more likely to answer the question that researchers want them to answer. By including the response choices, the survey reduces ambiguity. However, fixed-choice questions can obscure what people really think unless the choices are carefully designed to match the range of all possible responses to the question.

Regardless of the format used for questions, there are several rules to follow and pitfalls to avoid that will maximize the validity of your survey instrument. We will highlight these in the next section.

Write Clear and Meaningful Questions

All hope for achieving measurement validity is lost unless survey questions are clear and convey the intended meaning to respondents. You may be thinking that you ask people questions all the time and have no trouble understanding the answers you receive, so it may seem that writing clear and meaningful questions would not be difficult. But consider just a few of the differences between everyday conversations and standardized surveys:

- Survey questions must be asked of many people, not just one person.
- The same survey questions must be used with each person, not tailored to the specifics of a given conversation.
- Survey questions must be understood in the same way by people who differ in many ways.
- You will not be able to rephrase a survey question if someone does not understand it because that would result in a different question for that person.
- Survey respondents do not know you and so cannot be expected to share the nuances of expression that help you and your friends and family to communicate.

These features make a survey very different from natural conversation and make question writing a challenging and important task for survey researchers.

Questions must be very clear and specific about what is being asked of respondents. Note the differences in specificity between the rape-screening questions used by the NVAMW Survey and the NCVS displayed in Exhibit 6.1. It is logical that these multiple, behaviorally specific questions will be associated with greater disclosure by survey respondents compared to the one question about sexual intercourse posed by the NCVS. In fact, results of the two surveys indicate that the NVAMW Survey uncovers about four times as many rapes as does the NCVS (Bachman 2000).

In addition to writing clear and meaningful questions, there are several other rules to follow and pitfalls to avoid that we will highlight in the next section.

Avoid Confusing Phrasing

Good grammar is a basic requirement for clear questions. Clearly and simply phrased questions are most likely to have the same meaning for different respondents. So be brief and to the point.

Avoid Vagueness

Virtually all questions about behavior and feelings will be more reliable if they refer to specific times or events (Turner & Martin 1984: 300). Without a **reference period**, a researcher will not know how to interpret an answer. For example, the question "How often do you carry a method of self-protection such as pepper spray?" will produce answers that have no common reference period and therefore cannot reliably be compared with answers from other respondents. A more specific way to ask the question is, "In the last month, how many days did you carry a method of self-protection such as pepper spray?"

In general, research shows that the longer the reference period, the greater the under-reporting of a given behavior (Cantor 1984, 1985; Kobelarcik et al. 1983). For example, one survey asked, "During the past 12 months, about how many times did you see or talk to a medical doctor?"

When official records were checked, respondents forgot about 60% of their doctor visits (Goleman 1993: C11). In general, when information about mundane or day-to-day activities is solicited, reference periods should be no longer than "in the past month." However, when rare events are being measured, such as experiences with victimizations, "the last 6 months," as utilized by the NCVS, or "the past 12 months," as used by the NVAMW, are both acceptable.

Avoid Negatives and Double Negatives

Picture yourself answering the following question: "Do you disagree that juveniles should not be tried as adults if they commit murder?" It probably took a long time for you to figure out whether you would actually agree or disagree with this statement because it is written as a **double-negative question**. For example, if you think juveniles who commit murder should be tried as adults, you would actually agree with this statement. Even questions that are written with a single negative are usually difficult to answer. For example, suppose you were asked to respond to "I can't stop thinking about the terrorist attacks on 9/11" using a five-point response set of "very rarely" to "very often." A person who marks "very rarely" is actually saying, "I very rarely can't stop thinking about the terrorist attacks on 9/11." Confusing, isn't it? Even the most experienced survey researchers can unintentionally make this mistake, perhaps while trying to avoid some other wording problem.

Avoid Double-Barreled Questions

When a question is really asking more than one question it is called a **double-barreled question**. For example, the statement, "I believe we should stop spending so much money building prisons and put it into building more schools," is really asking respondents two different questions. Some respondents may believe we should stop building so many prisons but may not want the revenue to go into building more schools. Double-barreled questions can also show up in the response categories. For example, the item below is really asking two questions and would be better stated as such:

Do you know anyone who has ever used cocaine?

_____Yes _____No _____I have used cocaine

Avoid Making Either Disagreement or Agreement Disagreeable

People often tend to "agree" with a statement just to avoid seeming disagreeable. You can see the impact of this human tendency in a 1974 Michigan Survey Research Center survey that asked who was to blame for crime and lawlessness in the United States (Schuman & Presser 1981: 208). When one question stated that individuals were more to blame than social conditions, 60% of the respondents agreed. But when the question was rephrased so respondents were asked, in a balanced fashion, whether individuals or social conditions were more to blame, only 46% chose individuals.

You can take several steps to reduce the likelihood of agreement bias. As a general rule, you should present both sides of attitude scales in the question itself: "In general, do you believe that *individuals* or *social conditions* are more to blame for crime and lawlessness in the United States?" (Dillman 2000: 61–62). The response choices themselves should be phrased to make each one seem as socially approved, as "agreeable," as the others. You should also consider replacing a range of response alternatives that focus on the word "agree" with others. For example, "To what extent do you support or oppose the new health care plan?" (response choices range from "strongly support" to "strongly oppose") is probably a better approach than the question, "To what extent do you agree or disagree with the statement: 'The new health care plan is worthy of support'?" (response choices range from "strongly agree" to "strongly disagree").

When an illegal or socially disapproved behavior or attitude is the focus, we have to be concerned that some respondents will be reluctant to agree that they have ever done or thought such a thing. In this situation, the goal is to write a question and response choices that make agreement seem more acceptable. For example, Dillman (2000) suggests that we ask, "Have you ever taken anything from a store without paying for it?" rather than "Have you ever shoplifted something from a store?" (2000: 75). Asking about a variety of behaviors or attitudes that range from socially acceptable to socially unacceptable will also soften the impact of agreeing with those that are socially unacceptable.

Additional Guidelines for Fixed-Response Questions

Creating questions that are clear and meaningful is only half of the formula involved in creating a good survey instrument. The choices you provide respondents in fixed-choice questions are also important. In this section, we provide you with several rules that will help to ensure that the response choices you provide to your questions will also be clear and concise.

Response Choices Should Be Mutually Exclusive

When you want respondents to make only one choice, the fixed-response categories must not overlap. For example, if you were interested in the ways foot patrol officers spent their time while working, you might ask the following question:

On average, how much time do you spend on the job each week taking care of traffic violations?

Less than 1 hour

1–3 hours

3–6 hours

6–10 hours

10 hours or more

The choices provided for respondents in this question are not **mutually exclusive responses** because they overlap. Which choice would an officer select if he or she spent an hour a week on traffic violations? Choices that are mutually exclusive would look like this:

Less than 1 hour

2–3 hours

4–6 hours

7–10 hours

11 hours or more

Make the Response Categories Exhaustive

In addition to mutual exclusivity, fixed-response categories must also allow all respondents to select an option. Consider the same research question about foot patrol officers. Suppose we asked a question such as this:

In what activity do you spend the most time in an average week on the job?

traffic violations

disturbance-related issues

felony arrests

misdemeanor arrests

Regardless of how exhaustive we think the response categories are, there must always be an option for respondents who require another choice. Response categories can easily be made **exhaustive** if respondents are provided with a choice labeled:

Other, please specify: _____

Note, however, that "Other" should be used only after you have included all options that you believe to be relevant. Otherwise, a large percentage of respondents will select the "Other" category and you will have to spend time coding their responses.

Utilize Likert-Type Response Categories

Likert-type responses generally ask respondents to indicate the extent to which they agree or disagree with statements. Why the name? Well, this format is generally believed to have been developed by Rensis Likert back in the 1930s. Likert-type response categories list choices for respondents to select their level of agreement with a statement and may look something like this:

I think "three-strikes" laws that increase penalties for individuals convicted of three or more felonies will help to decrease the crime rate.

Strongly Agree	Agree	Disagree	Strongly Disagree
1	2	3	4

Minimize Fence-Sitting and Floating

Two related problems in question writing stem from the respondent's desire to choose an acceptable or socially desirable answer. There is no uniformly correct solution to these problems, so you must carefully select an alternative.

Fence-sitters are people who see themselves as neutral in their attitudes toward a particular issue. If you are truly interested in those who do not have strong feelings on an issue, one alternative is to provide a neutral or undecided response option. The disadvantage of these options is that they may encourage some respondents to take the easy way out rather than really thinking about their feelings. They may also provide an out for respondents who do not want to reveal how they truly feel about an issue. On the other hand, not providing respondents who really have no opinion on an issue with an option such as "undecided" can be very frustrating and may encourage them to leave the item blank. Whatever you decide, it is generally a good idea to provide respondents with instructions that ask them to "select the choice in each item that most closely reflects your opinion." This should help make all respondents feel more comfortable about their answers, particularly those who only slightly feel one way or the other.

Floaters are respondents who choose a substantive answer even when they do not know anything about a particular question. For example, research has shown that one-third of the public will provide an opinion on a proposed law they know nothing about if they are not provided with a "don't know" option (Schuman & Presser 1981). Of course, providing a "don't know" option has the same disadvantage as providing a neutral response option; its inclusion leads some people who have an option to take the easy way out and choose "don't know."

If you are really interested in informed opinions about an issue, it is best to provide detailed information about that issue when asking a question. For example, let us say we were interested in attitudes about the treatment of juvenile offenders by the criminal justice system. Suppose we asked respondents to provide their opinion to the following statement: "The Juvenile Justice Bill before Congress will help reduce crime committed by juveniles." Do you know what the Juvenile Justice Bill is? If we did not provide a "don't know" option, respondents who knew nothing about the Juvenile Justice Bill would be forced to select a response that would not be meaningful and may bias the results of the entire survey. Instead of a "don't know" option, another way to handle the problem is to provide details of the issue in which you are interested. As with all questions, there should be clear instructions about what the response options actually mean.

Utilize Filter Questions

The use of filter questions is important to ensure that questions are asked only of relevant respondents. For example, if you are interested in the utilization of police services by robbery victims, you would first need to establish victimization with a **filter question**. These filter questions create **skip patterns**. For example, respondents who answer no to one question are directed to skip ahead to another question, but respondents who answer yes go on to the **contingent question** or questions. That's why these questions are sometimes called contingency questions. Skip patterns should be indicated clearly with arrows or other direction in the questionnaire, as demonstrated in Exhibit 6.2.

Combining Questions in Indexes

Measuring variables with single questions is very popular. Public opinion polls based on answers to single questions are reported frequently in newspaper articles and TV newscasts: "Do you favor or oppose U.S. policy in . . .?" "If you had to vote today, for which candidate would you vote?" The primary problem with using a single question is that if respondents

EXHIBIT 6.2   Filter Questions and Skip Patterns

14. In the past 6 months, has anyone taken something from you by force or the threat of force?

_____ Yes (If yes, please answer questions 15 through 16)

_____ No (If no, please skip to question 17)

15. What was the approximate monetary value of the items taken?

_____ Under $50

_____ $51 to $99

_____ $100 to $299

_____ $300 to $500

_____ Over $500

16. Was the incident reported to the police?

_____ Yes

_____ No

17. How fearful are you of walking alone at night in your neighborhood?

_____ Extremely afraid

_____ Afraid

_____ Unafraid

_____ Extremely unafraid

misunderstand the question or have some other problem with the phrasing, there is no way to tell. Single questions are prone to this **idiosyncratic variation**, which occurs when individuals' responses vary because of their reactions to particular words or ideas in the question. Differences in respondents' backgrounds, knowledge, and beliefs almost guarantee that they will understand the same question differently. If some respondents do not know some of the words in a question, we will not know what the respondents' answers mean—if they answer at all. If a question is too complex, respondents may focus on different parts of the question. If prior experiences or culturally biased orientations lead different groups to interpret questions differently, answers will not have a consistent meaning.

If just one question is used to measure a variable, the researcher may not realize respondents had trouble with a particular word or phrase in the questions. Although writing carefully worded questions will help reduce idiosyncratic variation, the best option is to devise multiple rather than single questions to measure concepts.

When several questions are used to measure one concept, the responses may be combined by taking the sum or average of the responses. A composite measure based on this type of sum or average is called an **index** or **scale**. The idea is that idiosyncratic variation in response to single questions will average out, so the main influence on the combined measure will be the concept focused on by the questions. In addition, the index can be considered a more complete measure of the concept than can any one of the component questions.

Creating an index, however, is not just a matter of writing a few questions that seem to focus on one concept. Questions that seem to you to measure a common concept might seem to respondents to concern several different issues. The only way to know that a given set of questions does, in fact, form an index is to administer the questions to people similar to those you plan to study. If a common concept is being measured, people's responses to the different questions should display some consistency. Special statistics called **reliability measures** help researchers decide whether responses are consistent. Most respondent attitudes are complex and consist of many elements.

Be aware of response sets when constructing an index measuring attitudes. For example, some people tend to agree with almost everything asked of them, whereas others tend to disagree. Still others are prone to answer neutrally to everything if given the option. To decrease the likelihood of this happening, it is a good idea to make some statements favorable to a particular attitude and some unfavorable. In this way, respondents are forced to be more careful in their responses to individual items. Exhibit 6.3 displays a hypothetical set of questions designed to solicit respondents' attitudes toward police in their community.

When scoring indexes and scales made up of both favorable and unfavorable statements, you must remember to **reverse code** the unfavorable items. For example, marking "strongly agree" to the first item in Exhibit 6.3 should not be scored the same as a "strongly agree" response to the second item.

One index available in the NCVS is designed to measure what is referred to in criminological literature as *routine activities*. To explain crime victimization, the Routine Activities Theory focuses on the circumstances in which crimes are committed rather than on the circumstances of the offender. Thus, the routine patterns of work, play, and leisure time affect the convergence in time and place of the motivated offenders, the suitable targets, and the absence of guardians. To measure the extent to which respondents engage in routine activities away from the home, the NCVS asks three questions that are displayed in Exhibit 6.4.

EXHIBIT 6.3   Items in an "Attitude Toward Police" Index

1. I think police officers are generally fair to all people regardless of their race or ethnicity.

    _____ Strongly Agree _____ Agree _____ Disagree _____ Strongly Disagree

2. Police officers are given too much freedom to stop and frisk community residents.

    _____ Strongly Agree _____ Agree _____ Disagree _____ Strongly Disagree

3. I think if someone resisted arrest, even a little, most police officers would become assaultive if they thought they could get away with it.

    _____ Strongly Agree _____ Agree _____ Disagree _____ Strongly Disagree

4. Police officers put their lives on the line every day trying to make it safe for residents of this community.

    _____ Strongly Agree _____ Agree _____ Disagree _____ Strongly Disagree

5. I think the majority of police officers have lied under oath at least once.

    _____ Strongly Agree _____ Agree _____ Disagree _____ Strongly Disagree

6. The majority of police officers are honest and fair.

    _____ Strongly Agree _____ Agree _____ Disagree _____ Strongly Disagree

---

These questions measure different types of activities in which people routinely engage away from the home; when combined, these questions create a better measure of an individual's activities away from the home than would a single question.

Demographic Questions

Almost all questionnaires include a section on demographic information such as sex, age, race or ethnicity, income, and religion. For many research studies, these questions are important independent variables. For example, research has shown that all four of these factors are related to the probability of victimization. Many researchers, however, include demographic questions that are not necessary for purposes of their research. In particular, try to avoid this for questions on income, because it makes the questionnaire more intrusive than necessary. In fact, many respondents feel that questions about their income invade their privacy. If you believe income is an essential variable for your study, providing fixed responses that include a range of values to select from is less intrusive than asking respondents for specific annual incomes. This format was utilized by the NVAMW Survey, as shown in Exhibit 6.5.

Care should also be taken when writing questions about race and ethnicity. Many people are justifiably sensitive to these questions. Even the U.S. Bureau of the Census has

EXHIBIT 6.4   Example of an Index: NCVS Questions Used to Make Up an Index of Routine Activities Away From the Home

Before we get to the crime questions, I'd like to ask you about some of your usual activities. We have found that people with different lifestyles may be more or less likely to become victims of crime.

30. On average, during the past 6 months, that is since _____, 20 _____, how often have you gone shopping? For example, at drug, clothing, grocery, hardware, and convenience stores. (Read answer categories until respondent answers yes.)

_____ Almost every day (or more frequently)

_____ At least once a week

_____ At least once a month

_____ Less often

_____ Never

_____ Don't know

31. On average, during the past 6 months, how often have you spent the evening away from home for work, school, or entertainment? (Read answer categories until respondent answers yes.)

_____ Almost every day (or more frequently)

_____ At least once a week

_____ At least once a month

_____ Less often

_____ Never

_____ Don't know

32. On average, during the past 6 months, how often have you ridden public transportation? Do not include school buses. (Read answer categories until respondent answers yes.)

_____ Almost every day (or more frequently)

_____ At least once a week

_____ At least once a month

_____ Less often

_____ Never

_____ Don't know

EXHIBIT 6.5 Question on Income From the NVAMW Survey

Including income from all sources, such as work, child support, and AFDC, how much income did you personally receive in 1995 before taxes? Stop me when I get to the category that applies. Was it . . .

01	Less than $5,000
02	$5,001 to $10,000
03	$10,001 to $15,000
04	$15,001 to $20,000
05	$20,001 to $25,000
06	$25,001 to $35,000
07	$35,001 to $50,000
08	$50,001 to $80,000
09	$80,001 to $100,000
10	Over $100,001
11	(Volunteer) None
12	(Volunteer) Don't Know
13	(Volunteer) Refused

Source: Tjaden & Thoennes (2000).

been struggling with appropriate categories to offer respondents. In fact, the Bureau still utilizes two questions, one on race and one for respondent ethnicity (Hispanic or non-Hispanic), which is obviously problematic. Most survey researchers now include questions such as the following:

Which of the following best describes your racial or ethnic background? Please check one.

Asian

Black or African American

White or Caucasian

Hispanic (may be of any race)

Native American

Of Mixed Race or Ethnicity

Other (Please specify: _____)

Deciding which categories to include remains difficult. Some researchers still prefer to exclude the Mixed category, because they believe most respondents will identify primarily with one race.

Questions on marital status can also be tricky to compose. The traditional categories of married, single, divorced, and widowed, still used by unsavvy researchers, can be interpreted very differently by respondents. Why? Well, isn't someone currently divorced also single? And what about someone not officially divorced but separated? To avoid confusing respondents, the U.S. Bureau of the Census adopted the following response categories: Married, Separated, Widowed, Divorced, and Never Married.

Because demographic questions are usually perceived as private by respondents, some researchers place them in a section at the end of the questionnaire with an introduction reassuring respondents that the information will remain confidential. However, when the information being gathered in the rest of the questionnaire is even more sensitive, such as details of violence respondents may have experienced at the hands of a family member or intimate partner, some researchers opt to keep demographic questions near the beginning of the questionnaire. For example, the NVAMW Survey asked demographic questions after the first section, which asked respondents about their general perceptions of fear and safety.

Don't Forget to Pretest!

Adhering to the preceding question-writing guidelines will go a long way toward producing a useful questionnaire. However, simply asking what appear to be clear questions does not ensure that people have a consistent understanding of what you are asking. You need some external feedback, and the more of it the better.

No questionnaire should be considered ready for use until it has been **pretested**. Try answering the questionnaire yourself, and then revise it. Try it out on some colleagues or other friends, and then revise it. Then select a small sample of individuals from the population you are studying or one very similar to it, and try out the questionnaire on them. Audiotape the test interviews for later review or, for a written questionnaire, include in the pretest version some space for individuals to add comments on each key question.

Professional survey researchers have also developed a technique for evaluating questions called the **cognitive interview** (Fowler 1995). Although the specifics vary, the basic approach is to ask people test questions, then probe with follow-up questions to learn how they understood the question and what their answers mean.

Review the distribution of responses to each question, listen to the audiotapes, or read all the comments, and then code what you heard or read to identify problems in question wording or delivery. Revise any questions that respondents do not seem to interpret as you had intended or that are not working well for other reasons.

It takes several drafts to create a good questionnaire. By the time you have gone through just a couple of drafts, you may not be scanning the instrument as clearly as you think. A very honest illustration of this is provided by Don Dillman, the Director of the Social and Economic Sciences Research Center at Washington State University (Seltzer 1996). His research team was about ready to mail a questionnaire with the following response categories:

What is your opinion?

Strongly oppose   *Oppose*   *Neither*   *Favor*   *Strongly oppose*

A careful scrutiny of your questionnaire using the procedures outlined in this section will help you detect these and other problems.

ORGANIZATION MATTERS

Once the basic topics and specific variables for a questionnaire have been identified, they can be sorted into categories (which may become separate sections) and listed in tentative order. Throughout the question-writing process, the grouping of variables into sections and the ordering of questions within sections could be adjusted. These adjustments will in turn require changes in the specific questions, in an iterative process that leads to a polished, coherent questionnaire.

The first thing needed is a descriptive title for the questionnaire that indicates the overall topic. The title is essential because it sets the context for the entire survey. For example, the NCVS and the NVAMW Surveys are both interested in measuring the magnitude of crime victimization in the United States. The NVAMW Survey, however, was presented as a survey interested in a number of personal safety–related issues, including tactics used in conflict resolution. The NCVS is named as a crime survey and is a survey interested in obtaining information only about crimes. Unfortunately, some survey participants still may not view assaults by intimates and other family members as criminal acts.

In addition to the title, question order is important because this also can influence responses. Consider the issue of capital punishment. For nearly a decade after the 1976 Supreme Court case of *Gregg v. Georgia*, which made capital punishment constitutional under guided discretion statutes, proponents of the death penalty were quick to note public sentiment favoring the use of capital punishment. But refined public opinion polls reveal how this sentiment can change dramatically when respondents are given other choices. For example, a 1986 Gallup poll (Gallup 1986) revealed that 70% of those surveyed approved of the death penalty for murder. However, when respondents were given the alternative punishment of life imprisonment without the possibility of parole, the support declined to 55%. This suggests public opinion questions that simply ask whether the person approves of capital punishment for convicted murderers are a misleading indicator of the strength of support for the death penalty. The point to take away from these cases is that question order is extremely important.

There is no real cure for this potential problem, although the split-ballot technique may help the problem to at least be identified when the question order is reversed on a subset of the questionnaires. What is most important is to be aware of the potential for problems due to question order and carefully evaluate the likelihood of their occurrence in any particular questionnaire. Those who survey results should mention, at least in a footnote, the order in which key questions were asked when more than one such question was used (Labaw 1980). Questionnaires should conform to several other organizational guidelines as well:

- Major topic divisions within the questionnaire should be organized in separate sections, and each section introduced with a brief statement.
- Instructions should be used liberally to minimize respondent confusion. Instructions should explain how each type of question is to be answered (such as circling a number or writing a response) in a neutral way that is not likely to influence responses. Instructions also should route respondents through skip patterns.
- The questionnaire should look attractive, be easy to complete, and have substantial open space. Resist the temptation to cram as many questions as possible on to one page. Response choices should be printed in a font or format and location different from the questions (such as in all capital letters down the middle of the page).
- Response choices should be designated by numbers to facilitate coding and data entry after the questionnaire is completed.

The **cover letter** for a mailed questionnaire and the introductory statement read by interviewers in telephone or in-person interviews are critical to the survey's success. Similar to the context set by the title of the survey, the initial statement of the cover letter sets the tone for the entire questionnaire. For example, the first thing interviewers said to respondents of the NVAMW Survey was, "Hello, I'm _____ from SRBI, the national research organization. We are conducting a national survey on personal safety for the Center for Policy Research, under a grant from the federal government." Notice that, even though the survey's primary purpose was to uncover incidents of victimization, it was presented to respondents as a survey interested in issues of personal safety. This was done to increase the probability of respondents disclosing incidents of victimization even if they did not perceive them to be crimes. Also note that the introductory statement disclosed the researcher's affiliation and the project sponsor. In addition, the purposes of the survey should also be briefly described and a contact number should be included for those who wish to ask questions or register complaints.

SURVEY DESIGNS

The five basic survey designs are the mailed survey, group-administered survey, phone survey, in-person survey, and electronic survey. Exhibit 6.6 summarizes the typical features of the five different survey designs.

Each survey has some unique advantages and disadvantages:

Manner of administration. Mailed, group, and electronic surveys are completed by the respondents themselves. During phone and in-person interviews, however, the researcher or a staff person asks the questions and records the respondent's answers.

Questionnaire structure. Survey designs also differ in the extent to which the content and order of questions are structured in advance by the researcher. Most mailed, group, phone, and electronic surveys are highly structured, fixing in advance the content and order of questions and response choices. Some of these types of surveys, particularly mailed surveys, may include some open-ended questions. In-person interviews are often highly

EXHIBIT 6.6	Typical Features of the Five Survey Designs			
Design	**Manner of Administration**	**Setting**	**Questionnaire Structure**	**Cost**
Mailed survey	Self	Individual	Mostly structured	Low
Group survey	Self	Group	Mostly structured	Very low
Phone survey	Professional	Individual	Structured	Moderate
In-person interview	Professional	Individual	Structured or unstructured	High
Electronic survey	Self	Individual	Mostly structured	Very low

structured, but they may include many questions without fixed response choices. Moreover, some interviews may proceed from an interview guide rather than a fixed set of questions. In these relatively unstructured interviews, the interviewer covers the same topics with respondents but varies questions according to the respondent's answers to previous questions. Extra questions are added as needed to clarify or explore answers to the most important questions.

Setting. Most surveys are conducted in settings where only one respondent completes the survey at a time; most mail and electronic questionnaires and phone interviews are intended for completion by only one respondent. The same is usually true of in-person interviews, although sometimes researchers interview several family members at once. On the other hand, a variant of the standard survey is a questionnaire distributed simultaneously to a group of respondents, who complete the survey while the researcher (or assistant) waits. Students in classrooms are typically the group involved, although this type of group distribution also occurs in surveys of employees and members of voluntary groups.

Cost. As mentioned earlier, in-person interviews are the most expensive type of survey. Phone interviews are much less expensive, but surveying by mail is cheaper still. Electronic surveys are now the least expensive method because there are no interviewer costs, no mailing costs, and, for many designs, almost no costs for data entry. Of course, extra staff time and expertise is required to prepare an electronic questionnaire.

Because of their different features, the five designs vary in the types of errors to which they are most prone and the situations in which they are most appropriate. The rest of this section focuses on the unique advantages and disadvantages of each design.

Mailed, Self-Administered Surveys

A **mailed (self-administered survey)** is conducted by mailing a questionnaire to respondents, who then administer the survey themselves. The central concern in this method of survey administration is maximizing the response rate. The final response rate is unlikely to be much above 80%, and almost surely will be below 70% unless procedures to maximize the response rate are precisely followed. A response rate below 60% is a disaster, and even a 70% response rate is not much more than minimally acceptable. It is hard to justify the representativeness of the sample if more than a third of those surveyed fail to respond.

Some ways to maximize the response rate (Fowler 1988: 99–106; Mangione 1995: 79–82; Miller 1991: 144) include the following:

- Make the questionnaire attractive, with plenty of white space.
- Use contingent questions and skip patterns infrequently. When they are necessary, guide respondents visually through the pattern.
- Make individual questions clear and understandable to all the respondents. No interviewers will be on hand to clarify the meaning of the questions or probe for additional details.
- Use no more than a few open-ended questions. Respondents are likely to be put off by the idea of having to write out answers.
- Include a personalized and professional cover letter. Using an altruistic appeal (informing respondents that their response will do some good) seems to increase response rates.
- Have a credible research sponsor. According to one investigation, a sponsor known to respondents may increase the rate of response by as much as 17%. The next most credible sponsors are the state headquarters of an organization and then other people in a similar field. Publishing firms, college professors or students, and private associations elicit the lowest response rates.
- Write an identifying number on the questionnaire so you can determine the nonrespondents.
- A small incentive can help. Even a coupon or ticket worth $2 can be enough to increase the response rate.
- Include a stamped, self-addressed return envelope with the questionnaire.

Related to the threat of nonresponse in mailed surveys is the hazard of incomplete response. Some respondents may skip some questions or just stop answering questions at some point in the questionnaire. Fortunately, this problem does not often occur with well-designed questionnaires. Potential respondents who decide to participate in the survey will usually complete it.

Group-Administered Surveys

A **group-administered survey** is completed by individual respondents assembled in a group. The response rate is not usually a concern in surveys that are distributed and collected in a group setting because most group members will participate. The difficulty with this method is that assembling a group is seldom feasible because it requires a captive audience. With the exception of students, employees, members of the armed forces, and some institutionalized populations, most populations cannot be sampled in such a setting.

One issue of special concern with group-administered surveys is the possibility that respondents will feel coerced to participate and as a result will be less likely to answer questions honestly. Also, because administering a survey to a group requires the approval of the group's administrators and this sponsorship is made quite obvious by the fact that the survey is conducted on the organization's premises, respondents may infer that the researcher is not at all independent of the sponsor. No complete solution to this problem exists, but it helps to make an introductory statement that emphasizes the researcher's independence and gives participants a chance to ask questions about the survey.

Surveys by Telephone

In a **phone survey**, interviewers question respondents over the phone and then record respondents' answers. Phone interviewing has become a very popular method of conducting surveys in the United States because almost all families have phones. But two matters may undermine the validity of a phone survey: not reaching the proper sampling units and not getting enough complete responses to make the results generalizable.

Reaching Sampling Units

Today, drawing a random sample is easier than ever due to random digit dialing (Lavrakas 1987). A machine calls random phone numbers within designated exchanges, regardless of whether the numbers are published. When the machine reaches an inappropriate household (such as a business in a survey directed to the general population), the phone number is simply replaced with another.

The NVAMW Survey collected a national probability sample of 8,000 English- and Spanish-speaking women and 8,000 English- and Spanish-speaking men 18 years of age and older residing in households throughout the United States through random digit dialing (RDD).

Maximizing Response to Phone Surveys

Three issues require special attention in phone surveys. First, because people often are not home, multiple call-backs will be necessary for many sample members. In addition, interviewers must be prepared for distractions if the respondent is interrupted by other household members. Sprinkling interesting questions throughout the questionnaire may help to maintain respondent interest. In general, rapport between the interviewer and the respondent is likely to be lower with phone surveys than in-person interviews, as respondents may tire and refuse to answer all the questions (Miller 1991: 166).

Procedures can be standardized more effectively, quality control maintained, and processing speed maximized when phone interviewers are assisted by computers. This **computer-assisted telephone interview** has become known as **CATI**, and most large surveys are now performed in this way. There are several advantages to using CATI, but perhaps the foremost advantage is that data collection and data entry can occur concurrently. Second, the CATI system has several machine edit features that help to minimize data entry error. For example, by automatically assigning single-punch fields of appropriate width for each data item in the questionnaire, the CATI system eliminates the possibility of overpunching and the possibility of including blanks as legitimate values. Third, by programming the skip patterns into its data entry program, the CATI system ensures that the aggregated database is comprehensive and accurate.

In summary, phone surveying is the best method to use for relatively short surveys of the general population. Response rates in phone surveys tend to be very high, often above 80%, because few individuals will hang up on a polite caller or refuse to stop answering questions (at least within the first 30 minutes or so). The NVAMW Survey obtained a response rate of 72% in the female survey and 69% in the male survey.

In-Person Interviews

What is unique to the **in-person interview**, compared to the other survey designs, is the face-to-face social interaction between interviewer and respondent. If money is no object, in-person interviewing is often the best survey design.

In-person interviewing has several advantages. Response rates are higher for this survey design than for any other when potential respondents are approached by a courteous interviewer. In addition, in-person interviews can be much longer than mailed or phone surveys; the questionnaire can be complex, with both open-ended and closed-ended questions and frequent branching patterns; the order in which questions are read and answered can be controlled by the interviewer; the physical and social circumstances of the interview can be monitored; and respondents' interpretations of questions can be probed and clarified.

As with phone interviewing, computers can be used to increase control of the in-person interview. In a **computer-assisted personal interviewing (CAPI)** project, interviewers carry a laptop computer programmed to display the interview questions and process the responses that the interviewer types in, as well as to check that these responses fall within the allowed ranges. Interviewers seem to like CAPI, and the quality of the data obtained is at least as good as for a non-computerized interview (Shepherd et al. 1996). **Computer-assisted self interviewing (CASI)** is also an alternative. With audio-CASI, respondents interact with a computer-administered questionnaire by using a mouse and following audio instructions delivered via headphones. Audio-CASI is considered the most reliable way to administer questionnaires that probe sensitive or potentially stigmatizing information such as offending or victimization information (Miller et al. 1998; Tourangeau & Smith 1996; Turner et al. 1998). Wolf et al. (2006) used this technology to obtain information about the physical and sexual victimization experiences of male and female state prison inmates. They explain, "The survey was administered using audio-CASI (computed assisted self interviewing) and was available in English and Spanish. There were 30 computer stations set up at each facility and members of the research team were available to answer any questions and assist with the technology as needed."

Maximizing Response to Interviews

Even if the right balance is struck between maintaining control over interviews and achieving good rapport with respondents, in-person interviews can still have a problem. Due to the difficulty of catching all the members of a sample, response rates may suffer.

Several factors affect the response rate in interview studies. Contact rates tend to be lower in city centers, in part because of difficulties in finding people at home and gaining access to high-rise apartments and in part because of interviewer reluctance to visit some areas at night, when people are more likely to be home (Fowler 1988: 45–60). Households with young children or elderly adults tend to be easier to contact, whereas single-person house-holds are more difficult to reach (Groves & Couper 1998: 119–154).

Electronic Surveys

The widespread use of personal computers and the growth of the internet have created new possibilities for survey research. In 1999, 43% of American households were connected to the internet and another 22% had personal computers without internet connections (Nie & Erbring 2000). These percentages are growing rapidly; it is not unreasonable to think that use of the internet will soon become comparable to the use of telephones. As the propor-tion of the population that is connected increases, the internet will become the preferred medium for survey research on many topics.

Electronic surveys can be prepared in two ways (Dillman 2000: 352–354). **E-mail surveys** can be sent as messages to respondents' e-mail addresses. Respondents then mark their answers in the message and send them back to the researcher. This approach is easy for researchers to develop and for respondents to use. However, this approach is cumber-some for surveys that are more than four or five pages in length. By contrast, **web surveys** are designed on a server controlled by the researcher; respondents are then asked to visit the website and respond to the web questionnaire by checking answers. This approach requires more programming by the researcher and in many cases requires more skill on the part of the respondent. However, web surveys can be quite long, with questions that are inapplicable to a given respondent hidden from them so that the survey may actually seem much shorter than it is.

Web surveys are becoming the more popular form of internet survey because they are so flexible. The design of the questionnaire can include many types of graphic and typo-graphic features. Respondents can view definitions of words or instructions for answering questions by clicking on linked terms. Lengthy sets of response choices can be presented with pull-down menus. Pictures and audio segments can be added when they are useful. Because answers are recorded directly in the researcher's database, data entry errors are almost eliminated and results can be reported quickly.

The most important drawback to either internet survey approach is the large fraction of households that are not yet connected to the internet. For special populations with high rates of internet use, though, the technology makes possible fast and effective surveys. Also, access to a web survey must be limited to the sample members, perhaps by requiring use of a personal identification number (PIN) (Dillman 2000: 353–401).

Computerized **interactive voice response (IVR)** systems already allow the ease of internet surveys to be achieved with a telephone-based system. In IVR surveys, respondents receive automated calls and answer questions by pressing numbers on their touchtone phones or speaking numbers that are interpreted by computerized voice recognition soft-ware. These surveys can also record verbal responses to open-ended questions for later tran-scription. Although they present some difficulties when many answer choices must be used or skip patterns must be followed, IVR surveys have been used successfully with short ques-tionnaires and when respondents are highly motivated to participate (Dillman 2000: 402–411). When these conditions are not met, potential respondents may be put off by the impersonality of this computer-driven approach.

Mixed-Mode Surveys

Survey researchers increasingly are combining different survey designs. **Mixed-mode surveys** allow the strengths of one survey design to compensate for the weaknesses of another and can maximize the likelihood of securing data from different types of respondents. For example, a survey may be sent electronically to sample members who have e-mail addresses and mailed to those who do not. Alternatively, nonrespondents in a mailed survey may be interviewed in person or over the phone. As noted previously, an interviewer may use a self-administered questionnaire to present sensitive questions to a respondent.

A Comparison of Survey Designs

Which survey design should be used when? Group-administered surveys are similar in most respects to mailed surveys, except they require the unusual circumstance of having access to the sample in a group setting. We therefore do not need to consider this survey design by itself; what applies to mailed survey designs applies to group-administered survey designs, with the exception of sampling issues. Thus we can focus our comparison on the four survey designs that involve the use of a questionnaire with individuals sampled from a larger population: mailed surveys, phone surveys, in-person surveys, and electronic surveys. Exhibit 6.7 summarizes their strong and weak points.

The most important consideration in comparing the advantages and disadvantages of the four survey designs is the likely response rate they will generate. Because of the great weakness of mailed surveys in this respect, they must be considered the least preferred survey design from a sampling standpoint. However, researchers may still prefer a mailed survey when they have to reach a widely dispersed population and do not have enough financial resources to hire and train an interview staff or to contract with a survey organization that already has an interview staff available in many locations.

Contracting with an established survey research organization for a phone survey is often the best alternative to a mailed survey. The persistent follow-up attempts necessary to secure an adequate response rate are much easier over the phone than in person.

In-person surveys are clearly preferable in terms of the possible length and complexity of the questionnaire itself, as well as the researcher's ability to monitor conditions while the questionnaire is being completed. Mailed surveys often are preferable for asking sensitive questions, although this problem can be lessened in an interview by giving respondents a separate sheet to fill out on their own. Although interviewers may themselves distort results, either by changing the wording of questions or failing to record answers properly, this problem can be lessened by careful training, monitoring, and tape-recording the answers.

The advantages and disadvantages of electronic surveys must be weighed in light of the capabilities at the time the survey is to be conducted. At this time, too many people lack internet connections for general use of internet surveying, and too may people who have computers lack adequate computer capacity for displaying complex web pages.

These various points about the different survey designs lead to two general conclusions. First, in-person interviews are the strongest design and generally preferable when sufficient resources and a trained interview staff are available; telephone surveys have many of the advantages of in-person interviews at a much lower cost. Second, a decision about the best

EXHIBIT 6.7 Advantages and Disadvantages of Four Survey Designs

Characteristics of Design	In-Person Survey	Mail Survey	Phone Survey	Electronic Survey
Representative Sample				
Opportunity for inclusion is known				
For completely listed populations	High	High	High	Medium
For incompletely listed populations	High	Medium	Medium	Low
Selection within sampling units is controlled (e.g., specific family members must respond)	High	Medium	High	Low
Respondents are likely to be located	Medium	High	High	Low
If samples are heterogeneous	High	Medium	High	Low
If samples are homogeneous and specialized	High	High	High	High
Questionnaire Construction and Question Design				
Allowable length of questionnaire	High	Medium	Medium	Medium
Ability to include				
Complex questions	Medium	Low	High	High
Open questions	Low	High	High	Medium
Screening questions	Low	Low	High	
Tedious, boring questions	High	High	High	High
Ability to control question sequence	Low	High	High	High
Ability to ensure questionnaire completion	Medium	High	High	High
Distortion of Answers				
Odds of avoiding social desirability bias	High	Medium	Low	High
Odds of avoiding interviewer distortion	Low	High	Medium	
Odds of avoiding contamination by others	High	Medium	Medium	Medium
Administrative Goals				
Odds of meeting personnel requirements	High	High	Low	High
Odds of implementing quickly	Low	High	Low	High
Odds of keeping costs low	High	Medium	Low	High

Source: Adapted from Don A. Dillman, *Mail and Telephone Surveys: The Total Design Method.* Copyright © 1978 Don A. Dillman. Reprinted by permission of John Wiley & Sons, Inc.

survey design for any particular study must take into account the unique features and goals of the study.

ETHICAL ISSUES IN SURVEY RESEARCH

Survey research usually poses fewer ethical dilemmas than do experimental or field research designs. Potential respondents to a survey can easily decline to participate, and a cover letter or introductory statement that identifies the sponsors of and motivations for the survey gives them the information required to make this decision. The methods of data collection are quite obvious in a survey, so little is concealed from the respondents. The primary ethical issue in survey research involves protecting respondents.

Protection of Respondents

If the survey could possibly have any harmful effects for the respondents, these should be disclosed fully in the cover letter or introductory statement. The procedures used to reduce such effects should also be delineated, including how the researcher will keep interviews confidential and anonymous. In addition, surveys such as the NVAMW Survey and NCVS that attempt to measure sensitive subject matter such as rape and intimate-perpetrated assault should also have other protections in place. By asking respondents to recall incidents of abuse and violence, there is always the possibility of causing victims serious emotional trauma. How can researchers ameliorate the negative consequences that responding to these surveys may have? What responsibility do researchers have in providing respondents with safety should they need it? We believe these important questions have received far too little attention. Respondents in the NVAMW Survey were given a toll-free number they could call if they needed to suddenly hang up during the course of the interview (e.g., if they felt they were in danger). In addition, interviewers of the NVAMW Survey were instructed to contact an attending supervisor at the first sign a respondent was becoming upset or emotionally distraught. These supervisors were provided with a source book from the National Domestic Violence Coalition that listed rape crisis and domestic violence hotline numbers from around the country.

Confidentiality

Do any of the questions have the potential to embarrass respondents or otherwise subject them to adverse consequences such as legal sanctions? If the answer to this question is no— and it often is in surveys about general social issues—other ethical problems are unlikely. But if the questionnaire includes questions about attitudes or behaviors that are socially stigmatized or generally considered to be private, or questions about actions that are illegal, the researcher must proceed carefully and ensure that respondents' rights are protected.

The first step to take with potentially troublesome questions is to consider omitting or modifying them. If sensitive questions fall into this category, they probably should be omitted. There is no point in asking, "Have you ever been convicted of a felony?" if the answers are unlikely to be used in the analysis of survey results.

Many surveys—particularly surveys interested in delinquent or criminal offending behavior—do include some essential questions that might prove damaging to the subjects if their answers were disclosed. To prevent any possibility of harm to subjects due to disclosure of such information, it is critical to preserve subject confidentiality. No one other than research personnel should have access to information that could be used to link respondents to their responses, and even that access should be limited to what is necessary for specific research purposes. Only numbers should be used to identify respondents on their questionnaires, and the researcher should keep the names that correspond to these numbers in a safe, private location, unavailable to staff and others who might otherwise come across them. Follow-up mailings or contact attempts that require linking the ID numbers with names and addresses should be carried out by trustworthy assistants under close supervision.

Only if no identifying information about respondents is obtained can surveys provide true **anonymity** to respondents. In this way, no identifying information is ever recorded to link respondents with their responses. However, the main problem with anonymous surveys is that they preclude follow-up attempts to encourage participation by initial nonrespondents, and they prevent panel designs, which measure change through repeated surveys of the same individuals. In-person surveys rarely can be anonymous because an interviewer must in almost all cases know the name and address of the interviewee. However, phone surveys that are meant only to sample opinion at one point in time, as in political polls, can safely be completely anonymous. When no follow-up is desired, group-administered surveys also can be anonymous. To provide anonymity in a mail survey, the researcher should omit identifying codes from the questionnaire but could include a self-addressed, stamped postcard so the respondent can notify the researcher that the questionnaire has been returned, without being linked to the questionnaire itself (Mangione 1995: 69).

CONCLUSION

Survey research is an exceptionally efficient and productive method for investigating a wide array of social research questions. In addition to the potential benefits for social science, considerations of time and expense frequently make a survey the preferred data-collection method. One or more of the four survey designs reviewed in this chapter can be applied to almost any research question. It is no wonder that surveys have become the most popular research method in sociology and that they frequently influence discussion and planning about important social and political questions.

The relative ease of conducting at least some types of survey research leads many people to imagine that no particular training or systematic procedures are required. Nothing could be further from the truth. As a result of this widespread misconception, you will encounter a great many nearly worthless survey results. You must be prepared to carefully examine the procedures used in any survey before accepting its finding as credible. And if you decide to conduct a survey, you must be prepared to invest the time and effort required to follow proper procedures.

KEY TERMS

Anonymity	Interpretive question
Cognitive interview	Interview schedule
Computer-assisted personal interviewing (CAPI)	Likert-type responses
Computer-assisted self-interviewing (CASI)	Mailed (self-administered) survey
Contingent question	Mixed-mode survey
Cover letter	Mutually exclusive responses
Double-barreled question	Omnibus survey
Double-negative question	Open-ended question
Electronic survey	Phone survey
E-mail survey	Pretest
Exhaustive responses	Questionnaire
Fence-sitter	Reference period
Filter question	Reliability measures
Fixed-choice question	Reverse code
Floater	Scale
Group-administered survey	Skip pattern
Idiosyncratic variation Index	Split-ballot design
In-person interview	Survey research
Interactive voice response (IVR)	Web survey

HIGHLIGHTS

- Surveys are the most popular form of social research because of their versatility, efficiency, and generalizability. Many survey data sets, such as the General Social Survey (GSS), are available for social scientists to use in teaching and research.

- Surveys can fail to produce useful results due to problems in sampling, measurement, and overall survey design.

- A survey questionnaire or interview schedule should be designed as an integrated whole, with each question and section serving some clear purpose and complementing the others.

- Questions must be worded carefully to avoid confusing the respondents or encouraging a less-than-honest response. Inclusion of "don't know" choices and neutral responses may help, but the presence of such options also affects the distribution of answers. Open-ended questions can be used to determine the meaning that respondents attach to their answers. Answers to any survey questions may be affected by the questions that precede them in a questionnaire or interview schedule.

- Every questionnaire and interview schedule should be pretested on a small sample that is like the sample to be surveyed.

- The cover letter for a mailed questionnaire and the introductory statement for an interview should be credible, personalized, interesting, and responsible.

- Phone interviews using random digit dialing allow fast turnaround and efficient sampling.

- In-person interviews have several advantages over other types of surveys: They allow longer and more complex interview schedules, monitoring of the conditions when the questions are answered, probing for respondents' understanding of the questions, and high response rates.

- Electronic surveys may be e-mailed or posted on the web. At this time, use of the internet is not sufficiently widespread to allow e-mail or web surveys of the general population, but these approaches can be fast and efficient for populations with high rates of computer use.

- Mixed-mode surveys allow the strengths of one survey design to compensate for the weaknesses of another.

- Most survey research poses few ethical problems because respondents are able to decline to participate. This option should be stated clearly in the cover letter or introductory statement. When anonymity cannot be guaranteed, confidentiality must be assured.

EXERCISES

Discussing Research

1. Who does survey research and how do they do it? These questions can be answered through careful inspection of ongoing surveys and the organizations that administer them at www.ciser.cornell.edu/info/polls.shtml. Spend some time reading about the different survey research organizations, and write a brief summary of the types of research they conduct, the projects in which they are involved, and the resources they offer on their websites. What are the distinctive features of different survey research organizations?

2. Write 8 to 10 questions for a one-page questionnaire on fear of crime among students. Include some questions to measure characteristics (such as income or year in school) that might help to explain the attitudes. Make all but one of your questions closed-ended. What are some of the problems in trying to measure difficult concepts like "fear?" How about attitudes like "prejudice" and "intolerance?"

Finding Research

1. Go to the Social Information Gateway (SOSIG) at http://sosig.esrc.bris.ac.uk. Search SOSIG for electronic journal articles that use surveys to collect information on crime, criminal behavior, or criminal victimization. Find at least five articles and briefly describe each.

2. Go to the Research Triangle Institute website at www.rti.org. Click on "Tools and Methods," then "Surveys," and then "Survey Design and Development." Read about their methods for computer-assisted interviewing (under "Survey Methods") and their cognitive laboratory methods for refining questions (under "Usability Testing"). What does this add to your treatment of these topics in this chapter?

3. Go to The Question Bank at http://qb.soc.surrey.ac.uk/docs/home.htm. Go to the "Surveys" link and then click on one of the listed surveys or survey sections that interest you. Review 10 questions used in the survey, and critique them in terms of the principles for question writing that you have learned. Do you find any question features that might be attributed to the use of British English?

Critiquing Research

1. Read the original article reporting one of the surveys described in this book (check the text of the chapters for ideas). Critique the article using the questions presented in Appendix B as your guide. Focus particular attention on sampling, measurement, and survey design.

2. By interviewing two students, conduct a preliminary pretest of the questionnaire you wrote for Exercise 2 under "Discussing Research" (above). Follow up the closed-ended questions with open-ended questions that ask the students what they meant by each response or what came to mind when they were asked each question. Take account of the answers when you revise your questions.

3. Make any necessary revisions to the questionnaire you wrote in Exercise 2 under "Discussing Research" (above). Write a cover letter that presumes the survey will be administered to students in a class at your school. Submit the questionnaire and cover letter to your instructor for comment and evaluation.

Making Research Ethical

1. In this chapter, we posed the questions: "How can researchers ameliorate the negative consequences that responding to these surveys may have? What responsibility do researchers have in providing respondents with safety should they need it?" Write a short statement in response to each question.

2. Tjaden and Thoennes (2000) sampled adults with random digit dialing in order to study violent victimization from a nationally representative sample of adults. We already asked you about the ethical dilemmas of reporting victimizations in chapter 4. But what about respondents who are minors and are under the age of 18? What about children under the age of 12? Teachers and medical personnel are required by law to report cases they believe to represent incidents of child abuse. Should researchers have the same obligation? How would this affect large-scale surveys using random digit dialing in which you want to preserve the anonymity of respondents?

Developing a Research Proposal

1. Write 10 questions for a one-page questionnaire that concerns your proposed research question. Your questions should operationalize at least three of the variables on which you have focused, including at least one independent and one dependent variable (you may have multiple questions to measure some variables). Make all but one of your questions closed-ended. If you completed the "research proposal" exercises in chapter 3, you can select your questions from the ones you developed for those exercises.

2. Conduct a preliminary pretest of the questionnaire by conducting cognitive interviews with two students or other persons like those to whom the survey is directed. Follow up the closed-ended questions with open-ended probes that ask the students what they meant by each response or what came to mind when they were asked each question. Take account of the feedback you receive when you revise your questions.

3. Polish up the organization and layout of the questionnaire, following the guidelines in this chapter. Prepare a rationale for the order of questions in your questionnaire. Write a cover letter directed to the appropriate population that contains appropriate statements about research ethics (human subjects issues).

Performing Data Analysis in SPSS

Injuries are often sustained by victims of violent crime. Using NCS93.POR, a sample of incidents of violent crime for female victims from the National Crime Victimization Survey in 1993, you can explore what factors most often lead to injury for female victims of rape, robbery, and assault.

1. Browse the variables in the data set. What factors do you think are related to whether or not a victim of rape, robbery, or assault is injured?

2. Choose at least three of these variables, and state your hypotheses about the relationship between each of these variables and injury.

3. Generate cross-tabulations of your chosen variables and INJURY. (If you have had a statistics course, you may want to request the CHI-SQUARE statistic for each of the cross-tabulations.)

4. Describe the relationship you have found, noting the difference in the distribution of the dependent (row) variables between the categories of each independent (column) variable.

5. Do these relationships vary for the type of violent crime committed? Add the variable measuring the type of violent crime committed (TOC) as a CONTROL variable in your cross-tabulation request. Describe your results.

Student Study Site

The companion Student Study Website for *The Fundamentals of Research in Criminology and Criminal Justice* can be found at www.sagepub.com/frccjstudy.

Visit the Student Study Site to enhance your understanding of the chapter content and to discover additional resources that will take your learning one step further. You can enhance your understanding of the chapters by using the comprehensive study material, which includes interactive exercises, e-flashcards, web exercises, practice self-tests, and more. You will also find special features, such as Learning from Journal Articles, which incorporates SAGE's online journal collection.

Qualitative Methods and Data Analysis

In this chapter you will learn how qualitative methods were used to illuminate the relationships, both individually and collectively, that gang members have with other social institutions (Decker & Van Winkle 1996). Throughout the chapter, you will learn from a variety of other examples that some of our greatest insights into social processes can result from what appear to be very ordinary activities: observing, participating, listening, and talking.

But you will also learn that qualitative research is much more than just doing what comes naturally in social situations. Qualitative researchers must keenly observe respondents, sensitively plan their participation, systematically take notes, and strategically question respondents. They must also prepare to spend more time and invest more of their whole selves than often occurs with experiments or surveys. Moreover, if we are to have any confidence in the validity of a qualitative study's conclusions, each element of its design must be reviewed as carefully as the elements of an experiment or survey.

WHAT WE MEAN BY QUALITATIVE METHODS

"It's more like a family away from home. You're with your friends, you all stick together. They ain't going to let nothing happen to you, you ain't going to let nothing happen to them." This was one youth's reason for joining a gang. Such specific narrative information would not be easy to obtain from a structured survey. Thus, in an attempt to situate the origin, structure, and practices of street gangs within the social organizational context of the family and the larger community, Decker and Van Winkle (1996) obtained this information by conducting three years of fieldwork and interviews with 99 active gang members and 24 of their family members. As you will see, experimental or survey methodologies would be ill-suited to examine the unique institutional and cultural contexts of gang values and activities such as those uncovered by Decker and Van Winkle.

Qualitative methods refer to three distinctive research designs: **participant observation, intensive interviewing**, and **focus groups**. Participant observation and intensive interviewing are often used in the same project; focus groups combine some elements of these two approaches into a unique data-collection strategy.

Participant observation A qualitative method for gathering data that involves developing a sustained relationship with people while they go about their normal activities.

Intensive interviewing A qualitative method that involves open-ended, relatively unstructured questioning in which the interviewer seeks in-depth information on the interviewee's feelings, experiences, and perceptions (Lofland & Lofland 1984: 12).

Focus groups A qualitative method that involves unstructured group interviews in which the focus group leader actively encourages discussion among participants on the topics of interest.

Although these three qualitative designs differ in many respects, they share several features that distinguish them from experimental and survey research designs (Denzin & Lincoln 1994; Maxwell 1996; Wolcott 1995):

Collection primarily of qualitative rather than quantitative data. Any research design may collect both qualitative and quantitative data, but qualitative methods emphasize observations about natural behavior and artifacts that capture social life as it is experienced by the participants rather than in categories predetermined by the researcher.

Exploratory research questions, with a commitment to inductive reasoning. Qualitative researchers typically begin their projects seeking not to test preformulated hypotheses but to discover what people think and how and why they act in certain social settings. Only after many observations do qualitative researchers try to develop general principles to account for their observations.

A focus on previously unstudied processes and unanticipated phenomena. Previously unstudied attitudes and actions cannot adequately be understood with a structured set of questions or within a highly controlled experiment. Therefore, qualitative methods have their greatest appeal when we need to explore new issues, investigate hard-to-study groups, or determine the meaning people give to their lives and actions.

An orientation to social context, to the interconnections between social phenomena rather than to their discrete features. The context of concern may be a program, an organization, a case study, or a broader social context.

A focus on human subjectivity, on the meanings that participants attach to events and people give to their lives. "Through life stories, people account for their lives . . . The themes people create are the means by which they interpret and evaluate their life experiences and attempt to integrate these experiences to form a self-concept" (Kaufman 1986: 24–25).

A focus on the events leading up to a particular event or outcome instead of general causal explanations. With its focus on particular actors and situations and the processes that connect them, qualitative research tends to identify causes of particular events embedded within an unfolding, interconnected action sequence (Maxwell 1996: 20–21). The language of variables and hypotheses appears only rarely in the qualitative literature.

Reflexive research design. The design develops as the research progresses:

Each component of the design may need to be reconsidered or modified in response to new developments or to changes in some other component . . . The activities of collecting and analyzing data, developing and modifying theory, elaborating or refocusing the research questions, and identifying and eliminating validity threats are usually all going on more or less simultaneously, each influencing all of the others. (Maxwell 1996: 2–3)

Sensitivity to the subjective role of the researcher. Little pretense is made of achieving an objective perspective on social phenomena.

Origins of Qualitative Research

Anthropologists and sociologists laid the foundation for modern qualitative methods while doing **field research** in the early decades of the twentieth century. Dissatisfied with studies of native peoples that relied on second-hand accounts and inspection of artifacts, anthropologists Franz Boas and Bronislaw Malinowski went to live in or near the communities they studied. Boas visited Native American villages in the American Northwest; Malinowski lived among New Guinea natives. Neither truly participated in the ongoing social life of those they studied (Boas collected artifacts and original texts, and Malinowski reputedly lived as something of a noble among the natives he studied), but both helped to establish the value of intimate familiarity with the community of interest and thus laid the basis for modern anthropology (Emerson 1983: 2–5).

Many of sociology's field research pioneers were former social workers and reformers. Some brought their missionary concern with the spread of civic virtue among new immigrants to the Department of Sociology and Anthropology at the University of Chicago. Their successors continued to focus on sources of community cohesion and urban strain but came to view the city as a social science laboratory rather than as a focus for reform. They adopted the fieldwork methods of anthropology for studying the "natural areas" of the city and the social life of small towns (Vidich & Lyman 1994). By the 1930s, 1940s, and 1950s, qualitative researchers were emphasizing the value of direct participation in community life and sharing in subjects' perceptions and interpretations of events (Emerson 1983: 6–13).

Case Study: Life in the Gang

The use of fieldwork techniques to study gangs has a long tradition in a variety of cities, including Thrasher's (1927) classic study of gangs in Chicago, and others, including Whyte (1943), Hagedorn (1988), Vigil (1988), Padilla (1992), Sanchez-Jankowski (1991), and Moore (1978, 1991), who spent over two decades studying the "home-boys" of Hispanic *barrios* all over the country. All these researchers employed a fieldwork approach to the study of gangs rather than the more structured approaches offered by quantitative methods.

You can get a better feel for qualitative methods by reading the following excerpts from Decker and Van Winkle's (1996) book about gangs, *Life in the Gang: Family, Friends, and Violence*, and by reasoning inductively from their observations. See whether you can induce from these particulars some of the general features of field research. Ask yourself, "What were the research questions?" "How were the issues of generalizability, measurement, and causation approached?" "How did social factors influence the research?"

One of the first issues with which Decker and Van Winkle (1996) were challenged was precisely defining a gang. The term "gang" could refer to many groups of youth, including a high school Debate Society or the Young Republicans. After reviewing the literature,

Decker and Van Winkle developed a working definition of a gang as an "age-graded peer group that exhibits some permanence, engages in criminal activity, and has some symbolic representation of membership" (1996: 31). To operationalize who was a gang member, they relied on self-identification. "Are you claiming . . ." was a key screening question that was also verified, as often as possible, with other gang members.

There were several questions in which Decker and Van Winkle (1996) were interested:

> First, we were interested in motivations to join gangs, the process of joining the gang, the symbols of gang membership, the strength of associational ties, the structure or hierarchy within the gang, motivations to stay (or leave) the gang, and how this generation of St. Louis gangs began. The second set of issues concerned the activities gang members engaged in. These included such things as turf protection, drug sales and use, and violence, as well as conventional activities. A unique feature of our work is its focus on families. There has been little research examining specifically the links between gang members and their family members. For this reason, we have separated the family from our analysis of other social institutions and devote special attention to this relationship. (1996: 54–55)[1]

With these research questions in mind, Decker and Van Winkle (1996) explain why they chose a fieldwork approach: "A single premise guided our study; the best information about gangs and gang activity would come from gang members contacted directly in the field" (1996: 27). As stated earlier, Decker and Van Winkle combined two methods of qualitative data collection. With the help of a field ethnographer who spent the majority of each day "on the streets," direct observation was conducted along with the intensive interviewing conducted by Decker and Van Winkle.

Because they did not rely on structured questionnaires with fixed-response formats, their data are primarily qualitative rather than quantitative.

As for their method, it was inductive. First they gathered data. Then, as data collection continued, they figured out how to interpret the data, how to make sense of the social situations they were studying. Their analytic categories ultimately came not from social theory but from the categories by which the gang members themselves described one another and their activities and how they made sense of their social world. They provided the field of criminology with in-depth descriptions and idiographic connections of sequences of events that could not have been obtained through other methodologies. The goal of much qualitative research is to create a **thick description** of the setting being studied, a description that provides a sense of what it is like to experience that setting or group from the standpoint of the natural actors in that setting (Geertz 1973).

PARTICIPANT OBSERVATION

Other researchers have utilized a more direct observational strategy for studying gangs. For example, to illuminate the nuances and complexities of the role of a street gang in community social life, Venkatesh (1997) conducted intensive participant observation in Blackstone, a midsize public housing development located in a poor ghetto of a large Midwestern city. As Venkatesh describes, "Having befriended these gang members, I moved into their world, accompanying them into Blackstone and other spaces where they were actively involved in illicit economic activities, member recruitment, and the general expansion of their street-based organization" (1997: 4). As this quote eloquently depicts, participant observation, called fieldwork in anthropology, is a method of studying natural social processes as they happen (in the field rather than in the laboratory) and leaving them relatively undisturbed. It is the seminal field research method, a means for seeing the social world as the research subjects see it, in its totality, and for understanding subjects' interpretations of that world (Wolcott 1995: 66). By observing people and interacting with them in the course of their normal activities, participant observers seek to avoid the artificiality of experimental designs and the unnatural structured questioning of survey research (Koegel 1987: 8).

The term *participant observer* actually represents a continuum of roles (see Exhibit 7.2), ranging from being a complete observer who does not participate in group activities and is publicly defined as a researcher, to being a covert participant who acts just like other group members and does not disclose his or her research role. Many field researchers develop a role between these extremes, publicly acknowledging being a researcher but nonetheless participating in group activities. In some settings, it is possible to observe covertly without acknowledging being a researcher or participating.

Choosing a Role

The first concern of all participant observers is to decide what balance to strike between observing and participating and whether to reveal their role as researchers. These decisions must take into account the specifics of the social situation being studied, the researcher's own background and personality, the larger sociopolitical context, and ethical concerns. The balance of participating and observing that is most appropriate also changes many times during most projects. And the researcher's ability to maintain either a covert or an overt role will be challenged many times.

Complete Observation

In her study of community policing, Miller (1999) adopted the role of a complete observer. Community policing is an approach to policing that emphasizes building closer ties between police and members of the community. Miller was particularly interested in how gender affected the attitudes and behavior of neighborhood police officers (NPOs).

In **complete observation**, researchers try to see things as they happen, without disrupting the participants. Along with intensive interviews with police officers, Miller (1999) also observed police officers on their daily shifts:

Both neighborhood and patrol officers' shifts were observed, either on foot with neighborhood officers, or in squad cars with patrol officers. This component of

EXHIBIT 7.1   The Observational Continuum

the project also permitted gathering some observational information about citizens' reactions to police delivery of services . . . Typically, we tried to work the same shifts as the neighborhood police officers, and we shadowed the NPO and each corresponding patrol officer during the same shift. (1999: 232–233)

As clearly depicted in this quote, the "shadowing" is visible. Thus the researcher's very presence as an observer alters the social situation being observed. It is not natural in most social situations to have an observer present, who at some point will record their observations for research and publication purposes. The observer thus sees what individuals do when they are being observed, which is not necessarily what they would do without an observer. This is called a reactive effect, and the extent to which it can be a problem varies with the situation. In Miller's (1999) study, her long tenure as an observer made her presence commonplace, thereby serving to decrease the problem of **reactive effects**. She states,

> Since I had spent so many hours over eighteen months with the Jackson City Police Department [fictional name], I had grown to be a familiar face; this, I believe, decreased respondents' tendencies toward social desirability. Officers took my presence for granted in the briefing room, the hallways, the interview rooms, and in the field, including me in jokes and informal conversation in the coffee shop. (1999: 235)

In general, in social settings involving many people where observing while standing or sitting does not attract attention, the complete observer is unlikely to have much effect on the social processes. On the other hand, when the social setting involves few people and observing is unlike the usual activities in the setting, or when the observer differs in obvious respects from the participants, the complete observer is more likely to have an impact.

Participation and Observation

Most field researchers adopt a role that involves some active participation in the setting. Usually they inform at least some group members of their research interests, but then they participate in enough group activities to develop rapport with members and to gain a direct sense of what group members experience. This is not an easy balancing act.

In his classic study of corner gangs and other social organizations in the poor Boston community he called Cornerville, Whyte (1943) spent a large part of nearly four years trying to be accepted by the community and seen as a good fellow. He describes his efforts:

> My aim was to gain an intimate view of Cornerville life. My first problem, therefore, was to establish myself as a participant in the society so that I would have a position from which to observe. I began by going to live in Cornerville, finding a room with an Italian family . . . It was not enough simply to make the acquaintance of various groups of people. The sort of information that I sought required that I establish intimate social relations, and that presented special problems. Since illegal activities are prevalent in Cornerville, every newcomer is under suspicion . . . I put in a great deal of time simply hanging around with them [the men] and participating in their various activities. This active participation gave me something in common with them so that we had other things to talk about besides the weather. It broke down the social barriers and made it possible for me to be taken into the intimate life of the group. (1943: v–vii)[2]

Because of the great deal of time he spent with each gang and social organization he was studying, Whyte became accepted into each group and the community. The result was his famous book, *Street Corner Society* (1943). Sudhir Alladi Ventatesh's (2000) book, *American Project*, about the relationship between gangs and a public housing development, will almost certainly become a classic as well. In it, he describes the evolution of his research methodology from structured interviews to participant observation:

They read my survey instrument, informed me that I was "not going to learn shit by asking these questions," and said I would need to "hang out with them" if I really wanted to understand the experiences of African-American youth in the city. Over the next few months, I met with many of them informally to play racquetball, drink beer on the shores of Lake Michigan, attend their parties, and eat dinner with their families . . . Over an eighteen-month period, I logged notes on the activities of their gang, called the Black Kings. But it was the gang's relationship with other people in the housing development that piqued my interest. Gang members were also schoolchildren, nephews, churchgoers, fathers, husbands, and so on. They were "gang members" at certain times and in certain contexts, such as narcotics trafficking and meetings in open park space, but most of the time their lives were characterized by involvement with work, family, school, and peers. (2000: xiv)

Participating and observing have two clear ethical advantages. Because group members know the researcher's real role in the group, they can choose to keep some information or attitudes hidden. By the same token, the researcher can decline to participate in unethical or dangerous activities without fear of exposing his or her identity.

Even when researchers maintain a public identity as researchers, the ethical dilemmas arising from participation in group activities do not go away. In fact, researchers may have to prove themselves to group members by joining in some of their questionable activities. For example, police officers gave Van Maanen (1982) a nonstandard and technically prohibited pistol to carry on police patrols. Pepinsky (1980) witnessed police harassment of a citizen but did not intervene when the citizen was arrested. Trying to strengthen his ties with a local political figure in Cornerville, Whyte (1943) illegally voted multiple times in a local election.

Covert Participation

To lessen the potential for reactive effects and to gain entry to otherwise inaccessible settings, some field researchers have adopted the role of covert participant. By doing so they keep their research secret and do their best to act like other participants in a social setting or group. **Covert participation** is also known as *complete participation*. Laud Humphreys (1970) served as a "watch queen" so that he could learn about men engaging in homosexual acts in a public restroom. Randall Alfred (1976) joined a group of Satanists to investigate group members and their interaction. Goffman (1961) worked as a state hospital assistant while studying the treatment of psychiatric patients.

Although the role of covert participant lessens some of the reactive effects encountered by the complete observer, covert participants confront other problems. The following are a few examples:

- *Covert participants cannot openly take notes or use any obvious recording devices.* They must write up notes based solely on memory and must do so at times when it is natural for them to be away from group members.
- *Covert participants cannot ask questions that will arouse suspicion.* Thus they often have trouble clarifying the meaning of other participants' attitudes or actions.

- *The role of covert participation is difficult to play successfully.* Covert participants will not know how regular participants act in every situation in which the researchers find themselves. Suspicion that researchers are not "one of us" may then have reactive effects, obviating the value of complete participation (Erikson 1967).
- *Covert participants must keep up the act at all times while in the setting under study.* Researchers may experience enormous psychological strain, particularly in situations where they are expected to choose sides in intragroup conflict or to participate in criminal or other acts. Of course, some covert observers may become so wrapped up in their role that they adopt not just the mannerisms but also the perspectives and goals of the regular participants—they "go native." At this point, they abandon research goals and cease to critically evaluate their observations.

Ethical issues have been at the forefront of debate over the strategy of covert participation. Erikson (1967) argues that covert participation is by its very nature unethical and should not be allowed except in public settings. Covert researchers cannot anticipate the unintended consequences of their actions for research subjects, Erikson points out. In addition, other social research is harmed when covert research is disclosed, either during the research or upon its publication, because distrust of social scientists increases and access to research opportunities may decrease.

But a total ban on covert participation would "kill many a project stone dead" (Punch 1994: 90). Studies of unusual religious or sexual practices and institutional malpractice would rarely be possible. "The crux of the matter is that some deception, passive or active, enables you to get at data not obtainable by other means" (Punch 1994: 91). Therefore, some field researchers argue that covert participation is legitimate in some settings. If the researcher maintains the confidentiality of others, keeps commitments to others, and does not directly lie to others, some degree of deception may be justified in exchange for the knowledge gained (Punch 1994: 90).

Entering the Field

Entering the field, the setting under investigation, is a critical stage in a participant observation project because it can shape many subsequent experiences. Some background work is necessary before entering the field, at least enough to develop a clear understanding of what the research questions are likely to be and to review one's personal stance toward the people and problems likely to be encountered. With participant observation, researchers must also learn in advance about the participants' dress and their typical activities to avoid being caught completely unprepared.

Developing trust with at least one member of the research setting is a necessity in qualitative research. Such a person can become a valuable informant throughout the project, and most participant observers make a point of developing trust with at least one informant in a group under study. The entry gambit that finally worked for Whyte (1943) was to rely on a local community leader for introductions. A helpful social worker at the local settlement house introduced Whyte to "Doc," who agreed to help:

Well, any nights you want to see anything, I'll take you around. I can take you to the joints—gambling joints—I can take you around to the street corners. Just remember that you're my friend. That's all they need to know [so they won't bother you]. (1943: 291)

Miller (1999) gained access to the police department she studied through a chief of police who was extremely open to research. She also had two friends on the police force at the time of her study.

In short, field researchers must be very sensitive to the impression they make and the ties they establish when entering the field. This state of research lays the groundwork for collecting data from people who have different perspectives and for developing relationships that the researcher can use to surmount the problems that inevitably arise in the field.

Developing and Maintaining Relationships

Researchers must be careful to manage their relationships in the research setting so they can continue to observe and interview diverse members of the social setting throughout the long period typical of participant observation (Maxwell 1996: 66). Every action the researcher takes can develop or undermine this relationship. As Decker and Van Winkle (1996) describe, maintaining trust is the cornerstone to successful research engagement. They elaborate further:

We were able to maintain good field relations with our subjects by strictly observing our own commitment to the confidentiality of their statements. Since we interviewed many individuals from the same gang, it was often the case that one member would want to know what an earlier participant had told us. We refused to honor such inquiries, reminding them that the same confidentiality that applied to their own answers also covered those of their fellow gang members. The strict confidentiality we were committed to was respected by our subjects, and appeared to enhance our own credibility as "solid" in their eyes. (1996: 46)

Experienced participant observers (Whyte 1943: 300–306; Wolcott 1995: 91–95) have developed some sound advice for others seeking to maintain relationships in the field:

- Develop a plausible (and honest) explanation for yourself and your study.
- Maintain the support of key individuals in groups or organizations under study.
- Don't be too aggressive in questioning others (e.g., don't violate implicit norms that preclude discussion of illegal activity with outsiders). Being a researcher requires that you not simultaneously try to be the guardian of law and order.
- Don't fake social similarity with your subjects. Taking a friendly interest in them should be an adequate basis for developing trust.
- Avoid giving and receiving monetary or other tangible gifts, but do not violate norms of reciprocity. Living with other people, taking others' time for conversations, and going out for a social evening all create expectations and incur social obligations. You cannot be an active participant without occasionally

helping others. But you will lose your ability to function as a researcher if you are seen as someone who gives away money or other favors. Such small forms of assistance as an occasional ride to the store or advice on applying to college may strike the right balance.

- Be prepared for special difficulties and tensions if multiple groups are involved. It is hard to avoid taking sides or being used in situations of intergroup conflict.

Sampling People and Events

Decisions to study one setting or several settings and to pay attention to specific people and events will shape field researchers' ability to generalize about what they have found as well as the confidence that others can place in the results of their study. Limiting a particular study to a single setting allows a more intensive portrait of actors and activities in that setting, but also makes generalization of the findings questionable.

We may be reassured by information indicating that a typical case was selected for study or that the case selected was appropriate in some way for the research question. We also must keep in mind that many of the most insightful participant observation studies were conducted in only one setting and draw their credibility precisely from the researcher's thorough understanding of that setting. Nonetheless, studying more than one case or setting almost always strengthens the causal conclusions and makes the findings more generalizable (King, Keohane, & Verba 1994).

Decker and Van Winkle (1996) utilized the technique of snowball sampling. In addition, they chose to contact gang members directly, without the intervention of social service or criminal justice agencies, for several reasons, including their concern that they would be identified with law enforcement. To make their findings more generalizable, they interviewed members of several different gangs. Specifically, the snowball began with an earlier fieldwork project on active residential burglars (Wright & Decker 1994). The young members from this sample, along with contacts the field ethnographer had with several active street criminals, started the referral process. The initial interviewees then nominated other gang members as potential interview subjects.

Theoretical sampling is a systematic approach to sampling in participant observational research (Glaser & Strauss 1967). Decker and Van Winkle (1996) used this technique to ensure that various subgroups such as race, sex, or type of gang were represented within their sample. When field researchers discover in an investigation that particular processes seem to be important, implying that certain comparisons should be made or that similar instances should be checked, the researchers then choose new settings or individuals to study as well, as shown in Exhibit 7.2 (Ragin 1994: 98–101). Based on the existing literature and anecdotal knowledge, Decker and Van Winkle (1996) knew that not all gang members were young minority-group males. They describe their strategy to obtain a full range of gang members as follows:

> We aggressively pursued leads for female gangs and gang members as well as opportunities to locate older and nonblack gang members. These leads were more difficult to find and often caused us to miss chances to interview other gang members. Despite these "missed opportunities," our sample is strengthened in that

it more accurately represents the diverse nature of gangs and gang members in St. Louis. (1996: 43)

The resulting sample of gang members in Decker and Van Winkle's (1996) study represented 29 different gangs; 16 were affiliated with the Crips and 13 were affiliated with the Bloods. Thus Decker and Van Winkle's ability to draw from different gangs in developing conclusions gives us greater confidence in their study's generalizability.

Quota sampling also may be employed to ensure the representation of particular categories of participants. Using some type of intentional sampling strategy within a particular setting can allow tests of some hypotheses that would otherwise have to wait until comparative data could be collected from several settings (King, Keohane, & Verba 1994). When field

EXHIBIT 7.2   Theoretical Sampling

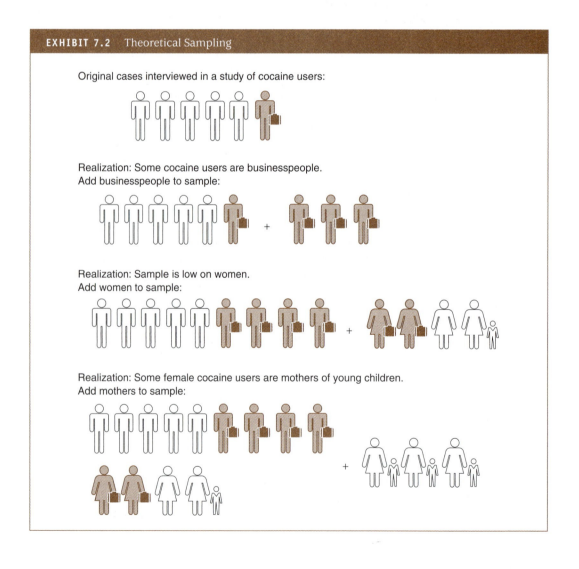

Original cases interviewed in a study of cocaine users:

Realization: Some cocaine users are businesspeople.
Add businesspeople to sample:

Realization: Sample is low on women.
Add women to sample:

Realization: Some female cocaine users are mothers of young children.
Add mothers to sample:

studies do not require ongoing, intensive involvement by researchers in the setting, the **experience sampling method** (ESM) can be used. The experiences, thoughts, and feelings of a number of people are randomly sampled as they go about their daily activities. Participants in an ESM study carry an electronic pager and fill out reports when they are beeped.

Taking Notes

Written **field notes** are the primary means of recording participant observation data (Emerson, Fretz, & Shaw 1995). Of course, written no longer means handwritten; many field researchers jot down partial notes while observing and then retreat to their computers to write up more complete notes on a daily basis. The computerized text can then be inspected and organized after it is printed out, or it can be marked up and organized for analysis using one of several computer programs designed especially for the task.

It is almost always a mistake to try to take comprehensive notes while engaged in the field; the process of writing extensively is just too disruptive. The usual procedure is to jot down brief notes about the highlights of the observation period. These brief notes, called **jottings**, then serve as memory joggers when writing the actual field notes at a later time. With the aid of the brief notes and some practice, researchers usually remember a great deal of what happened, as long as the comprehensive field notes are written within the next 24 hours, that night or upon arising the next day.

Usually, writing up notes takes as long as making the observations. Field notes must be as complete, detailed, and true to what was observed and heard as possible. Quotes should clearly be distinguished from the researcher's observations and phrased in the local vernacular; pauses and interruptions should be indicated. The surrounding context should receive as much attention as possible, and a map of the setting should always be included, with indications of where individuals were at different times.

Careful note-taking yields a big payoff for the researcher. On page after page, field notes will suggest new concepts, causal connections, and theoretical propositions. Social processes and settings can be described in rich detail, with ample illustrations.

Complete field notes must provide more than only a record of what was observed or heard. Notes also should include descriptions of the methodology: where researchers were standing while observing; how they chose people for conversation or observation; and what counts of people or events they made and why. Sprinkled throughout the notes should be a record of the researchers' feelings and thoughts while observing: when they were disgusted by some statement or act, when they felt threatened or intimidated, why their attention shifted from one group to another. Notes like these provide a foundation for later review of the likelihood of bias or inattention to some salient features of the situation.

Managing the Personal Dimensions

Our overview of participant observation is not complete without considering its personal dimensions. Because field researchers become a part of the social situation they are studying, they cannot help but be affected on a personal, emotional level. At the same time, those being studied react to researchers not just as researchers but as personal acquaintances— often as friends, sometimes as personal rivals. Managing and learning from this personal side of field research is an important part of any project.

The impact of personal issues varies with the depth of researchers' involvement in the setting. The more involved researchers are in multiple aspects of the ongoing social situation, the more important personal issues become and the greater the risk of "going native." Even when researchers acknowledge their role, "increased contact brings sympathy, and sympathy in its turn dulls the edge of criticism" (Fenno 1978: 277).

There is no formula for successfully managing the personal dimension of field research. It is much more art than science and flows more from the researcher's own personality and natural approach to other people than from formal training. Novice field researchers often neglect to consider how they will manage personal relationships when they plan and carry out their projects. Then, suddenly, they find themselves doing something they do not believe they should, just to stay in the good graces of research subjects, or juggling the emotions resulting from conflict within the group. As Whyte (1943) notes, these issues are even more salient when researchers place themselves in potentially dangerous situations. As Decker and Van Winkle (1996) explain:

> In part, gang members were of interest to us because of their involvement in violence. Because of this, we took steps to insure our own safety. One of the guiding principles was to limit the number of people being separately interviewed at the same time and location. In addition, we steadfastly avoided interviewing members of rival gangs at the same time. The field ethnographer carried a portable phone with him at all times, to insure that he could check in with us and we with him. Despite our best efforts, there were occasions when these precautions did not work. The field ethnographer witnessed several drive-by shootings while on the way to pick up interview subjects, and on one occasion, he saw three of our subjects shot while waiting to be picked up for an interview . . . Not all exposure to risk of physical danger comes through such obvious means, however; during one interview, when asked whether he owned any guns, a gang member reached into his coat pocket and pulled out a .32 caliber pistol. We assured him that we would have taken his word for it. (1996: 46)

If you plan a field research project, there are some general guidelines to follow:

- Take the time to consider how you want to relate to your potential subjects as people.
- Speculate about what personal problems might arise and how you will respond to them.
- Keep in touch with other researchers and personal friends outside the research setting.
- Maintain standards of conduct that make you comfortable as a person and that respect the integrity of your subjects (Whyte 1943: 300–317).

SYSTEMATIC OBSERVATION

Observations can be made in a more systematic, quantitative design that allows systematic comparisons and more confident generalizations. A researcher using systematic observation develops a standard form on which to record variation within the observed setting in terms of variables of interest. Such variables might include the frequency of some behavior(s), the particular people observed, the weather or other environmental conditions, and the number and state of repair of physical structures. In some systematic observation studies, records will be obtained from a random sample of places or times.

Case Study: Systematic Observation in Chicago Neighborhoods

You first learned about Robert Sampson and Stephen Raudenbush's (1999) study of disorder and crime in urban neighborhoods in chapter 4. In this section, we'll elaborate on their use of the method of systematic social observation of public spaces to learn about these neighborhoods. A **systematic observational** strategy increases the reliability of observational data by using explicit rules that standardize coding practices across observers (Reiss 1971). It is a method particularly well suited to overcoming one of the limitations of survey research on crime and disorder: Residents who are fearful of crime perceive more neighborhood disorder than do residents who are less fearful, even though both are observing the same neighborhood (Sampson & Raudenbush 1999: 606).

This ambitious multiple methods investigation combined observational research, survey research, and archival research. The observational component involved a stratified probability (random) sample of 196 Chicago census tracts. A specially equipped sport utility vehicle was driven down each street in these tracts at the rate of 5 miles per hour. Two video recorders taped the blocks on both sides of the street, while two observers peered out the vehicle's windows and recorded their observations in logs. The result was an observational record of 23,816 face blocks (the block on one side of the street is a face block). The observers recorded in their logs codes that indicated land use, traffic, physical conditions, and evidence of physical disorder (see Exhibit 7.3). The videotapes were sampled and then coded for 126 variables, including housing characteristics, businesses, and social interactions. Physical disorder was measured by counting such features as cigarettes or cigars in the street, garbage, empty beer bottles, graffiti, condoms, and syringes. Indicators of social disorder included adults loitering, drinking alcohol in public, fighting, and selling drugs.

Sampson and Raudenbush (1999) also measured crime levels with data from police records, census tract socioeconomic characteristics with census data, and resident attitudes and behavior with a survey. This study illustrates both the value of multiple methods and the technique of recording observations in a form from which quantitative data can be obtained. The systematic observations give us much greater confidence in the measurement of relative neighborhood disorder than we would have in unstructured descriptive reports or in responses of residents to survey questions. However, for some purposes, it might be more important to know how disordered the neighborhood is in the eyes of the residents, so interviews might be preferred or perhaps participant observation reports on "what it is really like."

EXHIBIT 7.3 Neighborhood Disorder Indicators Used in Systematic Observation Log

Variable	Category	Frequency
Physical Disorder		
Cigarettes, cigars on street or gutter	no	6,815
	yes	16,758
Garbage, litter on street or sidewalk	no	11,680
	yes	11,925
Empty beer bottles visible in street	no	17,653
	yes	5,870
Tagging graffiti	no	12,859
	yes	2,252
Graffiti painted over	no	13,390
	yes	1,721
Gang graffiti	no	14,138
	yes	973
Abandoned cars	no	22,782
	yes	806
Condoms on sidewalk	no	23,331
	yes	231
Needles or syringes on sidewalk	no	23,392
	yes	173
Political message graffiti	no	15,097
	yes	14
Social Disorder		
Adults loitering or congregating	no	14,250
	yes	861
People drinking alcohol	no	15,075
	yes	36
Peer group, gang indicators present	no	15,091
	yes	20
People intoxicated	no	15,093
	yes	18
Adults fighting or hostilely arguing	no	15,099
	yes	12
Prostitutes on street	no	15,100
	yes	11
People selling drugs	no	15,099
	yes	12

Source: Raudenbush, Stephen W. and Robert J. Sampson. 1999. "Ecometrics: Toward a Science of Asssessing Ecological Settings with Application to the Systematic Social Observation of Neighborhoods." *Sociological Methodology, 29:* 1–41. Reprinted with permission.

INTENSIVE INTERVIEWING

Asking questions is part of almost all participant observation (Wolcott 1995: 102–105). Many qualitative researchers employ intensive interviewing exclusively, without systematic observation of respondents in their natural setting. Unlike the more structured interviewing that may be used in survey research (discussed in chapter 6), intensive interviewing relies on open-ended questions. Qualitative researchers do not presume to know the range of answers that respondents might give, and they seek to hear these answers in the respondents' own words. Rather than asking standard questions in a fixed order, intensive interviewers allow the specific content and order of questions to vary from one interviewee to another.

What distinguishes intensive interviewing from more structured forms of questioning is consistency and thoroughness. The goal is to develop a comprehensive picture of the interviewees' background, attitudes, and actions, in their own terms; to "listen to people as they describe how they understand the worlds in which they live and work" (Rubin & Rubin 1995: 3). For example, even though Decker and Van Winkle (1996) had an interview guide, they encouraged elaboration on the part of their respondents and "went to great lengths to insure that each person we interviewed felt they had received the opportunity to tell their story in their own words" (1996: 45).

Random selection is rarely used to select respondents for intensive interviews, but the selection method still must be considered carefully. Researchers should try to select interviewees who are knowledgeable about the subject of the interview, who are open to talking, and who represent the range of perspectives (Rubin & Rubin 1995: 65–92). Selection of new interviewees should continue, if possible, at least until the **saturation point** is reached, the point when new interviews seem to yield little additional information (see Exhibit 7.4). As new issues are uncovered, additional interviewees may be selected to represent different opinions about these issues.

Research by Fleury-Steiner (2003) that examines the thoughts and emotions of jurors in death penalty cases is an excellent illustration of the tremendous insights that can be uncovered through intensive interviewing. In *Jurors' Stories of Death,* Fleury-Steiner reports on his work with the Capital Jury Project (CJP), which was a national study of the experiences of citizens who served as jurors on death penalty cases. To encourage respondents to tell stories about their experiences, the CJP survey explicitly asked jurors to tell interviewers about important moments during the trial and deliberations, and their impressions of the defendant. Fleury-Steiner states, "The goal of these questions was to facilitate jurors to construct their responses in their own ways . . . Given the leeway to answer as they saw fit, in many instances jurors' stories emerged when I least expected them to" (2003: 44).

Establishing and Maintaining a Partnership

Because intensive interviewing does not engage researchers as participants in subjects' daily affairs, the problems of entering the field are much reduced. However, the logistics of arranging long periods for personal interviews can still be fairly complicated. It is important to establish rapport with subjects by considering in advance how they will react to the interview arrangement and by developing an approach that does not violate their standards

EXHIBIT 7.4   The Saturation Point in Intensive Interviewing

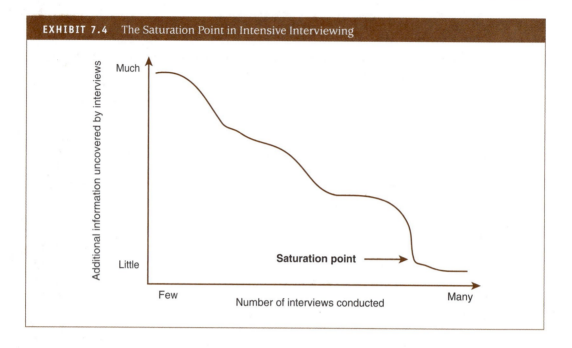

for social behavior. Interviewees should be treated with respect, as knowledgeable partners whose time is valued. (In other words, avoid being late for appointments.) A commitment to confidentiality should be stated and honored (Rubin & Rubin 1995).

But the intensive interviewer's relationship with the interviewee is not an equal partnership, for the researcher seeks to gain certain types of information and strategizes throughout to maintain an appropriate relationship (Kvale 1996: 6). In the first few minutes of the interview, the goal is to show interest in the interviewee and to clearly explain the purpose of the interview (Kvale 1996: 128). During the interview, the interviewer should maintain an appropriate distance from the interviewee, one that does not violate cultural norms; the interviewer should maintain eye contact and not engage in distracting behavior. An appropriate pace is also important; pause to allow the interviewee to reflect, elaborate, and generally not feel rushed (Gordon 1992). When an interview covers emotional or otherwise stressful topics, at the end the interviewer should give the interviewee an opportunity to unwind (Rubin & Rubin 1995: 138).

Asking Questions and Recording Answers

Intensive interviewers must plan their main questions around an outline of the interview topic. The questions should generally be short and to the point. More details can then be elicited through nondirective probes (such as "Can you tell me more about that?"), and follow-up questions can be tailored to answers to the main questions. Interviewers should strategize throughout an interview about how best to achieve their objectives while taking into account interviewees' answers.

Decker and Van Winkle's (1996) interview narrative illustrates this well:

Nearly half of the gang members identified leaders as persons who could provide
material advantage, thus ascribing a functional character to leadership within the
gang. Since half of our sample were in their early teens, someone with the ability
to procure cars, drugs, guns, or alcohol could play a valuable role in the gang.
Consequently, it was no surprise to find that over half of gang members identified
leaders as persons who could "deliver." Because of the situational nature of
leadership, persons moved in and out of this role. This was especially true in the
case of being able to provide drugs in large quantities for street sales:

Q: Does someone have more juice in the gang?
A: Yeah, you always got someone that got more juice.
Q: What is the type of person who usually has more juice?
A: The one who got the connection with the drugs.
Q: Who has the most juice?
A: Dude named T-Loc.
Q: Why does he have more juice than everybody else?
A: 'Cause he travels a lot. Gets the good stuff.
Q: What's the good stuff?
A: Like guns, cocaine, weed.
Q: What gives him the juice? (1996: 97–98)

Do you see how the interviewer actively encouraged the subject to elaborate on answers?
More importantly, intensive interviews can also uncover true meanings that questions uti-
lizing fixed formats would surely miss.

Tape recorders commonly are used to record intensive interviews. Most researchers who
have tape-recorded interviews feel that they do not inhibit most interviewees and, in fact,
are routinely ignored. The occasional respondent who is very concerned with his or her
public image may speak "for the tape recorder," but such individuals are unlikely to speak
frankly in any research interview. In any case, constant note-taking during an interview pre-
vents adequate displays of interest and appreciation by the interviewer and hinders the
degree of concentration that results in the best interviews.

FOCUS GROUPS

Focus groups are groups of unrelated individuals which are formed by a researcher and then
led in group discussion of a topic. The researcher asks specific questions and guides the discussion to ensure that group members address these questions, but the resulting information is qualitative and relatively unstructured. Unlike most other survey designs, focus
groups do not involve representative samples; instead, a few individuals are recruited for
the group who have the time to participate and who share key characteristics with the target population.

Most focus groups involve 7 to 10 people, a number that facilitates discussion by all in attendance. Although participants usually do not know one another, they are chosen so that they are relatively homogeneous, which tends to reduce their inhibitions in discussion. (Some researchers conduct discussion among groups of people who know one another, which may further reduce inhibitions.) Of course, the characteristics of individuals that determine their inclusion are based on the researcher's conception of the target population for the study. Focus group leaders must begin the discussion by creating the expectation that all will participate and that the researcher will not favor any particular perspective or participant.

Focus groups are interviewed to collect qualitative data using open-ended questions posed by the researcher (or group leader). Thus a focused discussion mimics the natural process of forming and expressing opinions and may give some sense of validity. The researcher may also want to conduct a more traditional survey, asking a representative sample of the target population to answer closed-ended questions, to weigh the validity of data obtained from the focus group. No formal procedure exists for determining the generalizability of focus group answers, but the careful researcher should conduct at least several focus groups on the same topic and check for consistency in the findings as a partial test of generalizability.

Focus group methods share with other field research techniques an emphasis on discovering unanticipated findings and exploring hidden meanings. Although they do not provide a means for developing reliable, generalizable results (the traditional strong suits of survey research), focus groups can be an indispensable aid for developing hypotheses and survey questions, for investigating the meaning of survey results, and for quickly assessing the range of opinion about an issue.

ANALYZING QUALITATIVE DATA

The distinctive features of qualitative data-collection methods are also reflected in the methods used to analyze the data collected. The focus on text, on qualitative data rather than on numbers, is the most important feature of qualitative analysis. The "text" that qualitative researchers analyze is most often transcripts of interviews or notes from participant observation sessions, but text can also refer to pictures or other images that the researcher examines.

Good qualitative data analyses are distinguished by their focus on the interrelated aspects of the setting, group, or person under investigation—the case—rather than breaking the whole into separate parts. The whole is always understood to be greater than the sum of its parts, and so the social context of events, thoughts, and actions becomes essential for interpretation. Within this framework, it does not really make sense to focus on two variables out of an interacting set of influences and test the relationship between just those two.

Qualitative data analysis is an iterative and reflexive process that begins as data are being collected rather than after data collection has ceased (Stake 1995). Next to her field notes or interview transcripts, the qualitative analyst jots down ideas about the meaning of the text and how it might relate to other issues. This process of reading through the data and interpreting them continues throughout the project. The analyst adjusts the data-collection process itself when it begins to appear that additional concepts need to be investigated or new relationships explored. This process is termed **progressive focusing** (Parlett & Hamilton 1976).

Progressive focusing The process by which a qualitative analyst interacts with the data and gradually refines his or her focus.

We want to reiterate the narrative from Venkatesh's (2000) study of gang life in a Chicago public housing project because it vividly illustrates how progressive focusing affects the entire research process as well:

[The African-American youth] read my survey instrument, informed me that "I was not going to learn shit by asking these questions," and said I would need to "hang out with them" if I really wanted to understand the experiences of African-American youth in the city. Over the next few months, I met with many of them informally to play racquetball, drink beer on the shores of Lake Michigan, attend their parties, and eat dinner with the families . . . Their views of life, getting ahead in America, the status of blacks, and "gangland" challenged some of my preconceived notions about these topics. (2000: xiv)

Qualitative Data Analysis as an Art

If you find yourself longing for the certainty of predefined measures and deductively derived hypotheses, you are beginning to understand the difference between setting out to analyze data quantitatively and planning to do so with a qualitative approach in mind. Or maybe you are now appreciating better the contrast between the positivist and interpretivist research philosophies that were summarized in chapter 2. Actually, the process of qualitative data analysis is even described by some as involving as much "art" as science, as a "dance," in the words of Miller and Crabtree (1999b). In this artful way, analyzing text involves both inductive and deductive processes. The researcher generates concepts and linkages between them based on reading the text and also checks the text to see whether those concepts and interpretations are reflected in it.

Qualitative Compared With Quantitative Data Analysis

With these points in mind, let us review the ways in which qualitative data analysis differs from quantitative analysis (Denzin & Lincoln 2000a: 8–10; Patton 2002: 13–14).

- a focus on meanings rather than on quantifiable phenomena;
- collection of many data on a few cases rather than few data on many cases;
- study in depth and detail, without predetermined categories or directions, rather than emphasis on analyses and categories determined in advance;
- conception of the researcher as an "instrument," rather than as the designer of objective instruments to measure particular variables;
- sensitivity to context rather than seeking universal generalizations;
- attention to the impact of the researcher's and others' values on the course of the analysis rather than presuming the possibility of value-free inquiry;
- a goal of rich descriptions of the world rather than measurement of specific variables.

You will also want to keep in mind features of qualitative data analysis that are shared with those of quantitative data analysis. Both qualitative and quantitative data analysis can involve making distinctions about textual data. You also know that textual data can be transposed to quantitative data through a process of categorization and counting. Some qualitative analysts also share with quantitative researchers a positivist goal of describing better the world as it "really" is, but others have adopted a postmodern goal of trying to understand how different people see and make sense of the world, without believing that there is any "correct" description.

TECHNIQUES OF QUALITATIVE DATA ANALYSIS

The most typical techniques that are shared by most approaches to qualitative data analysis include

- documentation of the data and the process of data collection;
- organization or categorization of the data into concepts;
- connection of the data to show how one concept may influence another;
- corroboration or legitimization, by evaluating alternative explanations, disconfirming evidence, and searching for negative cases; and
- representing the account (reporting the findings).

The analysis of qualitative research notes begins in the field, at the time of observation, interviewing, or both, as the researcher identifies problems and concepts that appear likely to help in understanding the situation. Simply reading the notes or transcripts is an important step in the analytic process. Researchers should make frequent notes in the margins to identify important statements and to propose ways of coding the data.

An interim stage may consist of listing the concepts reflected in the notes and diagramming the relationships among concepts (Maxwell 1996: 78–81). In a large project, weekly team meetings are an important part of this process. Miller (1999) described this process in her study of neighborhood police officers. Miller's research team met both to go over their field notes and to resolve points of confusion, as well as to dialogue with other skilled researchers who helped to identify emerging concepts:

> The fieldwork team met weekly to talk about situations that were unclear and to troubleshoot any problems. We also made use of peer-debriefing techniques. Here, multiple colleagues, who were familiar with qualitative data analysis but not involved in our research, participated in preliminary analysis of our findings. (1999: 233)

This process continues throughout the project and should assist in refining concepts during the report-writing phase, long after data collection has ceased. Let us examine each of the stages of qualitative research in more detail.

Documentation

As we noted earlier, the data for a qualitative study most often are notes jotted down in the field or during an interview—from which the original comments, observations, and feelings are reconstructed—or text transcribed from audiotapes. "The basic data are these observations and conversations, the actual words of people reproduced to the best of my ability from the field notes" (Diamond 1992: 7). What to do with all this material? Many field research projects have slowed to a halt because a novice researcher becomes overwhelmed by the quantity of information that has been collected. A one-hour interview can generate 20 to 25 pages of single-spaced text (Kvale 1996: 169). Analysis is less daunting, however, if the researcher maintains a disciplined transcription schedule.

The first formal analytical step is **documentation**. The various contacts, interviews, written documents, and whatever it is that preserves a record of what happened all need to be saved and listed. Documentation is critical to qualitative research for several reasons: It is essential for keeping track of what will be a rapidly growing volume of notes, tapes, and documents; it provides a way of developing an outline for the analytic process; and it encourages ongoing conceptualizing and strategizing about the text.

Making Sense of It: Conceptualization, Coding, and Categorizing

Identifying and refining important concepts is a key part of the iterative process of qualitative research. Sometimes conceptualizing begins with a simple observation that is interpreted directly, "pulled apart," and then put back together more meaningfully. Stake (1995) provides an example:

> More often, analytic insights are tested against new observations, the initial statement of problems and concepts is refined, the researcher then collects more data, interacts with the data again, and the process continues.

Miller (2000) provides an excellent illustration of this iterative process of conceptualization in her study of girls in gangs:

> I paid close attention to and took seriously respondents' reactions to themes raised in interviews, particularly instances in which they "talked back" by labeling a topic irrelevant, pointing out what they saw as misinterpretations on my part, or offering corrections. In my research, the women talked back the most in response to my efforts to get them to articulate how gender inequality shaped their experiences in the gang. Despite stories they told to the contrary, many maintained a strong belief in their equality within the gang . . . As the research progressed, I also took emerging themes back to respondents in subsequent interviews to see if they felt I had gotten it right. In addition to conveying that I was interested in their perspectives and experiences, this process also proved useful for further refining my analyses. (2000: 30)

The process described in this quote illustrates the reflexive nature of qualitative data collection and analysis. In qualitative research, the collection of data and their analysis are not typically mutually exclusive activities. This excerpt shows how the researcher first was alerted to a concept by observations in the field, then refined her understanding of this concept by investigating its meaning. By observing the concept's frequency of use, she came to realize its importance. Then she incorporated the concept into an explanatory model of student–patient relationships.

Examining Relationships and Displaying Data

Examining relationships is the centerpiece of the analytic process, because it allows the researcher to move from simple description of the people and settings to explanations of why things happened as they did with those people in that setting. The process of examining relationships can be captured in a **matrix** that shows how different concepts are connected, or perhaps what causes are linked with what effects.

Exhibit 7.5 provides an excellent example of a causal model developed by Baskin and Sommers (1998) to explain the desistance process for the sample of violent female offenders they interviewed in the state of New York. They described the process for the women who made it out of their lives of crime as follows:

> Desistance is a process as complex and lengthy as the process of initial involvement. It was interesting to find that some of the key concepts in initiation of deviance—social bonding, differential association, deterrence, age—were equally important in the process of desistance. We see the aging offender take the threat of punishment seriously, reestablish links with conventional society and sever associations with subcultural street elements. We found, too, that the decision to give up crime was triggered by a shock of some sort that was followed by a period of crisis. Anxious and dissatisfied, the women took stock of their lives and criminal activity. They arrived at a point at which the deviant way of life seemed senseless. (1998: 139)

Authenticating Conclusions

No set standards exist for evaluating the validity or "authenticity" of conclusions in a qualitative study, but the need to consider carefully the evidence and methods on which conclusions are based is just as great as with other types of research.

A qualitative researcher's conclusions should be assessed by his ability to provide a credible explanation for some aspect of social life. That explanation should capture group members' **tacit knowledge** of the social processes that were observed, not just their verbal statements about these processes. Tacit knowledge, "the largely unarticulated, contextual understanding that is often manifested in nods, silences, humor, and naughty nuances," is reflected in participants' actions as well as their words and in what they fail to state but nonetheless feel deeply and even take for granted (Altheide & Johnson 1994: 492–493). These features are evident in Whyte's (1955) analysis of Cornerville social patterns.

EXHIBIT 7.5   The Desistance Process for Violent Female Offenders (Baskin & Sommers 1998)

Stage 1: Problems Associated With Criminal Participation	
Socially Disjunctive Experiences Hitting rock bottom Fear of death Tiredness Illness	*Delayed Deterrence* Increased probability of punishment Increased difficulty in "doing time" Increased severity of sanctions Increasing fear
Assessment Reappraisal of life and goals Psychic change	
Decision Decision to quit or initial attempts at desistance Continuing possibility of criminal participation	
Stage 2: Restructuring of Self	
Public pronouncement of decision to end criminal participation Claim to a new identity	
Stage 3: Maintenance of the Decision to Stop	
Ability to successfully renegotiate identity Support of significant others Integration into new social networks Ties to conventional roles Stabilization of new social identity	

Source: Baskin, Deborah R. and Ira B. Sommers. 1998. *Casualties of Community Disorder: Women's Careers in Violent Crime.* Boulder, CO: Westview. Reprinted by permission of Westview Press, a member of the Perseus Books Group.

Comparing conclusions from a qualitative research project to those obtained by other researchers conducting similar projects can also increase confidence in their authenticity. Susan Miller's (1999) study of neighborhood police officers (NPOs) found striking parallels in the ways they defined their masculinity to processes reported in research about males in nursing and other traditionally female jobs:

> In part, male NPOs construct an exaggerated masculinity so that they are not seen as feminine as they carry out the social-work functions of policing. Related to this is the almost defiant expression of heterosexuality, so that the men's sexual orientation can never truly be doubted even if their gender roles are contested. Male patrol officers' language—such as their use of terms like "pansy police" to connote neighborhood police officers—served to affirm their own

heterosexuality . . . In addition, the male officers, but not the women, deliberately wove their heterosexual status into conversations, explicitly mentioning their female domestic partner or spouse and their children. This finding is consistent with research conducted in the occupational field. The studies reveal that men in female-dominated occupations, such as teachers, librarians, and pediatricians, over-reference their heterosexual status to ensure that others will not think they are gay. (1999: 222)

Reflexivity

Confidence in the conclusions from a field research study is also strengthened by an honest and informative account about how the researcher interacted with subjects in the field, what problems she encountered, and how these problems were or were not resolved. Such a "natural history" of the development of the evidence, sometimes termed **reflexivity**, enables others to evaluate the findings. Such an account is important first and foremost because of the evolving and variable nature of field research: To an important extent, the researcher "makes up" the method in the context of a particular investigation rather than applying standard procedures that are specified before the investigation begins.

Qualitative data analysts, more often than quantitative researchers, display real sensitivity to how a social situation or process is interpreted from a particular background and set of values and not simply based on the situation itself (Altheide & Johnson 1994). Researchers are only human, after all, and must rely on their own senses and process all information through their own minds. By reporting how and why they think they did what they did, they can help others determine whether, or how, the researchers' perspectives influenced their conclusions. "There should be clear 'tracks' indicating the attempt [to show the hand of the ethnographer] has been made" (Altheide & Johnson 1994: 493).

ALTERNATIVES IN QUALITATIVE DATA ANALYSIS

The qualitative data analyst can choose from many interesting alternative approaches. Of course, the research question under investigation should shape the selection of an analytic approach, but the researcher's preferences and experiences inevitably also will have an important influence on the method chosen. The alternative approaches we present here—ethnography, ethnomethodology, qualitative comparative analysis, narrative analysis, conversation analysis, case-oriented understanding, and grounded theory—give you a good sense of the different possibilities (Patton 2002).

Ethnography

Ethnography is the study of a culture or cultures that a group of people share (Van Maanen 1995: 4). As a method, it usually is meant to refer to the process of participant observation by a single investigator who immerses himself or herself in the group for a long period of time (often one or more years). Ethnographic research can also be called "naturalistic," because it seeks to describe and understand the natural social world as it really is, in all its richness and detail. There are no particular methodological techniques associated with ethnography, other than just "being there." The analytic process relies on the thoroughness and insight of the researcher to "tell it like it is" in the setting, as he or she experienced it.

Code of the Street, Anderson's (1999) award-winning study of Philadelphia's inner city, captures the flavor of this approach:

> My primary aim in this work is to render ethnographically the social and cultural dynamics of the interpersonal violence that is currently undermining the quality of life of too many urban neighborhoods . . . How do the people of the setting perceive their situation? What assumptions do they bring to their decision making? (1999: 10–11)[3]

Like most traditional ethnographers, Anderson (1999) describes his concern with being "as objective as possible" and using his training as other ethnographers do, "to look for and to recognize underlying assumptions, their own and those of their subjects, and to try to override the former and uncover the latter" (1999: 11).

From analysis of the data obtained in these ways, a rich description emerges of life in the inner city. Although we often do not "hear" the residents speak, we feel the community's pain in Anderson's (1999) description of "the aftermath of death":

> When a young life is cut down, almost everyone goes into mourning. The first thing that happens is that a crowd gathers about the site of the shooting or the incident. The police then arrive, drawing more of a crowd. Since such a death often occurs close to the victim's house, his mother or his close relatives and friends may be on the scene of the killing. When they arrive, the women and girls often wail and moan, crying out their grief for all to hear, while the young men simply look on, in studied silence . . . Soon the ambulance arrives. (1999: 138)

Anderson (1999) uses these descriptions as a foundation on which he develops the key concepts in his analysis, such as "code of the street":

> The "code of the street" is not the goal or product of any individual's action but is the fabric of everyday life, a vivid and pressing milieu within which all local residents must shape their personal routines, income strategies, and orientations to schooling, as well as their mating, parenting, and neighbor relations. (1999: 326)

This rich ethnographic tradition is being abandoned by some qualitative data analysts, however. Many have become skeptical of the ability of social scientists to perceive the social world in a way that is not distorted by their own subjective biases or to a receive impressions from the actors in that social world which are not altered by the fact of being studied (Van Maanen 2002). As a result, both specific techniques and alternative approaches to qualitative data analysis have proliferated. The next sections introduce several of these alternative approaches.

Ethnomethodology

Ethnomethodology focuses on the way that participants construct the social world in which they live—how they "create reality"—rather than on describing the social world itself. In fact, ethnomethodologists do not necessarily believe that we can find an objective reality; it is the way that participants come to create and sustain a sense of "reality" that is of interest. In the words of Gubrium and Holstein (1997), in ethnomethodology, as compared to the naturalistic orientation of ethnography, "The focus shifts from the scenic features of everyday life onto the ways through which the world comes to be experienced as real, concrete, factual, and 'out there.' An interest in members' methods of constituting their world supersedes the naturalistic project of describing members' worlds as they know them." (1997: 41)

Unlike the ethnographic analyst, who seeks to describe the social world as the participants see it, the ethnomethodological analyst seeks to maintain some distance from that world. The ethnomethodologist views a "code" of conduct like that described by Anderson (2003) not as a description of a real normative force that constrains social action, but as the way that people in the setting create a sense of order and social structure (Gubrium & Holstein 1997: 44–45). The ethnomethodologist focuses on how reality is *constructed*, not on what it *is*.

Qualitative Comparative Analysis

In previous chapters, we have discussed many studies that have attempted to explain violent crime. Another novel approach to the study of violence, specifically of homicide, was recently undertaken by Miethe, Regoeczi, and Drass (2004). In their book *Rethinking Homicide,* instead of focusing on the victim or the offender, they analyze the homicide situation as the unit of analysis, exploring the structure and process underlying the lethal outcome. They state, "Homicide situations are defined by the nexus of offender, victim, and offense elements in time and space. It is the combination of these elements, not their operation in isolation, which provides the context for lethal violence" (2004: xvii).

To analyze the homicide narratives from cases from four large cities in the United States, Miethe and colleagues used **qualitative comparative analysis** (QCA). They describe why QCA was the most appropriate methodology for their study:

> As an analytical method for case comparisons, QCA considers cases holistically, as complex configurations of attributes measured by a set of variables. It also assumes that events or outcomes are produced by variables acting together in combination. (Miethe et al., 2004: 50)

It is beyond the scope of this book to detail the process of QCA here. Readers who want more information should seek other sources (e.g., Amenta & Poulsen 1994). QCA actually combines elements of quantitative and qualitative analysis, and as such is a hybrid of sorts. For example, similar to a statistical analysis, QCA requires the specification of a model relating a set of independent variables to an outcome variable. But it examines the data holistically by developing typologies across a complex arrangement of cases and variables.

After their QCA analysis of over 400,000 homicides, Miethe and colleagues (2004) concluded that most homicides occur in situational contexts that have changed little over the past three decades. They found expressive homicides involving disputes and arguments to be more prevalent than instrumental homicides, with males being the primary perpetrators of both, but particularly of instrumental homicides. Like other research, they found that these conflicts often involved what many would call "trivial altercations" where alcohol was involved and where the victim often provoked the offender in some way (e.g., with an insult). This was particularly true for youth homicides, many of which contained elements of honor contests and issues of respect.

Narrative Analysis

Narrative "displays the goals and intentions of human actors; it makes individuals, cultures, societies, and historical epochs comprehensible as wholes" (Richardson 1995: 200). **Narrative analysis** focuses on "the story itself" and seeks to preserve the integrity of personal biographies or a series of events that cannot adequately be understood in terms of their discrete elements (Riessman 2002: 218). The coding for a narrative analysis is typically of the narratives as a whole, rather than of the different elements within them. The coding strategy revolves around reading the stories and classifying them into general patterns.

For example, Morrill et al. (2000: 534) read through 254 conflict narratives written by the ninth graders they studied and found four different types of stories:

1. *action tales,* in which the author represents himself or herself and others as acting within the parameters of taken-for-granted assumptions about what is expected for particular roles among peers;

2. *expressive tales,* in which the author focuses on strong, negative emotional responses to someone who has wronged him or her;

3. *moral tales,* in which the author recounts explicit norms that shaped his or her behavior in the story and influenced the behavior of others; and

4. *rational tales,* in which the author represents him- or herself as a rational decision maker navigating through the events of the story.[4]

Morrill et al. (2000: 553) summarize their classification of the youth narratives in a simple table that highlights the frequency of each type of narrative and the characteristics associated with each of them. How does such an analysis contribute to our understanding of youth violence? Morrill and colleagues first emphasize that their narratives "suggest that consciousness of conflict among youths—like that among adults—is not a singular entity, but comprises a rich and diverse range of perspectives" (2000: 551).

In this way, Morrill et al.'s (2000) narrative analysis allowed an understanding of youth conflict to emerge from the youths' own stories while also informing our understanding of broader social theories and processes.

Conversation Analysis

Conversation analysis is a specific qualitative method for analyzing ordinary conversation. Unlike narrative analysis, it focuses on the sequence and details of conversational interaction, rather than on the "stories" that people are telling. Like ethnomethodology (from which it developed), conversation analysis focuses on how reality is constructed, rather than on what it *is*. Three premises guide conversation analysis (Gubrium & Holstein 2000: 492):

1. Interaction is sequentially organized, and talk can be analyzed in terms of the process of social interaction rather than in terms of motives or social status.
2. Talk, as a process of social interaction, is contextually oriented; it is both shaped by interaction and creates the social context of that interaction.
3. These processes are involved in all social interaction, so no interactive details are irrelevant to understanding it.

Consider these premises as you read the following dialogue between British researcher Ann Phoenix (2003) and a boy she called "Thomas" in her study of notions of masculinity, bullying, and academic performance among 11- to 14-year-old boys in 12 London schools.

Thomas: *It's your attitude, but some people are bullied for no reason whatsoever just because other people are jealous of them . . .*

Q: *How do they get bullied?*

Thomas: *There's a boy in our year called James, and he's really clever and he's basically got no friends, and that's really sad because . . . He gets top marks in every test and everyone hates him. I mean, I like him.* (2003: 235)

Do you see how Thomas's presentation of himself reflected his interchange with the researcher as she probed his orientation? Do you imagine that his talk would have been quite different if this conversation had been with other boys?

Case-Oriented Understanding

A **case-oriented understanding** attempts to understand a phenomenon from the standpoint of the participants. The case-oriented understanding method reflects an interpretive research philosophy that is not geared to identifying causes but provides a different way to explain social phenomena. For example, Fischer and Wertz (2002) constructed such an explanation of the effect of being criminally victimized. They first recounted crime victims' stories and then identified common themes in these stories.

Their explanation began with a description of what they termed the process of "living routinely" before the crime: "He/she . . . feels that the defended against crime could never happen to him/her. I said, 'nah, you've got to be kidding.'"

In a second stage, "being disrupted," the victim copes with the discovered crime and fears worst outcomes: "You imagine the worst when it's happening . . . I just kept thinking my baby's upstairs." In a later stage, "reintegrating," the victim begins to assimilate the violation by taking some protective action: "But I clean out my purse now since then and I leave very little of that kind of stuff in there."

Finally, when the victim is "going on," he or she reflects on the changes the crime produced: "I don't think it made me stronger. It made me smarter."

You can see how Fischer and Wertz (2002: 288–290) constructed an explanation of the effect of crime on its victims through this analysis of the process of responding to the experience. This effort to "understand" what happened in these cases gives us a much better sense of why things happened as they did.

Grounded Theory

Theory development occurs continually in qualitative data analysis (Coffey & Atkinson 1996: 23). The goal of many qualitative researchers is to create **grounded theory**—that is, to inductively build up a systematic theory that is "grounded" in, or based on, the observations. The observations are summarized into conceptual categories, which are tested directly in the research setting with more observations. Over time, as the conceptual categories are refined and linked, a theory evolves (Glaser & Strauss 1967; Huberman & Miles 1994: 436). Exhibit 7.6 illustrates this process.

As observation, interviewing, and reflection continue, researchers refine their definitions of problems and concepts, and select indicators. They can then check the frequency and distribution of phenomena: How many people made a particular type of comment? How often did social interaction lead to arguments? Social system models may then be developed, which specify the relationships among different phenomena. These models are modified as researchers gain experience in the setting. For the final analysis, the researchers check their models carefully against their notes and make a concerted attempt to discover negative evidence that might suggest the model is incorrect.

EXHIBIT 7.6   The Development of Grounded Theory

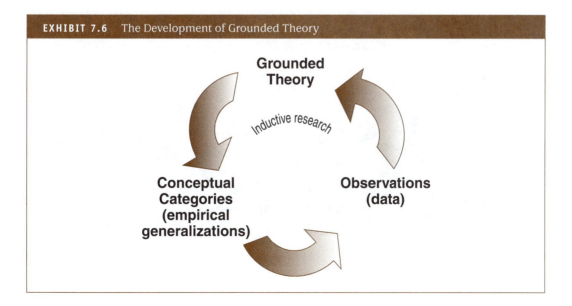

VISUAL SOCIOLOGY

For about 150 years, people have been creating a record of the social world with photography. This creates the possibility of "observing" the social world through photographs and films and of interpreting the resulting images as a "text." It is no surprise that visual sociology has been developed as a method both to learn how others "see" the social world and to create images of it for further study. As in the analysis of written text, however, the visual sociologist must be sensitive to the way in which a photograph or film "constructs" the reality that it depicts.

An analysis by Margolis (2004) of photographic representations of American Indian boarding schools provides an idea of the value of analysis of photographs (see Exhibit 7.7). On the left is a picture taken in 1886 of Chiricahua Apaches who had just arrived at the Carlisle Indian School in Carlisle, Pennsylvania. The school was run by a Captain Richard Pratt who, like many Americans in that period, felt tribal societies were communistic, indolent, dirty, and ignorant, while Western civilization was industrious and individualistic. So Captain Pratt set out to acculturate American Indians to the dominant culture. The second picture shows the result: the same group of Apaches looking like Europeans, not Native Americans, dressed in standard uniforms, with standard haircuts, and with more standard posture.

Many other pictures display the same type of transformation. Are these pictures each "worth a thousand words?" They capture the ideology of the school management, but we can be less certain that they document accurately the "before and after" status of the students.

Captain Pratt "consciously used photography to represent the boarding school mission as successful" (Margolis 2004: 79). While he clearly tried to ensure a high degree of conformity, there were accusations that the contrasting images were exaggerated to overemphasize the change (Margolis 2004: 78). Reality was being constructed, not just depicted, in these photographs.

EXHIBIT 7.7   Pictures of Chiricahua Apache Children Before and After Starting Carlisle Indian School, Carlisle, Pennsylvania, 1886

Chiricahua Apache Children Upon Arrival at Carlisle School.

Chiricahua Apache Children After 4 Months at Carlisle School.

Source: Margolis (2004: 78).

Visual sociology will certainly become an increasingly important aspect of qualitative analyses of social settings and the people in them. The result will be richer descriptions of the social world, but whether you examine or also produce pictures for such analyses, remember Darren Newbury's (2005) reminder to readers of his journal, *Visual Studies*, that "images cannot be simply taken of the world, but have to be made within it" (2005: 1). Pictures, like other "text," are partly a social construction.

Computer-Assisted Qualitative Data Analysis

The analysis process can be enhanced in various ways by using a computer. Programs designed for qualitative data can speed up the analysis process, make it easier for researchers to experiment with different codes, test different hypotheses about relationships, and facilitate diagrams of emerging theories and preparation of research reports (Coffey & Atkinson 1996; Richards & Richards 1994). The steps involved in **computer-assisted qualitative data analysis** parallel those used traditionally to analyze such text as notes, documents, or interview transcripts: preparation, coding, analysis, and reporting. We use two of the most popular programs to illustrate these steps: HyperRESEARCH and QSR NVivo. (See the Student Study Site, www.sagepub.com/frccjstudy, for an extended introduction to HyperRESEARCH. The software itself and the HyperRESEARCH tutorials are found on the study site as well.)

Text preparation begins with typing or scanning text in a word processor or, with NVivo, directly into the program's rich text editor. NVivo will create or import a rich text file. HyperRESEARCH requires that your text be saved as a text file (as "ASCII" in most word processors) before you transfer it into the analysis program. HyperRESEARCH expects your text data to be stored in separate files corresponding to each unique case, such as an interview with one subject.

Coding the text involves categorizing particular text segments. This is the foundation of much qualitative analysis. Either program allows you to assign a code to any segment of text (in NVivo, you drag through the characters to select them; in HyperRESEARCH, you click on the first and last words to select text). You can make up codes as you go through a document and also assign codes that you have already developed to text segments. You can also have the programs "autocode" text by identifying a word or phrase that should always receive the same code, or, in NVivo, by coding each section identified by the style of the rich text document, for example, each question or speaker (of course, you should check carefully the results of autocoding). Both programs also let you examine the coded text "in context," embedded in its place in the original document.

Analysis focuses on reviewing cases or text segments with similar codes and examining relationships among different codes. You may decide to combine codes into larger concepts. You may specify additional codes to capture more fully the variation among cases. You can test hypotheses about relationships among codes.

Reports from both programs can include text to illustrate the cases, codes, and relationships that you specify. You can also generate counts of code frequencies and then import these counts into a statistical program for quantitative analysis. However, the many types of analyses and reports that can be developed with qualitative analysis software do not lessen the need for a careful evaluation of the quality of the data on which conclusions are based.

In reality, using a qualitative data analysis computer program is not always as straightforward as it appears. Scott Decker and Barrik Van Winkle (1996) describe the difficulty they faced in using a computer program to identify instances of the concept of "drug sales":

> The software we used is essentially a text retrieval package . . . One of the dilemmas faced in the use of such software is whether to employ a coding scheme within the interviews or simply to leave them as unmarked text. We chose the first alternative, embedding conceptual tags at the appropriate points in the text. An example illustrates this process. One of the activities we were concerned with was drug sales. Our first chore (after a thorough reading of all the transcripts) was to use the software to "isolate" all of the transcript sections dealing with drug sales.
>
> One way to do this would be to search the transcripts for every instance in which the word "drugs" was used. However, such a strategy would have the disadvantages of providing information of too general a character while often missing important statements about drugs. Searching on the word "drugs" would have produced a file including every time the word was used, whether it was in reference to drug sales, drug use, or drug availability—clearly more information than we were interested in. However, such a search would have failed to find all of the slang used to refer to drugs ("boy" for heroin, "Casper" for crack cocaine) as well as the more common descriptions of drugs, especially rock or crack cocaine. (1996: 53–54)

Decker and Van Winkle solved this problem by parenthetically inserting conceptual tags in the text whenever talk of drug sales was found. This process allowed them to examine all the statements made by gang members about a single concept (drug sales). As you can imagine, though, this still left the researchers with many pages of transcripts material to analyze.

ETHICAL ISSUES IN QUALITATIVE RESEARCH

Qualitative research can raise some complex ethical issues. No matter how hard the field researcher strives to study the social world naturally, leaving no traces, the very act of research itself imposes something unnatural on the situation. It is up to the researchers to identify and take responsibility for the consequences of their involvement. Four main ethical issues arise: voluntary participation, subject wellbeing, identity disclosure, and confidentiality.

Voluntary Participation

Ensuring that subjects are participating in a study voluntarily is not often a problem with intensive interviewing and focus group research, but it is often a point of contention in participant observation studies. Few researchers or institutional review boards are willing to condone covert participation because it does not offer a way to ensure that participation by the subjects is voluntary. Even when the researcher's role is more open, interpreting the standard of voluntary participation still can be difficult. Practically, much field research would be impossible if the participant observer were required to request permission of everyone having some contact, no matter how minimal, with a group or setting being observed. And should the requirement of voluntary participation apply equally to every member of an organization being observed? What if the manager consents, the workers are ambivalent, and the union says no? Requiring everyone's consent would limit participant observation research only to settings without serious conflicts of interest.

The issue of voluntary participation is particularly important when interviewing or observing minors. At what age can individuals validly give their voluntary consent to participate in a project? It is customary for human subjects committees to want the consent of parents when their children are participating in research. This requirement poses a problem for research that may be investigating issues that parents or guardians may not want uncovered, such as abuse or neglect. In other instances, alerting parents or guardians about the nature of the study may compromise the confidentiality of the participants. For example, if Decker and Van Winkle (1996) had been forced to obtain parental approval for their gang member interviews, it would have violated the confidentiality they tried to provide to their respondents. To assure the human subjects committee that their participants understood their rights, Decker and Van Winkle obtained an advocate for each juvenile member of their sample. This advocate was responsible for making sure that the juveniles each understood their right to refuse or quit the interview at any time without penalty and the confidential nature of the project. Only after these issues were carefully explained did the participant sign a consent form.

Subject Wellbeing

Before beginning a project, every field researcher should carefully consider how to avoid harm to subjects. It is not possible to avoid every theoretical possibility of harm or to be sure that any project will not cause adverse consequences to any individual. Some of the Cornerville men read Whyte's book and felt discomfited by it (others found it enlightening). Direct harm to the reputations or feelings of particular individuals is what researchers must carefully avoid. They can do so in part by maintaining the confidentiality of research subjects. They must also avoid adversely affecting the course of events while engaged in a setting.

Jody Miller (2000) encountered a unique ethical dilemma while she was recruiting young women from a residential facility by paying them to refer other girls who were gang members to her research. These referral gratuities are common in snowball samples like this. Unfortunately, in this case one young woman decided to cash in on the deal by initiating new young women into her gang. The ethical dilemma regarding "subject wellbeing" in this case was that the initiation ceremony for this particular gang involved recruits to the gang being "beaten into the gang." Miller decided to stop conducting research at this location and ultimately lost several interviews. She states,

> It was a difficult decision to make because I had struggled for so long to locate gang girls in Columbus [Missouri]. Ultimately, I believe it was the right thing to do. My presence had stirred up trouble for the agency, and I had an ethical obligation to back away, regardless of the cost to me. (2000: 26)

Identity Disclosure

We have considered already the problems of identity disclosure, particularly in the case of covert participation. But how much disclosure about the study is necessary, and how hard should researchers try to make sure that their research purposes are understood? Less-educated subjects may not readily comprehend what a researcher is or be able to weigh the possible consequences of the research for themselves. Should researchers inform subjects if the study's interests and foci change while it is in progress? Current ethical standards require informed consent of research subjects; can this standard be met in any meaningful way if researchers do not fully disclose their identity? But isn't some degree of dissimulation a natural part of social life (Punch 1994: 91)? Can a balance be struck between the disclosure of critical facts and a coherent research strategy?

Confidentiality

Field researchers normally use fictitious names for the characters in their reports, but doing so does not always guarantee confidentiality for their research subjects. Individuals in the setting studied may be able to identify those whose actions are described and may thus become privy to some knowledge about their colleagues or neighbors that had formerly been kept from them. Researchers should thus make every effort to expunge possible identifying material from published information and to alter unimportant aspects of a description when necessary to prevent identity disclosure. In any case, no field research project should begin if it is clear that some participants will suffer serious harm by being identified in project publications.

Confidentiality is particularly important if the research is uncovering deviant or illegal behavior. In research such as Decker and Van Winkle's (1996), it was almost inevitable that their information about illegal activity would be revealed during the course of observing or interviewing. Because they had promised confidentiality to their interviewees, Decker and Van Winkle did not use specific information they gained about past crimes; they would only refer to this activity in an aggregate form to describe the activities of gang members in general. They state, "had we violated this promise [of confidentiality], we would have placed the lives of several individuals (including the field-worker) in jeopardy." In addition, Decker and Van Winkle told their subjects that they did not want to know about information concerning future crimes, as this information would not be protected by their pledge of confidentiality.

These ethical issues cannot be evaluated independently. The final decision to proceed must be made after weighing the relative benefits and risks to participants. Few qualitative research projects will be barred by consideration of these ethical issues, except for those involving covert participation. The more important concern for researchers is to identify the ethically troublesome aspects of their proposed research, resolve them before the project begins, and act on new ethical issues as they come up during the project. Combining methods is often the best strategy.

Ethics in Qualitative Data Analysis

Analyzing qualitative data also poses ethical issues. Miles and Huberman (1994: 293–295) suggest several specific questions that are of particular importance during the process of data analysis:

Intervention and advocacy. "What do I do when I see harmful, illegal, or wrongful behavior on the part of others during a study? Should I speak for anyone's interests besides my own? If so, whose interests do I advocate?" Maintaining what is called "guilty knowledge" may force the researcher to suppress some parts of the analysis so as not to disclose the wrongful behavior, but presenting "what really happened" in a report may prevent ongoing access and violate understandings with participants.

Research integrity and quality. "Is my study being conducted carefully, thoughtfully, and correctly in terms of some reasonable set of standards?" Real analyses have real consequences, so you owe it to yourself and those you study to adhere strictly to the analysis methods that you believe will produce authentic, valid conclusions.

Ownership of data and conclusions. "Who owns my field notes and analyses: I, my organization, my funders? And once my reports are written, who controls their diffusion?" Of course, these concerns arise in any social research project, but the intimate involvement of the qualitative researcher with participants in the setting studied makes conflicts of interest between different stakeholders much more difficult to resolve. Working through the issues as they arise is essential.

Use and misuse of results. "Do I have an obligation to help my findings be used appropriately? What if they are used harmfully or wrongly?" It is prudent to develop understandings early in the project with all major stakeholders that specify what actions will be taken in order to encourage appropriate use of project results and to respond to what is considered misuse of these results.

CONCLUSION

Qualitative research allows the careful investigator to obtain a richer and more intimate view of the social world than can be achieved with more structured methods. It is not hard to understand why so many qualitative studies have become classics in the literature. And the emphases in qualitative research on inductive reasoning and incremental understanding help to stimulate and inform other research approaches. Exploratory research to chart the dimensions of previously unstudied social settings and intensive investigations of the subjective meanings that motivate individual action are particularly well served by the techniques of participant observation, intensive interviewing, and focus groups.

The very characteristics that make qualitative research techniques so appealing restrict their use to a limited set of research problems. It is not possible to draw representative samples for study using participant observation, and for this reason the generalizability of any particular field study's results cannot really be known. Only the accumulation of findings from numerous qualitative studies permits confident generalization, but here again the time and effort required to collect and analyze the data make it unlikely that many particular field research studies will be replicated.

Even if qualitative researchers made an effort to replicate key studies, their notion of developing and grounding explanations inductively in the observations made in a particular setting would hamper comparison of findings. Measurement reliability is thereby hindered, as are systematic tests for the validity of key indicators and formal tests for causal connections.

In the final analysis, qualitative research involves a mode of thinking and investigating different from that used in experimental and survey research. Qualitative research is inductive and idiographic; experiments and surveys tend to be conducted in a deductive, quantitative framework. Both approaches can help social scientists learn about the social world; the proficient researcher must be ready to use either. Qualitative data are often supplemented with many quantitative characteristics or activities. And, as you have already seen, quantitative data are often enriched with written comments and observations, and focus groups have become a common tool of survey researchers seeking to develop their questionnaires. Thus the distinction between qualitative and quantitative research techniques is not always clear-cut.

KEY TERMS

Case-oriented understanding	Jottings
Complete observation	Matrix
Computer-assisted qualitative data analysis	Narrative analysis
Conversation analysis	Participant observation
Covert (complete) participation	Progressive focusing
Documentation	Qualitative comparative analysis (QCA)
Ethnography	Qualitative methods
Ethnomethodology	Reactive effect
Experience sampling method (ESM)	Reflexivity
Field notes	Saturation point
Field research	Systematic observation
Focus group	Tacit knowledge
Grounded theory	Theoretical sampling
Intensive interviewing	Thick description

HIGHLIGHTS

- Qualitative researchers tend to develop ideas inductively, try to understand the social context and sequential nature of attitudes and actions, and explore the subjective meanings that participants attach to events. They rely primarily on participant observation, intensive interviewing, and, in recent years, focus groups.

- Participant observers may adopt one of several roles for a particular research project. Each role represents a different balance between observing and participating, which may or may not include public acknowledgment of the researcher's real identity. Many field researchers prefer a moderate role, participating as well as observing in a group but publicly acknowledging the researcher role.

- Field researchers must develop strategies for entering the field, developing and maintaining relations in the field, sampling, and recording and analyzing data.

- Recording and analyzing notes is a crucial step in field research. Detailed notes should be recorded and analyzed daily to refine methods and to develop concepts, indicators, and models of the social system observed.

- Intensive interviews involve open-ended questions and follow-up probes, with the content and order of specific questions varying from one interview to the next.

- Focus groups combine elements of participant observation and intensive interviewing. They can increase the validity of attitude measurement by revealing what people say when presenting their opinions in a group context.

- Case studies use thick description and other qualitative techniques to provide a holistic picture of a setting or group.

- Narrative analysis attempts to understand a life or a series of events as they unfolded, in a meaningful progression.

- Grounded theory connotes a general explanation that develops in interaction with the data and is continually tested and refined as data collection continues.

- The four main ethical issues in field research concern voluntary participation, subject wellbeing, identity disclosure, and confidentiality.

EXERCISES

Discussing Research

1. Review the experiments and surveys described in previous chapters. Choose one and propose a field research design that would focus on the same research question but with participant observation techniques in a local setting. Propose the role that you would play in the setting, along the participant observation continuum, and explain why you would favor this role. Describe the stages of your field research study, including your plans for entering the field, developing and maintaining relationships, sampling, and recording and analyzing data. Then discuss what you would expect your study to add to the findings resulting from the study described in the book.

2. Develop an interview guide that focuses on a research question addressed in one of the studies in this book. Using this guide, conduct an intensive interview with one person who is involved with the topic in some way. Take only brief notes during the interview, and then write as complete a record of the interviews as you can immediately afterward. Turn in an evaluation of your performance as an interviewer and note-taker, together with your notes.

3. Find the Qualitative Research lesson in the interactive exercises on the Student Study Site, www.sagepub.com/frccjstudy. Answer the questions in this lesson in order to review the types of ethical issues that can arise in the course of participant observation research.

Finding Research

1. Go to the *Annual Review of Sociology*'s website by following the publication link at http://soc.AnnualReviews.org. Search for articles that use field research as the primary method of gathering data on gangs or delinquency. Find at least three articles and report on the specific method of field research used in each.

2. Search the web for information on focus groups (previous, upcoming, or ongoing) involving victims, offenders, fear of crime, crime prevention, or another criminological

topic. List the websites you find, and write a paragraph about the purpose of each focus group and the sample involved. How might these focus groups be used to influence public policy?

Critiquing Research

1. Read and summarize one of the qualitative studies discussed in this chapter or another classic study recommended by your instructor. Review and critique the study using the article review questions presented in Appendix B. What questions are answered by the study? What questions are raised for further investigation?

2. Read the complete text of one of the qualitative studies presented in this chapter and evaluate its conclusions for authenticity, using the criteria in this chapter.

3. Review one of the articles on the book Study Site, www.sagepub.com/frccjstudy, that used qualitative methods. Describe the data that were collected, and identify the steps used in the analysis. What type of qualitative data analysis was this? If it is not one of the methods presented in this chapter, describe its similarities to and differences from one of these methods. How confident are you in the conclusions, given the methods of analysis used?

Developing a Research Proposal

Add a qualitative component to your proposed study. You can choose to do this with a participant observation project or intensive interviewing. Choose the method that seems most likely to help answer the research question for the overall survey project.

1. For a participant observation component, propose an observational plan that would complement the overall survey project. Present in your proposal the following information about your plan:
   a. Choose a site and justify its selection in terms of its likely value for the research.
   b. Choose a role along the participation–observation continuum and justify your choice.
   c. Describe access procedures and note any likely problems.
   d. Discuss how you will develop and maintain relations in the site.
   e. Review any sampling issues.
   f. Present an overview of the way in which you will analyze the data you collect.

2. For an intensive interview component, propose a focus for the intensive interviews that you believe will add the most to findings from the survey project. Present in your proposal the following information about your plan:
   a. Present and justify a method for selecting individuals to interview.
   b. Write out three introductory biographical questions and five "grand tour" questions for your interview schedule.
   c. List at least six different probes you may use.
   d. Present and justify at least two follow-up questions for one of your grand tour questions.
   e. Explain what you expect this intensive interview component to add to your overall survey project.

3. Which qualitative data analysis alternative is most appropriate for the qualitative data you proposed to collect for your project? Using the approach, develop a strategy for using the techniques of qualitative data analysis to analyze your textual data.

Making Research Ethical

1. The April 1992 issue of the *Journal of Contemporary Ethnography* is devoted to a series of essays reevaluating Whyte's (1943) classic field study, *Street Corner Society*. A social scientist interviewed some of the people described in Whyte's book and concluded that the researcher had made methodological and ethical errors. Whyte and others offer able rejoinders and further commentary. Reading the entire issue of this journal will improve your appreciation of the issues that field researchers confront.

2. Covert participation may be the only way for researchers to observe the inner workings of some criminal or other deviant groups, but this strategy is likely to result in the researcher witnessing, and perhaps being asked to participate in, illegal acts. Do you think that covert participation is ever ethical? If so, under what conditions? Can the standards of "no harm to subjects," "identity disclosure," and "voluntary" participation be maintained in covert research?

3. A *New York Times* reporter (Wines 2006) recently talked about the dilemma many reporters have: whether or not to provide monetary or other compensation, like food or medical supplies, to people they interview for a story. In journalism, paying for information is a "cardinal sin" because journalists are "indoctrinated with the notion that they are observers." They are trained to report on situations, but not to influence a situation. This is what many scholars believe a researcher's role should be. Nevertheless, as we learned in this chapter, it is common in research to offer small gratuities for information and interviews. However, does paying for information unduly influence the truthfulness of the information being sought? What are your thoughts on paying for information? What if you were investigating the problems faced by families living below the poverty level and during an interview you noticed that the family refrigerator and cupboards were empty and the baby was crying from hunger? What is the ethical reaction? If you believe the most ethical response would be to provide food or money for food, is it fair that there is another family next door in the same condition who did not happen to be on your interview list? How should gratuities be handled?

Performing Data Analysis in SPSS

The YOUTH.POR data set includes some questions on opinions regarding friends' attitudes toward delinquent acts and the extent to which getting caught for committing a crime would negatively affect the respondent's life.

1. Describe the opinions about friends' attitudes and personal misfortune based on the frequencies for these variables (V77; V79; V109; V119).

2. What explanation can you develop (inductively) for these attitudes? Do you believe that either friends' attitudes toward delinquent acts or getting caught for committing a crime would influence behavior? Explain.

3. Propose a participant observation, a focus group, or an intensive interview study to explore these attitudes further. Identify the sample for the study, and describe how you would carry out your observations, focus groups, or interviews.

Student Study Site

The companion Student Study Website for *The Fundamentals of Research in Criminology and Criminal Justice* can be found at www.sagepub.com/frccjstudy.

Visit the Student Study Site to enhance your understanding of the chapter content and to discover additional resources that will take your learning one step further. You can enhance your understanding of the chapters by using the comprehensive study material, which includes interactive exercises, e-flashcards, web exercises, practice self-tests, and more. You will also find special features, such as Learning from Journal Articles, which incorporates SAGE's online journal collection.

NOTES

1. From *Life in the Gang: Family, Friends, and Violence* by Decker, S. H., Winkle, B. van, Blumstein, A., & Farrington, D. P., pp. 97–98, copyright © 1996. Reprinted with permission of Cambridge University Press.

2. From *Street Corner Society: The Social Structure of an Italian Slum*, pp. vndashvii, by Whyte, W. F., copyright © 1943. Reprinted with permission of The University of Chicago Press.

3. From *Code of the Street: Decency, Violence, and the Moral Life of the Inner City* by Elijah Anderson. Copyright © 1999 by Elijah Anderson. Used by permission of W. W. Norton & Company, Inc.

4. From Morrill, et al., "Telling Tales in School: Youth Culture and Conflict Narratives," *Law & Society Review* 34. Copyright © Blackwell. Reprinted with permission from Blackwell.

CHAPTER 8

Analyzing Content

Crime Mapping and Historical, Secondary, and Content Analysis

The research methods we have examined so far have relied on researchers collecting the data or information themselves. Increasingly, however, those interested in criminological research questions are relying on data previously collected by other investigators (Riedel 2000). As we noted in chapter 1, this is referred to as secondary data analysis. Secondary data analysis is simply the act of collecting or analyzing data that were originally collected for another purpose (Riedel 2000). Thus, if a researcher goes to a police department and personally compiles information from police reports to examine a research question, that researcher is still engaging in secondary data analysis because the police records were originally collected for another purpose.

In this chapter, we will tell you about a number of data sets, including surveys and official records, which are publicly available for research purposes. Then we examine several research methods that rely on secondary data, including historical events research, cross-cultural research, content analysis, and crime mapping. Next we highlight the strengths and weaknesses of all types of methods and illustrate the importance of triangulating two or more methods when possible. Because using data originally gathered for other purposes poses unique concerns for a researcher, we spend the latter part of the chapter highlighting these methodological issues.

WHAT IS SECONDARY DATA?

In general, there are four major types of secondary data: surveys, official statistics, official records, and other historical documents. Although a data set can be obtained by an agreement between two or more researchers, many researchers obtain data through the Inter-University Consortium for Political and Social Research (ICPSR) (www.icpsr.umich.edu). Data stored at ICPSR primarily include surveys, official records, and official statistics. ICPSR stores data and information for nearly 5,000 sources and studies, including those conducted independently and those conducted by the U.S. government.

Case Study: Gender and Offending

The research possibilities are almost limitless with the wealth of data already made available to researchers interested in issues of criminology and criminal justice. For example, Heimer and De Coster (1999) used the National Youth Survey to examine the mechanisms explaining variation in violent delinquency between male and female youth. Generally, studies of self-reported violent delinquency find gender ratios (self-reports of delinquency of males to females) ranging from approximately 1.1 to 5.3, depending on the specific aggressive offense being measured. These ratios show that, although males generally commit more violent acts than females, young females do engage in violence.

One of the primary mechanisms related to violent offending that Heimer and De Coster (1999) examined was "cultural definitions of violence." Specifically, according to differential association theory, interaction with others and social structural context are important because they shape the learning of violent definitions, which in turn affects the likelihood that youths engage in violent delinquency. Heimer and De Coster believed that one factor affecting the violent offending disparities between young males and females was that, on average, boys tend to acquire more violent definitions than girls. In addition, the "gender definitions" held by boys and girls are different: femininity often is equated with a high capacity for nurturance and a tendency toward passivity rather than aggressiveness. In contrast, masculinity tends to be equated with competitiveness, independence, rationality, and strength.

To operationalize the concepts of violent definitions and gender definitions, Heimer and De Coster (1999) used several questions in the National Youth Survey (NYS), which are displayed in Exhibit 8.1 along with the questions used to uncover incidents of violent offending. After statistically controlling for other important factors proven to be related to violent offending, such as socioeconomic status, age, prior violent delinquency, association with aggressive friends, and attachments to family, the results of the analyses of the NYS data provided support for both hypotheses. Heimer and De Coster concluded that girls are less violent than boys mainly because they are influenced more strongly by bonds to family, learn fewer violent definitions, and are taught that violence is inconsistent with the meaning of being female.

HISTORICAL EVENTS RESEARCH

The central insight behind historical methods is that we can improve our understanding of social processes when we make comparisons with other times and places. Although there are no rules for determining how far in the past the focus of research must be in order for it to be considered historical, in practice research tends to be considered historical when it focuses on a period prior to the experience of most of those conducting the research (Abbott 1994).

Historical research in the social sciences differs from traditional historical research because researchers seek to develop general theoretical explanations of historical events and processes instead of just detailed, "fact-centered" descriptions of them (Monkkonen 1994: 8). Social scientists do not ignore the details of historical events; rather, they "unravel" unique events to identify general patterns (Abrams 1982: 200). However, as in traditional history, the focus on the past presents special methodological challenges. Documents and

EXHIBIT 8.1   Questions From the National Youth Survey Used to Measure Violent Definitions, Gender Definitions, and Violent Delinquent Offending

Violent Delinquency

The below items were coded 1 = never; 2 = once or twice a year; 3 = once or twice every 2–3 months; 4 = once a month; 5 = once every 2–3 weeks; 6 = once a week; 7 = 2–3 times a week; 8 = once a day; 9 = 2–3 times a day.

How may times in the past year have you

   a) carried a hidden weapon other than a plain pocket knife?

   b) attacked someone with the idea of seriously hurting or killing them?

   c) been involved in gang fights?

   d) hit or threatened to hit a teacher or other adult at school?

   e) hit or threatened to hit your parents?

   f) hit or threatened to hit other students?

   g) had or tried to have sexual relations with someone against their will?

   h) used force (strong-arm methods) to get money or things from other students?

   i) used force (strong-arm methods) to get money or things from a teacher or adult at school?

   j) used force (strong-arm methods) to get money or things from other people (not teachers or students)?

Violent Definitions

The following questions were coded 1 = strongly disagree; 2 = disagree; 3 = neither agree nor disagree; 4 = agree; 5 = strongly agree.

   a) In order to gain respect from your friends, it is sometimes necessary to beat up on other kids.

   b) It is alright to beat up another person if he or she called you a dirty name.

   c) It is alright to beat up another person if he or she started the fight.

   d) Hitting another person is an acceptable way to get him or her to do what you want.

Gender Definitions

   a) In general, the father should have greater authority than the mother in the bringing up of children.

   b) Women with children should not work outside the home unless there is no one else to support the family.

   c) In a marriage, it is the woman's responsibility to care for any children and take care of the home.

   d) Women are too emotional to solve problems well.

   e) Women are physically and emotionally weaker than men and therefore need male protection and support.

Source: Heimer & De Coster (1999) "The Gendering of Violent Delinquency." *Criminology, 37*(2): 277–318. Reprinted with permission.

other evidence may have been lost or damaged, and what evidence there is may represent a sample biased toward those who were more newsworthy figures or who were more prone to writing. The feelings of individuals involved in past events may be hard, if not impossible, to reconstruct. Nonetheless, in many situations the historical record may support very systematic research on what occurred in the past. When research on past events does not follow processes for a long period of time, when it is basically cross-sectional, it is usually referred to as **historical events research**.

Case Study: Race, Rape, and Capital Punishment

In his book *The Martinsville Seven: Race, Rape, and Capital Punishment*, Eric Rise (1995) offers an in-depth example of historical events research. On January 8, 1949, a 32-year-old white woman in Martinsville, Virginia, accused seven young black men of violently raping her. These men became known as the "Martinsville Seven." Within two days of the allegation, state and local police had arrested and obtained confessions from each of the suspects. In a rapid succession of brief trials held over the course of 11 days, six separate juries convicted the defendants of rape and sentenced each to death. During the first week of February 1951, each of the "Martinsville Seven" died in the electric chair at the Virginia State Penitentiary. At a time when African Americans were beginning to assert their civil rights vigorously, the executions provided a stark reminder of the harsh treatment reserved for blacks who violated Southern racial codes.

In his analysis of the case, Rise (1995) examined a wealth of historical documents, including

- legal papers that the lawyers involved in the case made available to such archives as the Virginia State Library and Archives, and the United States National Archive;
- official transcripts of the cases from the Clerk's Office in Martinsville, Virginia;
- briefs and petitions to the Virginia State Supreme Court;
- related case law from the Supreme Court;
- annual reports from the Virginia Department of Corrections 1946–1951;
- newspaper accounts of the event from 16 local and national newspapers including the *Martinsville Bulletin*, *The New York Times*, and *The Washington Post*.

The large number of defendants, the rapid pace of the trials, and the specter of multiple executions attracted the attention of two national organizations, the National Association for the Advancement of Colored People (NAACP) and the Civil Rights Congress (CRC). In addition to the discriminatory nature of the jury's harsh sentences, Rise (1995) also found that another factor which obstructed justice in this case was the escalating tension and antagonisms between these two organizations. Ironically, both were trying to obtain justice for the Martinsville Seven.

The divergent manner in which each organization proposed to handle the cases highlighted fundamental disagreements over strategy, ingrained suspicions of motive, and fierce competition for membership. Because cooperation was never established through the appeals process, both organizations continued to pursue the cases in a manner consistent with their own ideological and institutional interests. The result, of course, was deadly.

Rise's (1995) analysis revealed the critical effect that this historical event had on subsequent developments. The revelation that capital sentencing disparities existed between white and African American defendants during the appeals process of the Martinsville Seven was significant for modern jurisprudence. Specifically, the Martinsville case was the first time attorneys presented in court equal protection arguments that challenged the racial disparity of death sentences for rape.

COMPARATIVE METHODS

The limitations of examining data from a single location have encouraged many social scientists to turn to comparisons among many geographical entities. Although comparative methods are often associated with cross-national comparisons, research examining smaller aggregates such as states and cities can also be subsumed under the comparative research umbrella. **Comparative research** methods allow for a broader vision about social relations than is possible with cross-sectional research limited to one location.

Case Study: The Comparative Crime Data File

One of the largest comparative research projects undertaken in criminology was the development of the Comparative Crime Data File (CCDF), which was created by Archer and Gartner (1984). Archer and Gartner articulated the need for comparative research in the field succinctly:

> The need for cross-national comparisons seems particularly acute for research on crime and violence since national differences on these phenomena are of a remarkable magnitude. In some societies, homicide is an hourly, highly visible, and therefore somewhat unexceptional cause of death. In other nations, homicides are so infrequent that, when they do occur, they receive national attention and lasting notoriety. (1984: 4)

The CCDF continues to be updated, but originally contained crime and violence data from 110 nations and 44 major international cities covering the period from approximately 1900 to 1970. In their work, Archer and Gartner (1984) examined many research questions using the CCDF. One of these questions is related to the idea that war might increase the level of postwar homicide within nations involved in wars. There are several theoretical models that speculate about the possible effects of wars on postwar violence within a nation. For example, the social solidarity model posits a wartime *decrease* in violence because of the increase in social solidarity among a nation's citizenry. At a more individual level, the violent veteran model predicts that postwar levels of violence within a nation will *increase* as a result of the violent acts of returning war veterans. At a societal level, the legitimization of violence model postulates that, during a war, a society reverses its prohibitions against killing and instead honors acts of violence that would be regarded as murderous in peacetime. This social approval or legitimation of violence, this model predicts, may produce a lasting reduction of inhibitions against taking human life, even after the war, thereby increasing levels of violence within nations.

To examine the effects of war on postwar violence, Archer and Gartner (1984) compared national rates of homicide before and after many wars, both small and large, including the two World Wars. Exhibit 8.2 displays the increase or decrease of homicide rates in combatant nations and a sample of control nations that were not involved in World War I and World War II. The researchers also controlled for a number of other factors related to war, including the number of combat deaths in war, whether nations were victorious or defeated, and whether the nation's postwar economics were improved or worsened, and for several types of homicide offenses committed by both men and women. The researchers found that most combatant nations in their analysis experienced substantial postwar increases in their rates of homicide after both small and large wars. Archer and Gartner concluded,

> The one model that appears to be fully consistent with the evidence is the legitimation of violence model, which suggests that the presence of authorized or sanctioned killing during war has a residual effect on the level of homicide in peacetime society. (1984: 96)

CONTENT ANALYSIS

Do media accounts of crime, such as newspaper and television news coverage, accurately portray the true nature of crime? Using the methodologies already discussed in this book may not be helpful for answering this question. Content analysis, however, would be. **Content analysis** is "the systematic, objective, quantitative analysis of message characteristics" (Neuendorf 2002: 1). Using this method, we can learn a great deal about popular culture and many other issues through studying the characteristics of messages delivered through the mass media and other sources.

The goal of a content analysis is to develop inferences from text (Weber 1985). You can think of a content analysis as a "survey" of some documents or other records of prior communication. In fact, a content analysis is a survey designed with fixed-choice responses so that it produces quantitative data that can be analyzed statistically.

Content analysis bears some similarities to qualitative data analysis, because it involves coding and categorizing text and identifying relationships among constructs identified in the text. However, since it usually is conceived as a quantitative procedure, content analysis overlaps with qualitative data analysis only at the margins, the points where qualitative analysis takes on quantitative features or where content analysis focuses on qualitative features of the text. Content analysis also bears some similarities to secondary data analysis, because it involves taking data or text that already exists and subjecting it to a new form of "analysis;" however, unlike secondary analysis of previously collected quantitative data, content analysis also involves sampling and measurement of primary data. Content analysis techniques can be used with all forms of messages, including visual images, sounds, and interaction patterns, as well as written text (Neuendorf 2002: 24–25).

EXHIBIT 8.2 Homicide Rate Changes in Combatant and Control Nations After World War I and World War II

Combatant Nations

Rates Decreased	Rates Remained Unchanged	Rates Increased
Australia (I)	England (I)	Belgium
Canada (I)	France (I)	Bulgaria
Hungary (I)	S. Africa (I)	Germany
Finland (II)	Canada (II)	Italy (I)
N. Ireland (II)		Japan (I)
U.S. (II)		Portugal (I)
		Scotland (I)
		U.S. (I)
		Australia (II)
		Denmark (II)
		England (II)
		France (II)
		Italy (II)
		Japan (II)
		Netherlands (II)
		New Zealand (II)
		Norway (II)
		Scotland (II)
		S. Africa (II)

Control Nations

Rates Decreased	Rates Remained Unchanged	Rates Increased
Norway (I)	Ceylon (I)	Finland (I)
Ceylon (II)	Chile (1)	Thailand (I)
Chile (II)	Netherlands (I)	Colombia (II)
El Salvador (II)		Sweden (I)
Ireland (II)		Turkey (II)
Switzerland (II)		
Thailand (II)		

Source: Archer & Gartner (1984), Table 4.1.

Identifying a Population of Documents or Other Textual Sources

The population of documents that is selected for analysis should be appropriate to the research question of interest. The units that are surveyed in a content analysis can range from newspapers, books, films, nomination speeches, or TV shows to persons referred to in other communications, themes expressed in documents, or propositions made in different statements. Words or other features of these units are then coded in order to measure the variables involved in the research question. The content analysis proceeds through several stages (Weber 1985).

Identify a population of documents or other textual sources for study. This population should be selected so that it is appropriate to the research question of interest. Perhaps the population will be all newspapers published in the United States, college student newspapers, nomination speeches at political party conventions, or "state of the nation" speeches by national leaders.

Determine the units of analysis. These could be newspaper articles, whole newspapers, speeches, or political conventions.

Select a sample of units from the population. The simplest strategy might be a simple random sample of documents. However, a stratified sample might be needed to ensure adequate representation of community newspapers in large and small cities, or of weekday and Sunday papers, or of political speeches during election years and in off years (see chapter 4).

Design coding procedures for the variables to be measured. This requires deciding what unit of text to code, such as words, sentences, themes, or paragraphs. Then the categories into which the units are to be coded must be defined. These categories may be broad, such as "supports democracy," or narrow, such as "supports universal suffrage."

Test and refine the coding procedures. Clear instructions and careful training of coders are essential.

Base statistical analyses on counting occurrences of particular items. These could be words, themes, or phrases. You will also need to test relations between different variables.

Developing reliable and valid coding procedures is not an easy task. The meaning of words and phrases is often ambiguous. As a result, coding procedures cannot simply categorize and count words; text segments in which the words are embedded must also be inspected before codes are finalized. Because different coders may perceive different meanings in the same text segments, explicit coding rules are required to ensure coding consistency. Special dictionaries can be developed to keep track of how the categories of interest are defined in the study (Weber 1985: 24–34).

After coding procedures are developed, their reliability should be assessed by comparing different coders' codes for the same variables. The criteria for judging quantitative content analyses of text are the same standards of validity applied to data collected with other quantitative methods. We must review the sampling approach, the reliability and validity of the measures, and the controls used to strengthen any causal conclusions.

Case Study: Crime and TV

Researchers interested in the media and crime have used content analysis in a number of ways. For example, scholars analyzing crime depictions presented in the media often conclude that newspaper and television coverage of crime is frequently inaccurate and misleading; stories disproportionately report violent crimes and reporters tend to focus attention on sensational matters such as the capture of a criminal or high-status offenders.

One type of television program presents vignettes depicting actual crimes in which theories of crime are dramatized. These dramatizations feature actors, actual photographs or film footage, and interviews conducted with participants and the police. Viewers are urged to call the police or program representatives with information related to the crime, and police officers are on standby in the television studio to take these calls. Two such programs are *America's Most Wanted* (AMW) and *Unsolved Mysteries* (UM).

To analyze the images these programs were sending to viewers, Cavender and Bond-Maupin (2000) conducted a content analysis of AMW and UM programs that aired between January 25 and May 31, 1989. All programs that aired during this time period were videotaped and a subsample of 16 episodes was randomly selected that contained 77 crime vignettes. The crime vignettes served as the study's units of analysis. The coding protocol used for data collection was focused on three aspects of the programs:

1. *Demographics.* Types of crime and general information on the crime, criminals, and victims.

2. *Characterizations.* Specific depictions of crime, criminals, and victims, such as brutality, dangerousness, or a victim's vulnerability.

3. *Worldview.* The relative safety of people and places, the terror and randomness of crime, and what the audience should do about crime.

Exhibit 8.3 presents the percentage of program vignettes that depicted offense types for both AMW and UM. Consistent with previous research, Cavender and Bond-Maupin (2000) found that these shows focused a majority of their attention on violent crime directed at persons. Corporate and political criminals were notably absent from the vignettes.

Cavender and Bond-Maupin (2000) concluded that the overwhelming majority of criminals on these shows were depicted as dangerous people who were beyond the help of social control or rehabilitation. In addition, both shows regularly featured criminals who were characterized with deviant psychological labels such as a "crazed killer, a psycho, a maniac," schizophrenic, emotionally disturbed, or showing no emotion. Other criminals were portrayed as Satanists, gang members, and drug dealers. On the other hand, victims were usually presented as upstanding citizens who you would like to have as a neighbor. The camera most often took the victims' perspective as well, achieving what Cavender and Bond-Maupin called the "good/evil dichotomy," with the victim and the audience aligned against the criminal. In sum, they concluded that the message sent to viewers by both programs was that danger lurks everywhere, awaiting the victim and, by implication, the viewer.

CRIME MAPPING

The image of crime mapping you probably have is one of a large map on a police precinct wall with push pins stuck all over it identifying the location of crime incidents. Although applied crime mapping like this has been used for over 100 years in policing, the type of crime mapping we will discuss here is related to mapping techniques used for traditional research purposes (e.g., testing theory about the causes of crime), not for investigative purposes.

EXHIBIT 8.3   Number and Percentage of Vignettes Depicted by the Programs *Unsolved Mysteries* and *America's Most Wanted*

	%	n
Murder	52	40
Theft or fraud extortion	13	10
Escape	12	9
Bank robbery or armed robbery	10	8
Illegal arms or terrorism	3	2
Unexplained death or missing	7	5
Rape	5	4
Kidnapping	5	4
Child molestation	5	4
Attempted murder	3	2
Drug dealing	3	2
Other	7	5

Source: Adapted from Cavender & Bond-Maupin (2000).

Case Study: Mapping Crime in Cities

Crime mapping for general research purposes has a long history in criminological research. **Crime mapping** for research purposes is generally used to identify the spatial distribution of crime along with the social indicators such as poverty and social disorganization that are similarly distributed across areas (e.g., neighborhood, census tracks). Although they were not the first researchers to use crime mapping, Shaw and McKay (1942) conducted a landmark analysis in criminology on juvenile delinquency in Chicago neighborhoods back in the 1930s. These researchers mapped thousands of incidents of juvenile delinquency and analyzed relationships between delinquency and various social conditions such as social disorganization. After analyzing rates of police arrests for delinquency, using police records to determine the names and addresses of those arrested in Chicago between 1927 and 1935, Shaw and McKay observed a striking pattern that persisted over the years. They found there was a linear decrease in rates of delinquency as the distance from the Loop (city center) increased. When rates of other community characteristics were similarly mapped (e.g., infant mortality, tuberculosis cases, percentage of families who own their own homes, percentage of foreign-born residents, percentage of families on relief), the conclusions were obvious. Shaw and McKay (1942) concluded,

It may be observed, in the first instance, that the variations in rates of officially recorded delinquents in communities of the city correspond very closely with variations in economic status. The communities with the highest rates of delinquents are occupied by these segments of the population whose position is most disadvantageous in relation to the distribution of economic, social, and cultural values. Of all the communities in the city, these have the fewest facilities for acquiring the economic goods indicative of status and success in our conventional culture . . . In the low-income areas, where there is the greatest deprivation and frustration, where, in the history of the city, immigrant and migrant groups have brought together the widest variety of divergent cultural traditions and institutions, and where there exists the greatest disparity between the social values to which the people aspire and the availability of facilities for acquiring these values in conventional ways, the development of crime as an organized way of life is most marked. (1942: 318–319)

Case Study: Gang Homicides in St. Louis, Missouri

Contemporary researchers interested in issues related to crime and criminology have access to more sophisticated computer technology that allows the creation of more enhanced crime maps. The purpose of crime maps, however, remains the same: to illuminate the relationship between some category of crime and corresponding characteristics such as poverty and disorganization across given locations. Rosenfeld, Bray, and Egley (1999) recently examined the mechanisms through which gangs facilitate violent offending in St. Louis, Missouri. The primary purpose of this research was to examine whether gang membership impels members to engage in violence or merely exposes them to violent persons and situations. Rosenfeld and colleagues compared gang-affiliated, gang-motivated, and nongang youth homicides occurring in St. Louis between 1985 and 1995. In one part of their analysis, they examined the spatial distribution of gang and nongang youth homicide in relation to attributes of the neighborhood context (e.g., economic deprivation) in which the incidents occurred.

Rosenfeld and colleagues (1999) did not rely on the police classification of homicides as gang-related; they coded homicide reports themselves. Operationally, a homicide was coded gang-motivated if it resulted from gang behavior or relationships, such as an initiation ritual, the "throwing" of gang signs, or a gang fight. A case was coded as gang-affiliated if the homicide involved a suspect or victim identified in the police report as a gang member but did not arise from gang activity. For example, an incident in which a gang member was killed during a robbery would be gang-affiliated but not gang-motivated. A youth homicide was coded as nongang-related if no indication of gang activity or affiliation was present in the case file, and the suspect was between 10 and 24 years of age. To examine the spatial relationship between these three types of homicides and the relationship they had to neighborhood disadvantage (such as economic deprivation or social disorganization) and instability (such as residents moving in and out of the neighborhood), the researchers used the census block group as their units of analysis. Exhibit 8.4 displays the map of block groups where gang-affiliated and gang-motivated homicides occurred, along with the extent of neighborhood disadvantage in each block for 1990–1995 (Rosenfeld, Bray, & Egley 1999). Exhibit 8.5 displays this same information for nongang youth homicides.

EXHIBIT 8.4 Neighborhoods in St. Louis Where Gang-Affiliated and Gang-Motivated Homicides Occurred

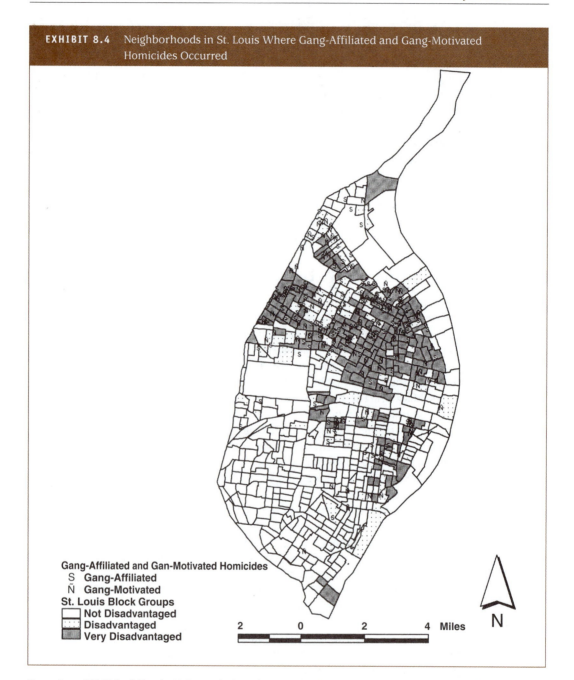

Gang-Affiliated and Gan-Motivated Homicides
S Gang-Affiliated
Ñ Gang-Motivated
St. Louis Block Groups
☐ Not Disadvantaged
⬚ Disadvantaged
▦ Very Disadvantaged

2 0 2 4 Miles

N

Source: Rosenfeld, Richard, Timothy M. Bray, and Arlen Egley (1999) "Facilitating Violence: A Comparison of Gang-Motivated, Gang-Affiliated, and Nongang Youth Homicides." *Journal of Quantitative Criminology, 15*(4): 496–516. Reprinted with permission.

EXHIBIT 8.5   Neighborhoods in St. Louis Where Nongang Homicides Occurred

8   **Non-Gang Youth Homicides**
St. Louis Block Groups

☐ **Not Disadvantaged**
▒ **Disadvantaged**
▓ **Very Disadvantaged**

2   0   2   4 Miles

N

Source: Rosenfeld, Richard, Timothy M. Bray, and Arlen Egley (1999) "Facilitating Violence: A Comparison of Gang-Motivated, Gang-Affiliated, and Nongang Youth Homicides." *Journal of Quantitative Criminology, 15*(4): 496–516. Reprinted with permission.

From these maps, you can see that both gang and nongang homicides were concentrated in disadvantaged areas. Other maps revealed a similar finding with regard to neighborhood instability: homicides were concentrated in neighborhoods with moderate levels of instability regardless of whether they were gang-affiliated, gang-motivated, or nongang-related. Rosenfeld and colleagues (1999) conclude,

> Our results offer powerful evidence of the clustering of both gang and nongang youth homicides in areas characterized by high levels of social-economic disadvantage and racial isolation. Although the accumulated evidence for gang facilitation of violence is quite compelling, our results serve as a reminder that concentrated disadvantage and racial isolation remain the fundamental sources of lethal violence in urban areas. (1999: 514)

These conclusions echo those made over half a century earlier by Shaw and McKay (1942). As such, we are compelled to note Ernest W. Burgess's words in the introduction of Shaw and McKay's original work:

> We must realize that the brightest hope in reformation is in changing the neighborhood and in control of the gang in which the boy moves, lives, and has his being and to which he returns after this institutional treatment . . . We must reaffirm our faith in prevention, which is so much easier, cheaper, and more effective than cure and which begins with the home, the play group, the local school, the church, and the neighborhood. (1942: xiii)

METHODOLOGICAL ISSUES WHEN USING SECONDARY DATA

Each of the methods we have discussed in this chapter presents unique methodological challenges. For example, in historical events research and comparative research, small numbers of cases, spotty historical records, variable cross-national record-keeping practices, and different cultural and linguistic contexts limit the confidence that can be placed in measures, samples, and causal conclusions. Just to identify many of the potential problems for a comparative historical research project requires detailed knowledge of the times and of the nations or other units investigated (Kohn 1987). This requirement often serves as a barrier to in-depth historical research and to comparisons between nations.

Analysis of secondary data presents several challenges, ranging from uncertainty about the methods of data collection to the lack of maximal fit between the concepts that the primary study measured and each of the concepts that are the focus of the current investigation. Responsible use of secondary data requires a good understanding of the primary data source.

Data quality is always a concern with secondary data, even when the data are collected by an official government agency. The need for concern is much greater in research across national boundaries, because different data-collection systems and definitions of key variables may have been used (Glover 1996). Census counts can be distorted by incorrect answers to census questions as well as by inadequate coverage of the entire population (see chapter 4; Rives & Serow 1988: 32–35). Social and political pressures may influence the success of a census in different ways in different countries. These influences on records are particularly acute for crime data. For example, Archer and Gartner (1984) note, "It is possible, of course, that many other nations also try to use crime rate fluctuations for domestic political purposes—to use 'good' trends to justify the current administration or 'bad' trends to provide a mandate for the next" (1984: 16).

Researchers who rely on secondary data inevitably make tradeoffs between their ability to use a particular data set and the specific hypotheses they can test. If a concept that is critical to a hypothesis was not measured adequately in a secondary data source, the study might have to be abandoned until a more adequate source of data can be found. Alternatively, hypotheses or even the research question itself may be modified in order to match the analytic possibilities presented by the available data (Riedel 2000: 53).

Measuring Across Contexts

One problem that historical and comparative research projects often confront is the lack of data from some historical periods or geographical units (Rueschemeyer, Stephens, & Stephens 1992: 4; Walters, James, & McCammon 1997). For example, the widely used U.S. Uniform Crime Reporting System did not begin until 1930 (Rosen 1995). Those measures that are available are not always adequate. What remains in the historical archives may be an unrepresentative selection of materials from the past. At various times, some documents could have been discarded, lost, or transferred elsewhere for a variety of reasons. "Original" documents may be transcriptions of spoken words or handwritten pages and could have been modified slightly in the process; they could also be outright distortions (Erikson 1966: 172, 209–210; Zaret 1996). When relevant data are obtained from previous publications, it is easy to overlook problems of data quality, but this simply makes it all the more important to evaluate the primary sources. Developing a systematic plan for identifying relevant documents and evaluating them is very important.

A somewhat more subtle measurement problem is that of establishing measurement equivalence. The meaning of concepts and the operational definition of variables may change over time and between nations or regions (Erikson 1966: xi). Individuals in different cultures may respond differently to the same questions (Martin & Kinsella 1995: 385). Alternatively, different measures may have been used for the same concepts in different nations and the equivalence of these measures may be unknown (van de Vijver & Leung 1997: 9).

The value of statistics for particular geographic units like counties may vary over time simply due to change in the boundaries of these units (Walters, James, & McCammon 1997). As Archer and Gartner (1984) note,

> These comparative crime data were recorded across the moving history of changing societies. In some cases, this history spanned gradual changes in the political and social conditions of a nation. In other cases, it encompassed transformations so acute that it seems arguable whether the same nation existed before and after. (1984: 15)

Sampling Across Time and Place

The simplest type of sample is the selection of one case for a historical study. Although a great deal can be learned from the intensive focus on one nation or other unit, the lack of a comparative element shapes the type of explanations that are developed.

Qualitative comparative historical studies are likely to rely on availability samples or purposive samples of cases. In an availability sample, researchers study a case or multiple cases simply because they are familiar with or have access to them. When using a purposive sampling strategy, researchers select cases because they reflect theoretically important distinctions. Quantitative historical comparative researchers often select entire populations of cases for which the appropriate measures can be obtained.

When geographic units like nations are sampled for comparative purposes, it is assumed that the nations are independent of each other in terms of the variables examined. Each nation can then be treated as a separate case for identifying possible chains of causes and effects. However, in a very interdependent world this assumption may be misplaced; nations may develop as they do because of how other nations are developing (and the same can be said of cities and other units). As a result, comparing the particular histories of different nations may overlook the influence of global culture, international organizations, or economic dependency. These common international influences may cause the same pattern of changes to emerge in different nations; looking within the history of these nations for the explanatory influences would lead to spurious conclusions. The possibility of such complex interrelations should always be considered when evaluating the plausibility of a causal argument based on a comparison between two apparently independent cases (Jervis 1996).

Identifying Causes

The restriction of historical research to one setting in the past limits possibilities for testing causal connections, because explanations applied to these events can seem arbitrary (Skocpol 1984: 365). The researcher can reduce this problem by making some comparisons with other events in the past or present. However, the interdependence of sampled units (noted in the previous section) may mean that several cases available for comparison should be treated as just one larger case. There may also be too many possible combinations of causal factors to test and not enough cases to test them with.

Some comparative researchers use a systematic method for identifying causes, developed by the English philosopher John Stuart Mill (1872), called the **method of agreement** (see Exhibit 8.6). The core of this approach is the comparison of nations (cases) in terms of similarities and differences on potential causal variables and the phenomenon to be explained. For example, suppose three nations that have all developed democratic political systems are compared in terms of four socioeconomic variables hypothesized by different theories to influence violent crime. If the nations differ in terms of three of the variables but are similar in terms of the fourth, this is evidence that the fourth variable influences violent crime.

The features of the cases selected for comparison have a large impact on the ability to identify influences using the method of agreement. Cases should be chosen for their difference in terms of key factors hypothesized to influence the outcome of interest and their similarity on other, possibly confounding, factors (Skocpol 1984: 383). For example, in order to understand how unemployment influences violent crime, you would need to select cases

EXHIBIT 8.6 John Stuart Mill's Method of Agreement

Variable	Case 1	Case 2	Case 3
A	Different	Different	Different
B	Different	Same	Same
C	Different	Different	Different
D[a]	Same	Same	Same
Outcome	Same	Same	Same

Source: Adapted from Skocpol (1984: 379).

a. D is considered the cause of the outcome.

for comparison that differ in unemployment rates, so that you could then see whether they differ in rates of violence (King, Keohane, & Verba 1994: 148–152).

With these cautions in mind, the combination of historical and comparative methods allows for rich descriptions of social and political processes in different nations or regions as well as for causal inferences that reflect a systematic, defensible weighing of the evidence. Data of increasingly good quality are available on a rapidly expanding number of nations, creating many opportunities for comparative research. We cannot expect one study comparing the histories of a few nations to control adequately for every plausible alternative causal influence, but repeated investigations can refine our understanding and lead to increasingly accurate causal conclusions (King, Keohane, & Verba 1994: 33).

COMBINING RESEARCH DESIGNS

Designing research means deciding how to measure empirical phenomena, how to identify causal connections, and how to generalize findings not as separate decisions, but in tandem, with each decision having implications for the others. The carefully controlled laboratory conditions that increased the causal validity of Bushman's (1995) experiments on media violence decreased the generalizability of his conclusions (see chapter 5). The representative sampling plan that increased the generalizability of Tjaden and Thoennes's (2000) national study of violent victimization limited their options for estimating causal effects (see chapter 6). The observations that underlay Decker and Van Winkle's (1996) descriptions of gang members would not be feasible in a national sample of gang members (see chapter 7).

Comparing Research Designs

It is not enough to ask of a study you critique, or one that you plan, such questions as, "Were the measures valid?" and "Were the causal conclusions justified?" You must also consider how the measurement approach might have affected the causal validity of the researcher's conclusions and how the sampling strategy might have altered the quality of measures. In fact, you must be concerned with how each component of the research design influenced the other components.

In the real world of social and criminological research, the boundaries separating different methods of data collection often overlap: experiments may be conducted in the field, surveys may involve some intensive open-ended questioning, and field research may utilize quantitative counts of phenomena or random samples of events. The central features of experiments, surveys, and qualitative methods provide distinct perspectives even when used to study the same social processes. Comparing subjects randomly assigned to a treatment and a comparison group, asking standard questions of the members of a random sample, and observing while participating in a natural social setting involve markedly different decisions about measurements, causality, and generalizability. No method can reasonably be graded as superior to the others, and each varies in its suitability to different research questions and goals.

In general, experimental designs are strongest for testing causal hypotheses and most appropriate for studies of treatment (see chapter 5). Because random assignment reduces the possibility of preexisting differences between treatment and comparison groups to small, specifiable, chance levels, many of the variables are controlled that might otherwise create a spurious association. But in spite of this clear advantage, experimental designs require a degree of control that cannot always be achieved outside of the laboratory. It can be difficult to ensure in real-world settings that a treatment was delivered as intended and that other influences did not intrude. As a result, what appears to be a treatment effect or noneffect may be something else altogether. Field experiments thus require careful monitoring of the treatment process.

Laboratory experiments permit much more control over conditions, but at the cost of less generalizable findings. People must volunteer for most laboratory experiments, so there is a good possibility that experimental subjects differ from those who do not volunteer. The problem of generalizability in an experiment using volunteers lessens only when the object of investigation is an orientation, a behavior, or a social process that is relatively invariable among people.

Most social science surveys rely on random sampling for their selection of cases from a larger population, and it is this feature that makes them preferable for maximizing generalizability (see chapter 4). When description of a particular large population is a key concern, survey research is likely to be the method of choice. Surveys are also often used to investigate hypothesized causal relationships, because many variables can be measured within a given survey, and repeated measurements are possible over time. If variables that might create spurious relations are included in the survey, they can be controlled statistically in the analysis, thus strengthening the evidence for or against a hypothesized causal relationship.

Qualitative methods presume an intensive measurement approach in which indicators of concepts are drawn from direct observation or in-depth commentary (see chapter 8). This approach is most appropriate when it is not clear what meaning people attach to a concept or what sense they might make of particular questions about it. Qualitative methods are also admirably suited to the exploration of new or poorly understood social settings, when it is not even clear what concepts would help to understand the situation. For these reasons, qualitative methods tend to be preferred when exploratory research questions are posed. But, of course, intensive measurement necessarily hampers the study of large numbers of cases or situations, resulting in the limitation of many field research efforts to small numbers of people or unique social settings.

When qualitative methods are used to study several individuals or settings that provide marked contrasts in a presumed independent variable, it becomes possible to evaluate causal hypotheses with these methods. However, for hypothesis testing, the impossibility of taking into account many possible extraneous influences in such limited comparisons makes qualitative methods a weak approach. Qualitative methods are more suited to the elucidation of causal mechanisms, and can be used to identify the multiple successive events that might have led to some outcome.

As discussed in this chapter, historical and comparative methods range from cross-national quantitative surveys to qualitative comparisons of social features and political events. Their suitability for exploration, description, explanation, and evaluation varies in relation to the particular method used, but they are essential for research on historical processes and national differences. If the same methods are used to study multiple eras or nations rather than just one nation at one time, the results are likely to be enhanced generalizability and causal validity.

In reality, none of these methods of data collection provides a foolproof means for achieving measurement validity, causal validity, or generalizability. Each will have some liabilities in a specific research application, and all can benefit from combination with one or more other methods (Sechrest & Sidani 1995). To benefit from this multiple-method approach, researchers have been using a triangulated methodology—that is, combining different methods in the same project to reveal different dimensions of the same phenomenon. It is to this subject that we now turn.

Triangulating Research Designs

The use of multiple methods to study one research question is called **triangulation**. The term suggests that a researcher can get a clearer picture of the social reality being studied by viewing it from several different perspectives. The term is actually derived from land surveying, where knowing a single landmark allows you to locate yourself only somewhere along a line in a single direction from the landmark. However, with two landmarks you can take bearings on both and locate yourself at their intersection.

Triangulation The use of multiple methods to study one research question.

Triangulation in Action: American Indian Homicide

When studying the social causes of homicide and other violence within contemporary American Indian communities, Bachman (1992) used triangulation. To examine the social causes of homicide within this population, she conducted in-depth interviews with American Indian homicide offenders who were incarcerated in state prisons in two states. In addition, she conducted national, state, and reservation-level statistical analyses to determine the social factors, such as levels of poverty and social disorganization, that were related to American Indian homicide rates at the aggregate level.

Bachman found that, compared with all other racial or ethnic groups, American Indians had some of the highest rates of homicide, sometimes reaching over 100 per 100,000 population on some reservations. Although other researchers had noted high rates of American Indian homicide, virtually no attempts were made to explore the factors that contributed to such high rates. Are the causal mechanisms that create these high rates the same as those that were documented in the population in general? Or are the social forces that were identified as increasing both African American and white homicide rates different from those forces that contribute to American Indian homicide? Because there was virtually no research examining the etiology of American Indian homicide, Bachman first wanted to gain some insight into an understanding of the structural and cultural conditions that may contribute to lethal violence at the individual level. Accordingly, she selected the qualitative method of intensive interviewing as her first method.

Bachman (1992) conducted face-to-face interviews with homicide offenders at two Midwestern state prisons. Offenders responded to a lengthy set of open-ended questions and probes concerning the circumstances surrounding their crime, their life before the crime, and their attitudes about crime in general. Bachman characterized the interview process as a conversation between two people getting to know one another rather than a rigid structure in which questions were formally addressed. An interview was usually ended not because there was nothing left to talk about, but because there was another interview scheduled or because the prisoner had to return to his cell for count (1992: 32).

Thus Bachman (1992) started with inductive research, beginning with qualitative interview data which were then used to develop (induce) a general explanation (a theory) to account for the data. The theoretical model that emerged from her interview data is displayed in Exhibit 8.7. The model combines the causal forces of social disorganization, economic deprivation, a culture of honor or violence, and the psychological mechanisms of culture conflict and perceived powerlessness with the intervening variable of alcohol or drug abuse. Also included in the theoretical guide is the antecedent variable to each of these concepts, internal colonialism. Although this concept was not explicitly derived from the qualitative analysis, Bachman explained, "No model explaining any phenomenon with regard to American Indians would be complete without acknowledgment of the colonization process to which our government has subjected this population" (p. 36).

This model assisted Bachman (1992) in subsequent quantitative analysis by providing a theoretical framework from which to start. Using this model as a guide along with the other relevant literature on the etiology of homicide, Bachman then performed deductive research in which she obtained American Indian homicide rates (dependent variable) and indicators of some of these theoretical constructs (independent variables) at the state and reservation levels to test three hypotheses:

1. The higher the level of social disorganization within a reservation community, the higher the rate of homicide.

2. The higher the level of economic deprivation within a reservation community, the higher the rate of homicide.

EXHIBIT 8.7 Theoretical Model for American Indian Homicide That Emerged From Bachman's Qualitative Interviews With American Indian Homicide Offenders

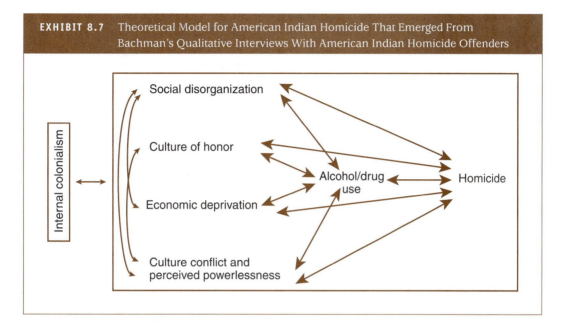

3. The more traditional and integrated a reservation community, the lower the rate of homicide.

Results indicated that American Indian communities with higher levels of both social disorganization and economic deprivation also had higher rates of homicide. She did not find support in her data for the third hypothesis. In addition to guiding her deductive research, the qualitative interview data also provided Bachman's (1992) research with a wealth of narratives that added meaning and depth to the statistical relationships that were found at the aggregate level. For example, many homicide offenders revealed what conditions of social disorganization and economic deprivation were like in their own lives.

As you can see, using triangulation in which both quantitative and qualitative methods are used to investigate the same research question has many advantages. In addition, finding support for relationships between independent and dependent variables at two different levels—the individual level and the community level—also provided validity to Bachman's (1992) conclusions that social disorganization and economic deprivation are both related to homicide in American Indian communities. Campbell and Fiske (1959) explain the validity-enhancing qualities of triangulation:

> If a hypothesis can survive the confrontation of a series of complementary methods of testing, it contains a degree of validity unattainable by one tested within the more constricted framework of a single method . . . Findings from this latter approach must always be subject to the suspicion that they are method-bound: Will the comparison totter when exposed to an equally prudent but different testing method? (1959: 82)

Choice of a data-collection method should be guided in part by the aspect of validity that is of most concern, but each aspect of validity must be considered in attempting to answer every research question. Experiments may be the preferred method when causal validity is a paramount concern, and surveys may be the natural choice if generalizability is critical. But generalizability must still be a concern when assessing the results of an experiment, and causal validity is a key concern in most social science surveys. Field research has unique value for measuring social processes as they happen, but the causal validity and generalizability of field research results are often open to question. A researcher should always consider whether data of another type should be collected in what is basically a single-method study, and whether additional research using different methods is needed before the research question can be answered with sufficient confidence.

The ability to apply diverse techniques to address different aspects of a complex research question is one mark of a sophisticated social researcher. Awareness that one study's findings must be understood in the context of a larger body of research, and the ability to speculate on how the use of different methods might alter a study's findings are prerequisites for informed criticism of social research. As social research methods and substantive findings continue to grow in number, these insights should stimulate more ambitious efforts to combine research methods and integrate many studies' findings.

But the potential for integrating methods and combining findings does not decrease the importance of single studies using just one method of data collection. The findings from well-designed studies in carefully researched settings are the necessary foundation for broader, more integrative methods. There is little point in combining methods that are poorly implemented or in merging studies that produced invalid results. Whatever the research question, we should consider the full range of methodological possibilities, make an informed and feasible choice, and then carefully carry out our strategy.

Finally, realistic assessment of the weaknesses as well as the strengths of each method of data collection should help you to remember that humility is a virtue in science. Advancement of knowledge and clear answers to specific research questions are attainable with the tools you now have in your methodological toolbox. Perfection is not a realistic goal, however. No matter what research method we use, our mental concepts cannot reflect exactly what we measured, our notions of causation cannot reveal a tangible causal force, and our generalizations cannot always extend beyond the cases that were actually studied. This is not cause for disillusionment, but it should keep us from being excessively confident in our own interpretations or unreasonably resistant to change. As you saw in chapter 2, research questions are never completely answered. Research findings regarding a particular question are added to the existing literature to inform future research, and the research circle continues.

ETHICAL ISSUES WHEN ANALYZING AVAILABLE DATA AND CONTENT

Analysis of historical documents or quantitative data collected by others does not create the potential for harm to human subjects that can be a concern when collecting primary data. It is still important to be honest and responsible in working out arrangements for data access when data must be obtained from designated officials or data archivists, but of course many data are easily accessed in libraries or on the web. Researchers who conclude that they are being denied access to public records of the federal government may be able to obtain the data by filing a Freedom of Information Act request. The FOIA stipulates that all persons have a right to access all federal agency records unless the records are specifically exempted (Riedel 2000: 130–131). Researchers who review historical or government documents must also try to avoid embarrassing or otherwise harming named individuals or their descendants by disclosing sensitive information.

Subject confidentiality is a key concern when original records are analyzed. Whenever possible, all information that could identify individuals should be removed from the records to be analyzed so that no link is possible to the identities of living subjects or the living descendants of subjects (Huston & Naylor 1996: 1698). When you used data that have already been archived, you need to find out what procedures were used to preserve subject confidentiality. The work required to ensure subject confidentiality probably will have been done for you by the data archivist. For example, the ICPSR examines carefully all data deposited in the archive for the possibility of disclosure risk. All data that might be used to identify respondents is altered to ensure confidentiality, including removal of information such as birth dates or service dates, specific incomes, or place of residence that could be used to identify subjects indirectly (see www.icpsr.edu/irb/statement/html). If all information that could be used in any way to identify respondents cannot be removed from a dataset without diminishing dataset quality (such as by preventing links to other essential data records), ICPSR restricts access to the data and requires that investigators agree to conditions of use that preserve subject confidentiality.

It is not up to you to decide whether there are any issues of concern regarding human subjects when you acquire a dataset for secondary analysis from a responsible source. The Institutional Review Board (IRB) for the Protection of Human Subjects at your college, university, or other institution has the responsibility to decide whether they need to review and approve proposals for secondary data analysis. The federal regulations are not entirely clear on this point, so the acceptable procedures will vary between institutions based on what their IRBs have decided.

Ethical concerns are multiplied when surveys are conducted or other data are collected in other countries. If the outside researcher lacks much knowledge of local norms, values, and routine activities, the potential for inadvertently harming subjects is substantial. For this reason, cross-cultural researchers should spend time learning about each of the countries in which they plan to collect primary data and strike up collaborations with researchers in those countries (Hantrais & Mangen 1996). Local advisory groups may also be formed in each country so that a broader range of opinion is solicited when key decisions must be made. Such collaboration can also be invaluable when designing instruments, collecting data, and interpreting results.

CONCLUSION

Historical and comparative social science investigations use a variety of techniques that range from narrative histories having much in common with qualitative methods to analyses of secondary data that in many respects are like traditional survey research. Each of these methods can help researchers gain new insights into processes like factors related to homicide offending. They encourage intimate familiarity with the course of development of the nations studied and thereby stimulate inductive reasoning about the interrelations among different historical events. Systematic historical and comparative techniques can be used to test deductive hypotheses concerning international differences as well as historical events.

Most historical and comparative methods encourage causal reasoning. They require the researcher to consider systematically the causal mechanism or historical sequences of events by which earlier events influence later outcomes. They also encourage attention to causal context, with a particular focus on the ways in which different cultures and social structures may result in different effects on other variables. There is much to be gained by continuing to use and develop these methods.

KEY TERMS

Comparative research
Content analysis
Crime mapping

Historical events research
Triangulation
Method of agreement

HIGHLIGHTS

- Secondary data analysis is the act of collecting or analyzing data that was originally collected for another purpose.
- In general, there are four major types of secondary data: surveys, official statistics, official records, and other historical documents including written text or media representations (e.g., trial transcripts, newspaper articles, television shows).
- The central insight behind historical and comparative methods is that we can improve our understanding of social processes when we make comparisons to other times and places.
- Content analysis is a tool for systematic analysis of documents and other textual data. It requires careful testing and control of coding procedures to achieve reliable measures.
- Crime mapping for research purposes is generally used to identify the spatial distribution of crime along with the social indicators such as poverty and social disorganization that are similarly distributed across areas (e.g., neighborhoods, census tracts).
- Using multiple research designs to answer the same research question, called triangulation, enhances generalizability, measurement validity, and causal validity.

EXERCISES

Discussing Research

1. What historical events have had a major influence on social patterns in the nation? The possible answers are too numerous to list, ranging from any of the wars to major internal political conflicts, economic booms and busts, scientific discoveries, and legal changes. Choose one such event in your own nation for this exercise. Find one historical book on

this event and list the sources of evidence used. What additional evidence would you suggest for a social science investigation of the event?

2. Select a current crime or political topic that has been the focus of news articles. Propose a content analysis strategy for this topic, using newspaper articles or editorials as your units of analysis. Your strategy should include a definition of the population, selection of the units of analysis, a sampling plan, and coding procedures for key variables. Now find an article on this topic and use it to develop your coding procedures. Test and refine your coding procedures with another article on the same topic.

Finding Research

1. Using your library's government documents collection or the U.S. Census website (www.census.gov), select one report by the U.S. Bureau of the Census about the population of the United States or some segment of it. Outline the report and list all the tables included in it. Summarize the report in two paragraphs. Suggest a historical or comparative study for which this report would be useful.

2. The Bureau of Justice Statistics (BJS) home page can be found at www.ojp.usdoj.gov/bjs. The site contains an extensive list of reports published by the BJS along with links to the data used in the reports. You can access tables of data that display phenomena over time and across various geographical locations.
   a. Using data and/or reports available from the National Crime Victimization Survey, conduct an analysis of the rates of violent victimization from 1993 until the most recent date the data report is available. What do you conclude about the trends of violent victimization?
   b. Find a report available on the site that makes cross-national comparisons. Summarize the methods by which the data were collected. Now summarize the findings of the report.

3. The National Institute of Justice has a wealth of information on crime mapping located at www.nicrs.org. Search the site for information on "crime mapping" and you will find that the site contains a multitude of information, including the latest technological advances in crime-mapping strategies for police departments as well as full-text articles discussing recent research that uses crime-mapping techniques. Select a report available online and summarize its findings.

Critiquing Research

1. Review the survey data sets available through the Inter-University Consortium for Political and Social Research (ICPSR), using either its published directory or its internet site (www.icpsr.umich.edu). Select two data sets that might be used to study a research question in which you are interested. Use the information ICPSR reports about them to answer Questions 1–5 in the section "Methodological Issues When Using Secondary Data" earlier in this chapter. Is the information adequate to answer these questions? What are the advantages and disadvantages of using one of these data sets to answer your research question compared to designing a new study?

2. Read the original article reporting one of the studies described in this chapter. Critique the article, using the article review questions presented in Appendix B as your guide. Focus particular attention on procedures for measurement, sampling, and establishing causal relations.

Making Research Ethical

1. Bachman (1992) found very high rates of homicide in her study of American Indian reservations. She reported this and other important and troubling findings in her book, *Death and Violence on the Reservation*. In your opinion, does a researcher have an ethical obligation to urge government officials or others to take action in response to social problems that they have identified? Why or why not?

2. Should any requirements be imposed on researchers who seek to study other cultures, in order to ensure that procedures are appropriate and interpretations are culturally sensitive? What practices would you suggest for cross-cultural researchers in order to ensure that ethical guidelines are followed? (Consider the wording of consent forms and the procedures for gaining voluntary cooperation.)

Developing a Research Proposal

Add a historical or comparative dimension to your proposed study.

1. Consider which of the four types of comparative-historical methods would best be suited to an investigation of your research question. Think of possibilities for qualitative and quantitative research on your topic with the method you prefer. Will you conduct a variable-oriented or case-oriented study? Write a brief statement justifying the approach you choose.

2. Review the possible sources of data for your comparative-historical project. Search the web and relevant government, historical, and international organization sites or publications. Search the social science literature for similar studies and read about the data sources they used.

3. Specify the hypotheses you will test or the causal sequences you will investigate. Describe what your cases will be (nations, regions, years, etc.). Explain how you will select cases. List the sources of your measures and describe the specific type of data you expect to obtain for each measure.

4. Review the list of potential problems in comparative-historical research and discuss those that you believe will be most troublesome in your proposed investigation. Explain your reasoning.

Performing Data Analysis in SPSS

1. Using the data set STATE2000, examine the rates of violence and murder across the four regions of the country (REGION). The best procedure to use for this is called MEANS. You can access this under ANALYZE, then COMPARE MEANS, then click on MEANS. In the Mean dialog box, place the rate of violence you wish to compare first (VIOLENT or MURDER) in the dependent variables box and REGION in the independent variable box. Summarize your findings.

   Now, using this same procedure, examine whether there are similar differences across regions for rates of poverty, which are often found to be associated with rates of violence. That is, geographical locations that have higher rates of poverty and overdeprivation also tend to have higher rates of violence. What do you conclude?

2. Because the GSS file is cross-sectional, we cannot use it to conduct historical research. However, we can develop some interesting historical questions by examining differences in the attitudes of Americans in different birth cohorts.

   a. Inspect the distributions of the same set of variables. Would you expect any of these attitudes and behaviors to have changed during the twentieth century? State your expectations in the form of hypotheses.

   b. Request a crosstabulation of these variables by birth COHORT.

   c. What appear to be the differences among the cohorts? Which differences do you think are due to historical change, and which do you think are due to the aging process? Which attitudes and behaviors would you expect to still differentiate the baby-boom generation and the post-Vietnam generation in 20 years?

Student Study Site

The companion Student Study Website for *The Fundamentals of Research in Criminology and Criminal Justice* can be found at www.sagepub.com/frccjstudy.

Visit the Student Study Site to enhance your understanding of the chapter content and to discover additional resources that will take your learning one step further. You can enhance your understanding of the chapters by using the comprehensive study material, which includes interactive exercises, e-flashcards, web exercises, practice self-tests, and more. You will also find special features, such as Learning from Journal Articles, which incorporates SAGE's online journal collection.

CHAPTER 9

Evaluation and Policy Analysis

In this chapter, we will provide you with an overview of evaluation research in the field of criminology and criminal justice. Although all the research we have discussed in this text is ultimately useful, evaluation research is inherently so because the results generally have an impact on policy choices in the immediate future. As such, evaluation research is often referred to as *applied research* because the findings can immediately be utilized and applied. We will first provide you with a brief history of evaluation research. Then, after describing the different types of evaluation research, we will provide you with case studies that illustrate the various methodologies used to assess the impacts of programs and policies in criminology and criminal justice.

WHY DO WE NEED EVALUATION?

Every year, the U.S. Department of Justice (DOJ) spends an average of $3 billion in grants to help state and local law enforcement and communities prevent and ameliorate the consequences of crime. But similar to virtually every government agency, very little money has been allocated by the DOJ to determine whether these prevention programs actually work. In 1996, Congress required the Attorney General to provide a "comprehensive evaluation of the effectiveness" of the programs that had been implemented with this money. Do not be alarmed if you think $3 billion is too much money to spend on prevention. By definition, virtually every aspect of the criminal justice system, as well as other government and private institutions, is considered preventive in nature. Not only does the money go for such stereotypical prevention programs as after-school recreation programs, but it also supports such efforts as community-oriented policing, drug raids, prisoner rehabilitation, boot camps, home confinement and electronic monitoring, job corps and vocational training for prison inmates, preschool education programs, and other programs too numerous to mention. Most of the Department of Justice money set aside for prevention, however, is allocated most heavily in police and prisons, with very little support for prevention programs in other institutions (Sherman et al. 1997). As the mandate from Congress suggests, evaluation plays an increasingly important role in the fields of criminology and criminal justice.

A BRIEF HISTORY OF EVALUATION RESEARCH

Evaluation research is not a method of data collection, like survey research or experiments, nor is it a unique component of research designs, like sampling or measurement. Instead, evaluation research is social research that is conducted for a distinctive purpose: to investigate social programs (such as substance abuse treatment programs, welfare programs, criminal justice programs, or employment and training programs). Rossi and Freeman (1989) define evaluation research as "the systematic application of social research procedures for assessing the conceptualization, design, implementation, and utility of social intervention programs" (1989: 18). What exactly does *systematic* mean? Well, regardless of the treatment or program being examined, evaluations are systematic because they employ social research approaches to gathering valid and reliable data. Note the plural *approaches* instead of the singular *approach*. Evaluation research covers the spectrum of research methods that we have discussed in this text.

For each project, an evaluation researcher must select a research design and a method of data collection that are useful for answering the particular research questions posed and appropriate for the particular program investigated.

You can see why we placed this chapter after most of the others in the text: When you review or plan evaluation research, you have to think about the research process as a whole and how different parts of that process can best be combined.

Although scientific research methods had been used prior to the 1950s (in fact as early as the 1700s) to evaluate outcomes of particular social experiments and programs, it was not until the end of the 1950s that social research became immersed in the workings of government with the common goal of improving society.

During the 1960s, the practice of evaluation research increased dramatically, not only in the United States but also around the world. One of the main initiatives that spawned this growth of evaluation research in the United States was the so-called War on Poverty that was part of the Great Society legislation of the 1960s. When the federal government began to take a major role in alleviating poverty and the social problems associated with it, such as delinquency and crime, the public wanted accountability for the tax dollars spent on such programs. Were these programs actually having their intended effects? Did the benefits outweigh the costs? During this time, the methods of social science were utilized like never before to evaluate this proliferation of new programs.

By the mid-1970s, evaluators were called on not only to assess the overall effectiveness of programs, but also to determine whether programs were being implemented as intended and to provide feedback to help solve programming problems as well. As an indication of the growth of evaluation research during this time, several professional organizations emerged to assist in the dissemination of ideas from the burgeoning number of social scientists engaged in this type of research in the United States, along with similar organizations in other countries (Patton 1997).

Professional evaluation researchers soon realized that it was not enough simply to perform rigorous experiments to determine program efficacy; they must also be responsible for making sure their results could be understood and utilized by the practitioners (e.g., government officials, corporations, and nonprofit agencies) to make decisions about scrapping or modifying existing programs. In addition, there was increased concern in the field regarding fiscal accountability, documenting the worth of social program expenditures in relation to their costs.

It was in this context that professional evaluators began discussing standards for the field of evaluation research. In 1981, a Joint Committee on Standards published the list of features all evaluations should have. These standards still exist today (Joint Committee 1994, as cited in Patton 1997: 17):

Utility: The utility standards are intended to ensure that an evaluation will serve the practical information needs of intended users.

Feasibility: The feasibility standards are intended to ensure that an evaluation will be realistic, prudent, diplomatic, and frugal.

Propriety: The propriety standards are intended to ensure that an evaluation will be conducted legally, ethically, and with due regard for the welfare of those involved in the evaluation, as well as those affected by its results.

Accuracy: The accuracy standards are intended to ensure that an evaluation will reveal and convey technically adequate information about the features that determine worth or merit of the program being evaluated.

To the surprise of many in the field, utility was at the top of the list. This conveyed the idea that an evaluation only met the standards if, in fact, it served the needs of intended users. Professionals in the field responded accordingly. For example, Patton (1997) developed the practice of and coined the term "utilization-focused evaluation" as a way to fulfill the utility standard. Utilization-focused evaluation offered both a philosophy of evaluation and a practical framework for designing and conducting evaluations. The primary premise of this method was that evaluations should be judged by their utility and actual use. Use concerned how real people in the real world applied evaluation findings and experienced the evaluation process.

EVALUATION BASICS

Exhibit 9.1 illustrates the process of evaluation research as a simple systems model. First, clients, customers, students, or some other persons or units—cases—enter the program as **inputs**. Students may begin a new DARE program, sex offenders may enter a new intense probation program, or crime victims may be sent to a victim advocate. Resources and staff required by a program are also program inputs.

Inputs Resources, raw materials, clients, and staff that go into a program.

Next, some service or treatment is provided to the cases. This may be attendance in a class, assistance with a health problem, residence in new housing, or receipt of special cash benefits. The process of service delivery (program process) may be simple or complicated, short or long, but it is designed to have some impact on the cases, as inputs are consumed and outputs are produced.

EXHIBIT 9.1   A Model of Evaluation

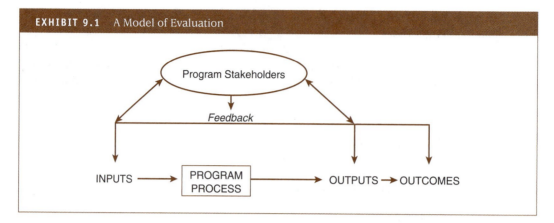

Source: Adapted from Martin, Lawrence L. & Peter M. Kettner. 1996. *Measuring the Performance of Human Service Programs.* Thousand Oaks, CA: Sage, Inc. Used with permission.

Program process The complete treatment or service delivered by the program.

The direct product of the program's service delivery process is its output. Program outputs may include clients served, case managers trained, food parcels delivered, or arrests made. The program outputs may be desirable in themselves, but they primarily serve to indicate that the program is operating.

Outputs The services delivered or new products produced by the program process.

Program **outcomes** indicate the impact of the program on the cases that have been processed. Outcomes can range from improved test scores or higher rates of job retention to fewer criminal offenses and lower rates of poverty. There are likely to be multiple outcomes of any social program, some intended and some unintended, some positive and others that are viewed as negative.

Outcomes The impact of the program process on the cases processed.

Variation in both outputs and outcomes in turn influences the inputs to the program through a **feedback** process. If not enough clients are being served, recruitment of new clients may increase. If too many negative side effects result from a trial medication, the trials may be limited or terminated. If a program does not appear to lead to improved outcomes, clients may go elsewhere.

Feedback Information about service delivery system outputs, outcomes, or operations that is available to any program inputs.

Evaluation research enters into this picture as a more systematic approach to feedback that strengthens the feedback loop through credible analyses of program operations and outcomes. Evaluation research also broadens this loop to include connections to parties outside of the program itself. A funding agency or political authority may mandate the research, outside experts may be brought in to conduct the research, and the evaluation research findings may be released to the public, or at least funders, in a formal report.

The evaluation process as a whole, and the feedback process in particular, can only be understood in relation to the interests and perspectives of program stakeholders. **Stakeholders** are those individuals and groups who have some basis of concern with the program. They might be clients, staff, managers, funders, or the public. The board of a program or agency, the parents or spouses of clients, the foundations that award program grants, the auditors who monitor program spending, the members of Congress are all potential program stakeholders, and each has an interest in the outcome of any program evaluation. Some may fund the evaluation, some may provide research data, some may review, and even approve, the research report (Martin & Kettner 1996: 3). Who the program stakeholders are and what role they play in the program evaluation will have tremendous consequences for the research.

Stakeholders Individuals and groups who have some basis of concern with the program.

Can you see the difference between evaluation research and traditional social science research? Unlike explanatory social science research, evaluation research is not designed to test the implications of a social theory; the basic issue is often just, "What is the program's impact?" Process evaluation often uses qualitative methods, but unlike traditional exploratory research, the goal is not to create a broad theoretical explanation for what is discovered; instead, the question is, "How does the program do what it does?" Unlike social science research, the researchers cannot design evaluation studies simply in accord with the highest scientific standards and the most important research questions; instead, it is program stakeholders who set the agenda but there is no sharp boundary between the two: In their attempt to explain how and why the program has an impact, and whether the program is needed, evaluation researchers often bring social theories into their projects.

EVALUATION ALTERNATIVES

Today, the field of evaluation research remains somewhat of a dichotomy. There are those who conduct evaluation research for the sake of knowledge alone, whereas others strive to make their products useful for some action (the more specific program evaluation research, such as that performed by Sherman and Berk, 1984, discussed in chapter 2). Regardless of the emphasis, however, all evaluation is empirical and data-driven. Both program evaluation and evaluation research in general offer empirical answers to questions of policy and policy effectiveness. Objective and empirical assessments of policies and programs are the cornerstone of the evaluation field.

Evaluation research may be undertaken for a variety of reasons: for management and administrative purposes, to test hypotheses derived from theory, to identify ways to improve the delivery of services, or to decide whether to continue, cut, or modify a particular program. The goal of evaluation research, however, is primarily the same as the goal for all social science research: to design and implement a study that is objective and grounded in the rules of scientific methodology. These methods run the gamut of the methods we have discussed in this text. They can range from the strictly quantitative experimental and quasi-experimental designs to the qualitative methodologies of observation and intensive interviewing.

Evaluation projects can focus on several questions related to the operation of social programs and the impact they have:

- Is the program needed? (evaluation of need)
- Can the program be evaluated? (evaluability assessment)
- How does the program operate? (process evaluation)
- What is the program's impact? (impact evaluation)
- How efficient is the program? (efficiency analysis)

The specific methods used in an evaluation research project depend, in part, on which of these questions is being addressed.

Do We Need the Program?

Is a new program needed or is an old one still required? Is there a need at all? A **needs assessment** attempts to answer these questions with systematic, credible evidence. The initial impetus for implementing programs to alleviate social problems and other societal ailments typically comes from a variety of sources, including advocacy groups, moral leaders, community advocates, and political figures. Before a program is designed and implemented, however, it is essential to obtain reliable information on the nature and the scope of the problem, and the target population in need of the intervention. Evaluation researchers often contribute to these efforts by applying research tools to answer such questions as "What is the magnitude of this problem in this community?" "How many people in this community are in need of this program?" "What are the demographic characteristics of these people (e.g., age, gender, and race or ethnicity)?" and "Is the proposed program or intervention appropriate for this population?"

Can the Program Be Evaluated?

Evaluation research will be pointless if the program itself cannot be evaluated. Yes, some type of study is always possible, but a study conducted specifically to identify the effects of a particular program may not be possible within the available time and resources. So researchers may carry out an **evaluability assessment** to learn this in advance, rather than expend time and effort on a fruitless project.

Knowledge about the program gleaned through the evaluability assessment can be used to refine evaluation plans. Because they are preliminary studies to "check things out," evaluability assessments often rely on qualitative methods. Program managers and key staff may be interviewed in depth, or program sponsors may be asked about the importance they attach to different goals. These assessments also may have an "action research" aspect, because the researcher presents the findings to program managers and encourages changes in program operations.

Is the Program Working as Planned?

What actually happens in a program? Once a program has been started, evaluators are often called on to document the extent to which implementation has taken place, whether the program is reaching the target individuals or groups, whether the program is actually operating as expected, and what resources are being expended in the conduct of the program. This is often called **process evaluation** or **program monitoring**. Rossi and Freeman (1989) define program monitoring as the systematic attempt by evaluation researchers to examine program coverage and delivery. Assessing program coverage consists of estimating the extent to which a program is reaching its intended target population; evaluating program delivery consists of measuring the degree of congruence between the plan for providing services and treatments and the ways they are actually provided.

Process evaluations are extremely important, primarily because there is no way to reliably determine whether the intended outcomes have occurred without being certain the program is working according to plan. For example, imagine you are responsible for determining whether an anti-bullying curriculum implemented in a school has been successful in decreasing the amount of bullying behavior by the students. You conduct a survey of the students both before and after the curriculum began and determine that rates of bullying have not significantly changed in the school since the curriculum started. After you write your report, however, you find out that, instead of being given in a five-day series of one-hour sessions as intended, the curriculum was actually crammed into a two-hour format delivered on a Friday afternoon. A process evaluation would have revealed this implementation problem. If a program has not been implemented as intended, there is obviously no need to ask whether it had the intended outcomes.

A process evaluation can take many forms. Because most government and private organizations inherently monitor their activities through such things as application forms, receipts, and stock inventories, it should be relatively easy to obtain quantitative data for monitoring the delivery of services. This information can be summarized to describe things such as the clients served and the services provided. In addition to this quantitative information, a process evaluation will also likely benefit from qualitative methodologies such as unstructured interviews with people using the service or program. Interviews can also be conducted with staff to illuminate what they perceive to be obstacles to their delivery of services.

Process evaluation can employ a wide range of indicators. Program coverage can be monitored through program records, participant surveys, community surveys, or utilizers versus dropouts and ineligibles. Service delivery can be monitored through service records completed by program staff, a management information system maintained by program administrators, or reports by program recipients (Rossi & Freeman 1989).

Qualitative methods are often a key component of process evaluation studies because they can be used to elucidate and understand internal program dynamics, even those that were not anticipated (Patton 2002: 159; Posavac & Carey 1997). Qualitative researchers may develop detailed descriptions of how program participants engage with each other, how the program experience varies for different people, and how the program changes and evolves over time.

Did the Program Work?

If a process study shows that the implementation of the program has been delivered to the target population as planned, the next role for an evaluator is to assess the extent to which the program achieved its goals. "Did the program work?" "Did the program have the intended consequences?" This question should by now be familiar to you; stated more like a research question we are used to, "Did the treatment or program (independent variable) effect change in the dependent variable?" It all comes back to the issue of causality. This part of the research is variously called impact analysis or impact evaluation.

Impact evaluation (or analysis) Analysis of the extent to which a treatment or other service has an effect.

The bulk of the published evaluation studies in our field are devoted to some type of impact assessment. Have new seat-belt laws increased rates of seat-belt usage? Have rape reform statutes increased the willingness of rape victims to report their victimizations to police? Are boot camps more likely to reduce recidivism among juveniles compared with more traditional juvenile detention settings? Have mandatory minimum sentencing guidelines decreased the probability that extra legal factors such as sex and race will affect an individual's sentence? The list could go on and on.

As in other areas of research, an experimental design is the preferred method for maximizing internal validity—that is, for making sure your causal claims about program impact are justified. Cases are assigned randomly to one or more experimental treatment groups and to a control group so that there is no systematic difference between the groups at the outset (see chapter 5). The goal is to achieve a fair, unbiased test of the program itself, so that the judgment about the program's impact is not influenced by differences between the types of people who are in the different groups. It can be a difficult goal to achieve, because the usual practice in social programs is to let people decide for themselves whether they want to enter a program or not and also to establish eligibility criteria that ensure people who enter the program are different from those who do not (Boruch 1997). In either case, a selection bias is introduced.

Of course, program impact may also be evaluated with quasi-experimental designs or survey or field research methods, without a randomized experimental design. But if current participants who are already in a program are compared with nonparticipants, it is unlikely that the treatment group will be comparable to the control group. Participants will probably be a selected group, different at the outset from nonparticipants. As a result, causal conclusions about program impact will be on much shakier ground. For instance, when a study at New York's maximum-security prison for women found that "Income Education [i.e., classes] is Found to Lower Risk of New Arrest," the conclusions were immediately suspect: The research design did not ensure that the women who enrolled in the prison classes were the same as those who had not enrolled in the classes, "leaving open the possibility that the results were due, at least in part, to self-selection, with the women most motivated to avoid reincarceration being the ones who took the college classes" (Lewin 2001).

Impact analysis is an important undertaking that fully deserves the attention it has been given in government program funding requirements. However, you should realize that more rigorous evaluation designs are less likely to conclude that a program has the desired effect; as the standard of proof goes up, success is harder to demonstrate.

Is the Program Worth It?

Whatever the program's benefits, are they sufficient to offset the program's costs? Are taxpayers getting their money's worth? What resources are required by the program? These efficiency questions can be the primary reason that funders require evaluation of the programs they fund. As a result, **efficiency analysis**, which compares program effects with costs, is often a necessary component of an evaluation research project.

A **cost-benefit analysis** must identify the specific program costs and the procedures for estimating the economic value of specific program benefits. This type of analysis also requires that the analyst identify whose perspective will be used in order to determine what can be considered a benefit rather than a cost.

A **cost-effectiveness analysis** focuses attention directly on the program's outcomes rather than on the economic value of those outcomes. In a cost-effectiveness analysis, the specific costs of the program are compared with the program's outcomes, such as the number of jobs obtained, the extent of improvement in reading scores, or the degree of decline in crimes committed. For example, one result might be an estimate of how much it cost the program for each job obtained by a program participant.

Efficiency analysis A type of evaluation research that compares program costs with program effects. It can be either a cost-benefit analysis or a cost-effectiveness analysis.

Cost-benefit analysis A type of evaluation research that compares program costs with the economic value of program benefits.

Cost-effectiveness analysis A type of evaluation research that compares program costs with actual program outcomes.

Social science training often does not give much attention to cost-benefit analysis, so it can be helpful to review possible costs and benefits with an economist or business school professor or student. Once potential costs and benefits have been identified, they must be measured. It is a need highlighted in recent government programs.

In addition to measuring services and their associated costs, a cost-benefit analysis must be able to make some type of estimation of how clients benefited from the program. Normally, this will involve a comparison of some indicators of client status before and after clients received program services, or between clients who received program services and a comparable group who did not.

A recent study of therapeutic communities provides a clear illustration. A therapeutic community is an alternative to the traditional correctional response to drug addiction, which is typically incarceration for those convicted of either the possession or trafficking of illegal substances. In therapeutic communities, abusers participate in an intensive, structured living experience with other addicts who are attempting to stay sober. Because the treatment involves residential support as well as other types of services, it can be quite costly. Are those costs worth it?

Sacks et al. (2002) conducted a cost-benefit analysis of a modified therapeutic community (TC). A total of 342 homeless mentally ill chemical abusers were randomly assigned to either a TC or a "treatment-as-usual" comparison group. Employment status, criminal activity, and utilization of health care services were each measured for the three months prior to entering treatment and the three months after treatment. Earnings from employment in each period were adjusted for costs incurred by criminal activity and utilization of health care services.

Was it worth it? The average cost of TC treatment for a client was $20,361. In comparison, the economic benefit (based on earnings) to the average TC client was $305,273, which declined to $273,698 after comparing post- to pre-program earnings, but was still $253,337 even after adjustment for costs. The resulting benefit-cost ratio was 13:1, although this ratio declined to only 5.2:1 after further adjustments (for cases with extreme values). Nonetheless, the TC program studied seems to have had a substantial benefit relative to its costs.

DESIGN DECISIONS

Once we have decided on, or identified, the goal or focus for a program evaluation, there are still important decisions to be made about how to design the specific evaluation project. The most important decisions are the following:

- Black box or program theory: Do we care how the program gets results?
- Researcher or stakeholder orientation: Whose goals matter most?
- Quantitative or qualitative methods: Which methods provide the best answers?
- Simple or complex outcomes: How complicated should the findings be?

Black Box Evaluation or Program Theory

The "meat and potatoes" of most evaluation research involves determining whether a program has the intended effect. If the effect occurred, the program "worked"; if the effect didn't occur, then some would say the program should be abandoned or redesigned. In this approach, the process by which a program has an effect on outcomes is often treated as a **black box**—that is, the focus of the evaluation researcher is on whether cases seem to have changed as a result of their exposure to the program, between the time they entered the program as inputs and when they exited the program as outputs (Chen 1990). The assumption is that program evaluation requires only the test of a simple input–output model. There may be no attempt to open the black box of the program process.

If an investigation of program process is conducted, a **program theory** may be developed. A program theory describes what has been learned about how the program has its effect. When a researcher has sufficient knowledge before the investigation begins, outlining a program theory can help to guide the investigation of program process in the most productive directions. This is termed a **theory-driven evaluation**.

A program theory specifies how the program is expected to operate and identifies which program elements are operational (Chen 1990: 32). In addition, a program theory specifies how a program is to produce its effects and so improves understanding of the relationship between the independent variable (the program) and the dependent variable (the outcome or outcomes).

Researcher or Stakeholder Orientation

Whose prescriptions specify how the program should operate, what outcomes it should try to achieve, or who it should serve? Most social science research assumes that the researcher specifies the research questions, the applicable theory or theories, and the outcomes to be investigated. Social science research results are most often reported in a professional journal or at professional conferences where scientific standards determine how the research is received. In program evaluation, however, the research question is often set by the program sponsors or the government agency that is responsible for reviewing the program. It is to these authorities that research findings are reported. Most often this authority also specifies the outcomes to be investigated. The first evaluator of the evaluation research is therefore the funding agency, not the professional social science community. Evaluation research is research for a client, and its results may directly affect the services, treatments, or even punishments (e.g., in the case of prison studies) that program users receive. In this case, the person who pays the piper gets to call the tune.

Should an evaluation researcher insist on designing the evaluation project and specifying its goals, or should they accept the suggestions and adopt the goals of the funding agency? What role should the preferences of program staff or clients play? What responsibility does the evaluation researcher have to politicians and taxpayers when evaluating government-funded programs? The different answers that various evaluation researchers have given to these questions are reflected in different approaches to evaluation (Chen 1990: 66–68).

Stakeholder approaches encourage researchers to be responsive to program stakeholders. Issues for study are to be based on the views of people involved with the program, and reports are to be made to program participants (Shadish, Cook, & Leviton 1991: 275–276). The program theory is developed by the researcher to clarify and develop the key stakeholders' theory of the program (Shadish et al. 1991: 254–255). In one stakeholder approach, termed *utilization-focused evaluation,* the evaluator forms a task force of program stakeholders who help to shape the evaluation project so that they are most likely to use its results (Patton 2002: 171–175). In evaluation research termed *action research* or *participatory research,* program participants are engaged with the researchers as coresearchers and help to design, conduct, and report the research. One research approach that has been termed *appreciative inquiry* eliminates the professional researcher altogether in favor of a structured dialogue about needed changes among program participants themselves (Patton 2002:177–185).

Social science approaches emphasize the importance of researcher expertise and maintenance of some autonomy in order to develop the most trustworthy, unbiased program evaluation. It is assumed that "evaluators cannot passively accept the values and views of the other stakeholders" (Chen 1990: 78). Evaluators who adopt this approach derive a program theory from information they obtain on how the program operates and extant social science theory and knowledge, not from the views of stakeholders.

Integrative approaches attempt to cover issues of concern to both stakeholders and evaluators, and to include stakeholders in the group from which guidance is routinely sought (Chen & Rossi 1987: 101–102). The emphasis given to either stakeholder or social concern is expected to vary with the specific project circumstances. Integrated approaches seek to balance the goal of carrying out a project that is responsive to stakeholder concerns with the goal of objective, scientifically trustworthy, and generalizable results. When the research is planned, evaluators are expected to communicate and negotiate regularly with key stakeholders and to take stakeholder concerns into account. Findings from preliminary inquiries are reported back to program decision makers so that they can make improvements in the program before it is formally evaluated. When the actual evaluation is conducted, the evaluation research team is expected to operate more autonomously, minimizing intrusions from program stakeholders.

Ultimately, evaluation research takes place in a political context, in which program stakeholders may be competing or collaborating to increase program funding or to emphasize particular program goals. It is a political process that creates social programs, and it is a political process that determines whether these programs are evaluated and what is done with evaluation findings (Weiss 1993:94). Developing supportive relations with stakeholder groups will increase the odds that political processes will not undermine evaluation practice.

Case Study: Problem-Oriented Policing in Violent Crime Areas

Several studies have found that over half of all crimes in a city are committed at a few criminogenic places within communities. These places have been called "hot spots" by some criminologists (Sherman, Gartin, & Buerger 1989; Weisburd, Maher, & Sherman 1992). Even within the most crime-ridden neighborhoods, it has been found that crime clusters at a few discrete locations while other areas remain relatively crime-free. The clustering of violent crime at particular locations suggests that there are important features or dynamics at these locations that give rise to violent situations. As such, focused crime prevention efforts should be able to modify these criminogenic conditions and reduce violence.

Problem-oriented policing strategies are increasingly utilized by urban jurisdictions to reduce crime in these high-activity crime places. Problem-oriented policing challenges officers to identify and analyze the causes of problems behind a string of criminal incidents. Once the underlying conditions that give rise to crime problems are known, police officers can then develop and implement appropriate responses. Braga et al. (1999) created a novel experiment designed to determine the effectiveness of problem-oriented policing to decrease the incidence of violent street crime in Jersey City, New Jersey. The methodology they employed for their study was a true randomized experimental design. Recall from chapter 5 that this design allows researchers to assume that the only systematic difference between a control and an experimental group is the presence of the intervention—in this case, the presence or absence of problem-oriented policing strategies.

To determine which places would receive the problem-oriented strategies and which places would not, 56 neighborhoods were matched into 28 pairs with equal levels of crime, which were then randomly assigned to receive the problem-oriented policing treatment (experimental places). Remember that a key feature of true experimental designs is this **random assignment**. The places that were not selected from the flip in each pair did not receive the new policing strategies (control places). The design of this experimental evaluation is illustrated in Exhibit 9.2.

In each of the experimental places, police officers from the Violent Crime Unit (VCU) of the Jersey City Police Department established networks consistent with problem-oriented policing. For example, community members were used as information sources to discuss the nature of the problems the community faced, the possible effectiveness of proposed responses, and the assessment of implemented responses. In most places, the VCU officers believed that the violence that distinguished these places from other areas of the city was closely related to the disorder of the place. Although specific tactics varied from place to place, most attempts to control violence in these places were actually targeted at the social disorder problems. For example, some tactics included cleaning up the environment of the place through aggressive order maintenance and making physical improvements such as securing vacant lots or removing trash from the street. The independent variable or treatment, then, was the use of problem-oriented policing, which comprised a number of specific tactics implemented by police officers to control the physical and social disorder at experimental violent places. In contrast, control places did not receive these problem-solving efforts; they received traditional policing strategies such as arbitrary patrol interventions and routine follow-up investigations by detectives. No problem-oriented strategies were employed.

Braga et al. (1999) examined the efficacy of these problem-oriented policing strategies by using three separate dependent variables: incident report data, citizen emergency calls for service within each place, and physical observation of each place during the pretest and posttest periods. This variable was used to indicate changes in both physical incivilities at

EXHIBIT 9.2 Randomized Experimental Design Used to Evaluate Problem-Oriented Policing Strategies

Places	Placement	Group	Pretest	Treatment/Condition	Posttest
56 high violent crime places	Random assignment	Experimental group	Citizen calls for police service	Problem-oriented policing	Citizen calls for police service
		Control group	Citizen calls for police service	Traditional policing	Citizen calls for police service

Source: Braga, Anthony A., David L. Weisburd, Elin J. Waring, Lorraine Green Mazerolle, William Spelman, and Francis Gajewski (1999) "Problem-Oriented Policing in Violent Crime Places: A Randomized Controlled Experiment." *Criminology, 37*(4): 541–580. Reprinted with permission.

places such as vacant lots, trash, graffiti, or broken windows and social incivilities such as drinking in public and loitering. These variables were measured for six-month preintervention and postintervention periods. If the problem-oriented policing approach was effective, then Braga and colleagues should have seen a decrease in incidents and emergency calls for service in the experimental areas in the posttest compared to the control areas. They should also have seen decreased signs of physical and social incivilities in the experimental areas compared to the control areas. Results indicated that the problem-oriented policing strategies examined in this evaluation research appear to have had a great deal of success in controlling and preventing crime.

STRENGTHS OF RANDOMIZED EXPERIMENTAL DESIGNS IN IMPACT EVALUATIONS

The research design used by Braga et al. (1999) meets all three criteria for a true experimental design. First, they used at least two comparison groups. In the Braga et al. research, some communities received the problem-oriented patrol strategies (experimental groups) while the other comparison communities received traditional police patrol (control groups). And finally, the assessment of change in the dependent variables used in their study was performed after the experimental condition (problem-oriented strategies) had been delivered.

Because the communities in Braga et al.'s (1999) study were randomly assigned to receive either problem-oriented or traditional patrol strategies, the relationship found between these strategies (independent variable) and the dependent variables (incidents of crime, etc.) are unambiguous. Braga and colleagues monitored their dependent variables both before and after the different policing strategies were implemented, so there is also no question that the strategies came before the change in the dependent variable. Finally, the random assignment of the communities to either the problem-oriented or traditional police conditions controlled for a host of possible extraneous influences that may have created spurious relationships.

The extent to which the findings of these studies can be generalized to the larger population, however, is another issue. Can Braga et al.'s (1999) findings be generalized to the larger population in New Jersey (sample generalizability) or to other states and communities (external validity)? Issues of sample generalizability, you will recall, are related to selecting a random sample from the population in the first place (random selection), not random assignment. However, because Braga and colleagues' study utilized several experimental and control communities, this increases the likelihood that their findings are generalizable to their respective populations. In addition, because the study was performed in the field (i.e., the real world) and not in a laboratory, their findings are more likely to be generalizable to the larger population.

WHEN EXPERIMENTS ARE NOT FEASIBLE

We have already learned that many research questions or situations are not amenable to a true experimental design. The same is true in evaluation research. There are many reasons why it may be impossible to use randomized experiments to evaluate the impacts of programs and policies. The primary reason why randomization is not possible in evaluation research is that the program is usually outside the control of the evaluator. As Rossi and Freeman (1989) state, "for political, human subject or other considerations, program staff, sponsors, or other powerful stakeholders resist randomization" (1989: 313). Obtaining the cooperation of the program staff and sponsors is often an obstacle in evaluation research. In fact, when there are several locations implementing similar programs, the sites included in an evaluation study may be selected based primarily on the cooperation of the staff and sponsors.

In general, quasi-experimental designs are the most powerful alternatives to true randomized experimental designs. The more alike the experimental and control groups are to each other, particularly on characteristics thought to be related to the intervention or treatment, the more confident we can be in a study's findings. In this section, we discuss two types of quasi-experimental designs that are often utilized in criminology and criminal justice to determine the impacts of programs. To illustrate the first type, a **nonequivalent control group design**, we use research that has been done to evaluate whether boot camps are more likely to reduce recidivism after release compared with traditional incarceration. The second type of quasi-experimental design we highlight is the **time series design**. To illustrate this design, we use a study that evaluated the impact of mandatory sentences for gun crimes.

Case Study: Boot Camps

Since their beginning in 1983 in Georgia, the use of correctional boot camps, sometimes called shock incarceration programs, has skyrocketed in both state and federal prison systems. For politicians and citizens alike, the notion of a strict, military-style punishment as an alternative to extended incarceration is attractive. Many questions remain, however, about the value of boot camps. Do they work? Because there are so many different types of boot camps (e.g., some have a military-style atmosphere whereas others do not), there is no easy answer to this question.

In 1990, Doris MacKenzie was the principal investigator of a study to evaluate boot camp program efficacy in eight states: Florida, Georgia, Illinois, Louisiana, New York, Oklahoma, South Carolina, and Texas. These sites were selected because they incorporated the core elements of a boot camp program, including (1) strict rules, discipline, and a military boot camp–like atmosphere; (2) mandatory participation in military drills and physical training; and (3) separation of program participants from other prison inmates.

The evaluation was extensive and resulted in many publications (Brame & MacKenzie 1996; MacKenzie 1994; MacKenzie et al. 1995; MacKenzie & Piquero 1994; MacKenzie & Souryal 1995). We will highlight the results of the impact assessments for recidivism here. To determine whether boot camps were more likely than traditional prison time to reduce recidivism after release, MacKenzie and colleagues utilized a quasi-experimental design. In each state, a sample of male boot camp program graduates was used as the experimental condition. Two other offender samples were used as comparison groups and usually included regular prison parolees, probationers, and boot camp dropouts. The individuals from all samples, however, met the eligibility requirements for the boot camp programs. This nonequivalent control group design is illustrated in Exhibit 9.3.

After being sentenced to probation or released from boot camps and prison, subjects were tracked for a follow-up period of up to two years of community supervision. Recidivism was measured by arrests and revocations for new crimes and/or for technical violations.

EXHIBIT 9.3   Nonequivalent Control Group Design Used to Evaluate Boot Camps

Source: Brame & MacKenzie (1996).

Were boot camps successful in meeting their goals? Results were mixed: Programs with more intensive long-term follow-up supervision had a decrease in recidivism while traditional boot camps without such long-term supervision did not.

The weakness of this quasi-experimental design lay in the fact that MacKenzie was not able to randomly assign offenders to the boot camps or the comparison treatments. Therefore, there is less confidence in the findings, primarily because there is no assurance that the offenders were equivalent before they received the treatments.

NONEXPERIMENTAL DESIGNS

Much research that is conducted to evaluate the effectiveness of programs or policies uses a **nonexperimental design** in which a single group is studied only once, after the treatment or program has been delivered. Unfortunately, such studies have absolutely no form of control or comparison. As such, they are "of almost no scientific value" (Campbell & Stanley 1996: 6). Nevertheless, because they are so common in evaluation research, we provide an illustration of their use.

Case Study: Vocational Education for Serious Juvenile Offenders—A One-Shot Design

Some of the earliest programs for crime reduction have been those that provide legitimate employment or employment skills to offenders or at-risk individuals. Most of these programs target adolescents. One of the myriad programs to provide vocational education for juvenile offenders is New Pride, Inc. This program has been providing vocational services to serious young offenders (14 through 18 years of age) for almost two decades.

The planners of New Pride, understandably, have a lot of faith in their program. Unfortunately, there have been few systematic attempts to evaluate the effectiveness of this program and others like it in either increasing employment or reducing recidivism (Bushway & Reuter 1997). For example, the results of the one-shot design methodology evaluation of the New Pride program performed by James and Granville (1984) are too scientifically deficient to be of value. This methodology is displayed in Exhibit 9.4.

Basically, a one-shot design measures the dependent variable after the treatment has been delivered for only those who received the treatment. James and Granville (1984) found that over 70% of those who completed the New Pride program were successfully reintegrated into the public school system, continued part-time employment, and were not rearrested within six months of program completion. Unfortunately, because there was no random assignment to another comparison group—in fact, no comparison group whatsoever—these results tell us very little. Perhaps the results would have been the same for youths who had received no vocational training. The problem is, we can never be sure when a one-shot design such as this is used.

QUALITATIVE AND QUANTITATIVE METHODS

Evaluation research that attempts to identify the effects of a treatment, law, or program typically is quantitative. It is fair to say that when there is an interest in comparing outcomes between an experimental and a control group, or tracking change over time in a systematic manner, quantitative methods are favored.

But qualitative methods can add much to quantitative evaluation research studies, including more depth, detail, nuance, and exemplary case studies (Patton 1997). Perhaps the greatest contribution qualitative methods can make in many evaluation studies is investigating program process—finding out what is "inside the black box." Although it is possible—even recommended—to track the process of service delivery with quantitative measures like staff contact hours, frequency of complaints, and the like, the goal of finding out what is happening to program clients and how clients experience the program can often best be achieved by observing program activities and interviewing staff and clients intensively.

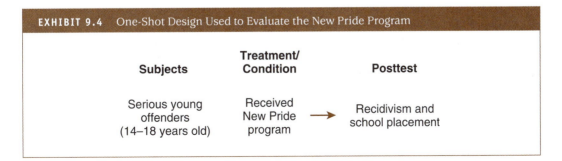

EXHIBIT 9.4 One-Shot Design Used to Evaluate the New Pride Program

Subjects	Treatment/ Condition	Posttest
Serious young offenders (14–18 years old)	Received New Pride program →	Recidivism and school placement

Source: James & Granville (1984).

Another good reason for using qualitative methods in evaluation research is the importance of learning how different individuals react to the treatment. Qualitative methods can also help in understanding how social programs actually operate. Complex social programs have many different features, and it is not always clear whether it is the combination of those features or some particular features that are responsible for the program's effect, or for the absence of an effect.

The more complex the social program, the more value qualitative methods can add to the evaluation process. For the most part, the strengths and weaknesses of methodologies used in evaluation research are those of the methods we have already discussed throughout this text. As Patton (1997) contends, "There are no perfect [evaluation] studies. And there cannot be, for there is no agreement on what constitutes perfection" (1997: 23). There are, however, methods that are better able to infer cause and effect. Because the basic question of most impact evaluations is, "Does program (cause) have its intended consequences (effect)?" there are basic methodological criteria we can use to judge the methods discussed in this chapter.

In their review of the crime prevention evaluation literature, Sherman et al. (1997) adopted a way to judge the "methodological rigor" of evaluation studies using a five-point scale. The researchers gave each study examined in their review a "scientific methods score" of 1 to 5, with 5 being the strongest scientific evidence. Studies were assigned a score based on the following criteria:

1. correlation between a crime prevention program and its intended outcome (e.g., a measure of crime or crime risk factors);

2. temporal sequence between the program and the crime or risk outcome clearly observed (e.g., program before outcome), or a comparison group present without demonstrated comparability to the treatment group;

3. a comparison between two or more groups or units, one with and one without the program and/or a long time series analysis;

4. a comparison between multiple groups or units with and without the program, controlling for other factors, or a nonequivalent comparison group that has only minor differences evident between the groups; and

5. random assignment to program (experimental group) and comparison (control groups).

Despite the fact that a randomized experiment is the best way to determine the impact of a program, it is also important to remember that the methodology selected for an evaluation project should be relevant to the policy makers and planners who intend to use the results. Although some researchers vehemently contend that only a randomized experimental design can provide reliable information on the impacts of a program, others just as vehemently disagree.

ETHICS IN EVALUATION

Evaluation research can make a difference in people's lives while it is in progress, as well as after the results are reported. Educational and vocational training opportunities in prison, the availability of legal counsel, and treatment for substance abuse are all potentially important benefits, and an evaluation research project can change both their type and their availability. This direct impact on research participants, and potentially their families, heightens the attention that evaluation researchers have to give to human subjects concerns. Although the particular criteria that are at issue and the decisions that are most ethical vary with the type of evaluation research conducted and the specifics of a particular project, there are always serious ethical as well as political concerns for the evaluation researcher (Boruch 1997: 13; Dentler 2002: 166).

Assessing needs, determining evaluability, and examining the process of treatment delivery have few special ethical dimensions. Cost-benefit analyses in themselves also raise few ethical concerns. It is when the focus is program impact that human subjects considerations multiply. What about assigning persons randomly to receive some social program or benefit? One justification given by evaluation researchers has to do with the scarcity of these resources. If not everyone in the population who is eligible for a program can receive it, due to resource limitations, what could be a fairer way to distribute the program benefits than through a lottery? Random assignment also seems like a reasonable way to allocate potential program benefits when a new program is being tested with only some members of the target recipient population. However, when an ongoing entitlement program is being evaluated and experimental subjects would normally be eligible for program participation, it may not be ethical simply to bar some potential participants from the programs. Instead, evaluation researchers may test alternative treatments or provide some alternative benefit while the treatment is being denied.

The Health Research Extension Act of 1985 (Public Law 99–158) mandated that the Department of Health and Human Services require all research organizations receiving federal funds to have an Institutional Review Board (IRB) to assess all research for adherence to ethical practice guidelines. We have already reviewed the federally mandated criteria (Boruch 1997: 29–33):

- Are risks minimized?
- Are risks reasonable in relation to benefits?
- Is the selection of individuals equitable (randomization implies this)?
- Is informed consent given?
- Are the data monitored?
- Are privacy and confidentiality assured?

Evaluation researchers must consider whether it will be possible to meet each of these criteria long before they even design a study.

The problem of maintaining subject confidentiality is particularly thorny because researchers in general are not legally protected from the requirements that they provide evidence requested in legal proceedings, particularly through the process known as "discovery." However, it is important to be aware that several federal statutes have been passed specifically to protect research data about vulnerable populations from legal disclosure requirements. For example, the Crime Control and Safe Streets Act (28 CFR Part 11) includes the following stipulation:

Copies of [research] information [about persons receiving services under the act or the subjects of inquiries into criminal behavior] shall be immune from legal process and shall not, without the consent of the persons furnishing such information, be admitted as evidence or used for any purpose in any action, suit, or other judicial or administrative proceedings. (Boruch 1997: 60)

It is important to realize that it is costly to society and potentially harmful to participants to maintain ineffective programs. In the long run, at least, it may be more ethical to conduct an evaluation study than to let the status quo remain in place.

CONCLUSION

In recent years, the field of evaluation research has become an increasingly popular and active research specialty within the fields of criminology and criminal justice. Many social scientists find special appeal in evaluation research because of its utility.

The research methods applied to evaluation research are no different from those covered elsewhere in this text; they can range from qualitative intensive interviews to rigorous randomized experimental designs. In process evaluations, qualitative methodologies can be particularly advantageous. However, the best method for determining cause and effect, or for determining whether a program had its intended consequences (impacts), is the randomized experimental design. Although this may not always be possible in the field, it is the "gold standard" with which to compare methodologies used to assess the impacts of all programs and/or policies.

KEY TERMS

Accuracy	Inputs
Black box evaluation	Judgment-oriented evaluation
Comparison group	Knowledge-oriented evaluation
Control group	Mechanisms
Cost-benefit analysis	Needs assessment
Cost-effectiveness analysis	Nonequivalent control group design
Efficiency analysis	One-shot design
Evaluation of efficiency	Outcomes
Evaluation of impact	Outputs
Evaluation of need	Program process
Evaluation of process	Program theory
Experimental designs	Propriety
Feasibility	Quasi-experimental design
Feedback	Random assignment
Formative evaluation	Stakeholders
Impact evaluation	Time series design
Improvement-oriented evaluation	Utility

HIGHLIGHTS

- The evaluation process as a whole, and the feedback process in particular, can be understood only in relation to the interests and perspectives of program stakeholders.
- The process by which a program has an effect on outcomes is often treated as a "black box," but there is good reason to open the black box and investigate the process by which the program operates and produces, or fails to produce, an effect.

- A program theory may be developed before or after an investigation of program process is completed. It may be either descriptive or prescriptive.
- There are five primary types of program evaluation: needs assessment, evaluability assessment, process evaluation (including formative evaluation), impact evaluation, and efficiency (cost-benefit) analysis.
- True randomized experiments are the most appropriate method for determining cause and effect, and as such, for determining the impact of programs and policies.
- Evaluation research raises complex ethical issues because it may involve withholding desired social benefits.

EXERCISES

Discussing Research

1. Read one of the articles reviewed in this chapter. Fill in the answers to the article review questions (Appendix B) not covered in the chapter. Do you agree with the answers to the other questions discussed in the chapter? Could you add some points to the critique provided by the author of the text or to the lessons on research design drawn from these critiques?

2. Propose a randomized experimental evaluation of a social program with which you are familiar. Include in your proposal a description of the program and its intended outcomes. Discuss the strengths and weaknesses of your proposed design.

Finding Research

1. Go to the American Evaluation Association website at www.eval.org. Choose "Publications" and then "Guiding Principles for Evaluator." What are the five guiding principles discussed in this document? Provide a summary of each principle.

2. How adequate are juvenile court records? Go to the Bureau of Justice Statistics website at http://blackstone.ojp.usdoj.gov/bjs/pub/ascii/pjjr.txt. Read the report and write a brief summary.

3. Describe the resources available for evaluation researchers at one of the following three websites:

   www.wmich.edu/evalctr

   www.stanford.edu/ ~ davidf/empowermentevaluation.html

   www.worldbank.org/oed

Critiquing Research

1. Evaluate the ethics of one of the studies reviewed in which human subjects were used. Sherman and Berk's (1984) study of domestic violence raises some interesting ethical issues, but there are also points to consider in most of the other studies. Which ethical guidelines (see chapter 2) seem most difficult to adhere to? Where do you think the line should be drawn between not taking any risks at all with research participants and developing valid scientific knowledge? Be sure to consider various costs and benefits of the research.

2. Find a recent article that evaluates a policy or program from a criminal justice policy journal such as *Crime and Public Policy*. Describe its strengths and weaknesses. Do the author(s) make claims about causality that are supported by their methodology?

Making Research Ethical

1. The Manhattan Bail Project randomly assigned some defendants with strong community ties to be recommended for release without bail and some not to be recommended. You learned in this chapter that they found a very high (99%) rate of appearance at trial for those released without bail, but of course the researchers did not know that this would be the case before they conducted the study. Would you consider this study design ethical? What if one of the persons in the 1% who did not come to trial murdered someone when they should have been at court? Are there any conditions when randomization should not be permitted when evaluating criminal justice programs?

2. A large body of evaluation research suggested that the DARE program was not effective in reducing drug use in schools, but many school and police officials, parents, and students insisted on maintaining the program without change for many years. Do you think that government agencies should be allowed to de-fund programs that numerous evaluation research studies have shown to be ineffective? Should government agencies be *required* to justify funding for social programs on the basis of evaluation research results?

Developing a Research Proposal

Imagine that you are submitting a proposal to the U.S. Justice Department to evaluate the efficacy of a new treatment program for substance abusers within federal correctional institutions.

1. What would your research question be if you proposed a process evaluation component to your research?

2. For the outcome evaluation, what is your independent variable and what would your dependent variable be? How would you operationalize both?

3. What type of research design would you propose to answer both the process evaluation and outcome evaluation components in your proposal?

Performing Data Analysis in SPSS

Do hospitals provide equal treatment across race and social class? Although the data available do not provide enough information for an in-depth evaluation of hospital procedures or quality of care, NCS93.POR enables you to explore the relationship between the total amount of medical expenses incurred as a result of injuries sustained from rape, robbery, or assault (MEDEXP) and the victim's family income (INCOME), race or ethnicity (PPRACE), and coverage by any medical insurance or other type of health benefits program (INSURANC).

1. Write at least three hypotheses about the relationship between medical expenses incurred from rape, robbery, or assault across race and social class based on the variables discussed above.

2. Obtain a frequency distribution for INCOME. Recode INCOME to measure victim's family income into three or four categories.

3. Select all cases in which the victim sustained injuries (YES = 1). Compare the mean amount of expenses incurred as a result of the victim's injuries across categories of each independent variable. Describe the results; be sure to note the number of victims for each category when interpreting your results.

4. Were your hypotheses supported? What conclusions do you make about these relationships? Can you determine whether hospitals provide equal treatment across race and social class based on these data? Explain.

Student Study Site

The companion Student Study Website for *The Fundamentals of Research in Criminology and Criminal Justice* can be found at www.sagepub.com/frccjstudy.

Visit the Student Study Site to enhance your understanding of the chapter content and to discover additional resources that will take your learning one step further. You can enhance your understanding of the chapters by using the comprehensive study material, which includes interactive exercises, e-flashcards, web exercises, practice self-tests, and more. You will also find special features, such as Learning from Journal Articles, which incorporates SAGE's online journal collection.

CHAPTER 10

Quantitative Data Analysis

"*Oh no, not data analysis and statistics!*" Perhaps most of you have been sailing along in this textbook understanding almost everything you have been reading and studying, if not immediately, then at least after a second reading or a classroom lecture. You probably feel relatively confident that you can design your own criminological research project, develop a measuring instrument, and collect your own data. Now, however, you hit the chapter that you may have been fearing all along: the chapter on data analysis and the use of statistics. This chapter describes what you need to do after your data have been collected. You now need to analyze what you have found, interpret it, and decide how to present your data so that you can most clearly make the points you wish to make.

We would like to state at the beginning, however, that you have relatively little to fear. If you can add, subtract, multiply, and divide, and are willing to put some effort into carefully reading the chapter, you will do well in the statistical analysis of your data. One helpful way to think of statistics is that it consists of a set of tools that you will use to examine your data to help you answer the questions that motivated your research in the first place. In the course of this chapter, we will add some fundamental tools to that toolbox.

This chapter will introduce several common statistics in social research and highlight the factors that must be considered in using and interpreting statistics. Think of it as a review of fundamental social statistics if you have already studied them, or as an introductory overview if you have not.

Two preliminary sections lay the foundation for studying statistics. In the first we discuss the role of statistics in the research process, returning to themes and techniques you already know. In the second preliminary section, we outline the process of acquiring data for statistical analysis. In the rest of the chapter, we explain how to describe the distribution of single variables and the relationship between variables. Along the way, we address ethical issues related to data analysis. This chapter will be successful if it encourages you to see statistics responsibly and evaluate them critically, and gives you the confidence necessary to seek opportunities for extending your statistical knowledge.

WHY WE NEED STATISTICS

Statistics play a key role in achieving valid research results, in terms of measurement, causal validity, and generalizability. Some statistics are useful primarily to describe the results of measuring single variables and to construct and evaluate multi-item scales. These statistics include frequency distributions, graphs, measures of central tendency and variation, and reliability tests. Other statistics are useful primarily in achieving causal validity, by helping us describe the association among variables and to control for, or otherwise take into account, other variables.

Crosstabulation is one technique for measuring association and controlling other variables and is introduced in this chapter. All these statistics are called **descriptive statistics** because they are used to describe the distribution of and relationship among variables.

It is also important for an analyst to choose statistics that are appropriate to the level of measurement of the variables to be analyzed. As you learned in chapter 3, numbers used to represent the values of variables may not actually signify different quantities, meaning that many statistical techniques will be inapplicable. Some statistics, for example, will only be appropriate when the variable you are examining is measured at the nominal level. Other kinds of statistics will require interval-level measurement. To use the right statistic, then, you must be very familiar with the measurement properties of your variables (and you thought that stuff would go away!).

Case Study: The Causes of Delinquency

Throughout this chapter, we will use research on the causes of delinquency for our examples. More specifically, our data will be a subset of a much larger study of a sample of approximately 1,200 high school students selected from the metropolitan and sub-urban high schools of a city in South Carolina. These students, all of whom were in the tenth grade, completed a questionnaire that asked about such things as how they spent their spare time; how they got along with their parents, teachers, and friends; their atti-tudes about delinquency; whether their friends committed delinquent acts; and their own involvement in delinquency. One specific hypothesis, derived from deterrence theory, predicts that youths who believe they are likely to get caught by the police for committing delinquent acts are less likely to commit delinquency than others. This hypothesis is shown in Exhibit 10.1. The variables from this study that we will use in our chapter examples are displayed in Exhibit 10.2.

EXHIBIT 10.1   Perceived Fear of Punishment and Delinquency

Fear of getting caught by police → Delinquency

EXHIBIT 10.2 List of Variables for Class Examples of Causes of Delinquency

Variable	SPSS Variable Name	Description
Gender	V1	Sex of respondent.
Age	V2	Age of respondent.
TV	V21	Number of hours per week the respondent watches TV.
Study	V22	Number of hours per week the respondent spends studying.
Supervision	V63	Do parents know where respondent is when he or she is away from home?
Friends think theft wrong	V77	How wrong respondent's best friends think is it to commit petty theft.
Friends think drinking wrong	V79	How wrong respondent's best friends think is it to drink liquor under age.
Punishment for drinking	V109	If respondent was caught drinking liquor under age and taken to court, how much of a problem it would be.
Cost of vandalism	V119	How much would respondent's chances of having good friends be hurt if he or she was arrested for petty theft.
Parental supervision	PARSUPER	Added scale from items that ask respondent if parents know where he or she is and who he or she is with when away from home. A high score means more supervision.
Friend's opinion	FROPINON	Added scale that asks respondent if his or her best friend thought that committing various delinquent acts was all right. A high score means more support for delinquency from friends.
Friend's behavior	FRBEHAVE	Added scale that asks respondent how many of his or her best friends commit delinquent acts.
Certainty of punishment	CERTAIN	Added scale that measures how likely respondent thinks it is that he or she will be caught by police if he or she were to commit delinquent acts. A high score means more fear of getting caught.
Morality	MORAL	Added scale that measures how morally wrong respondent thinks it is to commit diverse delinquent acts. A high score means strong moral inhibitions against committing delinquency.
Delinquency	DELINQ1	An additive scale that counts the number of times respondent admits to committing a number of different delinquent acts in the past year. The higher the score, the more delinquent acts committed.

PREPARING DATA FOR ANALYSIS

We used the Windows version of the Statistical Package for the Social Sciences (SPSS) for the analysis in this chapter; you will find examples of SPSS commands required to define and analyze data on the Student Study Site for this text, http://www.sagepub.com/frccjstudy.

DISPLAYING UNIVARIATE DISTRIBUTIONS

The first step in data analysis is usually to display the variation in each variable of interest in what are called *univariate frequency distributions*. For many descriptive purposes, the analysis may go no further. Frequency distributions and graphs of frequency distributions are the two most popular approaches for displaying variation; both allow the analyst to display the distribution of cases across the value categories of a variable. Graphs have the advantage over numerically displayed frequency distributions because they provide a picture that is easier to comprehend. Frequency distributions are preferable when exact numbers of cases with particular values must be reported, and when many distributions must be displayed in a compact form.

No matter which type of display is used, the primary concern of the data analyst is to accurately display the distribution's shape—that is, to show how cases are distributed across the values of the variable. Three features of the shape of a distribution are important: **central tendency**, **variability**, and **skewness** (lack of symmetry). All three of these features can be represented in a graph or in frequency distribution.

Central tendency The most common value (for variables measured at the nominal level) or the value around which cases tend to cluster (for a quantitative variable).

Variability The extent to which cases are spread out through the distribution or clustered in just one location.

Skewness The extent to which cases are clustered more at one or the other end of the distribution of a quantitative variable rather than in a symmetric pattern around the center. Skew can be positive (a "right skew"), with the number of cases tapering off in the positive direction, or negative (a "left skew"), with the number of cases tapering off in the negative direction.

A variable's level of measurement is the most important determinant of the appropriateness of particular statistics. For example, we cannot talk about the skewness (lack of symmetry) of a qualitative variable (measured at the nominal level). If the values of a variable cannot be ordered from lowest to highest, if the ordering of the values is arbitrary, we cannot say whether the distribution is symmetric because we could just reorder the values to make the distribution more (or less) symmetric. Some measures of central tendency and variability are also inappropriate for qualitative variables.

The distinction between variables measured at the ordinal level and those measured at the interval or ratio level should also be considered when selecting statistics to use, but social researchers differ on just how much importance they attach to this distinction. Many social researchers think of ordinal variables as imperfectly measured interval-level variables, and believe that in most circumstances statistics developed for interval-level variables also provide useful summaries for ordinal variables. Other social researchers believe that variation in ordinal variables will often be distorted by statistics that assume an interval level of measurement. We will touch on some of the details of these issues in the following sections on particular statistical techniques.

We will now examine graphs and frequency distributions that illustrate these three features of shape. Summary statistics used to measure specific aspects of central tendency and variability will be presented in a separate section. There is a summary statistic for the measurement of skewness, but it is used only rarely in published research reports and will not be presented here.

Graphs

A picture often is worth some unmeasurable quantity of words. Even for the statistically uninitiated, graphs can be easy to read, and they very nicely highlight a distribution's shape. They are particularly useful for exploring data because they show the full range of variation and identify data anomalies that might be in need of further study. And good, professional-looking graphs can now be produced relatively easily with software available for personal computers. There are many types of graphs, but the most common and most useful are bar charts, histograms, and frequency polygons. Each has two axes, the vertical axis (y-axis) and the horizontal axis (x-axis), and labels to identify the variables and the values with tick marks showing where each indicated value falls along the axis. The vertical y-axis of a graph is usually in frequency or percent units, whereas the horizontal x-axis displays the values of the variable being graphed. There are different kinds of graphs you can use to descriptively display your data, depending upon the level of measurement of the variable.

A **bar chart** contains solid bars separated by spaces. It is a good tool for displaying the distribution of variables measured at the nominal level and other discrete categorical variables because there is, in effect, a gap between each of the categories. In our delinquency data, one of the questions asked of respondents was whether their parents knew where they were when they were away from home. We graphed the responses to this question in a bar chart, which is shown in Exhibit 10.3. In this bar chart we report both the frequency count for each value and the percentage of the total that each value represents. The bar chart in Exhibit 10.3 indicates that very few of the respondents (only 16, or 1.3%) reported that their parents "never" knew where they were when they were not at home. Almost one-half (562, or 44.3%) of the youths reported that their parents "usually" knew where they were. What you can also see by noticing the height of the bars above "usually" and "always" is that most youths report that their parents provide very adequate supervision. You can also see that the most frequent response was "usually" and the least frequent was "never." Because the response "usually" is the most frequent value, it is called the mode or modal response. With ordinal data like these, the mode is the most appropriate measure of central tendency. (More about this later.)

A **histogram** is like a bar chart, but it has bars that are adjacent, or right next to each other, with no gaps. This is done to indicate that data displayed in a histogram, unlike the data in a bar chart, are quantitative variables that vary along a continuum (see the discussion of levels

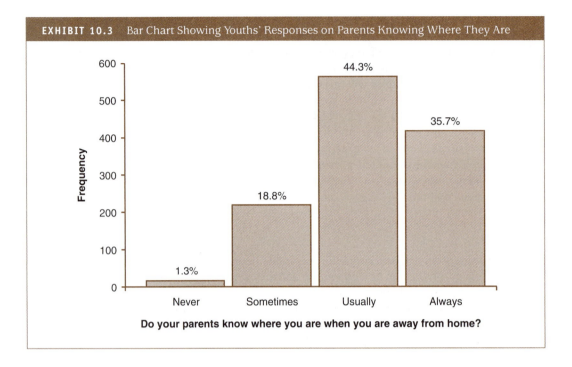

EXHIBIT 10.3 Bar Chart Showing Youths' Responses on Parents Knowing Where They Are

of measurement for variables in Chapter 3). Exhibit 10.4 shows a histogram from the delinquency data set we are using. The variable being graphed is the number of hours per week the respondent reported to be studying. Notice that the cases cluster at the low end of the values. In other words, there are a lot of youths who spend between 0 and 15 hours per week studying. After that, there are only a few cases at each different value with a "spike" occurring at 25, 30, 38, and 40 hours studied. This distribution is clearly not symmetric. In a symmetric distribution there is a lump of cases or a "spike" with an equal number of cases to the left and right of that spike. In the distribution shown in Exhibit 10.4, most of the cases are at the left end of the distribution (i.e., at low values) and the distribution trails off on the right side. The ends of a histogram like this are often called the tail of a distribution. In a symmetric distribution, the left and right tails are approximately the same length. As you can clearly see in Exhibit 10.4, however, the right tail is much longer than the left tail. When the tails of the distribution are uneven, the distribution is said to be asymmetrical or skewed. A skew is either positive or negative. When the cases cluster to the left and the right tail of the distribution is longer than the left, as in Exhibit 10.4, our variable distribution is **positively skewed**. When the cases cluster to the right side and the left tail of the distribution is long, our variable distribution is **negatively skewed**.

Frequency Distributions

A **frequency distribution** displays the number, the **percentage** (the relative frequencies), or both for cases corresponding to each of a variable's values or group of values. The

EXHIBIT 10.4 Histogram

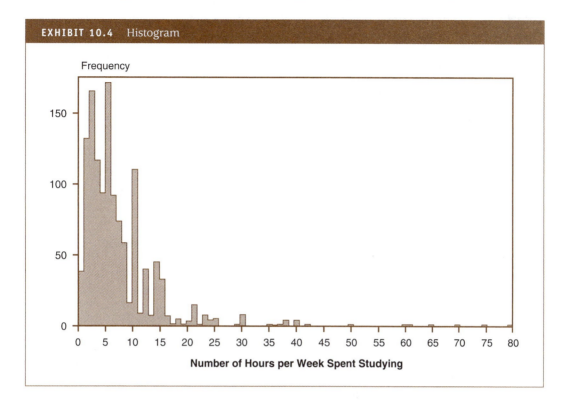

components of the frequency distribution should be clearly labeled, with a title, a stub (labels for the values of the variable), a caption (identifying whether the distribution includes frequencies, percentages, or both), and perhaps the number of missing cases. If percentages are presented rather than frequencies (sometimes both are included), the total number of cases in the distribution (**the base N**) should be indicated (see Exhibit 10.5). Remember that a percentage is simply a relative frequency. A percentage shows the frequency of a given value relative to the total number of cases times 100.

Ungrouped Data

Constructing and reading frequency distributions for variables with few values is not difficult. In Exhibit 10.5, we created the frequency distribution from the variable "Punishment for Drinking" found in the delinquency data set (see Exhibit 10.2). This variable asked the youths to respond to the following question, "How much of a problem would it be if you went to court for drinking liquor under age?" The frequency distribution in Exhibit 10.5 shows the frequency for each value and its corresponding percentage.

As another example of calculating the frequencies and percentages, suppose we had a sample of 25 youths and asked them their gender. From this group of 25 youths, 13 were male and 12 were female. The frequency of males (symbolized here by f) would be 13 and the frequency of females would be 12. The percentage of males would be 52%, calculated

EXHIBIT 10.5   Frequency Distribution

How much of a problem would it be if you went to court for drinking liquor under age?

Value	Frequency (f)	Percentage (%)
No problem at all	14	1.1
Hardly any problem	53	4.2
A little problem	196	15.4
A big problem	421	33.1
A very big problem	588	46.2
Total	1,272	100.0

by f / the total number of cases $\times$ 100 (13 / 25 $\times$ 100 = 52%). The percentage of females would be 12 / 25 $\times$ 100 = 48%.

In the frequency distribution shown in Exhibit 10.5, you can see that only a very small number of youths (14 out of 1,272) thought that they would experience "no problem" if they were caught and taken to court for drinking liquor under age. You can see that most, in fact 1,009, of these youths—or 79.3% of them—thought that they would have either "a big problem" or "a very big problem" with this.

Exhibit 10.5 is a frequency distribution of an ordinal-level variable; it has a very small number of discrete categories. In Exhibit 10.6, we provide an illustration of a frequency distribution with a continuous quantitative variable. This variable is one we have already looked at and graphed from the delinquency data, the number of hours per week the respondent spent studying. Notice that this variable, like many continuous variables in criminological research, has a large number of values. Although this is a reasonable frequency distribution to construct—you can, for example, still see that the cases tend to cluster in the low end of the distribution and are strung way out at the upper end—it is a little difficult to get a good sense of the distribution of the cases. The problem is that there are too many values to easily comprehend. It would be nice if we could simplify distributions like these that have a large number of different values. Well, we can. We can construct what is called a **grouped frequency distribution**.

Grouped Data

Many frequency distributions, such as that in Exhibit 10.6, and many graphs require grouping of some values after the data are collected. There are two reasons for grouping:

1. There are more than 15–20 values to begin with, a number too large to be displayed in an easily readable table.

EXHIBIT 10.6	Frequency Distribution With Continuous Quantitative Data: Hours Studied Per Week	

Value	Frequency (f)	Percentage (%)
0	38	3.0
1	132	10.4
2	165	13.0
3	116	9.1
4	94	7.4
5	171	13.4
6	92	7.2
7	73	5.7
8	58	4.6
9	16	1.3
10	110	8.6
11	9	0.7
12	40	3.1
13	7	0.6
14	45	3.5
15	32	2.5
16	7	0.6
17	5	0.4
18	4	0.3
19	1	0.1
20	15	1.2
21	8	0.6
22	1	0.1
23	1	0.1
24	4	0.3
25	5	0.4
29	1	0.1
30	8	0.6
35	1	0.1
37	1	0.1
40	4	0.3
42	1	0.1
50	1	0.1
60	1	0.1
61	1	0.1
65	1	0.1
70	1	0.1
75	1	0.1
80	1	0.1
Total	1,272	100.0

2. The distribution of the variable will be clearer or more meaningful if some of the values are combined.

Inspection of Exhibit 10.6 should clarify these reasons. In this distribution it is very difficult to discern any shape, much less the central tendency. What we would like to do now to make the features of the data more visible is change the values into intervals of values, or a range of values. For example, rather than having five separate values of 0, 1, 2, 3, 4 hours studied per week, we can have a range of values or an interval for the first value, such as 0–4 hours studied. Then we can get a count or frequency of the number of cases (and percentage of the total) that fall within that interval.

Once we decide to group values or categories, we have to be sure that in doing so we do not distort the distribution. Adhering to the following guidelines for combining values in a frequency distribution will prevent many problems.

- Categories should be logically defensible and preserve the distribution's shape.
- Categories should be mutually exclusive and exhaustive, so every case is classifiable in one and only one category.
- The first interval must contain the lowest value and the last interval must contain the highest value in the distribution.
- Each interval width, the number of values that fall within each interval, should be the same size.
- There should be between 7 and 13 intervals. This is a tough rule to follow. The key is not to have so few intervals that your data are clumped or clustered into only a few intervals (you will lose too much information about your distribution) and not to have so many intervals that the data are not much clearer than an ungrouped frequency distribution.

Let us use the data in Exhibit 10.6 on the number of hours studied by these youths to create a grouped frequency distribution. We will follow a number of explicit steps:

Step 1: Determine the number of intervals you think you want. This decision is arbitrary, but try to keep the number of intervals you have in the 7 to 13 range. For our example, let us say we initially decided we wanted to have 10 intervals. (Note: if you do your frequency distribution and it looks too clustered or there are too many intervals, redo your distribution with a different number of intervals.) Don't worry, there are no hard and fast rules for the correct number of intervals, and constructing a grouped frequency distribution is as much art as science. Just remember that the frequency distribution you make is supposed to convey information about the shape and central tendency of your data.

Step 2: Decide on the width of the interval (symbolized by w). The interval width is the number of different values that fall into your interval. For example, an interval width of 5 has five different values that fall into it, say, the values 0, 1, 2, 3, or 4 hours studied. There is a simple formula to approximate what your interval width should be given the number of intervals you decided on in the first step: determine the range of the data, where the range is simply the highest score in the distribution minus the lowest score. In our data, with the number of hours studied, the range is 80 because the high score is 80 and the low score is 0, so range $= 80 - 0 = 80$. Then determine the width of the interval by dividing the range by the number of intervals you want from Step 1. We wanted 10 intervals, so our interval width would be $w_i = 80 / 10 = 8$. We should therefore have an interval width of 8. If you use this simple formula for determining your interval width and you end up with a decimal, say 8.2 or 8.6, then simply round up or down to an integer.

Step 3: Make your first interval so that the lowest value falls into it. Our lowest value is 0 (for studied 0 hours per week), so our first interval begins with the value 0. Now, if the beginning of our first interval is 0 and we want an interval width of 8, is the last value of our interval 7 (with a first interval of 0–7 hours), or is the last value of our interval 8 (with a first interval of 0–8 hours)? One easy way to make a grouped frequency distribution is to do the following: Take the beginning value of your first interval (in our case, it is 0), and add the interval width to that value (8). This new value is the first value of your next interval. What we know, then, is that the first value of our first interval is 0, and the first value of our second interval is 8 (0–?, 8–?). This must mean that the last value to be included in our first interval is one less than 8, or 7. Our first interval, therefore, includes the ranges of values 0–7. If you count the number of different values in this interval you will find that it includes eight different values (0, 1, 2, 3, 4, 5, 6, 7). This is our interval width of 8.

Step 4: After your first interval is determined, the next intervals are easy. They must be the same width and not overlap (mutually exclusive). You must make enough intervals to include the last value in your variable distribution. The highest value in our data is 80 hours per week, so we construct the grouped frequency distribution as follows:

0–7

8–15

16–23

24–31

32–39

40–47

48–55

56–63

64–71

72–79

80–87

Notice that in order to include the highest value in our data (80 hours) we had to make 11 intervals instead of the 10 we originally decided upon in Step 1. No problem. Remember, the number of intervals is arbitrary and this is as much art as science.

Step 5: Count the number or frequency of cases that appear in each interval and their percentage of the total.

The completed grouped frequency distribution is shown in Exhibit 10.7. Notice that this grouped frequency distribution conveys the important features of the distribution of this data. Most of the data cluster at the low end of the number of hours studied. In fact, more than two-thirds of these youths studied fewer than eight hours per week. Notice also that the frequency of cases thins out at each successive interval. In other words, there is a long right tail to this distribution indicating a positive skew because fewer youths studied a high number of hours. Notice also that the distribution was created in such a way that the interval widths are all the same and each case falls into one and only one interval (i.e., the intervals are exhaustive and mutually exclusive). We would have run into trouble if we had two intervals like 0–7 and 7–14 because we would not know where to place those youths who spent seven hours a week studying. Should we put them in the first or second interval? If the intervals are mutually exclusive, as they are here, you will not run into these problems.

EXHIBIT 10.7   Example of a Grouped Frequency Distribution From Hours Studied

Value	Frequency (f)	Percentage (%)
0–7	881	69.26
8–15	317	24.92
16–23	42	3.30
24–31	18	1.42
32–39	2	0.16
40–47	5	0.39
48–55	1	0.08
56–63	2	0.16
64–71	2	0.16
72–79	1	0.08
80–87	1	0.08
Total	1,272	100.00

Note: Total may not equal 100.0% due to rounding error.

SUMMARIZING UNIVARIATE DISTRIBUTIONS

Summary statistics focus attention on particular aspects of a distribution and facilitate comparison among distributions. For example, suppose you wanted to report the rate of violent crimes for each city in the United States with over 100,000 in population. You could report each city's violent crime rate, but it is unlikely that two cities would have the same rate and you would have to report approximately 200 rates, one for each city. This would be a frequency distribution that many, if not most, people would find difficult to comprehend. One way to interpret your data for your audience would be to provide a summary measure that indicates what the average violent crime rate is in large U.S. cities. That is the purpose of the set of summary statistics called measures of *central tendency*. You would also want to provide another summary measure that shows the variability or heterogeneity in your data—in other words, a measure that shows how different the scores are from each other or from the central tendency. That is the purpose of the set of summary statistics called measures of *variation* or *dispersion*. We will discuss each type of measurement in turn.

Measures of Central Tendency

Central tendency is usually summarized with one of three statistics: the mode, the median, or the mean. For any particular application, one of these statistics may be preferable, but each has a role to play in data analysis. To choose an appropriate measure of central tendency, the analyst must consider a variable's level of measurement, the skewness of a quantitative variable's distribution, and the purpose for which the statistic is used. In addition, the analyst's personal experiences and preferences inevitably will play a role.

Mode

The mode is the most frequent value in a distribution. For example, refer to the data in Exhibit 10.7, which shows the grouped frequency distribution for the number of hours studied. The value with the greatest frequency in that data is the interval 0–7 hours; this is the mode of that distribution. Notice that the mode is the most frequently occurring value; it is not the frequency of that value. In other words, the mode in Exhibit 10.7 is 0–7 hours; the mode is not 881, which is the frequency of the modal category. When a variable distribution has one case or interval that occurs more often than the others, it is called a **unimodal** distribution.

Sometimes a distribution has more than one mode because there are two values that have the highest frequency. This distribution would be called **bimodal**. Some distributions are trimodal in that there are three distinctively high frequency values. And some distributions have no mode. In saying that there is no mode, though, you are communicating something very important about the data: that no case is more common than the others. Another potential problem with the mode is that it might happen to fall far from the main clustering of cases in a distribution. It would be misleading in this case, then, to say simply that the variable's central tendency was the same as the modal value.

Nevertheless, there are occasions when the mode is very appropriate. Most important, the mode is the only measure of central tendency that can be used to characterize the central tendency of variables measured at the nominal level. In Exhibit 10.8 we have the frequency distribution of the conviction offense for 1,000 offenders convicted in a criminal court. The central tendency of the distribution is property offense, because more of the 1,000 offenders were convicted of a property crime than any other crime. For the variable "type of offense convicted of," the most common value is property crime. The mode also is often referred to in descriptions of the shape of a distribution. The terms *unimodal* and *bimodal* appear frequently, as do descriptive statements such as "The typical (most probable) respondent was in her 30s." Of course, when the issue is determining the most probable value, the mode is the appropriate statistic.

Median

The **median** is the score in the middle of a rank-ordered distribution. It is, then, the score or point that divides the distribution in half (the 50th percentile). The median is inappropriate for variables measured at the nominal level because their values cannot be put in ranked order (remember, there is no "order" to nominal-level data), and so there is no meaningful middle position. To determine the median we simply need to do the following. First, rank-order the values from lowest to highest. If there is an odd number of scores then you can find the position of the median in the rank order of scores by using the following simple formula:

$$N + 1 \div 2$$

where N is equal to the total number of cases. If there is an even number of scores, then you can find the position of the median in the rank order of scores by finding the midpoint of the scores in the following two positions:

$$\text{Position } 1 = \frac{N}{2}$$

$$\text{Position } 2 = \frac{N+2}{2}$$

EXHIBIT 10.8 Frequency Distribution of Offense Convicted for 1,000 Offenders

Offense	Frequency (f)
Violent	125
Drug	210
Property	480
Public order	100
Other	85
Total	1,000

The midpoint of the two scores can be found by adding the scores in the two positions and dividing by 2. Please note that in both formulas you use the formula to find the position of the median; the formula does not give you the value of the median. Let us do an example.

In Exhibit 10.9, we first list a sample of nine U.S. cities and their rate of violent crime in 1994. In the bottom panel of Exhibit 10.9, we drop one of the cities (San Francisco) and are left with eight cities.

Let us determine the median for both lists. First, we rank-order the violent crime rates for the first list.

Rank	Crime Rate
1	1,322
2	1,461
3	1,530
4	1,589
5	1,861
6	1,887
7	1,916
8	2,059
9	3,571

EXHIBIT 10.9   Rate of Violent Crime for Selected U.S. Cities

City	Number of Violent Crimes per 100,000
Atlanta	3,571
Boston	1,916
Cleveland	1,530
Dallas	1,589
Los Angeles	2,059
New Orleans	1,887
New York	1,861
Philadelphia	1,322
San Francisco	1,461
Atlanta	3,571
Boston	1,916
Cleveland	1,530
Dallas	1,589
Los Angeles	2,059
New Orleans	1,887
New York	1,861
Philadelphia	1,322

Because we have an odd number of scores ($N = 9$), the position of the median is determined by $(9 + 1) / 2 = 10 / 2 = 5$. The median violent crime rate, then, is in the fifth position in this rank order. Starting either at the top of the scores and counting down to the fifth position or the bottom and counting up, we find that in the fifth position is the score 1,861 violent crimes per 100,000, which is the median violent crime rate for these nine U.S. cities. Now, let us find the median in the second list. We first rank-order these eight scores.

Rank	Crime Rate
1	1,322
2	1,530
3	1,589
4	1,861
5	1,887
6	1,916
7	2,059
8	3,571

Because we now have an even number of scores (notice that the violent crime rate for San Francisco is missing from this list), we know that the median position is the midpoint in between the fourth ($8 / 2 = 4$) and fifth ($[8 + 2] / 2$) positions. The score at the fourth position is 1,861 and at the fifth it is 1,887. The value of the median can now be found by adding these two scores and dividing by two. The median rate of violent crime is equal to $(1,861 + 1,887) / 2 = 1,874$ violent crimes per 100,000 population. Of the cities, 50% had a violent crime rate below 1,874 and 50% had a violent crime rate above 1,874.

Mean

The **mean** is simply the arithmetic average of all scores in a distribution. It is computed by adding up the value of all the cases and dividing by the total number of cases, thereby taking into account the value of each case in the distribution:

Mean = Sum of value of all cases / number of cases

The symbol for the mean is $\bar{X}$ (pronounced "x-bar"). In algebraic notation, the equation is

$$\bar{X} = \frac{\Sigma_1^n X_1}{N}$$

where x_i is a symbol for each ith score and i's go from 1 to N; N is the total number of cases. What the algebraic equation says to do is to sum all scores, starting at the first score and continuing until the last, or Nth, score; then divide this sum by the total number of cases (N).

We will calculate the mean rate of violent crime for the nine U.S. cities listed in Exhibit 10.9:

$$\bar{X} = \frac{(3,571 + 1,916 + 1,530 + 1,589 + 2,059 + 1,887 + 1,861 + 1,332 + 1,461)}{9}$$

$$= 1,910.7$$

The mean rate of violent crime for these nine U.S. cities, then, is 1,910.7 violent crimes per 100,000 population. Notice that in calculating the mean we do not first have to rank order the scores. The mean takes every score into account, so it does not matter whether we add 3,571 first, in the middle, or last.

Computing the mean requires adding up the values of the cases, so it makes sense to compute a mean only if the values of the cases can be treated as actual quantities—that is, if they reflect an interval or ratio level of measurement, or if they are ordinal and we assume that ordinal measures can be treated as interval. It would make no sense, however, to calculate the mean for a nominal level variable like racial or ethnic status, or for the variable gender. Thus both the median and the mean are inappropriate measures of central tendency for variables measured at the nominal level.

Median or Mean?

Both the median and the mean are used to summarize the central tendency of quantitative variables, but their suitability for a particular application must be assessed carefully.

The key issues to be considered in this assessment are the variable's level of measurement, the shape of its distribution, and the purpose of the statistical summary. Level of measurement is a key concern because, to calculate the mean, we must add up the values of all the cases, a procedure that assumes the variable is measured at the interval or ratio level. The shape of a variable's distribution should also be taken into account when deciding whether to use the median or the mean. When a distribution is perfectly symmetric (i.e., when the distribution is bell shaped), the distribution of values below the median is a mirror image of the distribution of values above the median, and the mean and median will be the same. But the values of the mean and median are affected differently by skewness, or the presence of cases with extreme values on one side of the distribution but not the other side. The median takes into account only the number of cases above and below the median point, not the value of these cases, so it is not affected in any way by extreme values. The mean is based on adding the value of all the cases, so it will be pulled in the direction of exceptionally high (or low) values. When the value of the mean is larger than the median, we know that the distribution is skewed in a positive direction, with proportionately more cases with lower than higher values. When the mean is smaller than the median, the distribution is skewed in a negative direction.

This differential impact of skewness on the median and mean is illustrated in Exhibit 10.10. The first list shows the crime rate per 1,000 residents for seven neighborhoods in a hypothetical city. The crime rates range from a low of 51.7 per 1,000 to 135.3 per 1,000. When we calculate the mean crime rate for these seven neighborhoods, we find that it is 94.8 crimes per 1,000; the median is 98.7 crimes per 1,000. Notice that this is a relatively symmetrical distribution, with the values of the mean and the median very comparable to each other. With these data both the mean and the median provide an accurate description of the central tendency.

In the second list of neighborhoods, we replace the neighborhood that had the highest crime rate (i.e., King's Crossing) with West Chester, which has a substantially higher crime rate: 697.5 per 1,000. It is then an unusually high score. When we calculate the mean for these data, we find that it is 175.1 per 1,000; it has increased from its previous value of 94.8. The median, however, remains the same; it is still 98.7 crimes per 1,000. When an unusually high score is added to a distribution, the mean thus gets inflated relative to the median.

EXHIBIT 10.10   Rates of Crime in Selected Neighborhoods

Community	Crime Rate per 1,000
Valley View	51.7
Glen Commons	63.1
Springdale	75.3
Green Acres	98.7
Oceanside	113.4
Meadowbrook	125.9
King's Crossing	135.3
Valley View	51.7
Glen Commons	63.1
Springdale	75.3
Green Acres	98.7
Oceanside	113.4
Meadowbrook	125.9
West Chester	697.5
Pleasantville	5.3
Glen Commons	63.1
Springdale	75.3
Green Acres	98.7
Oceanside	113.4
Meadowbrook	125.9
King's Crossing	135.3

In distributions that are positively skewed, the mean is of greater magnitude than the median. Notice also that, with this unusually high crime rate added, the median is still an accurate picture of the central tendency, whereas the mean of 175.1 is no longer accurate. In the third list of neighborhoods, we replace the neighborhood that has the lowest crime rate (i.e., Valley View) with Pleasantville, which has a substantially lower crime rate, 5.3 per 1,000. It is, then, an unusually low score. When we calculate the mean for these data, we find that it is 88.1 per 1,000; it has decreased from the value in the first list, which was 94.8. The median, however, remains the same; it is still 98.7 crimes per 1,000. When an unusually low score is added to a distribution, then, the mean gets deflated relative to the median. In distributions that are negatively skewed, the mean is less than the median. Notice also that, even with this unusually low crime rate added, the median is still an accurate picture of the central tendency, whereas the mean of 88.1 is no longer as accurate. This example illustrates one of the problems with using the mean as a measure of central tendency. If the data are skewed (either positively or negatively), then the mean will be affected by the extreme scores in the distribution and will not give as accurate an estimate of the central tendency of the data as the median. The lesson is that one should probably report both the mean and the median. In general, the mean is the most commonly used measure of central tendency for quantitative variables, because it takes into account the value of all cases in the distribution and it is the foundation for many other more advanced statistics. However, the mean's very popularity results in its use in situations for which it is inappropriate. Keep an eye out for this problem.

Measures of Variation

You have learned that central tendency is only one aspect of the shape of a distribution. Although the measure of center is the most important aspect for many purposes, it is still just a piece of the total picture. A summary of distributions based only on their central tendency can be very incomplete, even misleading. For example, three towns might have the same mean and median crime rate but still be very different in their social character due to the shape of the crime distributions. We show three distributions of community crime rates for three different towns in Exhibit 10.11. If you calculate the mean and median crime rate for each town, you will find that the mean and median crime rate are the same for all three. In terms of its crime rate, then, each community has the same central tendency. As you can see, however, there is something very different about these towns. Town A is a very heterogeneous town; crime rates in its neighborhoods are neither very homogeneous nor clustered at either the low or high end. Rather, the crime rates in its communities are spread out from one another. Crime rates in these neighborhoods are, then, very diverse. Town B is characterized by neighborhoods with very homogeneous crime rates; there are no real high or low crime areas because each neighborhood is not far from the overall mean of 62.4 crimes per 1,000. Town C is characterized by neighborhoods with either very low crime rates or very high crime rates. Crime rates in the first four neighborhoods are much lower than the mean (62.4 crimes per 1,000), whereas the last four neighborhoods are much higher than the mean. Although they share identical measures of central tendency, these three towns have neighborhood crime rates that are very different.

The way to capture these differences is with statistical measures of variation. Three popular measures of variation are the range, the variance, and the standard deviation (which is the most popular measure of variability). To calculate each of these measures, the variable must be at the interval or ratio level. Statistical measures of variation are used infrequently with qualitative variables, so these measures will not be presented here.

Range

The **range** is a simple measure of variation, calculated as the highest value in a distribution minus the lowest value:

Range = Highest value – Lowest value

It often is important to report the range of a distribution, to identify the whole range of possible values that might be encountered. However, because the range can be drastically

EXHIBIT 10.11   Neighborhood Crime Rates in Three Different Towns

Town A	Town B	Town C
19.5	58.1	8.9
28.2	59.7	15.4
35.7	60.1	18.3
41.9	62.7	21.9
63.2	63.2	63.2
75.8	63.9	103.5
92.0	64.2	104.2
95.7	64.5	110.7
109.4	65.0	105.3

altered by just one exceptionally high or low value (called an **outlier**), it does not do an adequate job of summarizing the extent of variability in a distribution. For our three towns in Exhibit 10.11, the range in crimes rates for Town A is 89.9 (109.4 – 19.5), for Town B it is 6.9 (65.0 – 58.7), and for Town C it is 106.4 (115.3 – 8.9).

Variance

If the mean is a good measure of central tendency, then it would seem that a good measure of variability would be the distance each score is away from the mean. Unfortunately, we cannot simply take the average distance of each score from the mean. One property of the mean is that it exactly balances negative and positive distances from it, so if we were to sum the difference between each score in a distribution and the mean of that distribution, it would always sum to zero. What we can do, though, is to square the difference of each score from the mean so the distance retains its value. This is the notion behind the variance as a measure of variability.

The **variance** is the average square deviation of each case from the mean, so it takes into account the amount by which each case differs from the mean. The equation to calculate the variance is

$$\sigma^2 = \frac{\Sigma_1^N (x - \bar{X})^2}{N}$$

In words, this formula says to take each score and subtract the mean, then square this difference, then sum all these differences, then divide this sum by N or the total number of scores. We will calculate the variance for the crime rate data from Town A in Exhibit 10.11.

X	$(X - \bar{X})$	$(X - \bar{X})^2$
19.5	$(19.5 - 62.4) = -42.9$	1,840.41
28.2	$(28.2 - 62.4) = -34.2$	1,169.64
35.7	$(35.7 - 62.4) = -26.7$	712.89
41.9	$(41.9 - 62.4) = -20.5$	420.25
63.2	$(63.2 - 62.4) = -0.8$	0.64
75.8	$(75.8 - 62.4) = 13.4$	179.56
92.0	$(92.0 - 62.4) = 29.6$	876.16
95.7	$(95.7 - 62.4) = 33.3$	1,108.89
109.4	$(109.4 - 62.4) = 47.0$	2,209.00
		$\Sigma(x - \bar{X}) = 8{,}517.44$

We can now determine that the variance is

$$\sigma^2 = \frac{8{,}517.44}{9} = 946.38$$

The variance of these data, then, is 946.38. The variance is used in many other statistics, although it is more conventional to measure variability with the closely related standard deviation than with the variance.

Standard Deviation

The **standard deviation** is simply the square root of the variance. It is the square root of the average squared deviation of each case from the mean:

$$\sigma = \sqrt{\frac{\Sigma_1^N (x - \bar{X})^2}{N}}$$

To find the standard deviation, simply calculate the variance and take the square root. For our example, the standard deviation is

$$\sigma = \sqrt{946.38} = 30.76$$

When the standard deviation is calculated from sample data, the denominator is supposed to be $N - 1$, rather than N, an adjustment that has no discernible effect when the number of cases is reasonably large.

The standard deviation has mathematical properties that make it the preferred measure of variability in many cases. In particular, the calculation of confidence intervals around sample statistics relies on an interesting property of normal curves. Areas under the normal curve correspond to particular distances from the mean, expressed in standard deviation units. If a variable is normally distributed, 68% of the cases will lie between plus and minus 1 standard deviation from the distribution's mean, and 95% of the cases will lie between 1.96 standard deviations above and below the mean. Cases that fall beyond plus or minus 1.96 standard deviations from the mean are termed outliers. Because of this property, the standard deviation tells us quite a bit about a distribution if the distribution is normal. This same property of the standard deviation enables us to infer how confident we can be that the mean (or some other statistic) of a population sampled randomly is within a certain range of the sample mean (see Chapter 4).

CROSSTABULATING VARIABLES

Most data analyses focus on relationships among variables to test hypotheses or just to describe or explore relationships. For each of these purposes, we must examine the association among two or more variables. **Crosstabulation (crosstab)** is one of the simplest methods for doing so. A crosstabulation displays the distribution of one variable for each category of another variable; it can also be called a *bivariate distribution*. Crosstabs also provide a simple tool for statistically controlling one or more variables while examining the associations among others. In this section, you will learn how crosstabs used in this way can help to test for spurious relationships and evaluate causal models. Crosstabulations are usually used when both variables are measured at either the nominal or ordinal level—that is, when the values of both variables are categories.

We are going to provide a series of examples of crosstabulations from our delinquency data. In our first example, the independent variable we are interested in is the youth's gender (VI, see Exhibit 10.2), and the dependent variable is the youth's self-reported involvement in delinquent behavior (DELINQ1). To use the delinquency variable in a crosstabulation, however, we first need to recode it into a categorical variable. We will make three approximately equal categories of self-reported delinquency: low, medium, and high.

Anyone who reported from zero to two delinquent acts is now coded as 1, or low delinquency; anyone reporting from three to 13 delinquent acts is now coded as 2, or medium delinquency; and anyone reporting more than 14 delinquent acts is now coded as 3, or high delinquency. If you were to do a frequency distribution of this new variable, DELINQ2, you would see that there are three approximately equal groups.

We are interested in the relationship between gender and delinquency because a great deal of delinquency theory would predict that males are more likely to be delinquent than females. The gender of the youth is the independent variable, and the level of self-reported delinquency is the dependent variable.

Exhibit 10.12 shows the crosstabulation of gender with DELINQ2. Some explanation of this table is in order. Notice that there are two values of gender (male and female) that comprise the two rows of the table, and three values of delinquency (low, medium, and high) that comprise the three columns of the table. Crosstabulations are usually referred to by the number of rows and columns the table has. Our crosstabulation in Exhibit 10.12 is a 2 × 3 (pronounced "two-by-three") table because there are two rows and three columns. Notice also that there are values at the end of each row and at the end of each column. These totals are referred to as the *marginals* of the table. These **marginal distributions** provide the sum of the frequencies for each column and each row of the table. For example, there are 680 females in the data and 592 males. These row marginals should sum to the total number of youths in the data set: 1,272. There are 450 youths who are low in delinquency, 348 youths who are medium in delinquency, and 251 youths who are high on the delinquency variable. These column marginals should also sum to the total number of youths in the data set: 1,272.

Now notice that there are 2 × 3 or 6 data entries in the table (let us ignore the percentages for now). These data entries are called the *cells* of the crosstabulation and represent the joint distribution of the two variables: gender and delinquency. The table in Exhibit 10.12 has six cells for the joint distribution of two levels of gender with three levels of delinquency. In other words, notice where the value for female converges with the value of low for delinquency. You see a frequency number of 275 in this cell. This frequency is how many times there is the joint occurrence of a female and low delinquency; it shows that 275 females were also low in delinquency. Moving to the cell to the right of this, we see that there are 182 females who were medium in delinquency, and moving to the right again we see that there are 223 females who are high in delinquency. The sum of these three numbers is equal to the total number of females, 680. The row for the males shows the joint distribution of males with each level of delinquency.

What we would like to know is whether there is a relationship or association between gender and delinquency. In other words, are males more likely to be delinquent than females? Because raw frequencies can provide a deceptive picture, we determine whether there is any relationship between our independent and dependent variables by looking at the percentages. Keep in mind that the idea in looking at relationships is that we want to know if variation on the independent variable has any effect on the dependent variable. To determine this, what we always do in crosstabulation tables is calculate our percentages on each value of the independent variable. For example, notice that in Exhibit 10.12 gender is our independent variable. We calculated our percentages so that for each value of gender the percentages would sum to 100% at the end of each row. The percentages for both females and males, therefore, sum to 100% at the end of the row. Now we take a given category of the dependent variable and ask what percentage of each independent variable value falls into that category of the dependent variable. Another way to say this is that we calculate our percentages on the independent variable and compare them on the dependent variable. We compare the percentages for different levels of the independent variable on the same category or level of the dependent variable.

EXHIBIT 10.12   Crosstabulation of Respondents' Gender by Delinquency

		SELF-REPORTED DELINQUENCY			
		Low	*Medium*	*High*	*Total*
GENDER	*Female*	275 40.4%	182 26.8%	223 32.8%	680 100%
	Male	175 29.6%	166 28.0%	251 42.4%	592 100%
	Total	450	348	474	1,272

In Exhibit 10.12, for example, notice that 40.4% of the female youths were low in delinquency, but only 29.6% of the males were low. This tells us that females are more likely to be low in delinquency than males. Now let us look at the high category. We can see that 32.8% of the females were high in delinquency and 42.4% of the males were high. Together, this tells us that females are more likely to be low in delinquency and males are more likely to be high in delinquency. There is, then, a relationship between gender and delinquency. Also notice that the independent variable was the row variable, and the dependent variable was the column variable. It does not always have to be this way; the independent variable could just as easily have been the column variable. The important general rule to remember is to always calculate your percentages on the levels of the independent variable (e.g., use marginal totals for the independent variable as denominators) and compare percentages on a level of the dependent variable.

In Exhibit 10.12, an association exists, although we can only say that it is a modest association. The percentage difference at the low and high ends of the delinquency variables is approximately 10 percentage points.

We provide another example of a crosstabulation in Exhibit 10.13. This is a 3 × 3 table that shows the relationship between how morally wrong a youth thinks delinquency is (the independent variable) and his or her self-reported involvement in delinquency (the dependent variable). This table reveals a very strong relationship between moral beliefs and delinquency. We can see that 5.6% of youths with weak moral beliefs are low on delinquency; this increases to 33.8% for those with medium beliefs and to 62.8% for those with strong moral beliefs. At the high end, over two-thirds (72.1%) of those youths with weak moral beliefs are high in delinquency, 29.4% of those with medium moral beliefs are high in delinquency, and only 16.9% of those youths with strong moral beliefs are high in delinquency. Clearly, then, having strong moral beliefs serves to effectively inhibit involvement in delinquent behavior. This is exactly what control theory would have us believe.

EXHIBIT 10.13   Crosstabulation of Respondents' Morals by Gender

		SELF-REPORTED DELINQUENCY			
		Low	*Medium*	*High*	*Total*
MORALS	*Weak*	20 5.6%	79 22.3%	256 72.1%	355 100%
	Medium	170 33.8%	185 36.8%	148 29.4%	503 100%
	Strong	260 62.8%	84 20.3%	70 16.9%	414 100%
	Total	450	348	474	1,272

You will find when you read research reports and journal articles that social scientists usually make decisions about the existence and strength of association on the basis of more statistics than just percentage differences in a crosstabulation table. A **measure of association** is a type of descriptive statistic used to summarize the strength of an association.

Inferential statistics are used in deciding whether it is likely that an association exists in the larger population from which the sample was drawn. Even when the association between two variables is consistent with the researcher's hypothesis, it is possible that the association was just due to chance or to the vagaries of sampling on a random basis (of course, the problem is even worse if the sample is not random). As we learned in Chapter 5, when an original relationship between an independent and dependent variable is actually caused by a third variable that is not controlled, the original relationship is termed **spurious.** It also is conventional in statistics to avoid concluding that an association exists in the population from which the sample was drawn unless the probability that the association was due to chance is less than 5%. In other words, a statistician normally will not conclude that an association exists between two variables unless he or she can be at least 95% confident that the association was not due to chance. Estimation of the probability that an association is not due to chance will be based on one of several inferential statistics, **chi-square** being the one used in most crosstabular analyses.

When an association passes muster in this way, when the analyst feels reasonably confident (at least 95% confident) that it was not due to chance, it is said that the association is statistically significant. **Statistical significance** means that an association is not likely to be due to chance, according to some criterion set by the analyst. Convention (and the desire to avoid concluding that an association exists in the population when it does not) dictates that the criterion be a probability less than 5%.

Controlling for a Third Variable

Crosstabulation can also be used to study the relationship between two variables while controlling for other variables. We will focus our attention on controlling for a third variable in this section, but we will say a bit about controlling for more variables at the section's end. We will examine three different uses for three-variable crosstabulation: identifying an intervening variable, testing a relationship for spuriousness, and specifying the conditions for a relationship. Each of these uses for three-variable crosstabs helps determine the validity of our findings, either by evaluating criteria for causality (nonspuriousness and identification of a causal mechanism) or by increasing our understanding of the conditions required for a relationship to hold, an indication of the crosspopulation generalizability of the findings. All three uses are aspects of **elaboration analysis**—the process of introducing control variables into a bivariate relationship in order to better understand or to elaborate the relationship (Rosenberg 1968). We will examine the gamma and chi-square statistics for each table in this analysis.

Intervening Variables

We have already discovered that females are less likely to be delinquent than males. Finding this relationship between gender and delinquency is just the beginning of our work, however. What we would now like to know and investigate is why this relationship exists.

What is it about females that makes them less likely to commit delinquent acts than males? Let us first rule out strictly biological factors, and explore some possible social reasons for this gender difference in delinquency. One possibility is that, because they are more closely supervised than males, females have fewer opportunities to be delinquent. In other words, females are under more strict parental supervision, and it is because they are under more strict supervision that they are less likely than males to commit delinquency. Notice that in this relationship the variable "parental supervision" intervenes between gender and delinquency. It explains why females are at lower risk for delinquency compared with males. To determine whether parental supervision intervenes in the relationship between gender and delinquency, and whether it explains this relationship, we must examine the relationship between gender and delinquency while controlling for difference in parental supervision. If parental supervision intervenes in the gender–delinquency relationship, the effect of controlling for this third variable would be to eliminate, or at least substantially reduce, the original relationship between gender and delinquency.

To examine this possibility, we first recode the parental supervision variable into two approximately equal levels: weak supervision and strong supervision. We then look at two **subtables** of the gender–delinquency relationship: once under the condition of weak parental supervision and once under the condition of strong parental supervision (see Exhibit 10.14). For ease of presentation, we will only report the cell percentages and not the frequencies. What we see is that, once parental supervision is controlled, there is no real relationship between gender and delinquency. That is, if males and females have the same amount of supervision from their parents, they do not differ that much in their risk of being delinquent. For example, among females with weak parental supervision, 46.0% are high in delinquency, and among males with weak parental supervision 49.6% are delinquent. There is less than four percentage points' difference between males and females in their risk of being high delinquents under these conditions. Among those with strong parental supervision, 19.8% of the females were high in delinquency and 23.6% of the males were high, less than four percentage points' difference.

These results would lead us to the conclusion that parental supervision intervenes in the relationship between gender and delinquency. A very important reason why females are less delinquent than males, therefore, is that females are under stricter supervision from their parents than males, and strong parental supervision leads to a reduced risk of delinquency.

Extraneous Variables

Another reason for introducing a third variable into a bivariate relationship is to see whether the original relationship is spurious due to the influence of an **extraneous variable**, which is a variable that causes both the independent and dependent variables. The only reason why the independent and dependent variables are related, therefore, is that they both are the effects of a common cause (another independent variable).

Exhibit 10.15 shows what a spurious relationship would look like. In this case, the relationship between x and y exists only because both are the effects of the common cause z. Controlling for z, therefore, will eliminate the x–y relationship. Ruling out possible extraneous variables will help to considerably strengthen the conclusion that the relationship between the independent and dependent variables is causal, particularly if all the variables that seem to have the potential for creating a spurious relationship can be controlled.

EXHIBIT 10.14   Crosstabulation of Respondents' Gender by Delinquency Within Levels of Parental Supervision

Weak Parental Supervision

GENDER	SELF-REPORTED DELINQUENCY			
	Low	Medium	High	Total
Female	26.1%	27.9%	46.0%	337
Male	23.2%	27.2%	49.6%	427
Total				764

$\chi^2 = 1.220$ ($p > .05$) Gamma = .067

Strong Parental Supervision

GENDER	SELF-REPORTED DELINQUENCY			
	Low	Medium	High	Total
Female	54.4%	25.7%	19.8%	343
Male	46.1%	30.3%	23.6%	165
Total				508

$\chi^2 = 3.193$ ($p > .05$) Gamma = .136

EXHIBIT 10.15   A Spurious Relationship Between x and y

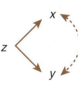

Original relationship between
x and y disappears

Notice that if a variable is acting as an extraneous variable, then controlling for it will cause the original relationship between the independent and dependent variables to disappear or substantially diminish. This was also the empirical test for an intervening variable. Therefore, the difference between intervening and extraneous variables is a logical one and not an empirical one. In both instances, controlling for the third variable will cause the original relationship to diminish or disappear. There should, therefore, be sound theoretical grounds for suspecting that a variable is acting as an intervening variable, explaining the relationship between the independent and dependent variables.

As an example of a possible extraneous relationship, we will look at the association between a youth's perception of the certainty of punishment and self-reported involvement in delinquency. Deterrence theory should lead us to predict a negative relationship between perceived certainty and delinquency. Indeed, this is exactly what we observe in our delinquency data. We will not show you the crosstabulation table, but when we looked at the relationship between perceived certainty and delinquency we found that 53.2% of youth who were low in certainty were high in delinquency; 39.1% of those who perceived medium certainty were high in delinquency; and only 23.6% of those who perceived a high certainty of punishment were high in delinquency. Youth who believed they would get caught if they engaged in delinquency, then, were less likely to be delinquent.

Someone may reasonably argue, however, that this discovered negative relationship may not be causal, but instead may be spurious. It could be suggested that what is actually behind this relationship is the extraneous variable, moral beliefs (see Exhibit 10.16). The argument is that those with strong moral inhibitions against committing delinquent acts think that punishment for morally wrongful actions is certain, *and* refrain from delinquent acts. Thus the observed negative relationship between perceived certainty and delinquency is really due to the positive effect of moral beliefs on perceived certainty, and the negative effect of moral beliefs on delinquency. If moral beliefs are actually the causal factor at work, then controlling for them will eliminate or substantially reduce the original relationship between perceived certainty and delinquency.

EXHIBIT 10.16   A Spurious Relationship Between Perceived Certainty and Delinquency

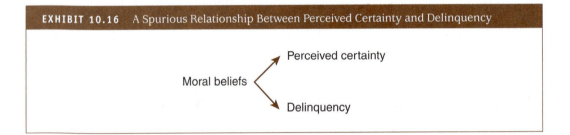

To look at this possibility, we examined the relationship between perceived certainty and delinquency under three levels of moral beliefs (weak, medium, and strong). The crosstabulations are shown in Exhibit 10.17. Although each of the subtables shows a negative relationship between moral beliefs and delinquency, in two of the subtables the relationship is weaker than it was in the original. Under the condition of strong moral beliefs, however, the original relationship is unchanged. What we would conclude from this elaboration analysis is that the variable "moral beliefs" is not acting as a very strong extraneous variable. Although some of the relationship between perceived risk and delinquency is due to their joint relationship with moral beliefs, we cannot dismiss the possibility that the perceived certainty of punishment has a causal influence on delinquent behavior.

Our goal in introducing you to crosstabulation has been to help you think about the association among variables and to give you a relatively easy tool for describing association.

EXHIBIT 10.17   Crosstabulation of Perceived Risk by Delinquency Within Levels of Moral Beliefs

Weak Moral Beliefs

	SELF-REPORTED DELINQUENCY			
PERCEIVED CERTAINTY	Low	Medium	High	Total
Low	3.8%	14.7%	81.4%	156
Medium	8.6%	27.3%	64.1%	128
High	4.2%	29.6%	66.8%	71
Total				355

$\chi^2 = 13.646$ ($p < .001$) Gamma $= -.271$

Medium Moral Beliefs

	SELF-REPORTED DELINQUENCY			
PERCEIVED CERTAINTY	Low	Medium	High	Total
Low	22.0%	42.5%	35.4%	127
Medium	33.9%	35.6%	30.5%	174
High	41.1%	34.2%	24.8%	202
Total				503

$\chi^2 = 13.646$ ($p < .001$) Gamma $= -.197$

Strong Moral Beliefs

	SELF-REPORTED DELINQUENCY			
PERCEIVED CERTAINTY	Low	Medium	High	Total
Low	42.7%	28.1%	29.2%	89
Medium	58.9%	17.7%	23.4%	107
High	72.9%	18.3%	8.7%	218
Total				414

$\chi^2 = 13.646$ ($p \leq .001$) Gamma $= -.393$

To read most statistical knowledge, in addition to the statistical techniques we have considered here and the inferential statistics we discussed previously, you should learn about the summary descriptive statistics used to indicate the strength and direction of association.

Until you do so, you will find it difficult to state with precision just how strong an association is. You also should learn about a different statistical approach to characterizing the association between two quantitative variables, called regression or correlation analysis. Statistics based on regression and correlation are used very often in the social sciences and have many advantages over crosstabulation, as well as some disadvantages. You will need to take a course in social statistics, however, to become proficient in the use of statistics based on regression and correlation.

ANALYZING DATA ETHICALLY: HOW NOT TO LIE ABOUT RELATIONSHIPS

It is when the data analyst begins to examine relationships among variables in some real data that social science research becomes most exciting. The moment of truth, it would seem, has arrived. Either the hypotheses are supported or not. But, in fact, this is also a time to proceed with caution, and to evaluate the analyses of others with even more caution. Once large data sets are entered into a computer, it becomes very easy to check out a great many relationships; when relationships are examined among three or more variables at a time, the possibilities become almost endless.

This range of possibilities presents a great hazard for data analysis. It becomes very tempting to search around in the data until something interesting emerges. Rejected hypotheses are forgotten in favor of highlighting what's going on in the data. It is not wrong to examine data for unanticipated relationships; the problem is that inevitably some relationships between variables will appear just on the basis of chance association alone. If you search hard and long enough, it will be possible to come up with something that really means nothing.

A reasonable balance must be struck between deductive data analysis to test hypotheses and inductive analysis to explore patterns in a data set. Hypotheses formulated in advance of data collection must be tested as they were originally stated; any further analyses of these hypotheses that involve a more exploratory strategy must be labeled as such in research reports. Serendipitous findings do not need to be ignored, but they must be reported. Subsequent researchers can try to deductively test the ideas generated by our explorations.

We also have to be honest about the limitations of using survey data to test causal hypotheses. The usual practice for those who seek to test a causal hypothesis with nonexperimental survey data is to test for the relationship between the independent and dependent variables, controlling for other variables that might possibly create spurious relationships. We must always think about the possibilities and be cautious in our causal conclusions.

CONCLUSION

This chapter has demonstrated how a researcher can describe phenomena in criminal justice and criminology, identify relationships among them, explore the reasons for these relationships, and test hypotheses about them. Statistics provide a remarkably useful tool for developing our understanding of the social world, a tool that we can use to test our ideas and generate new ones.

Unfortunately, to the uninitiated, the use of statistics can seem to end debate right there; you cannot argue with the numbers. But you now know better than that. The numbers will be worthless if the methods used to generate the data are not valid; and the numbers will be misleading if they are not used appropriately, taking into account the type of data to which they are applied. And even assuming valid methods and proper use of statistics, there is one more critical step, for the numbers do not speak for themselves. Ultimately, it is how we interpret and report the numbers that determines their usefulness. It is this topic we turn to in the next chapter.

KEY TERMS

Bar chart	Mode
Base N	Monotonic
Bimodal distribution	Negatively skewed
Central tendency	Outlier
Chi-square	Percentage
Crosstabulation (crosstab)	Positively skewed
Data cleaning	Probability average
Descriptive statistics	Range
Frequency distribution	Secondary data analysis
Grouped frequency distribution	Skewness
Histogram	Spurious
Inferential statistics	Standard deviation
Marginal distributions	Statistical significance
Mean	Unimodal distribution
Measure of association	Variability
Median	Variance

HIGHLIGHTS

- Bar charts, histograms, and frequency polygons are useful for describing the shape of distributions. Care must be taken with graphic displays to avoid distorting a distribution's apparent shape.

- Frequency distributions display variation in a form that can easily be inspected and described. Values should be grouped in frequency distributions in a way that does not alter the shape of the distribution. Following several guidelines can reduce the risk of problems.

- Summary statistics are often used to describe the central tendency and variability of distributions. The appropriateness of the mode, mean, and median vary with a variable's level of measurement, the distribution's shape, and the purpose of the summary.

- The variance and standard deviation summarize variability around the mean. The degree of skewness of a distribution is usually described in words rather than with a summary statistic.

- Crosstabulations should normally be percentaged within the categories of the independent variable.
- Inferential statistics are used with sample-based data to estimate the confidence that can be placed in a statistical estimate of a population parameter. Estimates of the probability that an association between variables may have occurred on the basis of chance are also based on inferential statistics.

EXERCISES

Discussing Research

1. Create frequency distributions from lists in the FBI Uniform Crime Reports on characteristics of arrestees in at least 100 cases (cites). You will have to decide on a grouping scheme for the distribution scheme of variables such as race, age, and crime committed, and how to deal with outliers in the frequency distribution.
   a. Decide what summary statistics to use for each variable of interest. How well were the features of each distribution represented by the summary statistics? Describe the shape of each distribution.
   b. Propose a hypothesis involving two of these variables, and develop a crosstabulation to evaluate the support for this hypothesis.
   c. Describe each relationship in terms of the four aspects of an association, after making percentages within each table within the categories of the independent variable. Which hypotheses appear to have been supported?

Finding Research

1. Search the web for a crime-related example of statistics. Using the key terms from this chapter, describe the set of statistics you have identified. What phenomena are described by this set of statistics? What relationships, if any, do the statistics identify?

2. Do a web search for information on a criminological subject that interests you. How much of the information you found relies on statistics as a tool for understanding the subject? How do statistics allow researchers to test their ideas about the subject and generate new ideas? Write your findings in a brief report, referring to the websites you found.

Critiquing Research

1. Become a media critic. For the next week, scan a newspaper or some magazines for statistics related to crime or criminal victimization. How many can you find using frequency distributions, graphs, and the summary statistics introduced in this chapter? Are these statistics used appropriately and interpreted correctly? Would any other statistics have been preferable or useful in addition to those presented?

Making Research Ethical

1. Review the frequency distributions and graphs in this chapter. Change one of these data displays so that you are "lying with statistics." You might consider using the graphic technique discussed by Orcutt & Turner (1993).

2. Consider the relationship between gender and delinquency that is presented in this chapter. What third variables do you think should be controlled in the analysis to better understand the basis for this relationship? How might criminal justice policies be affected by finding out that this relationship was due to differences in teacher expectations rather than to genetic differences in violence propensity?

Developing a Research Proposal

Use the General Social Survey data to add a pilot study to your proposal. A pilot study is a preliminary effort to test out the procedures and concepts that you have proposed to research.

1. Review the GSSCRJ2K variable list and identify some variables that have at least some connection to your research problem. If possible, identify one variable that might be treated as independent in your proposed research and one that might be treated as dependent.
2. Request frequencies for these variables.
3. Request a crosstabulation of the dependent variable by the independent variable (if you were able to identify any). If necessary, recode the independent variable to three or fewer categories.
4. Write a brief description of your findings and comment on their implications for your proposed research. Did you learn any lessons from this exercise for your proposal?

Performing Data Analysis in SPSS

1. Develop a description of homicide defendants and their sentence length from HOMICIDE.POR. Examine each characteristic with three statistical techniques: a graph, a frequency distribution, and a measure of central tendency.
2. Describe the distribution of each variable, noting any skewness and/or outliers.
3. Collapse the categories for defendant's age (DAGE) and sentence length (PRITIME). Examine the data distributions using a graph and frequency distribution. Does the general shape of the distributions change as a result of changing how the data are measured?
4. Look at the relationship between these two variables. Indicate which variable is the dependent variable and which variable is the independent variable.
5. Run a crosstabulation on these data (use your newly created categorical variables). Be sure to obtain percentiles for categories of the independent variable (either row or column).
6. Propose two variables that might create a spurious relationship between defendant's age and sentence length. Explain your thinking.

Reporting Research Results

The goal of research is not just to discover something but to communicate that discovery to a larger audience—other social scientists, government officials, your teachers, the general public, perhaps several of these audiences. Whatever the study's particular outcome, if the research report enables the intended audience to comprehend the results and learn from them, the research can be judged a success. If the intended audience is not able to learn about the study's results, the research should be judged a failure no matter how expensive the research, how sophisticated its design, or how much of yourself you invested in it.

The time for congratulations is when credible results are released and they serve some useful function, not when the research project is first approved. And if you have conducted a worthwhile research project, consider whether some of the results might be appropriate for more than one report to different audiences.

The primary goals of this chapter are to help you develop worthwhile reports for any research you conduct and guide you in evaluating reports produced by others. We begin by teaching you how to write research proposals, because a formal proposal lays the groundwork for a final research report. The next section highlights problems that are unique to the main types of reports: student papers and theses, journal articles, and unpublished reports for specific clients. The chapter's final sections present suggestions for writing and organizing reports, techniques for displaying statistical results, and ethical issues to be considered.

BEGINNING WITH A PROPOSAL

Be grateful for those who require you to write a formal research proposal and even more for those who give you constructive feedback. Whether your proposal is written for a professor, a thesis committee, an organization seeking practical advice, or a government agency that funds basic research, the proposal will force you to establish a problem statement and a research plan. Too many research projects begin without a clear problem statement or with only the barest of notions about which variables must be measured or what the analysis should look like. Such projects often wander along, lurching from side to side, then collapse entirely or just fizzle out with a report that is given little attention. So, even in circumstances when a proposal is not required, you should prepare one and present it to others for feedback. Just writing your ideas down will help you to see how they can be improved, and feedback in almost any form will help you to refine your plans.

A well-designed proposal can go a long way toward shaping the final research report and will make it easier to progress at later research stages. Every research proposal should have at least five sections, defined as follows:

1. *An introductory statement of the research problem.* Clarify the research question(s) that you are interested in studying and how this question was derived from the existing literature.

2. *A literature review.* Explain your problem in greater detail and build on what has already been reported in the literature on this topic.

3. *A methodological plan.* Detail the methods you will employ (including sample, variables, etc.) along with a discussion of how you will respond to the particular mix of opportunities and constraints you face.

4. *A budget.* Present a careful listing of the anticipated costs.

5. *An ethics statement.* Identify human subjects issues in the research and establish how you will respond to them in an ethical fashion.

If your research proposal will be competitively reviewed, it must present a compelling rationale for funding. It is not possible to overstate the importance of the research problem that you propose to study (see Chapter 2). If you propose to test a hypothesis, be sure it is one with plausible alternatives: "A boring hypothesis is one which, although likely to be correct, has no credible alternatives" (Dawes 1995: 93).

When you develop a research proposal, it will help to ask yourself a series of questions like those in Exhibit 11.1 (also see Herek 1995). The series of questions can serve as a map to preceding chapters in this book as well as a checklist of decisions that must be made throughout any research project. The questions are organized into five sections, each concluding with a checkpoint at which you should consider whether to proceed with the research as planned, modify the plans, or stop the project altogether. The sequential ordering of these questions obscures a bit the way they should be answered: not as single questions, one at a time, but as a unit, first as five separate stages and then as a whole.

RESEARCH REPORT GOALS

The research report will present research findings and interpretations in a way that reflects some combination of the researcher's goals, the research sponsor's goals, the concerns of the research subjects, and perhaps the concerns of a wider anticipated readership. Understanding the goals of these different groups will help the researcher begin to shape the final report even at the start of the research. In designing a proposal and in negotiating access to a setting for the research, commitments often must be made to produce a particular type of report, or at least cover certain issues in the final report. As the research progresses, feedback about the research from its subjects, sponsoring agencies, collaborators, or other interested parties may suggest the importance of focusing on particular issues in

EXHIBIT 11.1   Decisions in Research

PROBLEM FORMULATION (see Chapters 1–2)

1. Developing a research question
2. Assessing researchability of the problem
3. Consulting prior research
4. Relating to social theory
5. Choosing an approach:
   Deductive? Inductive? Descriptive?
6. Reviewing research guidelines

Checkpoint 1
Alternatives:
- Continue as planned.
- Modify the plan.
- STOP. Abandon the plan.

RESEARCH VALIDITY (see Chapters 3–5)

7. Establishing measurement validity:
   - How are concepts defined?
   - Choose a measurement strategy.
   - Assess available measures or develop new measures.
   - What evidence of reliability and validity is available or can be collected?

8. Establishing generalizability:
   - Was a representative sample used?
   - Are the findings applicable to particular subgroups?
   - Does the population sampled correspond to the population of interest?

9. Establishing causality:
   - What is the possibility of experimental or statistical controls?
   - How to assess the causal mechanism?
   - Consider the causal context.

10. Data required: Longitudinal or cross-sectional?
11. Units of analysis: Individuals or groups?
12. What are major possible sources of causal invalidity?

Checkpoint 2
Alternatives:
- Continue as planned.
- Modify the plan.
- STOP. Abandon the plan.

RESEARCH DESIGN (see Chapters 5–10)

13. Choosing a research design:
    - Experimental? Survey? Participant observation?
    - Historical, comparative? Multiple methods?

14. Secondary analysis? Availability of suitable data sets?
15. Assessing ethical concerns

(Continued)

EXHIBIT 11.1 (Continued)

Checkpoint 3
Alternatives:
- Continue as planned.
- Modify the plan.
- STOP. Abandon the plan.

DATA ANALYSIS (see Chapter 12)

18. Choosing a statistical approach:
- Statistics and graphs for describing data
- Identifying relationships between variables
- Deciding about statistical controls
- Testing for interaction effects
- Evaluating inferences from sample data to the population

Checkpoint 4
Alternatives:
- Continue as planned.
- Modify the plan.
- STOP. Abandon the plan.

REVIEWING, PROPOSING, REPORTING RESEARCH (see Chapter 13)

19. Clarifying research goals
20. Identifying the intended audience
21. Searching the literature and the Web
22. Organizing the text
23. Reviewing ethical and practical constraints

Checkpoint 5
Alternatives:
- Continue as planned.
- Modify the plan.
- STOP. Abandon the plan.

the final report. Social researchers traditionally have tried to distance themselves from the concerns of such interested parties, paying attention only to what is needed to advance scientific knowledge. But in recent years, some social scientists have recommended bringing these interested parties into the research and reporting process itself.

Advance Scientific Knowledge

Most social science research reports are directed to other social scientists working in the area of study, so they reflect orientations and concerns that are shared within this community of interest. The traditional scientific approach encourages a research goal to advance scientific knowledge by providing reports to other scientists. This approach also treats value considerations as beyond the scope of science: "An empirical science cannot tell anyone what he should do but rather what he can do and under certain circumstances what he wishes to do" (Weber 1949: 54). The idea is that developing valid knowledge about how society is organized or how we live our lives does not tell us how society should be organized or how we should live our lives. There should, as a result, be a strict separation between the determination of empirical facts and the evaluation of these facts as satisfactory or unsatisfactory (Weber 1949: 11). Social scientists must not ignore value considerations, which are viewed as a legitimate basis for selecting a research problem to study. After the research is over and a report has been written, many scientists also consider it acceptable to encourage government officials or private organizations to implement the findings. During a research project, however, value considerations are to be held in abeyance.

Shape Social Policy

Many social scientists seek to influence social policy through their writing. You have been exposed to several examples in this text, including all the evaluation research cited in Chapter 9. These particular studies, like much policy-oriented social science research, are similar to those that aim strictly to increase knowledge. In fact, these studies might even be considered contributions to knowledge first and to social policy debate second. What distinguishes the reports of these studies from strictly academic reports is their attention to policy implications.

Other social scientists who seek to influence social policy explicitly reject the traditional scientific, rigid distinction between facts and values (Sjoberg & Nett 1968). Bellah et al. (1985) have instead proposed a model of "social science as public philosophy," in which social scientists focus explicit attention on achieving a more just society:

> Social science makes assumptions about the nature of persons, the nature of society, and the relation between persons and society. It also, whether it admits it or not, makes assumptions about good persons and a good society and considers how far these conceptions are embodied in our actual society. (1985: 301)

This perspective suggests more explicit concern with public policy implications when reporting research results. But it is important to remember that we all are capable of distorting our research and our interpretations of research results to correspond to our own value preferences. The temptation to see what we want to see is enormous, and research reports cannot be deemed acceptable unless they avoid this temptation.

Organize Social Action

For the same reasons that value questions are traditionally set apart from the research process, many social scientists consider the application of research a nonscientific concern. William Foote Whyte has criticized this belief and proposed an alternative research and reporting strategy he calls **participatory action research**. Whyte (1991: 285) argues that social scientists must get "out of the academic rut" and engage in applied research to develop better understanding of social phenomena.

In participatory action research, the researcher involves some organizational members as active participants. Both the organizational members and the researcher are assumed to want to develop valid conclusions, to bring unique insights, and to desire change.

Dialogue With Research Subjects

Guba and Lincoln (1989: 44–45) have carried the notion of involving research subjects and others in the design and reporting of research one step further. What they call the **constructivist paradigm** is a methodology that emphasizes the importance of exploring how different stakeholders in a social setting construct their beliefs. This approach rejects the assumption that there is a reality around us to be studied and reported on. Instead, social scientists operating in the constructivist paradigm try to develop a consensus among participants in some social process about how to understand the focus of inquiry, a program that is often evaluated. A research report will then highlight different views of the social program and explain how a consensus can be reached.

Constructivist inquiry uses an interactive research process, in which a researcher begins an evaluation in some social setting by identifying the different interest groups in that setting and the stakeholder groups. The researcher goes on to learn what each group thinks and then gradually tries to develop a shared perspective on the problem being evaluated (Guba & Lincoln 1989: 42). This process involves four steps that can each be repeated many times in a given study:

1. Identify stakeholders and solicit their claims, concerns, and issues.
2. Introduce the claims, concerns, and issues of each stakeholder group to the other stakeholder groups and ask for their reactions.
3. Focus further information collection on claims, concerns, and issues about which understanding there is disagreement among stakeholder groups of research.
4. Negotiate with stakeholder groups about the information collected and attempt to reach consensus on the issues about which there is disagreement.

The researcher conducts an open-ended interview with the first respondent (R1) to learn about their thoughts and feelings on the subject of inquiry, their "construction" (C1). The researcher then asks this respondent to nominate a second respondent (R2), who feels very differently. The second respondent is then interviewed in the same way, but also is asked to comment on the themes raised by the previous respondent. The process continues until all major perspectives are represented, and then may be repeated again with the same set of respondents.

The final product is a case report:

> A case report is very unlike the technical reports we are accustomed to seeing in positivist inquiries. It is not a depiction of a "true" or "real" state of affairs . . . It does not culminate in judgments, conclusions, or recommendations except insofar as these are concurred on by relevant respondents.
>
> The case report helps the reader come to a realization (in the sense of making real) not only of the states of affairs that are believed by constructors [research respondents] to exist but also of the underlying motives, feelings, and rationales leading to those beliefs. The case report is characterized by a thick description that not only clarifies the all-important context, but that makes it possible for the reader vicariously to experience it. (Guba & Lincoln 1989: 180–181)

Although this is off the beaten social scientific track, the constructivist approach provides a useful way of thinking about how best to make sense of the complexity and subjectivity of the social world. Other researchers write reports intended to influence public policy and often their findings are ignored. Such neglect would be less common if social researchers gave more attention to the different meanings attached by participants to the same events, in the spirit of constructivist case reports.

TYPES OF RESEARCH REPORTS

Research projects designed to produce student papers and theses, applied research reports, and academic articles all have unique features that will influence the final research report. For example, student papers are written for a particular professor or for a thesis committee and often are undertaken with almost no financial resources and in the face of severe time constraints. Applied research reports are written for an organization or agency that usually also has funded the research and has expectations for a particular type of report. Journal articles are written for the larger academic community and will not be published until they are judged acceptable by some representatives of that community (e.g., after the article has gone through extensive peer review).

These unique features do not really match up so neatly with the specific types of research products. For example, a student paper that is based on a research project conducted in collaboration with a work organization may face some constraints for a project designed to produce an applied research report. An academic article may stem from an applied research project conducted for a government agency. An applied research report often can be followed by an academic article on the same topic. In fact, one research study may lead to all three types of research reports as students write course papers or theses for professors who write both academic articles and applied research reports.

Student Papers and Theses

What is most distinctive about a student research paper or thesis is the audience for the final product: a professor or, for a thesis, a committee of professors. In light of this, it is important for you to seek feedback early and often about the progress of your research and about your professor's expectations for the final paper. Securing approval of a research proposal is usually the first step, but it should not be the last occasion for seeking advice prior to writing the final paper. Do not become too anxious for guidance, however. Professors require research projects in part so that their students can work through, at least somewhat independently, the many issues they confront. A great deal of insight into the research process can be gained in this way. So balance your requests for advice with some independent decision making.

Most student research projects can draw on few resources beyond the student's own time and effort, so it is important that the research plan not be overly ambitious. Keep the paper deadline in mind when planning the project, and remember that almost every researcher tends to underestimate the time required to carry out a project.

The Thesis Committee

Students who are preparing a paper for a committee, usually at the M.A. or Ph.D. level, must be prepared to integrate the multiple perspectives and comments of committee members into a plan for a coherent final report. (The thesis committee chair should be the primary guide in this process; careful selection of faculty to serve on the committee is also important.) As much as possible, committee members should have complementary areas of expertise that are each important for the research project: perhaps one methodologist, one specialist in the primary substantive area of the thesis, and one specialist in a secondary area.

It is very important that you work with your committee members in an ongoing manner, both individually and collectively. In fact, it is vitally important to have a group meeting with all committee members at the beginning of the project to ensure everyone on the committee supports the research plan. Doing this will avoid obstacles that arise due to miscommunication later in the research process.

Journal Articles

It is the **peer review** process that makes preparation of an academic journal article most unique. Similar to a grant review, the journal's editor sends submitted articles to two or three experts, peers, who are asked whether the paper should be accepted more or less as is, revised and then resubmitted, or rejected. Reviewers also provide comments—which are sometimes quite lengthy—to explain their decision and to guide any required revisions. The process is an anonymous one at most journals; reviewers are not told the author's name, and the author is not told the reviewers' names. Although the journal editor has the final say, editors' decisions are normally based on the reviewers' comments.

This peer review process must be anticipated in designing the final report. Peer reviewers are not pulled out of a hat. They are expert in the field or fields represented in the paper and usually have published articles themselves in that field. It is critical that the author be familiar with the research literature and be able to present the research findings as a unique contribution to that literature. In most cases, this hurdle is much harder to jump with journal articles than with student papers or applied research reports. In fact, most leading journals have a rejection rate of over 90 %, so that hurdle is quite high indeed. Of course, there is also a certain luck of the draw in peer review. One set of two or three reviewers may be inclined to reject an article that another set of reviewers would accept. But in general, the anonymous peer review process results in higher quality research reports because articles are revised prior to publication in response to the suggestions and criticisms of the experts.

Criminological and criminal justice research is published in a myriad of journals within several disciplines, including criminology, law, sociology, psychology, and economics. As a result, there is no one formatting style by which all criminological literature abides. If, for example, you are submitting your paper to a psychology-related journal, you must abide by the formatting style dictated by the *Publication Manual of the American Psychological Association*. The easiest way to determine how to format a paper for a particular journal is to examine recent volumes of the journal and format your paper accordingly. There are numerous articles available on the Student Study Site for this text, www.sagepub.com/frccjstudy.

Despite the slight variations in style across journals, there are typically seven standard sections within a journal article in addition to the title page:

1. *Abstract.* This should be a concise and nonevaluative summary of your research paper (no more than 120 words) that describes the research problem, the sample, the method, and the findings.

2. *Introduction.* The body of a paper should open with an introduction that presents the specific problem under study and describes the research strategy. Before writing this section, you should consider the following questions: What is the point of the study? How do the hypotheses and the research design relate to the problem? What are the theoretical implications of the study, and how does the study relate to previous work in the area? What are the theoretical propositions tested, and how were they derived? A good introduction answers these questions in a few paragraphs by summarizing the relevant argument and the data, giving the reader a sense of what was done and why.

3. *Literature Review.* Discuss the relevant literature in a way that relates each previous study cited to your research, not in an exhaustive historical review. Citation of and specific credit to relevant earlier works is part of the researcher's scientific and scholarly responsibility. It is essential for the growth of cumulative science. This section should demonstrate the logical continuity between previous research and the research at hand. At the end of this section, you are ready to conceptually define your variables and formally state your hypotheses.

4. *Method.* Describe in detail how the study was conducted. Such a description enables the reader to evaluate the appropriateness of your methods and the reliability and the validity of your results. It also permits experienced investigators to replicate the study if they so desire. In this section, you can include subsections that describe the sample, the independent and dependent variables, and the analytical or statistical procedure you will use to analyze the data.

5. *Results.* Summarize the results of the statistical or qualitative analyses performed on the data. It can include tables and figures that summarize findings. If statistical analyses are performed, tests of significance should also be highlighted.

6. *Discussion.* Take the opportunity to evaluate and interpret your results, particularly with respect to your original hypotheses and previous research. Here, you are free to examine and interpret your results as well as draw inferences from them. In general, this section should answer the following questions: What have I contributed to the literature here? How has my study helped to resolve the original problem? What conclusions and theoretical implications can I draw from my study? What are the limitations of my study? What are the implications for future research?

7. *References.* All citations in the manuscript must appear in the reference list, and all references must be cited in the text.

Applied Reports

Unlike journal articles, applied reports are usually commissioned by a particular government agency, corporation, or nonprofit organization. As such, the most important problem that applied researchers confront is the need to produce a final report that meets the funding organization's expectations. This is called the hired gun problem. Of course, the extent to which being a hired gun is a problem varies greatly with the research orientation of the funding organization and with the nature of the research problem posed. The ideal situation is to have few constraints on the nature of the final report, but sometimes research reports are suppressed or distorted because the researcher comes to conclusions that the funding organization does not like.

Applied reports that are written in a less highly charged environment can face another problem—even when they are favorably received by the funding organization, their conclusions are often ignored. This problem can be more a matter of the organization not really knowing how to use research findings than of them not wanting to use them. And this is not just a problem of the funding organization; many researchers are prepared only to present their findings, without giving any thought to how research findings can be translated into organizational policies or programs.

An Advisory Committee

An advisory committee can help the applied researcher avoid the problems of incompatible expectations for the final report and insufficient understanding of how to use the research results, without adopting the more engaged strategy of Whyte's participatory action research or Guba and Lincoln's (1989) constructivist inquiry. An advisory committee should be formed before the start of the project to represent the various organizational segments with stakes in the outcomes of the research. The researcher can use the committee as a source of intelligence about how particular findings may be received and as a sounding board for ideas about how the organization or agency can use research findings. Perhaps most important, an advisory committee can help the researcher work out many problems in research design, implementation, and data collection. Because an advisory committee is meant to comprise all stakeholders, it is inevitable that conflicts will arise between advisory group members. In our experience, however, these conflicts almost invariably can be used to strategize more effectively about the research design and the final product.

CURBING THE FRUSTRATIONS OF WRITING

"Perfectionism is the voice of the oppressor, the enemy of the people. It will keep you cramped and insane your whole life and it is the main obstacle between you and a shitty first draft." (Lamott 1994: 28)

We often hear lamentations from students such as, "It is impossible to know where to begin," or "I have a hard time getting started." To this we say only, "Begin wherever you are most comfortable but begin early!" You do not have to start with the introduction; start in the method section if you prefer. The main point is to begin somewhere and then keep typing, keep typing, and keep typing! It is always easier to rewrite a paper than it is to write the first draft. The fine art of writing is really in the rewriting!

Those of you who began with a research proposal have a head start; you will find that the final report is much easier to write. It is very disappointing to discover that something important was left out when it is too late to do anything about it. And we do not need to point out that students (and professional researchers) often leave final papers (and reports) until the last possible minute (often for understandable reasons, including other coursework and job or family responsibilities). But be forewarned: The last-minute approach does not work for research reports.

A successful report must be well organized and clearly written. Getting to such a product is a difficult but not impossible goal. Consider the following principles formulated by experienced writers (Booth, Colomb, & Williams 1995: 150–151):

- Start with an outline.
- Respect the complexity of the task, and do not expect to write a polished draft in a linear fashion. Your thinking will develop as you write, causing you to reorganize and rewrite.
- Leave enough time for dead ends, restarts, revisions, and so on, and accept the fact that you will discard much of what you write.
- Write as fast as you comfortably can. Do not worry about spelling, grammar, and so on until you are polishing things up.
- Ask all the people whom you trust for their reactions to what you have written.
- Write as you go along, so you have notes and report segments drafted even before you focus on writing the report.

It is important to remember that no version of a manuscript is ever final. As you write, you will get new ideas about how to organize the report. Try them out. As you review the first draft, you will see many ways to improve your writing. Focus particularly on how to shorten and clarify your statements. Make sure each paragraph concerns only one topic. Remember the golden rule of good writing: writing is revising!

Another useful tip is called reverse outlining. After you have written a first complete draft, outline it on a paragraph-by-paragraph basis, ignoring the actual section headings you used. See if the paper you wrote actually fits the outline you planned. How could the organization be improved?

And perhaps most importantly, leave yourself enough time so that you can revise—several times if possible—before turning in the final draft.

A well-written research report requires (to be just a bit melodramatic) blood, sweat, and tears and more time than you will at first anticipate. But the process of writing one will help you to write the next. And the issues you consider, if you approach your writing critically, will be sure to improve your subsequent research projects and sharpen your evaluations of others.

Those of you interested in a more focused discussion of writing in general (e.g., grammar, elements of style, emotional aspects of writing) should see Becker (1986), Booth, Colomb, and Williams (1995), Mullins (1977), Strunk and White (1979), and Turabian (1967).

ETHICS AND REPORTING

It is at the time of reporting research results that the researcher's ethical duty to be honest becomes paramount. Here are some guidelines.

- *Provide an honest accounting of how the research was carried out and where the initial research design had to be changed.* Readers do not have to know about every change you made in your plans and each new idea you had, but they should be informed about major changes in hypotheses or research design.
- *Maintain a full record of the research project so that questions can be answered if they arise.* Many details will have to be omitted from all but the most comprehensive reports, but these omissions should not make it impossible to track down answers to specific questions about research procedures that may arise in the course of data analysis or presentation.
- *Avoid "lying with statistics" or using graphs to mislead.*
- *Acknowledge the sponsors of the research.* In part, this is so that others can consider whether this sponsorship may have tempted you to bias your results in some way; and thank staff who made major contributions.
- *Be sure that the order of authorship for coauthored reports is discussed in advance and reflects agreed-upon principles. Be sensitive to coauthors' needs and concerns.*

Ethical research reporting should not mean ineffective reporting. You need to tell a coherent story in the report and to avoid losing track of the story in a thicket of minuscule details. You do not need to report every twist and turn in the conceptualization of the research problem or the conduct of the research, but be suspicious of reports that do not seem to admit to the possibility of any room for improvement. Social science is an ongoing enterprise in which one research report makes its most valuable contribution by laying the groundwork for another, more sophisticated, research project. Highlight important findings in the research report, but use the research report also to point out what are likely to be the most productive directions for future researchers.

CONCLUSION

Much research lacks one or more of the three legs of validity—measurement validity, causal validity, or generalizability—and sometimes contributes more confusion than understanding about particular issues. Top journals generally maintain very high standards, partly because they have good critics in the review process and distinguished editors who make the final acceptance decisions. But some daily newspapers do a poor job of screening, and research reporting standards in many popular magazines, TV shows, and books are often abysmally poor. Keep your standards high and your view critical when reading research reports, but not so high or so critical that you turn away from studies that make tangible contributions to the literature, even if they do not provide definitive answers. And don't be so intimidated by the need to maintain high standards that you shrink from taking advantage of opportunities to conduct research yourself.

Of course, social research methods are no more useful than the commitment of the researchers to their proper application. Research methods, like all knowledge, can be used poorly or well, for good purposes or bad, when appropriate or not. A claim that a belief is based on social science research in itself provides no extra credibility. As you have learned throughout this book, we must first learn which methods were used, how they were applied, and whether interpretations square with the evidence. To investigate the social world, we must keep in mind the lessons of research methods.

KEY TERMS

Constructivist paradigm
Participatory action research
Peer review

HIGHLIGHTS

- Proposal writing should be a time for clarifying the research problem, reviewing the literature, and thinking ahead about the report that will be required.

- Relations with research subjects and consumers should be developed in a manner that achieves key research goals and preparation of an effective research report. The traditional scientific approach of minimizing the involvement of research subjects and consumers in research decisions has been challenged by proponents of participatory action research and adherents of the constructivist paradigm.

- Research reports should include an introductory statement of the research problem, a literature review, a methodology section, a findings section with pertinent data displays, and a conclusions section that identifies any weaknesses in the research design and points out implications for future research and theorizing. This basic report format should be modified according to the needs of a particular audience.

- All reports should be revised several times and critiqued by others before they are presented in final form.

- The central ethical concern in research reporting is to be honest. This honesty should include providing a truthful accounting of how the research was carried out, maintaining a full record about the project, using appropriate statistics and graphs, acknowledging the research sponsors, and being sensitive to the perspectives of coauthors.

EXERCISES

Discussing Research

1. Select a recent article published in a peer-reviewed criminological journal and answer the following questions: How effective is the article in conveying the design and findings of the research? Could the article's organization be improved at all? Are there bases for disagreement about the interpretation of the findings?

2. Call a local criminal justice official and arrange for an interview. Ask the official about his or her experience with applied research reports and his conclusions about the value of social research and the best techniques for reporting to practitioners.

Finding Research

1. Go to the National Science Foundation's Law and Social Science Program website at www.nsf.gov/sbe/ses/law/start.htm. What are the components that the National Science Foundation's Law and Social Science Program looks for in a proposed piece of research? Write a detailed outline for a research proposal to study a subject of your choice to be submitted to the National Science Foundation for funding.

2. Go to the Ethics, Public Policy, and Public Administration site at http://plsc.uark.edu/book/ books/ethics/index.htm. Choose "Cases" and then "Integrity and Separations" (No. 14). Read the case "Integrity and Separations." Briefly describe the issues surrounding social science research, methods, reporting research results, and ethics in the case. Now return to the home page of the Ethics site. Choose "Set of Questions" and answer the "Questions for Consideration" in terms of the case "Integrity and Separations."

3. Using the web, find five different examples of criminological research projects that have been completed. Briefly describe each. How does each differ in its approach to reporting the research results? To whom do you think the author(s) of each is "reporting" (i.e., who is the "audience")? How do you think the predicted audience has helped to shape the author's approach to reporting the results? Be sure to note the websites at which you located each of your five examples.

Critiquing Research

1. Rate four criminological journal articles for overall quality of the research and for effectiveness of the writing and data displays. Discuss how each could have been improved.

2. How firm a foundation do social research methods provide for understanding the social world? Stage an in-class debate, with the pro and con arguments focusing on the variability of social research findings across different social contexts and the difficulty of understanding human subjectivity.

Making Research Ethical

1. You learned in Chapter 2 about the controversy resulting from Ehrlich's (1975) failure to make his data on the impact of capital punishment available for reanalysis by other researchers. Would you recommend legal regulations about the release of research data? What would those regulations be? Would they differ depending on the researcher's source of funding? Would you allow researchers exclusive access to their own data for some period of time after they have collected it?

2. Full disclosure of sources of research as well as of other medically related funding has become a major concern for medical journals. Should researchers publishing in criminology and criminal justice journals also be required to fully disclose all sources of funding? Should full disclosure of all previous funds received by criminal justice agencies be required in each published article? What about disclosure of any previous jobs or paid consultations with criminal justice agencies? Write a short justification of the regulations you propose.

Developing a Research Proposal

Now it is time to bring all the elements of your proposal together.

1. Organize the proposal material you wrote for previous chapters in a logical order. Based on your research question, select the most appropriate research method as your primary method (see Chapters 5–8).

2. To add a multiple component to your research design, select another research method that could add knowledge about your research question.

3. Rewrite the entire proposal, adding an introduction. Also add sections that outline a budget and state the limitations of your study.

Performing Data Analysis in SPSS

1. How do friends' opinions and support for delinquent activities influence levels of delinquency among youth? A combined frequency display of the distributions of a series of YOUTH.POR variables will help you to answer this question.

   a. Obtain a frequency distribution and descriptive statistics for friends' attitudes toward delinquent acts index (FROPINION), index of friends' engagement in delinquent acts (FRBEHAVE), and the delinquency index at time 11 (DELINQ1).

   b. Using the mean as the measure of center, recode the three indexes to measure low and high levels of each variable (e.g., all values below the mean represent low levels of a given variable and all values above the mean represent high levels of the given variable).

   c. Use the percentages in these distributions to prepare a combined frequency display.

   d. Discuss what you have learned about the influence of friends' delinquent tendencies on delinquency levels among youth.

Student Study Site

The companion Student Study Website for *The Fundamentals of Research in Criminology and Criminal Justice* can be found at www.sagepub.com/frccjstudy.

   Visit the Student Study Site to enhance your understanding of the chapter content and to discover additional resources that will take your learning one step further. You can enhance your understanding of the chapters by using the comprehensive study material, which includes interactive exercises, e-flashcards, web exercises, practice self-tests, and more. You will also find special features, such as Learning from Journal Articles, which incorporates SAGE's online journal collection.

Conducting Literature Reviews and Finding Information

Social Research Foundations—
How to Conduct a Literature Review

Case Study: Arrest and Domestic Violence

How do we find prior research on questions of interest? You may already know some of the relevant material from prior coursework or your independent reading, but that would not be enough. When you are about to launch an investigation of a new research question, you must apply a very different standard than when you are studying for a test or just seeking to learn about domestic violence. You need to find reports of previous investigations that sought to answer the same research question that you wish to answer, not just those that were about a similar topic. If there are no prior studies of exactly the same research question on which you wish to focus, you should seek to find reports from investigations of very similar research questions. Once you have located reports from prior research similar to the research you wish to conduct, you may expand your search to include investigations about related topics or studies that used similar methods.

Sometimes, you will find that someone else has already reviewed the literature on your research question in a special review article or book chapter. For example, Chalk and Garner (2001) published an excellent review of the research on arrest and domestic violence in the journal *New Directions for Evaluation*. Most of the research articles you find will include a literature review. These reviews can help a lot, but they are no substitute for reviewing the literature yourself. No one but you can decide what is relevant for your research question and the research circumstances you will be facing: the setting you will study, the timing of your study, the new issues that you want to include in your study, and your specific methods. And you cannot depend on any published research review for information on the most recent work. New research results about many questions appear continually in scholarly journals and books, in research reports from government agencies and other organizations, and on Websites all over the world; you will need to check for new research such as this yourself.

Finding Information

Conducting a thorough search of the research literature and then reviewing critically what you have found is an essential foundation for any research project. Fortunately, much of this information can be identified online, without leaving your desktop, and an increasing number of published journal articles can be downloaded directly to your own computer (depending on your particular access privileges). But just because there is a lot available online does not mean that you need to find it all. Keep in mind that your goal is to find reports of prior research investigations, which means that you should focus on scholarly journals that choose articles for publication after they have been reviewed by other social scientists: "refereed" journals. Newspaper and magazine articles just will not do, although you may find some that raise important issues or even that summarize social science research investigations.

Every year, the Web offers more and more useful material, including indexes of the published research literature. You may find copies of particular rating scales, reports from research in progress, papers that have been presented at professional conferences, and online discussions of related topics. This section reviews the basic procedures for finding relevant research information in both the published literature and on the Web, but keep in mind that the primary goal is to identify research articles published in refereed journals.

Searching the Literature

The social science literature should be consulted at the beginning and end of an investigation. Even while an investigation is in progress, consultations with the literature may help to resolve methodological problems or facilitate supplementary explorations. As with any part of the research process, the method you use will affect the quality of your results. You should try to ensure that your search method includes each of the steps below.

Specify your research question. Your research question should be neither so broad that hundreds of articles are judged relevant nor so narrow that you miss important literature. "Is informal social control effective?" is probably too broad. "Does informal social control reduce rates of burglary in large cities?" is probably too narrow. "Is informal social control more effective in reducing crime rates than policing?" provides about the right level of specificity.

Identify appropriate bibliographic databases to search. Criminal Justice Abstracts and *Sociological Abstracts* may meet many of your needs, but if you are studying a question about medical consequences or other health issues, you should also search in *Medline*, the database for searching the medical literature. If your focus is on mental health, you will also want to include a search in the online *Psychological Abstracts* database, *PsycINFO*, or the version that also contains the full text of articles since 1985, *PsycARTICLES*. To find articles that refer to a previous publication, such as Sherman and Berk's (1984) study of the police response to domestic violence, the *Social Science Citation Index* would be helpful. In addition, the search engine Google now offers anyone with Web access Google Scholar (which indexes and searches the full text of selected journals) and Google Print (which digitizes and searches the full text of the books that are owned by selected research libraries). (At the time this book went to press, the Google Print project was on hold due to copyright concerns raised by some publishers, while the search engine and directory Yahoo! was starting a similar venture that focused only on older books that are no longer covered by copyright law; Hafner, 2005: C1.)

Choose a search technology. For most purposes, an online bibliographic database that references the published journal literature will be all you need. However, searches for unpopular topics or very recent literature may require that you also search Websites or bibliographies of relevant books.

Create a tentative list of search terms. List the parts and subparts of your research question and any related issues that you think are important: "informal social control," "policing," "influences on crime rates," and perhaps "community cohesion and crime." List the authors of relevant studies. Specify the most important journals that deal with your topic.

Narrow your search. The sheer number of references you find can be a problem. For example, searching for "social capital" resulted in 2,293 citations in *Sociological Abstracts*. Depending on the database you are working with and the purposes of your search, you may want to limit your search to English-language publications, to journal articles rather than conference papers or dissertations (both of which are more difficult to acquire), and to materials published in recent years.

Refine your search. Learn as you go. If your search yields too many citations, try specifying the search terms more precisely. If you have not found much literature, try using more general terms. Whatever terms you search first, do not consider your search complete until you have tried several different approaches and have seen how many articles you find. A search for "domestic violence" in *Sociological Abstracts* on September 11, 2005, yielded 1,569 hits; adding "effects" or "influences" as required search terms dropped the number of hits to 370.

Use Boolean search logic. It is often a good idea to narrow down your search by requiring that abstracts contain combinations of words or phrases that include more of the specific details of your research question. Using the Boolean connector "and" allows you to do this, whereas using the connector "or" allows you to find abstracts containing different words that mean the same thing. Exhibit A.1 provides an example.

Use appropriate subject descriptors. Once you have found an article that you consider to be appropriate, take a look at the "descriptors" field in the citation (see Exhibit A.2). You can then redo your search after requiring that the articles be classified with some or all of these descriptor terms.

Check the results. Read the titles and abstracts you have found, and identify the articles that appear to be most relevant. If possible, click on these article titles and generate a list of their references. See if you find more articles that are relevant to your research question but that you have missed so far. You will be surprised (I always am) at how many important articles your initial online search missed.

Read the articles. Now, it is time to find the full text of the articles of interest. If you are lucky, some of the journals you need will be available to patrons of your library in online versions, and you will be able to link to the full text just by clicking on a "full text" link. But many

EXHIBIT A.1   Use of Boolean Connectors in a Literature Search

journals, specific issues of some journals, or both will be available only in print; in this case, you will have to find them in your library or order a copy through interlibrary loan.

Refer to a good book for even more specific guidance. Fink's (2004) *Conducting Research Literature Reviews: From the Internet to Paper* is an excellent guide.

You may be tempted to write up a "review" of the literature based on reading the abstracts or using only those articles available online, but you will be selling yourself short. Many crucial details about methods, findings, and theoretical implications will be found only in the body of the article, and many important articles will not be available online. To understand, critique, and really learn from previous research studies, you must read the important articles, no matter how you have to retrieve them.

If you have done your job well, you will now have more than enough literature as background for your own research, unless it is on a very obscure topic (see Exhibit A.3). (Of course, ultimately your search will be limited by the library holdings you have access to and by the time you have to order or find copies of journal articles, conference papers, and perhaps dissertations that you cannot obtain online.) At this point, your main concern is to construct a coherent framework in which to develop your research question, drawing as many lessons as you can from previous research. You may use the literature to

EXHIBIT A.2   Checking Standard Subject Matter Descriptors

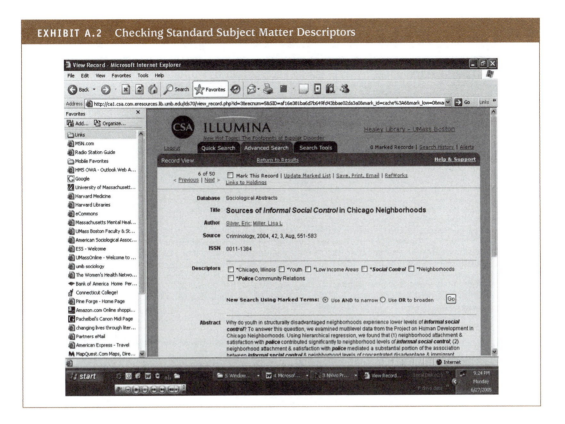

identify a useful theory and hypotheses to be reexamined, to find inadequately studied specific research questions, to explicate the disputes about your research question, to summarize the major findings of prior research, and to suggest appropriate methods of investigation.

Be sure to take notes on each article you read, organizing your notes into standard sections: Theory, Methods, Findings, Conclusions. In any case, write the literature review so that it contributes to your study in some concrete way; do not feel compelled to discuss an article just because you have read it. Be judicious. You are conducting only one study of one issue; it will only obscure the value of your study if you try to relate it to every tangential point in related research.

Don't think of searching the literature as a one-time-only venture, something that you leave behind as you move on to your "real" research. You may encounter new questions or unanticipated problems as you conduct your research or as you burrow deeper into the literature. Searching the literature again to determine what others have found in response to these questions or what steps they have taken to resolve these problems can yield substantial improvements in your own research. There is so much literature on so many topics that often it is not possible to figure out in advance every subject you should search the literature for or what type of search would be most beneficial.

EXHIBIT A.3 A Search in *Sociological Abstracts* on Informal Control

Another reason to make searching the literature an ongoing project is that the literature is always growing. During the course of one research study, whether it takes only one semester or several years, new findings will be published and relevant questions will be debated. Staying attuned to the literature and checking it at least when you are writing up your findings may save your study from being outdated.

Searching the Web

The World Wide Web provides access to vast amounts of information of many different sorts (Ó Dochartaigh 2002). You can search the holdings of other libraries and download the complete text of government reports, some conference papers, and newspaper articles. You can find policies of local governments, descriptions of individual social scientists and particular research projects, and postings of advocacy groups. It is also hard to avoid finding a lot of information in which you have no interest, such as commercial advertisements, third-grade homework assignments, or college course syllabi. In 1999, there were already about 800 million publicly available pages of information on the Web (Davis 1999). Today, there may be as many as 15 billion pages on the Web (Novak 2003).

After you are connected to the Web with a browser such as Microsoft Internet Explorer or Netscape Navigator, you can use three basic strategies for finding information: direct addressing (i.e., typing in the address, or uniform resource locator [URL], of a specific site); browsing (i.e., reviewing online lists of Websites); and searching (i.e., Google is currently the most popular search engine for searching the Web). For some purposes, you will need to use only one strategy; for other purposes, you will want to use all three.

Exhibit A.4 illustrates the first problem that you may encounter when searching the Web: the sheer quantity of resources that are available. It is a much bigger problem than when searching bibliographic databases. On the Web, less is usually more. Limit your inspection of Websites to the first few pages that turn up in your list (they are ranked by relevance). See what those first pages contain, and then try to narrow your search by including some additional terms. Putting quotation marks around a phrase that you want to search will also help to limit your search; for example, searching for "informal social control" on Google (on September 11, 2005) produced 31,100 sites, compared to the roughly 15,500,000 sites retrieved when we omitted the quotes wherein Google searched "informal" and "social" and "control."

EXHIBIT A.4   Google Search Results for "Informal Social Control"

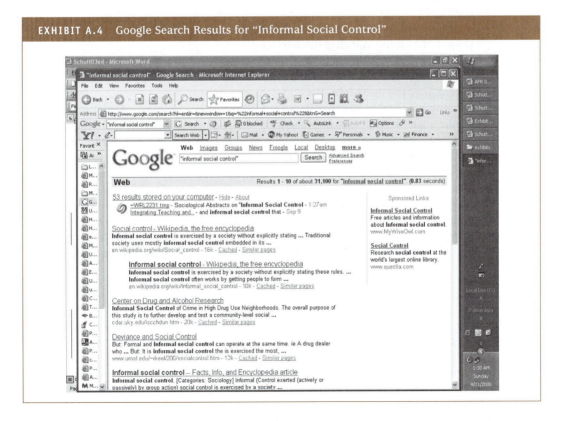

Remember the following warnings when you conduct searches on the Web:

- *Clarify your goals.* Before you begin the search, jot down the terms that you think you need to search for as well as a statement of what you want to accomplish with your search. This will help to ensure that you have a sense of what to look for and what to ignore.
- *Quality is not guaranteed.* Anyone can post almost anything, so the accuracy and adequacy of the information you find are always suspect. There is no journal editor or librarian to evaluate quality and relevance.
- *Anticipate change.* Websites that are not maintained by stable organizations can come and go very quickly. Any search will result in attempts to link to some URLs that no longer exist.
- *One size does not fit all.* Different search engines use different procedures for indexing Websites. Some attempt to be all-inclusive, whereas others aim to be selective. As a result, you can get different results from different search engines (e.g., Google or Yahoo!) even though you are searching for the same terms.
- *Be concerned about generalizability.* You might be tempted to characterize police department policies by summarizing the documents you find at police department Websites. But how many police departments are there? How many have posted their policies on the Web? Are these policies representative of all police departments? To answer all these questions, you would have to conduct a research project just on the Websites themselves.
- *Evaluate the sites.* There is a lot of stuff out there, so how do you know what is good? Some Websites contain excellent advice and pointers on how to differentiate the good from the bad.
- *Avoid Web addiction.* Another danger of the enormous amount of information available on the Web is that one search will lead to another and to another and so on. There are always more possibilities to explore and one more interesting source to check. Establish boundaries of time and effort to avoid the risk of losing all sense of proportion.
- *Cite your sources.* Using text or images from Web sources without attribution is plagiarism. It is the same as copying someone else's work from a book or article and pretending that it is your own. Record the Web address (URL), the name of the information provider, and the date on which you obtain material from the site. Include this information in a footnote to the material that you use in a paper.

Reviewing Research

Effective review of the prior research you find is an essential step in building the foundation for new research. You must assess carefully the quality of each research study, consider the implications of each article for your own plans, and expand your thinking about your research question to take account of new perspectives and alternative arguments. It is through reviewing the literature and using it to extend and sharpen your own ideas and methods that you become a part of the social science community. Instead of being just one individual studying an issue that interests you, you are building on an ever-growing body of knowledge that is being constructed by the entire community of scholars.

The research information you find on various Web sites comes in a wide range of formats and represents a variety of sources. *Caveat emptor* (buyer beware) is the watchword when you search the Web; following review guidelines such as those we have listed will minimize, but not eliminate, the risk of being led astray. By contrast, the published scholarly journal literature that you find in databases such as *Sociological Abstracts* and *Psychological Abstracts* follows a much more standard format and has been subject to a careful review process. There is some variability in the contents of these databases: some journals publish book reviews, comments on prior articles, dissertation abstracts, and conference papers. However, most literature you will find on a research topic in these databases represents peer-reviewed articles reporting analyses of data collected in a research project. These are the sources on which you should focus. This section concentrates on the procedures you should use for reviewing these articles. These procedures also can be applied to reviews of research monographs: books that provide much more information from a research project than that contained in a journal article.

Reviewing the literature is really a two-stage process. In the first stage, you must assess each article separately. This assessment should follow a standard format such as that represented by the "Questions to Ask About a Research Article" in Appendix B. However, you should keep in mind that you cannot adequately understand a research study if you just treat it as a series of discrete steps, involving a marriage of convenience among separate techniques. Any research project is an integrated whole, so you must be concerned with how each component of the research design influenced the others, for example, how the measurement approach might have affected the causal validity of the researcher's conclusions and how the sampling strategy might have altered the quality of measures.

The second stage of the review process is to assess the implications of the entire set of articles (and other materials) for the relevant aspects of your research question and procedures and then to write an integrated review that highlights these implications. Although you can find literature reviews that consist simply of assessments of one published article after another—that never get beyond stage one in the review process—your understanding of the literature and the quality of your own work will be much improved if you make the effort to write an integrated review.

In the next two sections, we will show how you might answer many of the questions in Appendix B as we review a research article about domestic violence. We will then show how the review of a single article can be used within an integrated review of the body of prior research on this research question. Because at this early point in the text you will not be familiar with all the terminology used in the article review, you might want to read through the more elaborate article review in Appendix C later in the course.

A Single-Article Review: Formal and Informal Deterrents to Domestic Violence

Anthony Pate and Edwin Hamilton at the National Police Foundation designed one of the studies funded by the U.S. Department of Justice to replicate the Minneapolis Domestic Violence Experiment. This section examines the article that resulted from that replication, which was published in the *American Sociological Review* (Pate & Hamilton 1992). The numbers in brackets refer to the article review questions in Appendix B.

The Research Question. Like Sherman and Berk's (1984) original Minneapolis study, Pate and Hamilton's (1992) Metro-Dade spouse assault experiment sought to test the deterrent effect of arrest in domestic violence cases, but with an additional focus on the role of informal social control [1]. The purpose of the study was explanatory because the goal was to explain variation in the propensity to commit spouse abuse [2]. Deterrence theory provided the theoretical framework for the study, but this framework was broadened to include the proposition by Williams and Hawkins (1986) that informal sanctions such as stigma and the loss of valued relationships augment the effect of formal sanctions such as arrest [3]. Pate and Hamilton's literature review referred, appropriately, to the original Sherman and Berk research, to the other studies that attempted to replicate the original findings, and to research on informal social control [4].

There is no explicit discussion of ethical guidelines in the article, although reference is made to a more complete unpublished report [6]. Clearly, important ethical issues had to be considered, given the experimental intervention in the police response to serious assaults, but the adherence to standard criminal justice procedures suggests attention to the welfare of victims as well as the rights of suspects. We will consider these issues in more detail later in this chapter.

The Research Design. Developed as a follow-up to the original Minneapolis experiment, the Metro-Dade experiment exemplified the guidelines for scientific research that were presented in Chapter 2 [5]. It was designed systematically, with careful attention to specification of terms and clarification of assumptions, and focused on the possibility of different outcomes rather than certainty about one preferred outcome. The major concepts in the study, formal and informal deterrence, were defined clearly [7] and then measured with straightforward indicators: arrest or nonarrest for formal deterrence and marital status and employment status for informal deterrence. However, the specific measurement procedures for marital and employment status were not discussed, and no attempt was made to determine whether they captured adequately the concept of informal social control.

Three hypotheses were stated and also related to the larger theoretical framework and prior research [8]. The study design focused on the behavior of individuals [11] and collected data over time, including records indicating subsequent assault up to 6 months after the initial arrest [12]. The project's experimental design was used appropriately to test for the causal effect of arrest on recidivism [13]. The research project involved all eligible cases, rather than a sample of cases, but there were a number of eligibility criteria that narrowed the ability to generalize these results to the entire population of domestic assault cases in the Metro-Dade area or elsewhere [14]. There is a brief discussion of the 92 eligible cases that were not given the treatment to which they were assigned, but it does not clarify the reasons for the misassignment [15].

The Research Findings and Conclusion. Pate and Hamilton's (1992) analysis of the Metro-Dade experiment was motivated by concern with effect of social context because the replications in other cities of the original Minneapolis domestic violence experiment had not had consistent results [19]. Their analysis gave strong support to the expectation that informal social control processes are important: As they had hypothesized, arrest had a deterrent effect on suspects who were employed but not on those who were unemployed (see Exhibit A.5).

EXHIBIT A.5   Percentage of Suspects With a Subsequent Assault by Employment Status and Arrest Status

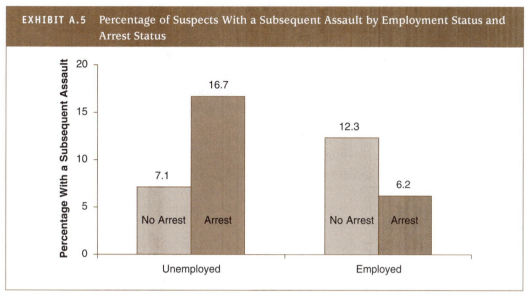

Source: Pate & Hamilton (1992: 695). Reprinted with permission.

However, marital status had no such effect [20]. The subsequent discussion of these findings gives no attention to the implications of the lack of support for the effect of marital status [21], but the study represents an important improvement over earlier research that had not examined informal sanctions [22]. The need for additional research is highlighted, and the importance of the findings for social policy are discussed: Pate and Hamilton suggest that their finding that arrest deters only those who have something to lose (e.g., a job) must be taken into account when policing policies are established [23].

Overall, the Pate and Hamilton (1992) study represents an important contribution to understanding how informal social control processes influence the effectiveness of formal sanctions such as arrest. Although the use of a population of actual spouse assault cases precluded the use of very sophisticated measures of informal social control, the experimental design of the study and the researchers' ability to interpret the results in the context of several comparable experiments distinguishes this research as exceptionally worthwhile. It is not hard to understand why these studies continue to stimulate further research and ongoing policy discussions.

An Integrated Literature Review: When Does Arrest Matter?

The goal of the second stage of the literature review process is to integrate the results of your separate article reviews and develop an overall assessment of the implications of prior research. The integrated literature review should accomplish three goals: (1) summarize prior research, (2) critique prior research, and (3) present pertinent conclusions (Hart 1998: 186–187).

Summarize prior research. Your summary of prior research must focus on the particular research questions that you will address, but you also may need to provide some more general background. Hoyle and Sanders (2000: 14) begin their *British Journal of Criminology* research article about mandatory arrest policies in domestic violence cases with what they term a "provocative" question: What is the point of making it a crime for men to assault their female partners and ex-partners? They then review the different theories and supporting research that has justified different police policies: the "victim choice" position, the "pro-arrest" position, and the "victim empowerment" position. Finally, they review the research on the "controlling behaviors" of men that frames the specific research question on which they focus: how victims view the value of criminal justice interventions in their own cases (p. 15).

Ask yourself three questions about your summary of the literature:

1. *Have you been selective?* If there have been more than a few prior investigations of your research question, you will need to narrow your focus to the most relevant and highest quality studies. Do not cite a large number of prior articles "just because they are there."

2. *Is the research up-to-date?* Be sure to include the most recent research, not just the "classic" studies.

3. *Have you used direct quotes sparingly?* To focus your literature review, you need to express the key points from prior research in your own words. Use direct quotes only when they are essential for making an important point (Pyrczak 2005: 51–59).

Critique prior research. Evaluate the strengths and weakness of the prior research. In addition to all the points you develop as you answer the Article Review Questions in Appendix B, you should also select articles for review that reflect work published in peer-reviewed journals and written by credible authors who have been funded by reputable sources. Consider the following questions as you decide how much weight to give each article:

1. *How was the report reviewed prior to its publication or release?* Articles published in academic journals go through a rigorous review process, usually involving careful criticism and revision. Top refereed journals may accept only 10% of submitted articles, so they can be very selective. Dissertations go through a lengthy process of criticism and revision by a few members of the dissertation writer's home institution. A report released directly by a research organization is likely to have had only a limited review, although some research organizations maintain a rigorous internal review process. Papers presented at professional meetings may have had little prior review. Needless to say, more confidence can be placed in research results that have been subject to a more rigorous review.

2. *What is the author's reputation?* Reports by an author or team of authors who have published other work on the research question should be given somewhat greater credibility at the outset.

3. *Who funded and sponsored the research?* Major federal funding agencies and private foundations fund only research proposals that have been evaluated carefully and ranked highly by a panel of experts. They also often monitor closely the progress of the research. This does not guarantee that every such project

report is good, but it goes a long way toward ensuring some worthwhile products. On the other hand, research that is funded by organizations that have a preference for a particular outcome should be given particularly close scrutiny (Locke, Silverman, & Spirduso 1998: 37–44).

Present pertinent conclusions. Do not leave the reader guessing about the implications of the prior research for your own investigation. Present the conclusions you draw from the research you have reviewed. As you do so, follow several simple guidelines:

- Distinguish clearly your own opinion of prior research from conclusions of the authors of the articles you have reviewed.
- Make it clear when your own approach is based on the theoretical framework you are using rather than on the results of prior research.
- Acknowledge the potential limitations of any empirical research project. Do not emphasize problems in prior research that you cannot avoid either (Pyrczak 2005: 53–56).
- Explain how the unanswered questions raised by prior research or the limitations of methods used in prior research make it important for you to conduct your own investigation (Fink 2004: 190–192).

A good example of how to conclude an integrated literature review is provided by an article based on the replication in Milwaukee of the Minneapolis Domestic Violence Experiment. For this article, Paternoster et al. (1997) sought to determine whether police officers' use of fair procedures when arresting assault suspects would lessen the rate of subsequent domestic violence. Paternoster et al. conclude that there has been a major gap in the prior literature: "Even at the end of some seven experiments and millions of dollars, then, there is a great deal of ambiguity surrounding the question of how arrest impacts future spouse assault" (p. 164). Specifically, they note that each of the seven experiments focused on the effect of arrest itself but ignored the possibility that "particular kinds of police procedure might inhibit the recurrence of spouse assault" (p. 165).

So Paternoster et al. (1997) ground their new analysis in additional literature on procedural justice and conclude that their new analysis will be "the first study to examine the effect of fairness judgments regarding a punitive criminal sanction (arrest) on serious criminal behavior (assaulting one's partner)" (p. 172).

SEARCHING THE WEB

To find useful information on the Web, you have to be even more vigilant than when you search the literature directly. With billions of webpages on the Internet, there is no limit to the amount of time you can squander and the volume of useless junk you can find as you conduct your research on the Web. However, we can share with you some good ways to avoid the biggest pitfalls.

Direct Addressing

Knowing the exact address (i.e., URL) of a useful Web site is the most efficient way to find a resource on the Web.

Professional Organizations

- American Society of Criminology (http://www.asc41.com)
- American Sociological Association (http://www.asanet.org)
- American Psychological Association (http://www.apa.org)

Government Sites

- U.S. Office of Justice Programs (http://www.ojp.usdoj.gov)
- U.S. Bureau of the Census (http://www.census.gov)

Journals and Newspapers

- *Annual Review of Sociology* (http://www/annualreviews.org)
- *The New York Times* (http://www.nytimes.com)

Bibliographic Formats for Citing Electronic Information

- Electronic reference formats suggested by the American Psychological Association (http://www.apastyle.org/elecref.html)
- Karla Tonella's Guide to Citation Style Guides (http://bailiwick.lib.uiowa.edu/journalism/cite.html) contains more than a dozen links to online style guides
- Style Sheets for Citing Resources (print and electronic) (http://www.lib.berkeley.edu/TeachingLib/Guides/Internet/Style.html)

When you find Web sites that you expect you will return to often, you can save their addresses as "bookmarks" or "favorites" in your Web browser. However, since these can very quickly multiply, you should try to be selective.

Browsing Subject Directories

Subject directories (also called guides, indexes, or clearinghouses) contain links to other Web resources that are organized by subject. They vary in quality and authoritativeness, but a good one can be invaluable to your research and save you much time. The main advantage to using subject directories is that they contain links to resources that have been selected, evaluated, and organized by human beings and thus present a much more manageable number of resources. If the person managing the guide is an expert in the field of concern, or just a careful and methodological evaluator of Web resources, the guide can help you to identify good sites that contain useful and trustworthy information, and you can avoid wading through thousands of "hits" and evaluating all the sites yourself.

There are general and specialized directories. The following are three examples of general directories:

- Yahoo! (http://www.yahoo.com) is often mistaken for a search engine, but it is actually a subject directory, and a monster one at that. It also functions as a portal or a gateway for a collection of resources that can be customized by the user. Unlike search engines, when you search Yahoo!, you are not searching across the Web but rather just within the Web pages that Yahoo! has cataloged. Yahoo! has a subject directory for the social sciences with more specific listings, including one for social work (http://dir.yahoo.com/social_science/social_work/). Yahoo! also links to versions of its site in about 20 countries, which would be good to go to when conducting extensive research on one of those countries (http:world .yahoo.com/).
- Open Directory (http://dmoz.org) is the largest Web directory with four million sites (Hock 2004), and unlike Yahoo!, it is not a portal. In fact, other directories and search engines such as Yahoo! and Google use it. It has 16 top-level categories, including Social Sciences.
- Librarians' Index to the Internet (http://lii.org) is a small and highly selective Web directory produced by the Library of California.

The following are some examples of specialized subject directories:

- Argus Clearinghouse (http://www.clearinghouse.net/searchbrowse.html) is a guide to subject directories on the Internet, and it classifies them under subject headings.
- BUBL INK (http://bubl.ac/uk/link) contains over 12,000 links covering all academic areas.
- Social Sciences Virtual Library (http://www.clas.ufl.edu/users/gthursby/socsci/) includes listings for anthropology, demographics, psychology, social policy and evaluation, sociology, women's studies, and other areas.
- INFOMINE: Scholarly Internet Resource Collections (http://infomine.ucr.edu/) is produced by librarians across several campuses of the University of California system, and it includes a subject directory for the social sciences.
- SOSIG, Social Science Information Gateway (http://www.sosig.ac/uk), is a British site that aims to be comprehensive. It is classified according to the Dewey Decimal System, the classification system used by most public libraries.

Many other Internet subject directories are maintained by academic departments, professional organizations, and individuals. It is often hard to determine whether a particular subject directory such as this is up-to-date and reasonably comprehensive, but you can have some confidence in subject directories published by universities or government agencies. *The Internet Research Handbook* is an excellent source for more information on subject directories (Ó Dochartaigh 2002).

EXHIBIT A.6 The Results of a Google Title Search

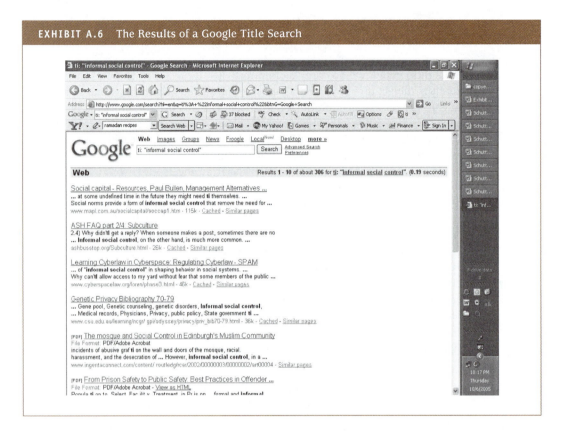

Search Engines

Search engines are powerful Internet tools. It is already impossible to imagine life without them. The biggest problem is the huge number of results that come back to you. If the number of results is still unmanageable, you can try a title search. Exhibit A.6 shows the results of typing the following into the Google search box: ti: "informal social control." This search will retrieve those pages that have that phrase in their title as opposed to anywhere in the page. This practice usually results in a dramatically smaller yield of results. If you are looking for graphical information such as a graph or a chart, you can limit your search to those pages that contain an image. On Google, this just requires clicking on the "Images" link located above the search box.

There are many search engines, and none will give you identical results when you use them to search the Web. Different search engines use different strategies to find Web sites and offer somewhat different search options for users. Due to the enormous size of the Web and its constantly changing content, it simply is not possible to identify one search engine that will give you completely up-to-date and comprehensive results. You can find the latest information about search engines at http://searchenginewatch.com. Hock's (2004)

The Extreme Searcher's Internet Handbook contains a wealth of information on specific search engines. Although there are many search engines, you may find the following to be particularly useful for general searching:

- Google (http://www.google.com) has become the leading search engine for many users in recent years. Its coverage is relatively comprehensive, and it does a good job of ranking search results by their relevancy (based on the terms in your search request). Google also allows you to focus your search just on images, discussions, or directories.
- AlltheWeb (http://www.alltheweb.com) is a more recent comprehensive search engine that also does a good job of relevancy ranking and allows searches restricted to images and so on.
- Microsoft's search engine (http://search.msn.com) adds a unique feature: Editors review and pick the most popular sites. As a result, your search request may result in a Popular Topics list that can help you to focus your search.
- Teoma (http://teoma.com) is one of the newest search engines and has a unique Resources section that links users to specialized directories.

In conclusion, use the appropriate tool for your searches. Do not use a search engine in place of searching literature that is indexed in tools such as *Sociological Abstracts*. Bookmark the key sites that you find in your area of interest. Become familiar with subject directories that cover your areas of interest, and look there before going to a search engine. And when you do use a search engine, take a moment to learn about how it works and what steps you should take to get the best results in the least amount of time.

APPENDIX B

Questions to Ask About a Research Article

1. What is the basic research question or problem? Try to state it in just one sentence. (Chapter 2)

2. Is the purpose of the study explanatory, evaluative, exploratory, or descriptive? Did the study have more than one purpose? (Chapter 1)

3. Was the theoretical framework presented? What was it? Did it seem appropriate for the research question addressed? Can you think of a different theoretical perspective that might have been used? (Chapter 2)

4. What prior literature was reviewed? Was it relevant to the research problem? To the theoretical framework? Does the literature review appear to be adequate? Are you aware of (or can you locate) any important omitted studies? (Chapter 2)

5. How well did the study live up to the guidelines for science? Do you need additional information in any areas to evaluate the study? To replicate it? (Chapter 2)

6. Did the study seem consistent with current ethical standards? Were any trade-offs made between different ethical guidelines? Was an appropriate balance struck between adherence to ethical standards and use of the most rigorous scientific practices? (Chapter 2 and in each methods chapter)

7. What were the major concepts in the research? How, and how clearly, were they defined? Were some concepts treated as unidimensional that you think might best be thought of as multidimensional? (Chapter 3)

8. Were any hypotheses stated? Were these hypotheses justified adequately in terms of the theoretical framework? In terms of prior research? (Chapter 2)

9. What were the independent and dependent variables in the hypothesis or hypotheses? Did these variables reflect the theoretical concepts as intended? What direction of association was hypothesized? Were any other variables identified as potentially important? (Chapter 2)

10.   Did the instruments used—the measures of the variables—seem valid and reliable? How did the author attempt to establish this? Could any more have been done in the study to establish measurement validity? (Chapter 3)

11.   What were the units of analysis? Were they appropriate for the research question? If some groups were the units of analysis, were any statements made at any point that are open to the ecological fallacy? If individuals were the units of analysis, were any statements made at any point that suggest reductionist reasoning? (Chapter 4)

12.   Was the study design cross-sectional or longitudinal, or did it use both types of data? If the design was longitudinal, what type of longitudinal design was it? Could the longitudinal design have been improved in any way, as by collecting panel data rather than trend data, or by decreasing the dropout rate in a panel design? If cross-sectional data were used, could the research question have been addressed more effectively with the longitudinal data? (Chapter 5)

13.   Were any causal assertions made or implied in the hypotheses or in subsequent discussion? What approach was used to demonstrate the existence of causal effects? Were all three criteria for establishing causal relationships addressed? What, if any, variables were controlled in the analysis to reduce the risk of spurious relationships? Should any other variables have been measured and controlled? How satisfied are you with the internal validity of the conclusions? (Chapters 5, 6)

14.   Was a sample or the entire population of elements used in the study? What type of sample was selected? Was a probability sampling method used? Did the authors think the sample was generally representative of the population from which it was drawn? Do you? How would you evaluate the likely generalizability of the findings to other populations? (Chapter 4)

15.   Was the response rate or participation rate reported? Does it appear likely that those who did not respond or participate were markedly different from those who did participate? Why or why not? Did the author(s) adequately discuss this issue? (Chapters 4, 6)

16.   Was an experimental, survey, participant observation, or some other research design used? How well was this design suited to the research question posed and the specific hypotheses tested, if any? Why do you suppose the author(s) chose this particular design? How was the design modified in response to research constraints? How was it modified in order to take advantage of research opportunities? (Chapters 6–10)

17.   Was an evaluation research design used? Which type was it? What was the primary purpose of the evaluation? (Chapter 11)

18.   Were multiple methods used? Were findings obtained with different methods complementary? (Chapter 11)

19.   Was any attention given to social context? To biological processes? If so, what did this add? If not, would it have improved the study? Explain. (Chapter 5)

20.   Summarize the findings. How clearly were statistical and/or qualitative data presented and discussed? Were the results substantively important? (Chapters 9, 12)

21. Did the author(s) adequately represent the findings in the discussion and/or conclusions sections? Were conclusions well grounded in the findings? Are any other interpretations possible? (Chapter 13)

22. Compare the study to others addressing the same research question. Did the study yield additional insights? In what ways was the study design more or less adequate than the design of previous research? (Chapters 2, 10, 12)

23. What additional research questions and hypotheses are suggested by the study's results? What light did the study shed on the theoretical framework used? On social policy questions? (Chapters 2, 10, 12)

How to Read
a Research Article

The discussions of research articles throughout the text may provide all the guidance you need to read and critique research on your own. But reading about an article in bits and pieces in order to learn about particular methodologies is not quite the same as reading an article in its entirety in order to learn what the research discovered. The goal of this appendix is to walk you through an entire research article, answering the review questions introduced in Appendix B. Of course, this is only one article, and our "walk" will take different turns from one taken by a review of other articles, but after this review you should feel more confident when reading other research articles on your own.

For this example, we will use an article by Alarid, Burton, and Cullen (2000) on gender and crime among felony offenders (reprinted in this volume on pp. C-8–C-31). It focuses on a topic important to explaining the similarities and differences between male and female offending patterns as well as to questions of the generalizability of central criminological theoretical perspectives. Moreover, the article is published in a reputable criminological journal, the *Journal of Research in Crime and Delinquency,* indicating the article makes an important contribution to what is known about the etiology of criminal offending across gender groups.

We have reproduced below each of the article review questions from Appendix B, followed by our answers to them. After each question, we indicate the article page or pages that we are referring to. You can also follow our review by reading through the article itself and noting our comments.

   1. *What is the basic research question or problem? Try to state it in just one sentence.*
      (Chapter 2)

The clearest statement of the research question actually consists of two questions: "[Can] social control and differential association theories . . . help account for participation in crime among young adult male and female felons?" (p. 174 in the original article). Prior to this point, the authors focus on the research problem, describing the limitations of past research and why exploring social control and differential association theories across gender groups among felony offenders is important.

2. *Is the purpose of the study explanatory, evaluative, exploratory, or descriptive? Did the study have more than one purpose?* (Chapter 1)

This study is exploratory in nature. The literature review (pp. 171–174) makes it clear that the primary purpose of this research is exploratory since new ground is being covered based on the limitations of past research. In addition, the problem statement indicates the exploratory character of the study: It "attempts to test the generality of social control and differential association theories to a population that has been infrequently studied" (p. 173).

3. *Was the theoretical framework presented? What was it? Did it seem appropriate for the research question addressed? Can you think of a different theoretical perspective that might have been used?* (Chapter 2)

This study uses two theoretical perspectives, "social control" and "differential association." This framework is very appropriate for the research questions addressed because this study explores the applicability of these theories to adult populations and their generalizability across gender groups. Because the research question focuses specifically on the applicability and generalizability of these specific theoretical perspectives, no other theoretical framework would be applicable.

4. *What prior literature was reviewed? Was it relevant to the research problem? To the theoretical framework? Does the literature review appear to be adequate? Are you aware of (or can you locate) any important omitted studies?* (Chapter 2)

Literature is reviewed from the article's first page until the "method" section (pp. 171–174). All the literature seems relevant to the particular problem as well as the general theoretical framework. The first few paragraphs generalize the findings of several studies that measures of both theories are related to criminal involvement (pp. 171–172). The authors then discuss the limited focus of previous studies and their rationale for selecting social control and differential association as their focus for this study (pp. 172–174). We leave it to you to find out whether any important studies were omitted.

5. *How well did the study live up to the guidelines for science? Do you need additional information in any areas to evaluate the study? To replicate it?* (Chapter 2)

It would be best to return to this question after reading the whole article. The study clearly involves a test of ideas against empirical reality to the extent that reality could be measured; it was carried out systematically and disclosed, as far as we can tell. Because the authors used a sample of newly incarcerated felons, it may be difficult for others to replicate the authors' findings. Drawing from previous research, the authors make some general assumptions about what factors best measure social control and differential association (p. 177). However, in previous studies, those factors measuring social control and differential association have been applied primarily to juvenile populations (p. 172). Intuitively, the same measures or indicators may not be applicable to adult populations (e.g., parental attachment and peer attachment), but we have no empirical evidence of this. The authors also assume respondents' reports of past criminal behavior are valid (pp. 177–178). It appears these are reasonable assumptions, but they are unproved assumptions that could be challenged. This is not in itself a criticism of the research, since some assumptions must be made in any study. The authors specified the meaning of key terms, as required in scientific research. The authors did search for regularities or patterns in their data, thus living up to another guideline. A skeptical stance toward current knowledge is apparent in the literature review and in the authors' claim that "social control and differential association theory appear to have general effects" on young adult felons and across gender groups (pp. 189–190). They encourage the development of new theories but emphasize the importance of "older" theoretical perspectives and their application to underresearched topics (p. 192). The study thus seems to exemplify adherence to basic scientific guidelines and to be very replicable.

6. *Did the study seem consistent with current ethical standards? Were any trade-offs made between different ethical guidelines? Was an appropriate balance struck between adherence to ethical standards and use of the most rigorous scientific practices?* (Chapter 2)

To the best of our knowledge, the study was consistent with current ethical standards. "All data were collected directly from the participants themselves" (p. 175). In accordance with the ASA code of ethics, participation in the study was voluntary, and the participants gave their informed consent to participate. The reporting seems honest and open. The original survey used by the authors is not likely to have violated any ethical guidelines concerning the treatment of human subjects, although it would be necessary to inspect the survey instrument itself to evaluate this.

7. *What were the major concepts in the research? How, and how clearly, were they defined? Were some concepts treated as unidimensional that you think might best be thought of as multidimensional?* (Chapter 3)

There are two key concepts in this study, social control and differential association. These concepts are the focus of the study and are discussed at length. These concepts, however, were not defined so that a layperson would understand what these concepts mean.

8. *Were any hypotheses stated? Were these hypotheses justified adequately in terms of the theoretical framework? In terms of prior research?* (Chapter 2)

Three hypotheses are stated, although they are labeled as theoretical predictions, which are derived from previous research (p. 173). The first hypothesis is that social control will account for variation in offending across gender groups. The second hypothesis is that differential association will account for variation in offending across gender groups. Finally, the third hypothesis is that the effect of the competing theory will be spurious.

9. *What were the independent and dependent variables in the hypothesis(es)? Did these variables reflect the theoretical concepts as intended? What direction of association was hypothesized? Were any other variables identified as potentially important?* (Chapter 2)

The dependent variable for this study is past criminal activity. For purposes of analysis, past criminal behavior is divided into three subscales resulting in four dependent variables: general crime (the total of all criminal activities), violent crime, property crime, and drug crime (p. 177). There are eight independent variables included in this study. The independent variables for the first hypothesis include five social control indicators. These include marital/partner attachment (0 = not married/unattached and 1 = married/attached), attachment to parents (a three-item composite index, higher values represent stronger attachment), attachment to friends (a two-item index, higher values represent stronger attachment), involvement in conventional activities (a two-item index measuring how much free time individual has, higher values represent more free time), and moral belief in the law (measured by a two-item index with higher values representing stronger belief) (pp. 178–180).

The independent variables for the second hypothesis include three indicators of differential association. These include individual definitions toward crime (a five-item index, higher values represent greater tolerance of criminal behavior), others' definitions toward crime (a three-item index, higher values represent greater association with individuals who hold favorable definition toward violating the law), and criminal friends (continuous variable indicating the number of close friends who have broken the law) (pp. 180–182).

Can you identify the variables in the final hypothesis?

10. *Did the instruments used—the measures of the variables—seem valid and reliable? How did the author attempt to establish this? Could any more have been done in the study to establish measurement validity?* (Chapter 3)

The measurement of the dependent variable was straightforward. The authors report the scale used has been identified as a valid and reliable self-report assessment of antisocial behavior (p. 176). In addition, reliability was assessed using Cronbach's alpha method, which indicated the general scale and the subscales are a reliable measure of criminal behavior. The measurement of the independent variables was also straightforward. The authors report the scales used have been identified as valid measures of social control and differential association indicators. In addition, Cronbach's alpha reliability testing shows the measures are reliable.

11. *What were the units of analysis? Were they appropriate for the research question? If some groups were the units of analysis, were any statements made at any point that are open to the ecological fallacy? If individuals were the units of analysis, were any statements made at any point that suggest reductionist reasoning?* (Chapter 4)

The authors sampled young adult, first-time felony offenders sentenced to a residential court-ordered boot camp program. The units of analysis are appropriate for the research question. No statements were made at any point that suggest reductionist reasoning.

12. *Was the study design cross-sectional or longitudinal, or did it use both types of data? If the design was longitudinal, what type of longitudinal design was it? Could the longitudinal design have been improved in any way, as by collecting panel data rather than trend data, or by decreasing the dropout rate in a panel design? If cross-sectional data were used, could the research question have been addressed more effectively with the longitudinal data?* (Chapter 5)

The survey was cross-sectional. The research question could have been addressed more effectively with longitudinal data that followed people from childhood into adulthood, since many of the authors' interpretations reflect their interest in how individuals' past experiences shape their propensity for criminal behavior.

13. *Were any causal assertions made or implied in the hypotheses or in subsequent discussion? What approach was used to demonstrate the existence of causal effects? Were all three criteria for establishing causal relationships addressed? What, if any, variables were controlled in the analysis to reduce the risk of spurious relationships? Should any other variables have been measured and controlled? How satisfied are you with the internal validity of the conclusions?* (Chapter 5)

The explanatory hypotheses indicate that the authors were concerned with causality. However, the lack of previous research on their chosen population suggests an exploratory approach to causality. In order to reduce the risk of spuriousness in the presumed causal relationships, three control variables were included in the analysis: age, race/ethnicity, and gender (p. 188); these variables have been shown to be strongly related to criminal activity. There are other variables that might have created a spurious relationship, but at least several of the most likely contenders have been controlled. For example, some of the differences in social control and differential association measures may be due to social class—that is, individuals who were raised in more affluent families are more likely to have had greater social control in their lives and less opportunity to be involved with individuals who favor, or at least justify, criminal behavior. Income has also been shown to be negatively related to criminal activity—that is, the higher an individual's income, the less likely he or she is to engage in criminal activity.

14. *Was a sample or the entire population of elements used in the study? What type of sample was selected? Was a probability sampling method used? Did the authors think the sample was generally representative of the population from which it was drawn? Do you? How would you evaluate the likely generalizability of the findings to other populations?* (Chapter 4)

The sample was a nonrandom (nonprobability) sample of young, first-time felony offenders. A purposive sampling technique was used when sampling women, the authors "focused [their] efforts on obtaining responses from the entire [female] population . . . in the program over a 15-month period" (p. 175). The authors did not focus on sampling the entire male population; therefore, the authors obtained an availability sample of males sentenced to the program over the same time period. The authors admit the sample is not representative of "felony crimes committed by men and women in prison, [but] closely resembles first-time felony offenders in other shock incarceration programs as an alternative to jail or prison incarceration" (p. 176). Do you believe the authors can generalize their findings to similar populations? Why or why not?

15. *Was the response rate or participation rate reported? Does it appear likely that those who did not respond or participate were markedly different from those who did participate? Why or why not? Did the author(s) adequately discuss this issue?* (Chapters 4, 6)

The response rate was reported. The authors obtained responses from 122 of 124 (or 98.4%) female offenders and 1,031 (or 85.9%) of male offenders (p. 175). With the exception of female offenders, the authors did not discuss differences among those who did and did not participate in the study. Of the two female offenders who did not participate in the study, one did not speak English and the other woman escaped from the facility (p. 175). In general, it is reasonable to believe those who did not participate in the study were not markedly different from those who did participate. The large sample of males and females obtained for this study should have provided good variability.

16. *Was an experimental, survey, participant observation, or some other research design used? How well was this design suited to the research question posed and the specific hypotheses tested, if any? Why do you suppose the author(s) chose this particular design? How was the design modified in response to research constraints? How was it modified in order to take advantage of research opportunities?* (Chapters 5–9)

Survey research was the method of choice and probably was used for this article because it provided the most cost-effective means of gathering data. Survey research seems appropriate for the research questions posed.

17. *Was an evaluation research design used? Which type was it? What was the primary purpose of the evaluation?* (Chapter 9)

This study did not use any type of evaluation research.

18. *Were multiple methods used? Were findings obtained with different methods complementary?* (Chapter 8)

This study used only survey methods.

19. *Was any attention given to social context? To biological processes? If so, what did this add? If not, would it have improved the study? Explain.* (Chapter 5)

Social context is given attention in this study on an individual level. The majority of social control and differential association indicators are measures of social conditions and experiences of the respondents. However, no attention is given to the potential importance of larger social contexts, such as neighborhood or region of the country. Biological factors that may increase the propensity for criminality are not considered in this study.

20. *Summarize the findings. How clearly were statistical and/or qualitative data presented and discussed? Were the results substantively important?* (Chapters 7, 10)

Statistical data are presented clearly using descriptive statistics, examination of bivariate relationships, and multiple regression analysis (a multivariate statistical technique) that highlight the most central findings. No qualitative data are presented. The findings seem substantively important, since they identify social control and differential association theories that can be applied to adult populations across gender groups (pp. 184–188).

21. *Did the author(s) adequately represent the findings in the discussion and/or conclusion sections? Were conclusions well grounded in the findings? Are any other interpretations possible?* (Chapter 11)

The findings are well represented in the discussion and conclusion section (pp. 188–192). The authors point out in their literature review that the focus for testing social control and differential association theories data is often limited to juvenile delinquent populations and frequently fails to consider possible differences between males and females. The findings suggest these theoretical perspectives can be applied to adult criminal populations and are important in explaining variation in criminal behavior across gender groups. You might want to consider what other interpretations of the findings might be possible. Remember that other interpretations are always possible for particular findings—it is a question of the weight of the evidence, the persuasiveness of the theory used, and the consistency of the findings with other research.

22. *Compare the study to others addressing the same research question. Did the study yield additional insights? In what ways was the study design more or less adequate than the design of previous research?* (Chapters 2, 11)

This study investigated the relationship between social control and differential association on a population that had not previously received much attention (young adult felony offenders). This helped the authors to gain additional insights into the influence of social control and differential association on young adults across gender groups.

23. *What additional research questions and hypotheses are suggested by the study's results? What light did the study shed on the theoretical framework used? On social policy questions?* (Chapters 2, 11)

The authors suggest no additional research questions or hypotheses. However, the study does shed light on the importance of "traditional" theoretical perspectives in explaining variation in criminal behavior among adults across gender groups. The authors note the importance of new theoretical paradigms but emphasize "that the value of 'older' theoretical perspectives should be remembered and . . . applied to underresearched topics" (p. 192).

Gender and Crime Among Felony Offenders

Assessing the Generality of
Social Control and Differential Association Theories

LEANNE FIFTAL ALARID

VELMER S. BURTON, JR.

FRANCIS T. CULLEN

Although often tested empirically on high school samples, differential association and social control theories have only infrequently been used to explain offending by felons. Based on a sample of 1,153 newly incarcerated felons, the authors examine the ability of differential association and social control theories to explain self-reported offending across types of crime and gender groups. Overall, the analyses lend support to both perspectives and suggest that they are "general" theories of crime. It also appears, however, that differential association theory has more consistent effects, especially for men. Parental attachment is a significantly stronger predictor of female than male participation in violent crime. These results indicate that future studies of criminal behavior risk being misspecified if they do not include measures of these "traditional" theories of crime.

Since the 1969 publication of Hirschi's *Causes of Delinquency*, social control or control theory and differential association or "cultural deviance" theory have competed vigorously against one another for the status of the preeminent microlevel sociological theory of crime (see also Kornhauser 1978). Even today, spirited exchanges occur in which the logical and empirical

NOTE: Reprinted from the *Journal of Research in Crime and Delinquency*, Vol. 37, No. 2, May 2000, 171–199. © Sage, Inc. A previous version of this article was presented at the 1995 meeting of the Academy of Criminal Justice Sciences.

adequacy of the theories is debated (see Akers 1996, 1998; Costello 1997; Hirschi 1996; Matsueda 1988, 1997). These paradigms continue to guide research (see, e.g., Akers 1998; Sampson and Laub 1993) not only because of their theoretical parsimony and elegance but also because they accrue a measure of empirical support (Akers 1996; Krohn 1995).

Although noteworthy exceptions exist, most of the tests of social control and differential association theory have been conducted using self-report surveys on juveniles. Particularly instructive are empirical studies in which measures of both theories have been incorporated in the analysis. In general, this research suggests that measures of both theories are related to delinquent or adult criminal involvement, although in some studies, the strength of the differential association variables is greater (Benda 1994; Conger 1976; Kandel and Davies 1991; Macdonald 1989; Matsueda 1982; Matsueda and Heimer 1987; McGee 1992; see also Akers 1998; Burton 1991; Krohn 1995).

A key concern, however, is the generality of social control and differential association theories. These perspectives typically have been seen as having the ability to explain various forms of crime for all people (see, e.g., Akers 1998; Hirschi 1969; Sampson and Laub 1993; Sutherland and Cressey 1955). Clearly, the theoretical power of each of these perspectives hinges on their ability to achieve the status of a general theory. Accordingly, a central empirical and thus theoretical issue is whether social control and differential association theories can explain criminal behavior that extends beyond the delinquency found among community samples of youth.

There have been studies conducted on adult samples that have found support for differential association/social learning theory (Akers 1998; Akers and LaGreca 1988, 1991; Akers et al. 1989; Boeringer, Shehan, and Akers 1991; Dull 1983; Orcutt 1987; Tittle, Burke, and Jackson 1986). Research on social control theory with adult samples also suggests that adult social bonds may reduce criminal behavior (Horney, Osgood, and Marshall 1995; Lasley 1988; Sampson and Laub 1993). Even so, the empirical literature assessing whether social control and differential association theories can explain adult criminal behavior remains limited, especially when one searches for studies that include in their analyses measures of both theoretical perspectives.[1] Among the few adult studies testing social control versus differential association theory, the results show mixed support for both perspectives. Thus, two studies using community samples of adults found stronger support for differential association theory (Burton 1991; Macdonald 1989), while another study revealed that social control theory was better able to account for variation in arrests for men and women drug offenders (Covington 1985).

Even with this research, however, there are typically two limitations. First, especially with adult samples, studies often do not explore whether the effects of variables measuring traditional criminological theories vary by gender. Traditional theories have been criticized for their perceived inability to explain female criminality (Adler 1975; Daly and Chesney-Lind 1988; Leonard 1982) and for ignoring how gender-related factors—such as patriarchal power relations—differentially shape the involvement of gender groups in crime (Heidensohn 1985; Messerschmidt 1993) and victimization (Chesney-Lind and Shelden 1992). In turn, it is argued that scholars should formulate separate or different theories of crime for women (Leonard 1982; Messerschmidt 1993; Naffine and Gale 1989; Smart 1976).

Second, tests of social control and differential association theory have only infrequently been conducted on samples that include a high base rate of serious offending. As a result, we have only limited information on whether these theories explain more than relatively minor forms of criminal involvement. As Messner and Rosenfeld (1994: 47) note, this "neglect of serious offending by contemporary criminologists" means that it is necessary to employ "other ways of obtaining information from people who commit serious crimes (e.g., they can be interviewed in prison)." Although still not widespread, criminologists increasingly are undertaking tests of criminological theories that employ serious offenders interviewed in prison or in the community (see Covington 1985; Horney and Marshall 1992; Horney et al. 1995; Longshore, Turner, and Stein 1996; Sampson and Laub 1990, 1993).

Among this body of research on samples of adult offenders, however, research testing social control and differential association theories is rare; research that conducts such studies by gender is virtually nonexistent. The only known exception is Covington's (1985) study of adult heroin addicts in which an attempt is made to explain self-reported total arrests and arrests for property crimes. Covington's analysis revealed that measures of social control were better predictors of women's criminal involvement in property crime and in both men's and women's involvement in overall offending behaviors; differential association measures, however, were able to explain men's property arrests.[2]

In light of the status of the existing research, the current study attempts to test the generality of social control and differential association theories to a population that has been infrequently studied: young adult felons drawn from the inner city. Social control and differential association theories were selected because they have been found, among existing sociological theories, to have the most consistent empirical support in studies of juveniles.[3] Social control theory is also used to explain adult crime in recent important studies (Horney et al. 1995; Sampson and Laub 1993). These theories both predict that their effects will be general—that is, they will account for variation in offending and that this effect will hold for males and females.

These theories also predict that the effects of the competing theory will be spurious (Hirschi 1969). The spuriousness issue is important because most tests with adults have not included measures of both theories (e.g., Horney et al. 1995; Sampson and Laub 1993). As such, findings from previous theoretical tests could be misspecified if the effects of differential association variables account for the findings of social control variables.

Based on previous research on community samples of adults and juveniles that have used both sets of measures, we would anticipate that both variables will have effects. Like members of the community, offenders can be expected to vary in their levels of social control (Horney et al. 1995; Sampson and Laub 1993). We can also expect variation in differential associations and crime-related attitudes. Still, given the lack of previous research testing these theories with a population of offenders extensively involved in crime, the relationship of the theories to criminal involvement remains to be empirically determined.

Thus, the purpose of this article is to test the generality of social control and differential association theories with a sample of young adult felons drawn from the inner city. The study also has the advantage of including males and females. Using a self-report survey, the study examines both overall offending and involvement in specific forms of criminal conduct. By testing the two theories against each other, the central focus will be to discern which theory—if not both theories—can explain variation in offending among young adult men and women felony offenders from an urban area. That is, are social control and differential association theories mainly explanations of juvenile delinquency, or can they help account for participation in crime among young adult male and female felons?

METHOD

The procedures used to test differential association and social control theory with 1,153 felony women and men in a community corrections program have been organized into four categories: (1) data collection, (2) sample characteristics, (3) dependent variables, and (4) independent variables.

Data Collection

Data for this study were gathered from felons sentenced to a residential court-ordered boot camp program in Harris County, Texas, which includes the Houston metropolitan area. The boot camp program was designed for a 17- to 25-year-old male or female adult who had been convicted as a first-time felon and had been sentenced to prison. Offenders were considered for the program by judges as a "last stop before prison." The type of convicted offender (violent, property, or drug) in this program was thus a reflection of judicial discretion.

The three-month coed program emphasized discipline, physical labor, and drills and offered GED education, life skills, and drug awareness classes. The program housed a maximum capacity of 30 women in one smaller barrack and approximately 240 men in five program barracks, with a sixth housing barrack available for incoming "new boots." Up to 48 men entered the program as a cohort, were housed in the same barracks, and graduated together three months later. Since only about 2 women entered the program every week, there were no distinct female cohorts. Rather, female "new boots" were mixed with more senior women offenders, and the barracks never filled to capacity during the data collection period. For both women and men, the residential stay in the boot camp program was an alternative to jail or prison incarceration. The program was followed by a two-year period of intensive supervision probation in the community (Burton et al. 1993).

Data were collected on participants who entered the boot camp between June 1992 and September 1993. Since a smaller number of women were sentenced to boot camp, we focused our efforts on obtaining responses from the entire population of 124 women in the program over a 15-month time period. Out of the female population in the boot camp program, we were successful at obtaining consent from 122 (or 98.4%) of the women. One woman who did not participate could not understand or speak English, while another woman escaped from the facility prior to our weekly visit. Of approximately 1,200 males who entered the program during that time period, we collected questionnaire responses from 1,031 (or 85.9%) of the men offenders.

All data were collected directly from the participants themselves, who completed a paper-and-pencil questionnaire in the facility housing barracks within two weeks of their arrival. The male cohorts completed their surveys in a group setting with one trained researcher available to answer questions. The women participants completed their surveys individually with one trained research team member (recall that only two to three women entered the program weekly). We do not believe that the differences in the two data collection methods were significant enough to affect response reliability or validity. The benefits of obtaining a high response rate for the women outweighed any negative effects caused by conducting the men's questionnaire sessions in larger groups. A total of 1,153 usable questionnaires were completed, 10.6% by women respondents.

TABLE C.1: Sample Characteristics

Characteristic	Women (n = 122)	Men (n = 1,031)
Age (17-28 years)	20.6	19.5
Race/ethnicity (percentage)		
African American	44.3	44.4
Caucasian	45.1	31.4
Hispanic	10.7	23.8
Formal education (years)	10.5	10.3
Marital/partner attachment		
(percentage attached)	32.0	35.1
Number of children (percentage)		
None	46.7	69.8
One	30.3	21.3
Two	9.8	6.1
Three or more	13.1	2.9
Median household income (in dollars)	16,800	27,500
Current conviction (percentage)		
Drug	41.8	28.9
Person	19.7	19.5
Property	38.5	51.6

Sample Characteristics

The sample characteristics of the 1,031 men and 122 women indicated that the vast majority lived in the inner city or surrounding urban area at the time of arrest for their most recent conviction. Men and women were both between the ages of 17 and 28 years, with the average age calculated at 19.5 for men and 20.6 years for women. The African American composition of both samples was identical (44%). However, there were more Caucasian women (45.1%) than men (31.4%), and there were more Hispanic men than women (23.8% and 10.7%, respectively). The amount of formal education completed ranged between 6th grade and three years of higher education, with a mean of a 10th-grade education. Single/unattached women (68.0%) and men (64.9%) comprised the majority of the sample relative to married and cohabiting women and men.

The demographic differences between the men and women in the sample were number of children, median household income, and current conviction. First, about 46.7% of women and 69.8% of men had no dependent children. Of all the fathers and mothers, the women more often reported being the primary caretaker and sole financial respondent for the children. As primary caretakers, the women lived in households that generated much lower incomes than men. The median household income for women (most with children) was $16,800, while men's reported annual household income was $27,500.

As for the most recent conviction, crimes of violence were comparably represented by gender; in the sample, 19.7% of women and 19.5% of men were violent offenders. More women (41.8%) than men (28.9%) were convicted of a drug offense. Bear in mind that the offense type of each convicted offender (violent, property, or drug) does not represent felony crimes committed by men and women in prison. Even though women are increasingly being sentenced for felony drug offenses as a result of the war on drugs (Immarigeon and Chesney-Lind 1993;

U.S. Bureau of Justice Statistics 1994), our sample more closely resembles first-time felony offenders in other shock incarceration programs as an alternative to jail or prison incarceration (MacKenzie and Brame 1994).

Dependent Variables

Dependent variable measures for the analysis were originally derived from Elliott and Ageton's (1980) scale of delinquent behaviors offenses found in the National Youth Survey (NYS). The NYS is currently "the most highly respected self-report assessment of antisocial behavior" (Caspi et al. 1994). We adjusted certain measures to apply to our young adult sample. Respondents were asked whether they had ever committed 35 different deviant and criminal acts (Hindelang, Hirschi, and Weis 1981). Our prevalence dimension of crime measures offense participation or the number of crime types committed. Other researchers have preferred the use of the prevalence measure of variety:

> Variety scores are useful for individual-differences research for several reasons. First, they show the extent of involvement in different types of crimes. . . . Second, they are less skewed than frequency scores. Third, they give equal weight to all delinquent acts, unlike frequency scores, which give more weight to minor crimes that are committed more frequently (e.g., underage drinking) and less weight to serious, less frequent crimes (e.g., rape). (Caspi et al. 1994: 170-71)[4]

In the current study, one point was assigned if a respondent admitted involvement in a specific act; if respondents did not admit involvement, no points were assigned. The general crime scale was summed to obtain a composite score, which ranged from 0 to 35. Items in the general crime scale have been employed in previous tests of criminological theories using samples of adults (Burton et al. 1993, 1994, 1998). In addition, we distinguished type of criminal behavior by dividing the offenses into three subscales: violent, property, and drug. Table C.2 shows the means, standard deviations, and reliability for all dependent and independent variables used in the analysis.

Using Cronbach's (1951) alpha method, the 35-item general crime scale was reliable at .82 for women and .90 for men; the 15-item property crime subscale had a reliability level for women and men of .72 and .85, respectively; the 11-item drug subscale was .76 for women and .81 for men; and the 9-item violent crime subscale was reliable for females at .61 and .66 for males (see the appendix for individual offenses included in each subscale and accompanying frequencies separated by gender). Table C.2 shows that men admitted past involvement in an average of nine crimes: three drug offenses, four property crimes, and two violent crimes. Women engaged in an average of nine total crimes: four drug offenses, three property crimes, and two violent crimes. Although the property crime rate differed slightly for men and women, the types of drug offenses and violent crimes committed by both men and women were similar (see English 1993).[5]

Independent Variables

The items used in this study to measure social control and differential association variables were all drawn from previous theoretical tests (see Burton 1991; Burton et al. 1993,

TABLE C.2: Individual Dependent and Independent Variables by Gender

Variable	Number of Items	Women		Men		Sample F-Ratio
		Reliability	Mean (SD)	Reliability	Mean (SD)	
Dependent						
General crime	35	.82	8.57 (5.12) (range: 0-26)	.90	9.49 (6.85) (range: 0-31)	2.06
Violent crime	9	.61	1.64 (1.25) (range: 0-6)	.66	1.72 (1.70) (range: 0-9)	0.27
Property crime	15	.72	2.98 (2.60) (range: 0-11)	.85	4.19 (3.76) (range: 0-17)	11.99**
Drug crime	11	.76	3.96 (2.55) (range: 0-11)	.81	3.62 (2.72) (range: 0-11)	1.68
Independent						
Social control						
Marital/partner attachment	1	—	0.32 (0.47)	—	0.35 (0.48)	0.48
Parental attachment	3	.75	15.25 (2.98)	.64	14.87 (3.02)	1.77
Peer attachment	2	.81	6.84 (2.91)	.73	7.68 (2.79)	9.58**
Involvement	2	.69	6.44 (2.89)	.56	6.09 (2.69)	1.82
Belief	2	.63	8.88 (2.41)	.51	8.11 (2.40)	11.23**
Differential association						
Individual definitions	5	.77	10.97 (4.95)	.62	11.98 (4.52)	5.30*
Others' definitions	3	.71	9.50 (3.79)	.66	10.11 (3.61)	3.11
Criminal friends	1	—	2.87 (1.66)	—	2.77 (1.85)	0.30

*$p < .05$. **$p < .01$.

1994, 1998; Fiftal 1993; Matsueda 1982).[6] Participants in our sample responded to each item by using a 6-point Likert-type scale that ranged from *strongly agree* (6) to *strongly disagree* (1). Some responses were recoded so that a high score on an item indicated the presence of differential association or social control. The reliability of each composite independent theory measure was checked by Cronbach's (1951) alpha method. Finally, factor analysis was performed on each composite measure to ensure that each of the individual measures loaded on one factor. The mean, standard deviation, and reliability of each independent variable, separated by gender, can be found in Table C.2.

Social Control Theory

Hirschi's (1969) social control theory was originally formulated to rival differential association or "cultural deviance" theory as an explanation of why some juveniles conform and others engage in delinquency. More recent research has applied this perspective to adult criminality. Social control theory asserts that individuals with strong ties to family and friends (Covington 1985; Sampson and Laub 1990, 1993) will be protected from criminal involvement. In this study, we measure the adult social bond by marital attachment, attachment to parents, attachment to friends, involvement, and belief.[7]

Marital/partner attachment. Attachment to a significant other of the opposite sex by cohabiting or marriage is perceived as providing informal social control by protecting individuals from participation in criminal and other antisocial activities (Rand 1987; Sampson and Laub 1993). In our analysis, we use marital/partner attachment status as one of the adult social bond measures (0 = not married/unattached and 1 = married/ attached).

Attachment to parents. We include three items to measure attachment to parents to determine the effect of longstanding connections to parents by gender: "Throughout my life, I have had a lot of respect for my mother and father" (LaGrange and White 1985; Rosenbaum 1987). The second item asks whether respondents have "gotten along" well with their parents throughout their lives. This measure is modified from previous tests of social control (Eve 1978; Simons et al. 1980). The third component states, "My family is the most important thing in my life." The level of reliability for the attachment-to-parents scale is .75 for women and .64 for men.

Attachment to friends. The bond to friends is an important part of conventional attachment. The items used in the questionnaire yielded a reliability level of .81 for women and .73 for men. Respondents were asked to respond to the following two items: "It is important for me to spend time with my friends," and "My friends are a very important part of my life" (Agnew 1985; Burton 1991; Canter 1982; Friedman and Rosenbaum 1988; Hindelang 1973; Johnson, Marcos, and Bahr 1987; Matsueda 1982; Paternoster and Triplett 1988; Rosenbaum 1987).

Involvement. Involvement in conventional activities is measured by how much free time individuals have (Agnew 1985; Burton 1991; Canter 1982; Johnson 1979; Rosenbaum 1987). The following two items (reliable at .69 for women and .56 for men) were borrowed from Burton's (1991) study: "Between work, family, and community activities, I don't have much free time," and "Before coming here, I had a lot of free time on my hands."

Belief. Finally, the conventional bond is measured by moral belief in the law, specifically in the police, as measured by the following statement: "I have a lot of respect for the police" (Hindelang 1973; Hirschi 1969). The second item, "It is all right to get around the law if you can get away with it," was also used by Hirschi (1969) in previous tests. The two items have a reliability level of .63 for women and .51 for men.

Differential Association Theory

According to Sutherland's (1947) theory of differential association, individuals develop internalized definitions that are favorable or nonfavorable toward violating the law. As individual exposure to procriminal values, patterns, and associates increases, the likelihood of criminal involvement also increases. As in previous studies, we use three differential association variables to measure the likelihood of criminal exposure: individual definitions toward the law, others' definitions toward the law, and number of criminal friends.

Individual definitions toward crime. The five-item scale measuring individual definitions toward crime examined an individual's degree of tolerance for criminal behavior, the moral validity of violating the law, and the level of agreement with committing criminal acts.

Cronbach's (1951) alpha reliability for the scale for women is .77 and .62 for men. To measure disapproval toward violating the law, we asked for a response to the following item: "No matter how small the crime, breaking the law is a serious matter" (Akers et al. 1989; Jackson, Tittle, and Burke 1986; Short 1960). A second item, "It is morally wrong to break the law," also assessed anticriminal definitions (see Jackson et al. 1986; Matsueda 1989; Silberman 1976; Tittle et al. 1986). In contrast, to measure adults' willingness to violate the law, three items were included: "Sometimes you just don't have any choice but to break the law" (Krohn, Lanza-Kaduce, and Akers 1984; Short 1960), "If someone insulted me, I would be likely to hit or slap them," and "If breaking the law really doesn't hurt anyone, and you can make a quick buck doing it, then it's really not all that wrong" (Burton 1991).

Others' definitions toward crime. According to Sutherland (1947), criminal behavior is influenced primarily through exposure to other individuals holding definitions favorable toward violating the law. Relying on previous tests of differential association (Akers et al. 1979; Cressey 1953; Dull 1983; Griffen and Griffen 1978; Jaquith 1981; Johnson et al. 1987; Short 1960; Tittle et al. 1986), we included the following item: "Many of the people I associate with think it's okay to break the law if you can get away with it." The second item is designed to determine the type of people (criminal or noncriminal) with whom an individual associates. Thus, respondents were presented with the following item: "Most of the people I associate with would never break the law." In previous research, items similar to this have been related to delinquent involvement (Akers et al. 1989; Krohn et al. 1984; Jackson et al. 1986; Orcutt 1987). Finally, the third item assesses the extent to which individuals are "often in situations where people encourage [them] to do something illegal." This three-item scale has a reliability coefficient of .71 for women and .66 for men.

Criminal friends. Many empirical tests of differential association theory have relied on the number of criminal associates as evidence of interaction with criminal members within an individual's primary group (see, e.g., Akers et al. 1979; Dull 1983; Johnson et al. 1987; Warr and Stafford 1993; Winfree, Griffith, and Sellers 1989). In our study, we apply a measure of the actual number of criminal friends in our model by asking, "In the last 12 months, how many of your five closest friends have done something they could have gotten arrested for?"

FINDINGS

We assessed the bivariate relationships between the eight independent variables and crime by zero-order correlations. Tables C.3 and C.4 show that for the sample as a whole, all three of the differential association variables (individual definitions, others' definitions, and number of criminal friends) were significantly and directly correlated with property, violent, and drug offenses.[8] Similarly, these tables reveal that the social control variables of attachment to parents, involvement in conventional activities, and belief in the law were significantly and inversely correlated with criminal behavior. On the other hand, marriage reduced involvement only in property crime, and attachment to peers was positively correlated with all types of crime.[9]

TABLE C.3: Zero-Order Correlations of Theoretical Variables and Crime Scales (men)

	General Crime	Violent Crime	Property Crime	Drug Crime	Peer Attachment	Parental Attachment	Marital/Partner Attachment	Involvement	Individual Belief	Other Definitions	Criminal Definitions	Friends
General crime	1.00											
Violent crime	.75**	1.00										
Property crime	.91**	.60**	1.00									
Drug crime	.80**	.44**	.53**	1.00								
Peer attachment	.15**	.09**	.14**	.13**	1.00							
Parent attachment	-.23**	-.16**	-.22**	-.18**	-.05	1.00						
Marital/partner attachment	-.05	-.01	-.10**	-.00	-.07*	.04	1.00					
Involvement	-.19**	-.12**	-.20**	-.14**	-.10**	-.01	.10**	1.00				
Belief	-.25**	-.24**	-.20**	-.18**	-.02	.21**	-.02	.18**	1.00			
Individual definitions	.27**	.29**	.24**	.18**	.04	-.22**	-.02	-.17**	-.54**	1.00		
Others' definitions	.37**	.32**	.34**	.24**	.02	-.18**	-.07*	-.28**	-.29**	.28**	1.00	
Criminal friends	.39**	.30**	.37**	.29**	.02	-.12**	-.09**	-.22**	-.27**	.27**	.42**	1.00

*p < .05. **p < .01.

TABLE C.4: Zero-Order Correlations of Theoretical Variables and Crime Scales (women)

	General Crime	Violent Crime	Property Crime	Drug Crime	Peer Attachment	Parental Attachment	Marital/Partner Attachment	Involvement	Individual Belief	Other Definitions	Criminal Definitions	Friends
General crime	1.00											
Violent crime	.61**	1.00										
Property crime	.86**	.41**	1.00									
Drug crime	.83**	.32**	.50**	1.00								
Peer attachment	.32**	.13	.31**	.27**	1.00							
Parent attachment	-.35**	-.24**	-.33**	-.25**	-.12	1.00						
Marital/partner attachment	-.30**	-.09	-.29**	-.26**	-.20*	.08	1.00					
Involvement	-.26**	-.38**	-.13	-.19*	-.10	-.12	-.07	1.00				
Belief	-.22*	-.17*	-.19*	-.16	-.13	.27**	.10	.09	1.00			
Individual definitions	.28**	.23*	.21	.24**	.19*	-.20*	-.01	-.16	-.50**	1.00		
Others' definitions	.47**	.35**	.35**	.42**	.17	-.24**	-.00	-.32**	-.18*	.33**	1.00	
Criminal friends	.31**	.22**	.28**	.23**	.03	-.10	-.00	-.13	-.12	.14	.28**	1.00

*p < .05. **p < .01.

General Criminal Behavior and Gender

Following the bivariate analysis, we used ordinary least squares (OLS) regression to examine the effects of independent variables on dependent variables. The first dependent variable (general crime) was regressed on three control variables (age, race, and gender), five social control variables, and three differential association variables.[10] Race was dummy coded (white vs. non-white), while age was a continuous variable. Regression coefficients were determined with all variables entered simultaneously into the equation. Table C.5 shows the standardized and unstandardized regression coefficients for men and women when both theories were regressed against each other. Gender groups were analyzed both independently and together.

Social control. Table C.5 shows that three out of five social control variables were significantly related to the overall measure of criminal behavior for the sample. Attachment to peers was significantly and positively related to criminal behavior. Attachment to parents and involvement in conventional activities were significantly and inversely related to involvement in criminal behavior. Those who got along well with their parents and considered them an important part of their lives were less likely to engage in criminal behavior. Furthermore, respondents who were immersed in time-consuming activities (i.e., work, family, and community activities) were also less likely to commit crimes.

We conducted a difference of slopes test on the significant unstandardized regression coefficients and their corresponding standard errors to determine if any significant differences existed between men and women. When conducting a hypothesis test of two samples of this nature, we relied on the formula suggested by Paternoster et al. (1998).

TABLE C.5: Effects of Social Control and Differential Association Variables on General Crime: Standardized Betas (unstandardized *B* coefficients) Reported

Variable Name	Women (n = 122)		Men (n = 1,031)		Women and Men (N = 1,153)	
Social control						
Marital/partner attachment						
(0 = not attached)	.21	(2.27)**	.01	(.08)	.02	(.33)
Parental attachment	−.31	(−.53)**	−.09	(−.21)**	−.12	(−.32)**
Peer attachment	.07	(.12)	.06	(.16)*	.07	(.16)*
Involvement	−.24	(−.43)**	−.06	(−.16)*	−.07	(−.18)*
Belief	.03	(.05)	−.06	(−.17)	−.05	(−.15)
Differential association						
Individual definitions	.11	(.11)	.12	(.19)**	.12	(.17)**
Others' definitions	.18	(.31)*	.16	(.31)**	.16	(.30)**
Criminal friends	.16	(.50)*	.26	(.98)**	.26	(.94)**
Control variables						
Age	−.08	(−.15)	.03	(.08)	.01	(.04)
Gender (0 = male)	—	—	—	—	−.05	(−.93)
Race (0 = non-white)	.22	(2.23)**	.19	(2.75)**	.19	(2.64)**
R^2		.51		.29		.30

*$p < .05$. **$p < .01$.

We found that attachment to parents ($z = -2.214$) was a significantly stronger predictor of female ($b = -.533$; $SE = .129$) as opposed to male ($b = -.208$; $SE = .070$) crime participation. On the other hand, there were no significant differences between women and men and the level of involvement as a predictor of criminal participation. The effect, then, of involvement on participation in crime is similar for men and women.

One of the strongest predictors for a woman's involvement in crime was whether she lived with a mate or was married. The significance of this relationship was not in the predicted direction of social control theory, which would hypothesize that family relationships, including marriage, insulate against criminal involvement. On the other hand, marital attachment was not significant for predicting men's criminal behavior.

One factor that was significantly related to men's participation in crime was peer attachment. Young men who were attached to their friends were more likely to engage in criminal behavior—a relationship in the direction opposite to that predicted by social control theory. Other studies have interpreted peer attachment and increased criminal involvement as indirect support for differential association theory, depending on whether the friends were delinquent (Conger 1976).[11]

Differential association. In Table C.5, others' definitions and criminal friends significantly predicted both male and female involvement in crime. A difference of slopes test on criminal friends indicated there were no significant differences between women and men; the effect of criminal friends on participation in crime is similar for men and women.

Individual definitions, although in the expected direction for women, were significant only for men. Furthermore, for men, differential association variables had stronger effects than social control theory variables in predicting their participation in crime. For women, there was some tendency for the social control variables to have stronger effects. The overall explanatory power for both theories in the model for women was $R^2 = .51$ and for men was .29.

Control variables. Race/ethnicity significantly predicted criminal involvement for women and men. Specifically, Anglo men and women were more likely to have been involved in crime than non-white individuals. Age was not a significant predictor of overall rates of criminal behavior. To more precisely measure the nature of gender differences and similarities for overall crime, a separate *t*-test for independent samples was conducted using unstandardized partial regression coefficients while using gender as the grouping variable. Results indicated that the mean for the men (9.88) was significantly higher than for women (8.56) for the general crime scale.

Type of Criminal Behavior and Gender

Table C.6 shows the contribution of social control and differential association theories to individually and simultaneously explain young men's and women's involvement in drug, property, and violent crimes.

Social control. A consistent and significant predictor of all three crime types for women was parental attachment. Parental attachment was also significant in the direction predicted by

TABLE C.6: Effects of Social Control and Differential Association Variables on Drug, Property, and Violent Crime: Standardized Betas (and unstandardized coefficients) Reported

Variable Name	Drug Crime			Property Crime			Violent Crime		
	Women	Men	Sample	Women	Men	Sample	Women	Men	Sample
Social control									
Marital/partner attachment	.16 (.89)*	.04 (.24)	.06 (.33)*	.21 (1.17)**	-.04 (-.32)	-.02 (-.18)	.08 (.21)	.02 (.07)	.02 (.08)
Parental attachment	-.18 (-.15)*	-.06 (-.05)	-.06 (-.07)*	-.29 (-.26)**	-.10 (-.12)**	-.12 (-.18)**	-.29 (-.12)**	-.06 (-.04)*	-.10 (-.07)**
Peer attachment	-.02 (-.02)	.06 (.06)	.06 (.06)*	.15 (.14)	.06 (.08)*	.07 (.09)*	.01 (.00)	.06 (.04)	.05 (.03)
Involvement	-.22 (-.20)**	-.07 (-.07)*	-.09 (-.08)**	-.10 (-.09)	-.07 (-.10)*	-.07 (-.09)*	-.34 (-.15)**	.01 (.01)	-.02 (-.01)
Belief	.01 (.01)	-.08 (-.09)*	-.07 (-.08)*	.02 (.02)	-.02 (-.03)	-.02 (-.03)	.01 (.01)	-.05 (-.04)	-.04 (-.03)
Differential association									
Individual definitions	.11 (.06)	.08 (.05)*	.09 (.05)*	.06 (.03)	.10 (.08)**	.09 (.08)**	.09 (.02)	.15 (.06)**	.14 (.05)**
Others' definitions	.15 (.18)*	.08 (.06)*	.10 (.08)**	.14 (.21)*	.16 (.16)**	.15 (.15)**	.10 (.03)	.17 (.08)**	.16 (.07)**
Criminal friends	.15 (.22)*	.23 (.34)**	.22 (.33)**	.17 (.23)*	.24 (.50)**	.24 (.48)**	.05 (.04)	.18 (.17)**	.17 (.16)**
Control variables									
Age	.14 (.14)*	.16 (.20)**	.16 (.19)**	-.18 (-.18)*	-.06 (-.11)*	-.08 (-.13)**	-.23 (-.11)**	-.03 (-.02)	-.04 (-.03)
Gender (0 = male)	—	—	.01 (.06)	—	—	-.09 (-1.04)**	—	—	-.01 (.07)
Race (0 = non-white)	.44 (2.25)**	.26 (1.51)**	.28 (1.62)**	.03 (.14)	.13 (1.07)**	.12 (.96)**	-.07 (-.17)	.02 (.08)	-.00 (-.00)
R^2	.49	.23	.25	.40	.25	.26	.36	.18	.19

*$p < .05$. **$p < .01$.

social control theory for men's property and violent crime. Attachment to parents served as an effective insulator for men and women against criminal involvement, a finding consistent in delinquency studies (Burton et al. 1995). A difference of slopes test indicated that the effect of parental attachment ($z = -2.136$) was a significantly stronger predictor for women ($b = -.122$; $SE = .036$) than for men ($b = -.036$; $SE = .018$) for violent crime participation. The effect of parental attachment on property crime ($z = 1.62$) is similar for males and females since the difference was found to be not statistically significant.

Lack of involvement in conventional activities significantly predicted men's and women's participation in drug crime, as well as women's violent crime and men's property crime. Difference of slopes tests verified that lack of involvement in activities has similar effects for men's and women's involvement in drug crime and overall crime participation.

Marital attachment significantly predicted women's involvement in drug and property crimes but not in the direction predicted by social control theory. In other words, women who were married or living with a mate or boyfriend were more likely to be involved in drugs and/or property offenses. Marital attachment for men, however, did not insulate against or foster crime.

Differential association. For men, all three measures of differential association theory were significantly and positively related to all three types of crime. Thus, when criminal behavior was separated by type, differential association theory more consistently explained men's participation in drug, property, and violent criminal behaviors than did social control theory. For women, though, both differential association and social control theory were related to explaining female drug and property offenses, while social control variables were stronger predictors of women's participation in violent crime. Difference of slopes tests were conducted to detect significant effects on others' definitions and criminal friends between men and women. None of the differences was statistically significant for participation in property, drug, or overall crime. In other words, the effects of criminal friends and others' definitions on criminal participation were similar for men and women.

Control variables. Of the three control variables, age and race/ethnicity were the most consistent and strongest predictors of differences in rates of offending for men and women. As the age of male and female adults increased, involvement in drug crimes also significantly increased, while male and female property and female violent crimes significantly decreased. Anglo men and women were more likely to have been involved in drug crime than non-white men and women. Also, Anglo men were more likely than were African American and Hispanic men to have been involved in property crime.

The only type of crime that varied by gender was property offenses. Men were more likely than women to have committed crimes against property. For independent samples, *t*-tests were conducted for each of the three subscales, using unstandardized partial regression coefficients. Gender was used in each *t*-test as the grouping variable to more precisely measure the nature of gender differences and similarities for drug, property, and violent offenses. Results confirmed that the mean for the men (4.37) was significantly higher than for women (2.98) for the property crime subscale. However, for drug offenses, there was no difference between men (3.75) and women (3.94). The same held true for the violent crime subscale, in which men (1.77) were found to have a mean similar to that of women (1.64).

DISCUSSION

If psychology is sometimes referred to as the "science of college sophomores," then criminology might earn the label of the "science of high school sophomores"; while psychologists run experiments on their students, criminologists rely, over and over again, on samples of adolescents in school. To be sure, such self-report research is important and has considerably advanced our understanding of crime causation. Nonetheless, the skewness in focusing on adolescents and on minor delinquencies means that the applicability of criminological theory to serious and adult offending for men and women has been examined too infrequently.

A strategy employed episodically to rectify this omission has been to test theories on samples of convicted offenders, who have higher base rates of serious criminality (see, e.g., Covington 1985; Horney et al. 1995; Longshore et al. 1996; Sampson and Laub 1993). Building on this research, we have attempted to assess the generality of social control and differential association theories and to explain self-report crime across gender among first-time convicted felons serving a three-month sentence in a shock probation program, as an alternative to jail or prison incarceration. Several salient results were found.

First, both social control theory and differential association theory appear to have general effects. For the sample as a whole, the support for differential association is especially strong and consistent: The three differential association variables are significantly related to the general crime scale and to the drug, property, and violent crime subscales. Note that many studies that assess differential association use only the single measure of "number of delinquent peers." In a cross-sectional study, the peer-delinquency relationship is subject to the claim of spuriousness—that it is merely a case of "birds of a feather flocking together" (see Gottfredson and Hirschi 1990; Hirschi 1969). In our analysis, however, it is noteworthy that the attitudinal measures of others' definitions and one's own individual definitions also are related to all the crime scales for the sample. Some additional support for differential association theory can be drawn from the positive relationships of peer attachment to all the crime measures for the sample. This result is contrary to Hirschi's (1969) prediction. Furthermore, to the extent that the members of the sample are likely to have delinquent friends, then such attachment might be viewed as an indicator of differential association.

The findings for the social control measures are less impressive but nonetheless offer support for the perspective. Parental attachment had a consistent negative relationship to all of the crime measures for the sample. It appears, therefore, that bonds to parents have continuing effects on serious felons into early adulthood (Sampson and Laub 1993). Furthermore, with the exception of violent crime, involvement in conventional activities was negatively and significantly associated with the crime measures. Previous research on social control theory exploring the relationship between involvement and criminality has revealed mixed findings. While some studies have reported that involvement has few effects on offending (see, e.g., Hirschi 1969), others have found that involvement in conventional activities has a significant and inverse relationship both to minor forms of deviance (Agnew 1985; Friedman and Rosenbaum 1988; Rosenbaum 1987) and to adult offending behavior (Fiftal 1993; Lasley 1988).

Second, the analyses suggest that the "traditional" criminological perspectives can account for offending across the genders. This is not to say, however, that gender-specific theories could not expand our understanding not only of female crime but also of male criminal participation (see, e.g., Chesney-Lind 1989; Hagan 1989; Messerschmidt 1993). Still, the data reveal that differential association and social control variables—albeit with some variation—have similar effects across male and female felons. In fact, for every crime measure, the amount of explained variation is higher for the female sample than it is for the male sample. Furthermore, our results are consistent with a recent meta-analysis of predictors of criminal behavior, which reports that antisocial attitudes/associates and parental/family factors have similar effects for males and females (Andrews and Bonta 1994:68).

Some differences do emerge, however, when analyzing the effects of theoretical variables by gender. We should caution that making interpretations is difficult because the large sample size for the male offenders (1,031 men vs. 122 women) means that the analyses of the males have more power to detect statistically significant relationships. With this caveat stated, it appears that the differential association variables have consistent effects not only across crime types but also across male and female offenders. Only with individual definitions are any gender differences apparent; even here, the relationships, though not significant for women, are in the same direction.

In contrast, the effects of social control variables were stronger for the women than for the men in our sample. We found that the effects of parental attachment significantly and inversely affected males' offending, but the impact of parental attachment on females was significantly stronger for participation in violent offenses. This difference between men and women was not found for property crime, and parental attachment was not significant for male drug crime participation. The effect of a lack of parental attachment as a significant predictor of female violent crime is especially noteworthy for furthering our understanding of female offending.

Covington's (1985) analysis revealed that measures of social control theory were stronger predictors of adult women's criminal involvement. She suggests that as adolescents, females generally are exposed to more parental supervision than male adolescents. Thus, females may be more negatively influenced when familial relations are problematic or when parental supervision is reduced or nonexistent. Covington raises the additional possibility that these findings indicate differential perception of female and male adolescent offending by the juvenile justice system. While male adolescent offending may stem from a variety of causes, "many of the early female [juvenile] arrests may have been based on their detached and unsupervised status as juveniles rather than serious criminality" (Covington 1985:350).

We should note that with the exception of violent crime, being married or attached to a male partner was positively and significantly related to criminal involvement for women. For males, female partner attachment had no effects on any crime scale. The result for males is consistent with Sampson and Laub (1993), who found that marriage only had effects on their sample of former delinquents when marital quality is taken into account (see also Laub, Nagin, and Sampson 1998). Unfortunately, we do not have detailed information on the nature of the marital relationship to disentangle why marriage or attachment fosters criminality.

From a differential association perspective, it may be that the female felons in the sample are involved with men who reinforce their criminality. Research on battered women offenders found that being involved in intimate violent relationships was a main pathway to increasing the risk of offending (Richie 1996). Another possibility is that women from abusive, dysfunctional homes—those who are at a high risk for offending (see, e.g., Chesney-Lind 1989)—attempt to escape family victimization through early marriages and attachments (Miller 1986). These attachments, in turn, influenced the roles these women played in criminal behavior in relation to men (see Alarid et al. 1996). Future research should take into account the quality of the marital relationship, as well as the role that battering and intimate abuse have on subsequent involvement with the criminal justice system.

Another noteworthy finding is that for both males and females, being Caucasian was associated with higher rates of self-reported crime for every scale with the exception of violent offending. These differences could reflect racial differences in criminal justice processing: Compared to minorities, whites had to have more involvement in self-reported crime before being arrested and incarcerated.

An added finding that may have resulted from decisions made during prosecutorial and judicial case processing was the offending patterns of men and women. While men reported having committed more overall crime than women, particularly more property offenses, women and men did not differ significantly in the type and number of drug and violent crimes. These similarities may mean that judges who sentenced young, first-time felony offenders to shock incarceration as a prison alternative were impartial to gender.

In closing, the analyses reported here lend continuing support to the traditional theories of social control and, especially, differential association/social learning. Importantly, the data support the claim that these are "general" theories, explaining variations in self-report criminality among felony offenders and across men and women. As Cole (1975) demonstrates, however, the fate of crime and deviance theories does not always or usually hinge on their empirical vitality but on whether newer "paradigms" offer fresh research opportunities. New theories, of course, should be welcomed and their explanatory power assessed. But in doing so, we would caution that the value of "older" perspectives should be remembered and, as in our research, applied to underresearched topics.

APPENDIX   Prevalence of Self-Reported Criminal Behavior: "Have You Ever . . . ?"

	Women n (%)		Men n (%)	
Property crime subscale (15 items)				
1. Avoided paying at restaurants, the movie theater, etc.?	29	(23.8)	346	(33.7)*
2. Knowingly bought, held, sold stolen property?	50	(41)	531	(51.8)*
3. Taken someone else's vehicle without their permission?	33	(27)	379	(36.9)*
4. Taken anything ($5 or less) from your job?	11	(9)	152	(14.8)
5. Taken anything (between $5 and $50) from your job?	11	(9)	118	(11.5)
6. Taken anything (over $50) from your job?	3	(2.5)	102	(10.0)**
7. Taken anything ($5 or less) from someone (other than work)?	46	(37.7)	317	(31.0)
8. Taken anything (between $5 and $50) from someone (other than work)?	25	(20.5)	306	(30.0)*
9. Taken anything (over $50) from someone else (other than work)?	31	(25.4)	346	(33.7)

10. Damaged/destroyed property belonging to relative/family of origin?	15	(12.3)	166	(16.2)
11. Purposely damaged/destroyed property belonging to an employer?	2	(1.6)	59	(5.7)*
12. Purposely damaged/destroyed property belonging to spouse/partner/friend (someone other than family of origin or an employer)?	22	(18.0)	327	(31.9)**
13. Broken into a building/vehicle?	25	(20.5)	423	(41.2)**
14. Stolen or attempted to steal a motor vehicle?	19	(15.6)	314	(30.6)**
15. Thrown objects at cars/property?	41	(33.6)	419	(40.9)
Drug crime subscale (11 items)				
1. Drank alcoholic beverages before age 21?	92	(75.4)	788	(76.8)
2. Drove a car while drunk?	51	(41.8)	471	(46.0)
3. Bought/provided beer/liquor for someone under 21?	51	(41.8)*	340	(33.2)
4. Had marijuana/hashish?	86	(70.5)**	572	(55.8)
5. Used hallucinogens/LSD?	26	(21.3)	226	(22.0)
6. Had amphetamines?	17	(13.9)	129	(12.6)
7. Had barbiturates?	14	(11.5)	91	(8.9)
8. Had heroin?	6	(4.9)	32	(3.1)
9. Had cocaine?	60	(49.2)**	278	(27.1)
10. Sold marijuana?	34	(27.9)	359	(35.2)
11. Sold hard drugs (cocaine, crack, heroin)?	46	(37.7)	435	(42.5)
Violent crime subscale (9 items)				
1. Been involved in a gang fight?	25	(20.5)	232	(22.6)
2. Used physical force to get money from a relative/family of origin?	4	(3.3)	48	(4.7)
3. Used physical force to get money from someone at work?	1	(0.8)	35	(3.4)
4. Used physical force to get money from someone, a family member, or someone at work?	12	(9.8)	151	(14.7)
5. Hit or threatened to hit a relative/member of family of origin?	42	(34.4)	337	(32.9)
6. Hit or threatened to hit someone at work?	5	(4.1)	144	(14.0)**
7. Hit or threatened to hit friend/partner/spouse?	80	(65.6)**	528	(51.7)
8. Had or tried to have sex with someone against their will?	1	(0.8)	31	(3.0)
9. Attacked someone with the idea of seriously hurting/killing them?	30	(24.6)	264	(25.7)

NOTE: Women, $N = 122$; men, $N = 1,031$.

*$p < .05$. **$p < .01$.

NOTES

1. There have been several adult tests of social control and differential association measures assessed against deterrence, low self-control, social learning, strain, or subcultural theory measures (see, e.g., Burton et al. 1994; Ginsberg and Greenley 1978; Makkai and Braithwaite 1991; Tittle 1980).

2. Covington's (1985) tests of social control and differential association theories differed from the variables presented in this study. For example, involvement was not included as a social control variable, and individual definitions toward crime were not included as a differential association variable.

3. Strain theory, a fundamental perspective that also offers explanations on criminal behavior, was not included in the final analysis. Although Agnew's (1985) general strain theory has received some empirical support, Merton's (1938) social strain theory has received less support in previous studies. We originally included social strain variables that tested relative deprivation and blocked opportunities for both men and women in the data set. The variables measuring blocked opportunities were not reliable (.44) and were not used in the analysis. The variables measuring relative deprivation (reliable at .74) were regressed separately with all dependent crime variables. Relative deprivation was not significant for women for any type of crime and was significant only for male property crime but not for male drug or violent offenses. When relative deprivation was regressed against social control theory and/or differential association theory, relative deprivation had no effect for any type of crime.

4. Incidence data (how many times in the past year) were collected on all criminal behaviors but were not used due to a low reliability of the incidence subscales. The 35-item general crime incidence scale was, however, reliable at .61.

5. We are not suggesting that women are becoming more violent in their criminal involvement, especially as they relate to the women's self-reported involvement of violent crime, particularly the three "hit or threatened to hit" measures in the violent crime subscale (see appendix). The similarities in self-reported crime participation by women and men in our study can be accounted for in part by English (1993: 373), who found that incarcerated adult women and men prisoners had similar participation rates for assault, robbery, motor vehicle theft, fraud, and dealing drugs. Our data show, however, that women and men participate in a wide variety of criminal behaviors, from less serious to more serious, which may or may not be related to their conviction offense.

6. A potential weakness of our measures is the varying time frame of our independent and dependent variables (e.g., the time frame for "peer attachment" and "marital attachment" is current, the time frame for "criminal friends" is in the past year, while the time frame for the dependent measure of prevalence is lifetime). We are largely assuming that our measures of our independent variables are relatively stable over time. Furthermore, we believe that our analysis has merit despite these issues. Future research would benefit from longitudinal analysis to determine the stability of theoretical variables over time.

7. Commitment, an element of Hirschi's (1969) social bond, was not used in the analysis due to its low reliability.

8. Men and women were also analyzed separately using correlations between differential association variables with the dependent variables. Our analyses revealed that a significant correlation existed between all variables. For the sample as a whole, the three differential association measures are more highly correlated with each other than are the five measures of social control. This may increase the likelihood of finding greater consistency with differential association measures.

9. When bivariate correlations were analyzed separately by gender, a mixed portrayal emerged for social control variables. Attachment to parents for both men and women was significantly and inversely related to all types of crime. For men, attachment to friends, involvement, and belief were significantly related to all crime types, with the exception of marital attachment, which was significant only for property crime. For women, attachment to friends and marital attachment were related to drug and property crimes but not violent crime. On the other hand, involvement was significantly related to women's drug and violent crimes but not women's property offenses. Finally, belief was significantly related to women's property crime and violent crime but was not significantly related to women's drug crime.

10. We separately analyzed the control variables with each of the theories before regressing them together as shown in Table C.5. The results of the separate regressions show a significant relationship between age, race, and self-reported offending behavior. Age was inversely related to crime—that is, as age increased, less crime was committed. Men and women of color reported they committed significantly less crime than did Caucasian men and women. When social control theory was introduced into the equation with the three control variables, all social control variables, except for marital attachment, were significantly related to criminal offending. All social control variables were significant in the predicted direction, except for attachment to friends. When social control variables were removed and differential association variables were regressed with the three control variables, all three differential association variables were significantly and directly related to crime in the predicted direction.

11. To detect the presence of an interaction between peer attachment and criminal friends, we introduced a multiplicative term into each regression equation. A hierarchical F-test indicated that an interaction effect was not present for women, but an interaction existed for men for drug, property, and general crime scales (Jaccard, Turrisi, and Wan 1990). The difference between the R^2 values in the main effect and interactive models indicated that the interaction contributed less than 1 percent to each model (.63 percent for drug, .89 percent for general crime, and .90 percent for property offenses).

REFERENCES

Adler, Freda. 1975. *Sisters in Crime: The Rise of the New Female Offender.* New York: McGraw-Hill.

Agnew, Robert. 1985. "Social Control Theory and Delinquency: A Longitudinal Test." *Criminology* 23:47-61.

Akers, Ronald L. 1996. "Is Differential Association/Social Learning Cultural Deviance Theory?" *Criminology* 34:229-47.

_____. 1998. *Social Learning and Social Structure: A General Theory of Crime and Deviance.* Boston: Northeastern University Press.

Akers, Ronald L., Marvin Krohn, Lonn Lanza-Kaduce, and Marcia Radosevich. 1979. "Social Learning and Deviant Behavior: A Specific Test of a General Theory." *American Sociological Review* 44:636-55.

Akers, Ronald L., and Anthony LaGreca. 1988. "Alcohol, Contact with the Legal System, and Illegal Behavior among the Elderly." In *Older Offenders,* edited by Belinda Mccarthy and Robert Langworthy. New York: Praeger.

_____. 1991. "Alcohol Use among the Elderly: Social Learning, Community Context, and Life Events." In *Society, Culture, and Drinking Patterns Re-Examined,* edited by David J. Pittman and Helene Raskin White. New Brunswick, NJ: Rutgers Center of Alcohol Studies.

Akers, Ronald L., Anthony LaGreca, John Cochran, and Christine Sellers. 1989. "Social Learning Theory and Alcohol Behavior among the Elderly." *Sociological Quarterly* 30:625-38.

Alarid, Leanne Fiftal, Velmer S. Burton, James W. Marquart, Francis T. Cullen, and Steven J. Cuvelier. 1996. "Women's Roles in Serious Offenses: A Study of Adult Felons." *Justice Quarterly* 13:431-54.

Andrews, D. A., and James Bonta. 1994. *The Psychology of Criminal Conduct.* Cincinnati, OH: Anderson.

Benda, Brent B. 1994. "Testing Competing Theoretical Concepts: Adolescent Alcohol Consumption." *Deviant Behavior* 15:375-96.

Boeringer, Scot, Constance L. Shehan, and Ronald L. Akers. 1991. "Social Contexts and Social Learning in Sexual Coercion and Aggression: Assessing the Contribution of Fraternity Membership." *Family Relations* 40:558-64.

Burton, Velmer S. 1991. "Explaining Adult Criminality: Testing Strain, Differential Association, and Control Theories." Ph.D. dissertation, University of Cincinnati.

Burton, Velmer S., Francis T. Cullen, T. David Evans, Leanne Fiftal Alarid, and R. Gregory Dunaway. 1998. "Gender, Self-Control, and Crime." *Journal of Research in Crime and Delinquency* 35:123-47.

Burton, Velmer S., Francis T. Cullen, T. David Evans, and R. Gregory Dunaway. 1994. "Reconsidering Strain Theory: Operationalization, Rival Theories, and Adult Criminality." *Journal of Quantitative Criminology* 10:213-40.

Burton, Velmer S., Francis T. Cullen, T. David Evans, R. Gregory Dunaway, Sesha R. Kethineni, and Gary L. Payne. 1995. "The Impact of Parental Controls on Delinquency." *Journal of Criminal Justice* 23:111-26.

Burton, Velmer S., James W. Marquart, Steven J. Cuvelier, Robert J. Hunter, and Leanne Fiftal. 1993. "The Harris County CRIPP Program: An Outline for Evaluation, Part 1." *Texas Probation* 8:1-8.

Canter, Rachelle J. 1982. "Family Correlates of Male and Female Delinquency." *Criminology* 20:149-67.

Caspi, Avshalom, Terrie E. Moffitt, Phil A. Silva, Magda Stouthamer-Loeber, Robert F. Krueger, and Pamela S. Schmutte. 1994. "Are Some People Crime Prone? Replications of the Personality-Crime Relationship across Countries, Genders, Races, and Methods." *Criminology* 32:163-95.

Chesney-Lind, Meda. 1989. "Girls' Crime and Woman's Place: Toward a Feminist Model of Female Delinquency." *Crime & Delinquency* 35:5-29.

Chesney-Lind, Meda, and Randall G. Shelden. 1992. *Girls, Delinquency, and Juvenile Justice.* Pacific Grove, CA: Brooks/Cole.

Cole, Stephen. 1975. "The Growth of Scientific Knowledge: Theories of Deviance as a Case Study." In *The Idea of Social Structure: Papers in Honor of Robert K. Merton,* edited by Lewis A. Coser. New York: Harcourt Brace.

Conger, Rand. 1976. "Social Control and Social Learning Models of Delinquency: A Synthesis." *Criminology* 14:17-40.

Costello, Barbara. 1997. "On the Logical Adequacy of Cultural Deviance Theories." *Theoretical Criminology* 1:403-28.

Covington, Jeanette. 1985. "Gender Differences in Criminality among Heroin Users." *Journal of Research in Crime and Delinquency* 22:329-53.

Cressey, Donald. 1953. *Other People's Money.* Glencoe, IL: Free Press.

Cronbach, Lee J. 1951. "Coefficient Alpha and the Internal Structure of Tests." *Psychometrika* 16:297-334.

Daly, Kathleen, and Meda Chesney-Lind. 1988. "Feminism and Criminology." *Justice Quarterly* 5:497-538.

Dull, R. Thomas. 1983. "Friend's Use and Adult Drug and Drinking Behavior: A Further Test of Differential Association Theory." *Journal of Criminal Law and Criminology* 74:1608-19.

Elliott, Delbert S., and Suzanne S. Ageton. 1980. "Reconciling Race and Class Differences in Self-Reported and Official Estimates of Delinquency." *American Sociological Review* 45:95-110.

English, Kim. 1993. "Self Reported Crime Rates of Women Prisoners." *Journal of Quantitative Criminology* 9:357-82.

Eve, Raymond. 1978. "A Study of the Efficacy of Interactions of Several Theories for Explaining Rebelliousness among High School Students." *Journal of Criminal Law and Criminology* 69:115-25.

Fiftal, Leanne E. 1993. "Assessing Adult Female Criminality: Testing Differential Association and Social Control Theories." Master's thesis, Sam Houston State University.

Friedman, Jennifer, and Dennis P. Rosenbaum. 1988. "Social Control Theory: The Salience of Components of Age, Gender, and Type of Crime." *Journal of Quantitative Criminology* 4:363-81.

Ginsberg, Irving J., and James R. Greenley. 1978. "Competing Theories of Marijuana Use: A Longitudinal Study." *Journal of Health and Social Behavior* 19:22-34.

Gottfredson, Michael R., and Travis Hirschi. 1990. *A General Theory of Crime.* Stanford, CA: Stanford University Press.

Griffin, Brenda S., and Charles T. Griffin. 1978. "Marijuana Use among Students and Peers." *Drug Forum* 7:155-65.

Hagan, John. 1989. *Structural Criminology.* New Brunswick, NJ: Rutgers University Press.

Heidensohn, Frances M. 1985. *Women and Crime.* New York: Macmillan.

Hindelang, Michael J. 1973. "Causes of Delinquency: A Partial Replication and Extension." *Social Problems* 20:471-87.

Hindelang, Michael J., Travis Hirschi, and Joseph G. Weis. 1981. *Measuring Delinquency.* Beverly Hills, CA: Sage.

Hirschi, Travis. 1969. *Causes of Delinquency.* Berkeley: University of California Press.

———. 1996. "Theory without Ideas: Reply to Akers." *Criminology* 34:249-56.

Horney, Julie, and Ineke Haen Marshall. 1992. "Risk Perceptions among Serious Offenders: The Role of Crime and Punishment." *Criminology* 30:575-94.

Horney, Julie, D. Wayne Osgood, and Ineke Haen Marshall. 1995. "Criminal Careers in the Short-Term: Intra-Individual Variability in Crime and Its Relation to Local Life Circumstances." *American Sociological Review* 60:655-73.

Immarigeon, Russ, and Meda Chesney-Lind. 1993. "Women's Prisons: Overcrowded and Overused." In *It's a Crime: Women and Justice,* edited by Roslyn Muraskin and Ted Alleman. Englewood Cliffs, NJ: Regents/Prentice Hall.

Jaccard, James, Robert Turrisi, and Choi K. Wan. 1990. *Interaction Effects in Multiple Regression.* Newbury Park, CA: Sage.

Jackson, Elton F., Charles R. Tittle, and Mary Jean Burke. 1986. "Offense-Specific Models of the Differential Association Process." *Social Problems* 33:335-56.

Jaquith, Susan M. 1981. "Adolescent Marijuana and Alcohol Use: An Empirical Test of Differential Association Theory." *Criminology* 19:271-80.

Johnson, Richard. 1979. *Juvenile Delinquency and Its Origins: An Integrated Theoretical Approach.* Cambridge, MA: Cambridge University Press.

Johnson, Richard E., Anastasios C. Marcos, and Stephen J. Bahr. 1987. "The Role of Peers in the Complex Etiology of Adolescent Drug Use." *Criminology* 25:323-40.

Kandel, Denise, and Mark Davies. 1991. "Friendship Networks, Intimacy, and Illicit Drug Use in Young Adulthood: A Comparison of Two Competing Theories." *Criminology* 29:441-69.

Kornhauser, Ruth. 1978. *Social Sources of Delinquency.* Chicago: University of Chicago Press.

Krohn, Marvin. 1995. "Control and Deterrence Theories of Criminality." In *Criminology: A Contemporary Handbook,* 2nd ed., edited by Joseph F. Sheley. Belmont, CA: Wadsworth.

Krohn, Marvin, Lonn Lanza-Kaduce, and Ronald Akers. 1984. "Community Context and Theories of Deviant Behavior: An Examination of Social Learning and Social Bonding Theories." *The Sociological Quarterly* 25:353-71.

LaGrange, Randy L., and Helene Raskin White. 1985. "Age Differences in Delinquency: A Test of Theory." *Criminology* 23:19-45.

Lasley, James R. 1988. "Toward a Control Theory of White-Collar Offending." *Journal of Quantitative Criminology* 4:347-62.

Laub, John H., Daniel S. Nagin, and Robert J. Sampson. 1998. "Trajectories of Change in Criminal Offending: Good Marriages and the Desistance Process." *American Sociological Review* 63:225-38.

Leonard, Eileen B. 1982. *Women, Crime, and Society: A Critique of Theoretical Criminology.* New York: Longman.

Longshore, Douglas, Susan Turner, and Judith A. Stein. 1996. "Self-Control in a Criminal Sample: An Examination of Construct Validity." *Criminology* 34:209-28.

Macdonald, Patrick T. 1989. "Competing Theoretical Explanations of Cocaine Use: Differential Association Versus Control Theory." *Journal of Contemporary Criminal Justice* 5:73-88.

MacKenzie, Doris Layton, and Robert Brame. 1994. "Shock Incarceration and Positive Adjustment during Community Supervision: A Multi-Site Evaluation." Presented at the annual meeting of the Academy of Criminal Justice Sciences, June, Chicago.

Makkai, Toni, and John Braithwaite. 1991. "Criminological Theories and Regulatory Compliance." *Criminology* 29:191-220.

Matsueda, Ross L. 1982. "Testing Control Theory and Differential Association: A Causal Modeling Approach." *American Sociological Review* 47:489-504.

_____. 1988. "The Current State of Differential Association Theory." *Crime & Delinquency* 34:277-306.

_____. 1989. "The Dynamics of Moral Beliefs and Minor Deviance." *Social Forces* 68:428-57.

_____. 1997. "'Cultural Deviance Theory': The Remarkable Persistence of a Flawed Term." *Theoretical Criminology* 1:429-52.

Matsueda, Ross L., and Karen Heimer. 1987. "Race, Family Structure, and Delinquency: A Test of Differential Association and Social Control Theories." *American Sociological Review* 52:826-40.

McGee, Zina T. 1992. "Social Class Differences in Parental and Peer Influence on Adolescent Drug Use." *Deviant Behavior* 13:349-72.

Merton, Robert. 1938. "Social Theory and Anomie." *American Sociological Review* 3:672-82.

Messerschmidt, James W. 1993. *Masculinities and Crime.* Lanham, MD: Rowman & Littlefield.

Messner, Steven F., and Richard Rosenfeld. 1994. *Crime and the American Dream.* Belmont, CA: Wadsworth.

Miller, Eleanor M. 1986. *Street Woman.* Philadelphia, PA: Temple University Press.

Naffine, Ngaire, and Fay Gale. 1989. "Testing the Nexus: Crime, Gender, and Unemployment." *British Journal of Criminology* 29:144-56.

Orcutt, James. 1987. "Differential Association and Marijuana Use: A Closer Look at Sutherland (with a Little Help from Becker)." *Criminology* 25:341-58.

Paternoster, Raymond, Robert Brame, Paul Mazerolle, and Alex Piquero. 1998. "Using the Correct Statistical Test for the Equality of Regression Coefficients." *Criminology* 36:859-66.

Paternoster, Raymond, and Ruth Triplett. 1988. "Disaggregating Self-Reported Delinquency and Its Implications for Theory." *Criminology* 26:591-625.

Rand, Alicia. 1987. "Transitional Life Events and Desistance from Delinquency and Crime." In *From Boy to Man: From Delinquency to Crime,* edited by Marvin Wolfgang, Terence P. Thornberry, and Robert M. Figlio. Chicago: University of Chicago Press.

Richie, Beth E. 1996. *Compelled to Crime: The Gender Entrapment of Battered Black Women.* New York: Routledge Kegan Paul.

Rosenbaum, James L. 1987. "Social Control, Gender and Delinquency: An Analysis of Drug, Property and Violent Offenders." *Justice Quarterly* 4:117-32.

Sampson, Robert J., and John H. Laub. 1990. "Crime and Deviance over the Life Course: The Salience of Adult Social Bonds." *American Sociological Review* 55:609-27.

_____. 1993. *Crime in the Making.* Cambridge, MA: Harvard University Press.

Short, James F. 1960. "Differential Association as a Hypothesis: Problems of Empirical Testing." *Social Problems* 8:14-24.

Silberman, Matthew. 1976. "Toward a Theory of Deterrence." *American Sociological Review* 41:442-61.

Simons, Ronald L., Martin G. Miller, and Stephen M. Aigner. 1980. "Contemporary Theories of Deviance and Female Delinquency: An Empirical Test." *Journal of Research in Crime and Delinquency* 17:42-57.

Smart, Carol. 1976. *Women, Crime and Criminology: A Feminist Critique.* Boston: Routledge Kegan Paul.

Sutherland, Edwin H. 1947. *Principles of Criminology.* 4th ed. Philadelphia, PA: Lippincott.

Sutherland, Edwin H., and Donald Cressey. 1955. *Principles of Criminology.* Philadelphia, PA: Lippincott.

Tittle, Charles R. 1980. *Sanctions and Social Deviance.* New York: Praeger.

Tittle, Charles, Mary Jean Burke, and Elton Jackson. 1986. "Modeling Sutherland's Theory of Differential Association: Toward an Empirical Clarification." *Social Forces* 65:405-32.

U.S. Bureau of Justice Statistics. 1994. *Special Report, March, 1994.* Washington DC: Government Printing Office.

Warr, Mark, and Mark Stafford. 1993. "Age, Peers, and Delinquency." *Criminology* 31:17-40.

Winfree, L. Thomas Curt, T. Griffiths, and Christine Sellers. 1989. "Social Learning Theory, Drug Use and American Indian Youths: A Cross-Cultural Test." *Justice Quarterly* 6:395-418.

Table of Random Numbers

Appendix D

Line/Col.	(1)	(2)	(3)	(4)	(5)	(6)	(7)	(8)	(9)	(10)	(11)	(12)	(13)	(14)
1	10480	15011	01536	02011	81647	91646	69179	14194	62590	36207	20969	99570	91291	90700
2	22368	46573	25595	85393	30995	89198	27982	53402	93965	34095	52666	19174	39615	99505
3	24130	48360	22527	97265	76393	64809	15179	24830	49340	32081	30680	19655	63348	58629
4	42167	93093	06243	61680	07856	16376	39440	53537	71341	57004	00849	74917	97758	16379
5	37570	39975	81837	16656	06121	91782	60468	81305	49684	60672	14110	06927	01263	54613
6	77921	06907	11008	42751	27756	53498	18602	70659	90655	15053	21916	81825	44394	42880
7	99562	72905	56420	69994	98872	31016	71194	18738	44013	48840	63213	21069	10634	12952
8	96301	91977	05463	07972	18876	20922	94595	56869	69014	60045	18425	84903	42508	32307
9	89579	14342	63661	10281	17453	18103	57740	84378	25331	12566	58678	44947	05585	56941
10	85475	36857	43342	53988	53060	59533	38867	62300	08158	17983	16439	11458	18593	64952
11	28918	69578	88231	33276	70997	79936	56865	05859	90106	31595	01547	85590	91610	78188
12	63553	40961	48235	03427	49626	69445	18663	72695	52180	20847	12234	90511	33703	90322
13	09429	93969	52636	92737	88974	33488	36320	17617	30015	08272	84115	27156	30613	74952
14	10365	61129	87529	85689	48237	52267	67689	93394	01511	26358	85104	20285	29975	89868
15	07119	97336	71048	08178	77233	13916	47564	81056	97735	85977	29372	74461	28551	90707
16	51085	12765	51821	51259	77452	16308	60756	92144	49442	53900	70960	63990	75601	40719
17	02368	21382	52404	60268	89368	19885	55322	44819	01188	65255	64835	44919	05944	55157
18	01011	54092	33362	94904	31273	04146	18594	29852	71585	85030	51132	01915	92747	64951
19	52162	53916	46369	58586	23216	14513	83149	98736	23495	64350	94738	17752	35156	35749
20	07056	97628	33787	09998	42698	06691	76988	13602	51851	46104	88916	19509	25625	58104
21	48663	91245	85828	14346	09172	30168	90229	04734	59193	22178	30421	61666	99904	32812
22	54164	58492	22421	74103	47070	25306	76468	26384	58151	06646	21524	15227	96909	44592
23	32639	32363	05597	24200	13363	38005	94342	28728	35806	06912	17012	64161	18296	22851
24	29334	27001	87637	87308	58731	00256	45834	15398	46557	41135	10367	07684	36188	18510
25	02488	33062	28834	07351	19731	92420	60952	61280	50001	67658	32586	86679	50720	94953
26	81525	72295	04839	96423	24878	82651	66566	14778	76797	14780	13300	87074	79666	95725
27	29676	20591	68086	26432	46901	20849	89768	81536	86645	12659	92259	57102	80428	25280
28	00742	57392	39064	66432	84673	40027	32832	61362	98947	96067	64760	64584	96096	98253
29	05366	04213	25669	26422	44407	44048	37937	63904	45766	66134	75470	66520	34693	90449
30	91921	26418	64117	94305	26766	25940	39972	22209	71500	64568	91402	42416	07844	69618
31	00582	04711	87917	77341	42206	35126	74087	99547	81817	42607	43808	76655	62028	76630
32	00725	69884	62797	56170	86324	88072	76222	36086	84637	93161	76038	65855	77919	88006
33	69011	65797	95876	55293	18988	27354	26575	08625	40801	59920	29841	80150	12777	48501

Line/Col.	(1)	(2)	(3)	(4)	(5)	(6)	(7)	(8)	(9)	(10)	(11)	(12)	(13)	(14)
34	25976	57948	29888	88604	67917	48708	18912	82271	65424	69774	33611	54262	85963	03547
35	09763	83473	73577	12908	30883	18317	28290	35797	05998	41688	34952	37888	38917	88050
36	91567	42595	27958	30134	04024	86385	29880	99730	55536	84855	29080	09250	79656	73211
37	17955	56349	90999	49127	20044	59931	06115	20542	18059	02008	73708	83317	36103	42791
38	46503	18584	18845	49618	02304	51038	20655	58727	28168	15475	56942	53389	20562	87338
39	92157	89634	94824	78171	84610	82834	09922	25417	44137	48413	25555	21246	35509	20468
40	14577	62765	35605	81263	39667	47358	56873	56307	61607	49518	89656	20103	77490	18062
41	98427	07523	33362	64270	01638	92477	66969	98420	04880	45585	46565	04102	46880	45709
42	34914	63976	88720	82765	34476	17032	87589	40836	32427	70002	70663	88863	77775	69348
43	70060	28277	39475	46473	23219	53416	94970	25832	69975	94884	19661	72828	00102	66794
44	53976	54914	06990	67245	68350	82948	11398	42878	80287	88267	47363	46634	06541	97809
45	76072	29515	40980	07391	58745	25774	22987	80059	39911	96189	41151	14222	60697	59583
46	90725	52210	83974	29992	65831	38857	50490	83765	55657	14361	31720	57375	56228	41546
47	64364	67412	33339	31926	14883	24413	59744	92351	97473	89286	35931	04110	23726	51900
48	08962	00358	31662	25388	61642	34072	81249	35648	56891	69352	48373	45578	78547	81788
49	95012	68379	93526	70765	10593	04542	76463	54328	02349	17247	28865	14777	62730	92277
50	15664	10493	20492	38391	91132	21999	59516	81652	27195	48223	46751	22923	32261	85653
51	16408	81899	04153	53381	79401	21438	83035	92350	36693	31238	59649	91754	72772	02338
52	18629	81953	05520	91962	04739	13092	97662	24822	94730	06496	35090	04822	86772	98289
53	73115	35101	47498	87637	99016	71060	88824	71013	18735	20286	23153	72924	35165	43040
54	57491	16703	23167	49323	45021	33132	12544	41035	80780	45393	44812	12515	98931	91202
55	30405	83946	23792	14422	15059	45799	22716	19792	09983	74353	68668	30429	70735	25499
56	16631	35006	85900	98275	32388	52390	16815	69298	82732	38480	73817	32523	41961	44437
57	96773	20206	42559	78985	05300	22164	24369	54224	35083	19687	11052	91491	60383	19746
58	38935	64202	14349	82674	66523	44133	00697	35552	35970	19124	63318	29686	03387	59846
59	31624	76384	17403	53363	44167	64486	64758	75366	72152	31601	12614	33072	60332	92325
60	78919	19474	23632	27889	47914	02584	37680	20801	05607	39339	34806	08930	85001	87820
61	03931	33309	57047	74211	63445	17361	62825	39908	73144	91284	68833	25570	38818	46920
62	74426	33278	43972	10119	89917	15665	52872	73823	16553	88662	88970	74492	51805	99378
63	09066	00903	20795	95452	92648	45454	09552	88815	86064	51125	79375	97596	16296	66092
64	42238	12426	87025	14267	20979	04508	64535	31355	00033	29472	47689	05974	52468	16834
65	16153	08002	26504	41744	81959	65642	74240	56302	33310	67107	77510	70625	28725	34191
66	21457	40742	29820	96783	29400	21840	15035	34537	33310	06116	95240	15957	16572	06004

(Continued)

Appendix D (Continued)

Line/Col.	(1)	(2)	(3)	(4)	(5)	(6)	(7)	(8)	(9)	(10)	(11)	(12)	(13)	(14)
67	21581	57802	02050	89728	17937	37621	47075	42080	97403	48626	68995	43805	33386	21597
68	55612	78095	83197	33732	05810	24813	86902	60397	16489	03264	88525	42786	05269	92532
69	44657	66999	99324	51281	84463	60563	79312	93454	68876	25471	93911	25650	12682	73572
70	91340	84979	46949	81973	37949	61023	43997	15263	80644	43942	89203	71795	99533	50501
71	91227	21199	31935	27022	84067	05462	35216	14486	29891	68607	41867	14951	91696	85065
72	50001	38140	66321	19924	72163	09538	12151	06878	91903	18749	34405	56087	82790	70925
73	65390	05224	72958	28609	81406	39147	25549	48542	42627	45233	57202	94617	23772	07896
74	27504	96131	83944	41575	10573	08619	64482	73923	36152	05184	94142	25299	84387	34925
75	37169	94851	39117	89632	00959	16487	65536	49071	39782	17095	02330	74301	00275	48280
76	11508	70225	51111	38351	19444	66499	71945	05422	13442	78675	84081	66938	93654	59894
77	37449	30362	06694	54690	04052	53115	62757	95348	78662	11163	81651	50245	34971	52924
78	46515	70331	85922	38329	57015	15765	97161	17869	45349	61796	66345	81073	49106	79860
79	30986	81223	42416	58353	21532	30502	32305	86482	05174	07901	54339	58861	74818	46942
80	63798	64995	46583	09765	44160	78128	83991	42865	92520	83531	80377	35909	81250	54238
81	82486	84846	99254	67632	43218	50076	21361	64816	51202	88124	41870	52689	51275	83556
82	21885	32906	92431	09060	64297	51674	64126	62570	26123	05155	59194	52799	28225	85762
83	60336	98782	07408	53458	13564	59089	26445	29789	85205	41001	12535	12133	14645	23541
84	43937	46891	24010	25560	86355	33941	25786	54990	71899	15475	95434	98227	21824	19585
85	97656	63175	89303	16275	07100	92063	21942	18611	47348	20203	18534	03862	78095	50136
86	03299	01221	05418	38982	55758	92237	26759	86367	21216	98442	08303	56613	91511	75928
87	79626	06486	03574	17668	07785	76020	79924	25651	83325	88428	85076	72811	22717	50585
88	85636	68335	47539	03129	65651	11977	02510	26113	99447	68645	34327	15152	55230	93448
89	18039	14367	61337	06177	12143	46609	32989	74014	64708	00533	35398	58408	13261	47908
90	08362	15656	60627	36478	65648	16764	53412	09013	07832	41574	17639	82163	60859	75567
91	79556	29068	04142	16268	15387	12856	66227	38358	22478	73373	88732	09443	82558	05250
92	92608	82674	27072	32534	17075	27698	98204	63863	11951	34648	88022	56148	34925	57031
93	23982	25835	40055	67006	12293	02753	14827	22235	35071	99704	37543	11601	35503	85171
94	09915	96306	05908	97901	28395	14186	00821	80703	10426	75647	76310	88717	37890	40129
95	50937	33300	26695	62247	69927	76123	50842	43834	86654	70959	79725	93872	28117	19233
96	42488	78077	69882	61657	34136	79180	97526	43092	04098	73571	80799	76536	71255	64239
97	46764	86273	63003	93017	31204	36692	40202	35275	57306	55543	53203	18098	47625	88684
98	03237	45430	55417	63282	90816	17349	88298	90183	36600	78406	06216	95787	42579	90730
99	86591	81482	52667	61583	14972	90053	89534	76036	49199	43716	97548	04379	46370	28672
100	38534	01715	94964	87288	65680	43772	39560	12918	86537	62738	19636	51132	25739	56947

Source: Beyer (1968).

References

Abbott, Andrew. 1992. "From Causes to Events: Notes on Narrative Positivism." *Sociological Methods* 20 (May): 428–455.

Abbott, Andrew. 1994. "History and Sociology: The Lost Synthesis." In *Engaging the Past: The Uses of History Across the Social Sciences*, 77–112. Durham, NC: Duke University Press.

Abrams, Philip. 1982. *Historical Sociology.* Ithaca, NY: Cornell University Press.

Agnew, R. 1986. "Work and Delinquency Among Juveniles Attending School." *Journal of Criminal Justice* 9: 19–41.

Alarid, Leanne Fiftal, Velmer S. Burton, Jr., and Francis T. Cullen, 2000. "Gender and Crime Among Felony Offenders: Assessing the Generality of Social Control and Differential Association Theories." *Journal of Research in Crime and Delinquency* 37: 171–199.

Alfred, Randall. 1976. "The Church of Satan." In *The New Religious Consciousness,* edited by Charles Glock and Robert Bellah, 180–202. Berkeley: University of California Press.

Altheide, David L. and John M. Johnson. 1994. "Criteria for Assessing Interpretive Validity in Qualitative Research." In *Handbook of Qualitative Research,* edited by Norman K. Denzin and Yvonna S. Lincoln, 485–499. Thousand Oaks, CA: Sage.

Amenta, E. and J. D. Poulsen. 1994. "Where to Begin: A Survey of Five Approaches to Selecting Independent Variables for Qualitative Comparative Analysis." *Sociological Methods and Research* 23(1): 22–53.

American Sociological Association. 1997. *Code of Ethics.* Washington, DC: American Sociological Association.

Anderson, Elijah. 1999. *Streetwise: Race, Class, and Change in an Urban Community.* Chicago: University of Chicago Press.

Anderson, Elijah. 2003. "Jelly's Place: An Ethnographic Memoir." *Symbolic Interaction* 26: 217–237.

Archer, Dane and Rosemary Gartner. 1984. *Violence and Crime in Cross-National Perspective.* New Haven, CT: Yale University Press.

Asmussen, Kelly J. and John W. Creswell. 1995. "Campus Response to a Student Gunman." *Journal of Higher Education,* 66(5): 575–591.

Babor, Thomas F., Robert S. Stephens, and G. Alan Marlatt. 1987. "Verbal Report Methods in Clinical Research on Alcoholism: Response Bias and Its Minimization." *Journal of Studies on Alcohol* 48(5): 410–424.

Bachman, Ronet. 2000. "A Comparison of Annual Incidence Rates and Contextual Characteristics of Intimate Perpetrated Violence Against Women from the National Crime Victimization Survey (NCVS) and the National Violence Against Women Survey (NVAWS)." *Violence Against Women* 6(8): 839–867.

Bachman, Ronet and Linda Saltzman. 1995. "Violence Against Women: Estimates from the Redesigned National Crime Victimization Survey." *Bureau of Justice Statistics Special Report.* Washington, DC: U.S. Department of Justice.

Bandura, Albert, Dorothea Ross, and Sheila A. Ross. 1963. "Imitation of Film-Mediated Aggressive Models." *Journal of Abnormal and Social Psychology* 66: 3–11.

Barringer, Felicity. 1993. "Majority in Poll Back Ban on Handguns." *The New York Times,* June 4, p. A14.

Baskin, D. R. and I. B. Sommers. 1998. *Casualties of Community Disorder: Women's Careers in Violent Crime.* Boulder, CO: Westview Press.

Becker, Howard S. 1963. *The Outsiders: Studies in the Sociology of Deviance.* New York: Free Press.

Becker, Howard S. 1986. *Writing for Social Scientists.* Chicago: University of Chicago Press. (This can be ordered directly from the American Sociological Association, 1722 N Street NW, Washington, DC 20036, 202–833–3410.)

Bellah, Robert N., Richard Madsen, William M. Sullivan, Ann Swidler, and Steven M. Tipton. 1985. *Habits of the Heart: Individualism and Commitment in American Life.* New York: Harper & Row.

Bench, L. L. and T. D. Allen. 2003. "Investigating the Stigma of Prison Classification: An Experimental Design." *The Prison Journal* 83(4): 367–382.

Bennet, Lauren, Lisa Goodman, and Mary Ann Dutton. 1999. "Systematic Obstacles to the Criminal Prosecution of a Battering Partner: A Victim Perspective." *Journal of Interpersonal Violence.* 14: 761–772.

Beyer, William H. (Ed.). 1968. *CRC Handbook for Tables for Probability and Statistics,* 2nd ed. Boca Raton, FL: CRC Press.

Binder, Arnold and James W. Meeker. 1993. "Implications of the Failure to Replicate the Minneapolis Experimental Findings." *American Sociological Review* 58 (December): 886–888.

Black, Donald J. (Ed.). 1984. *Toward a General Theory of Social Control.* Orlando, FL: Academic Press.

Booth, Wayne C., Gregory G. Colomb, and Joseph M. Williams. 1995. *The Craft of Research.* Chicago: University of Chicago Press.

Boruch, Robert F. 1997. *Randomized Experiments for Planning and Evaluation: A Practical Guide.* Thousand Oaks, CA: Sage.

Braga, A. A., D. L. Weisburd, E. J. Waring, L. G. Mazerolle, W. Spelman, and F. Gajewski. 1999. "Problem-Oriented Policing in Violent Crime Places: a Randomized Controlled Experiment." *Criminology* 37(4): 541–580.

Brame, R. and D. L. MacKenzie. 1996. "Shock Incarceration and Positive Adjustment During Community Supervision: A Multisite Evaluation." In *Correctional Boot Camps: A Tough Intermediate Sanction,* edited by D. L. MacKenzie and E. E. Herbert, Washington, DC: National Institute of Justice, U.S. Department of Justice.

Brener, Nancy D., Thomas R. Simon, Etienne G. Krug, and Richard Lowry. 1999. "Recent Trends in Violence-Related Behaviors Among High School Students in the United States." *Journal of the American Medical Association* 282(5): 133–147.

Brewer, J. and Hunter, A. 1989. *Multimethod Research: A Synthesis of Styles.* Newbury Park, CA: Sage.

Bridges, George S. and Joseph G. Weis. 1989. "Measuring Violent Behavior: Effects of Study Design on Reported Correlates of Violence," In *Violent Crime, Violent Criminals,* edited by Neil Alan Weiner and Marvin E. Wolfgang, pp. 14–34. Newbury Park, CA: Sage.

Broder, David S. 2000. "Don't Toy With the Census." *Washington Post,* April 4, p. A29.

Bureau of Justice Statistics. 1994. *Sourcebook of Criminal Justice Statistics: 1994.* Washington, DC: U.S. Department of Justice.

Bureau of Justice Statistics. 1995. *Sourcebook of Criminal Statistics: 1995.* Washington, DC: U.S. Department of Justice.

Bureau of Justice Statistics. 2002. "Nation's Violent Crime Victimization Rate Falls 10 Percent." Press Release, September 9. Retrieved from www.ojp.usdoj.gov/bjs/pub/press/cv01pr.htm.

Bureau of Justice Statistics. 2006. "Prison Statistics." Retrieved from www.ojp.usdoj.gov/bjs/prisons.htm.

Burt, Martha R. 1996. "Homelessness: Definitions and Counts." Pp. 15–23 in *Homelessness in America,* edited by Jim Baumohl. Phoenix, AZ: Oryx.

Bushman, Brad J. 1995. "Moderating Role of Trait Aggressiveness in the Effects of Violent Media on Aggression." *Journal of Personality and Social Psychology* 69(5): 950–960.

Bushway, S. and P. Reuter. 1997. "Labor Markets and Crime Risk Factors." In *Preventing Crime: What Works, What Doesn't, What's Promising,* edited by L. W. Sherman, D. Gottfredson, D. MacKenzie,

J. Eck, P. Reuter, and S. Bushway. Unpublished report by the Department of Criminology and Criminal Justice, University of Maryland.

Butterfield, Fox. 1996. "After 10 Years, Juvenile Crime Begins to Drop." *The New York Times,* August 9, pp. A1, A25.

Buzawa, Eva S. and Carl G. Buzawa. 1996. *Domestic Violence: The Criminal Justice Response,* 2nd ed. Thousand Oaks, CA: Sage.

Campbell, Donald T. and M. Jean Russo. 1999. *Social Experimentation.* Thousand Oaks, CA: Sage.

Campbell, Donald T. and Julian C. Stanley. 1996. *Experimental and Quasi-Experimental Designs for Research.* Chicago: Rand McNally.

Campbell, Richard T. 1992. "Longitudinal Research." In *Encyclopedia of Sociology,* edited by Edgar F. Borgatta and Marie L. Borgatta, 1146–1158. New York: Macmillan.

Campbell, T. T. and D. W. Fiske. 1959. "Convergent and Discriminant Validity by the Multi-Trait, Multi-Method Matrix." *Psychological Bulletin* 56: 126–139.

Cantor, David. 1984. *Comparing Bounded and Unbounded Three and Six Month Reference Periods in Rate Estimation.* Washington, DC: Bureau of Social Science Research.

Cantor, David. 1985. "Operational and Substantive Differences in Changing the NCS Reference Period." In *Proceedings of the American Statistical Association, Social Statistics Section* (pp. 125–137). Washington, DC: American Statistical Association.

Cao, L., A. Adams, and V. J. Jensen. 1997. "A Test of the Black Subculture of Violence Thesis: A Research Note." *Criminology* 35(2): 367–379.

Catalano. Shannan. 2006. *Criminal Victimization, 2005.* (NCJ 214644.) Washington, D.C.: U.S. Department of Justice, Bureau of Justice Statistics.

Cavender, Gray and Lisa Bond-Maupin. 2000. "Fear and Loathing on Reality Television: An Analysis of *America's Most Wanted* and *Unsolved Mysteries.*" In *Criminology: Perspectives,* edited by Steven Cooper, 51–57. Bellevue, WA: Coursewise.

Chalk, Rosemary and Joel H. Garner. 2001. "Evaluating Arrest for Intimate Partner Violence: Two Decades of Research and Reform." *New Directions for Evaluation* 90:9–23.

Chen, H. 1990. *Theory-Driven Evaluations.* Newbury Park, CA: Sage.

Coffey, Amanda and Paul Atkinson. 1996. *Making Sense of Qualitative Data: Complementary Research Strategies.* Thousand Oaks, CA: Sage.

Converse, J. M. 1984. Attitude measurement in psychology and sociology: The early years. Pp. 3–40, in *Surveying Subjective Phenomena, vol. 2,* edited by Charles F. Turner and Elizabeth Martin. New York: Russell Sage.

Cook, Philip J. and John H. Laub. 1998. "The Epidemic in Youth Violence." In *Youth Violence: Crime and Justice* (vol. 24), edited by Michael Tonry and Mark H. Moore. Chicago: University of Chicago Press.

Cook, Thomas D. and Donald T. Campbell. 1979. *Quasi-Experimentation: Design and Analysis Issues for Field Settings.* Chicago: Rand McNally.

Costner, Herbert L. 1989. "The Validity of Conclusions in Evaluation Research: A Further Development of Chen and Rossi's Theory-Driven Approach." *Evaluation and Program Planning* 12: 345–353.

Davis, Ryan. 1999. "Study: Search Engines Can't Keep Up With Expanding Net." *The Boston Globe,* July 8, pp. C1 C3.

Dawes, Robyn. 1995. "How Do You Formulate a Testable Exciting Hypothesis?" In *How to Write a Successful Research Grant Application: A Guidance for Social and Behavioral Scientists,* edited by Willo Pequegnat and Ellen Stover, 93–96. New York: Plenum Press.

Decker, Scott H. and Barrik Van Winkle. 1996. *Life in the Gang: Family, Friends, and Violence.* Cambridge, England: Cambridge University Press.

Dentler, Robert A. 2002. *Practicing Sociology: Selected Fields.* Westport, CT: Praeger.

Denzin, Norman K. and Yvonna S. Lincoln. 1994. "Introduction: Entering the Field of Qualitative Research." In *Handbook of Qualitative Research,* edited by Norman K. Denzin and Yvonna S. Lincoln, 1–17. Thousand Oaks, CA: Sage.

Denzin, Norman K. and Yvonna S. Lincoln, ed. 2000. *The Handbook of Qualitative Research.* 2nd ed. Thousand Oaks, CA: Sage.

Dewan, Shaila K. 2004a. "As Murders Fall, New Tactics Are Tried Against Remainder." *The New York Times,* December 31, pp. A24–A25.

Dewan, Shaila K. 2004b. "New York's Gospel of Policing by Data Spreads Across U.S." *The New York Times,* April 26, pp. A1, C16.

Diamond, Timothy. 1992. *Making Gray Gold: Narratives of Nursing Home Care.* Chicago: University of Chicago Press.

Dillman, Don A. 1978. *Mail and Telephone Surveys: The Total Design Method.* New York: Wiley.

Dillman, Don A. 2000. *Mail and Internet Surveys: The Tailored Design Method,* 2nd ed. New York: John Wiley & Sons.

Duggan, Paul, Michael D. Shear, and Marc Fisher. 1999. "Killers Fused Violent Fantasy, Reality." *The Washington Post,* April 22, p. A1.

Dunford, Franklyn W., David Huizinga, and Delbert Elliott. 1990. "The Role of Arrest in Domestic Assault: The Omaha Police Experiment." *Criminology* 28: 183–206.

Ehrlich, I. 1975. "The Deterrent Effect of Capital Punishment: a Question of Life and Death." *American Economic Review* 65: 397–417.

Emerson, Robert M. (Ed.). 1983. *Contemporary Field Research.* Prospect Heights, IL: Waveland Press.

Emerson, Robert M., Rachel I. Fretz, and Linda L. Shaw. 1995. *Writing Ethnographic Fieldnotes.* Chicago: University of Chicago Press.

Erikson, Kai T. 1966. *Wayward Puritans: A Study in the Sociology of Deviance.* New York: Wiley.

Erikson, Kai T. 1967. "A Comment on Disguised Observation in Sociology." *Social Problems* 12: 366–373.

Farrington, David P. 1977. "The Effects of Public Labeling." *British Journal of Criminology* 17(2): 112–125.

Felson, Richard B., Allen E. Liska, Scott J. South, and Thomas L. McNulty. 1994. "The Subculture of Violence and Delinquency: Individual versus School Context Effects." *Social Forces* 73(1): 155–174.

Fenno, Richard F. Jr. 1978. *Home Style: House Members in Their Districts.* Boston: Little, Brown.

Fink, Arlene. 1998. *Conducting Research Literature Reviews: From Paper to the Internet.* Thousand Oaks, CA: Sage.

Fischer, Constance T. and Frederick J. Wertz. 2002. "Empirical Phenomenological Analyses of Being Criminally Victimized." In *The Qualitative Researcher's Companion,* edited by A. Michael Huberman and Matthew B. Miles, 275–304. Thousand Oaks, CA: Sage.

Fleury-Steiner, Benjamin. 2003. *Jurors' Stories of Death: How America's Death Penalty Invests in Inequality.* Ann Arbor: University of Michigan Press.

Fowler, Floyd J. 1988. *Survey Research Methods,* rev. ed. Newbury Park, CA: Sage.

Fowler, Floyd J. 1995. *Improving Survey Questions: Design and Evaluation.* Thousand Oaks, CA: Sage.

Fraker, Thomas and Rebecca Maynard. 1987. "Evaluating Comparison Group Designs with Employment-Related Programs." *Journal of Human Resources* 22(2): 194–227.

Gallup, G. 1986. *Public Opinion, 1985.* Wilmington, DE: Scholarly Resources Press.

Garner, Joel, Jeffrey Fagan, and Christopher Maxwell. 1995. "Published Findings from the Spousal Assault Replication Program: A Critical Review." *Journal of Quantitative Criminology* 11: 3–28.

Geertz, Clifford. 1973. "Thick Description: Toward an Interpretive Theory of Culture." Pp. 3–30 in *The Interpretation of Cultures,* edited by Clifford Geertz. New York: Basic Books.

Glaser, Barney G. and Anselm L. Strauss. 1967. *The Discovery of Grounded Theory: Strategies for Qualitative Research.* London: Weidenfeld and Nicholson.

Glover, Judith. 1996. "Epistemological and Methodological Considerations in Secondary Analysis." In *Cross-National Research Methods in the Social Sciences,* edited by Linda Hantrais and Steen Mangen, 28–38. New York: Pinter.

Goffman, Erving. 1961. *Asylums: Essays on the Social Situation of Mental Patients and Other Inmates.* Garden City, NY: Doubleday.

Goldfinger, Stephen M., Russell K. Schutt, Larry J. Seidman, Winston M. Turner, Walter E. Penk, and George S. Tolomiczenko. 1996. "Self-Report and Observer Measures of Substance Abuse Among Homeless Mentally Ill Persons in the Cross-Section and Over Time." *The Journal of Nervous and Mental Disease* 184(11): 667–672.

Goleman, Daniel. 1993. "Pollsters Enlist Psychologists in Quest for Unbiased Results." *The New York Times,* September 7, pp. C1, C11.

Gordon, Raymond. 1992. *Basic Interviewing Skills.* Itasca, IL: Peacock.

Gregg v. Georgia, 428 U.S. 153 (1976).

Grinnell, Frederick. 1992. *The Scientific Attitude,* 2nd ed. New York: Guilford Press.

Grossman, David C., Jolly J. Neckerman, Thomas D. Koepsell, Ping-Yu Liu, Kenneth N. Asher, Kathy Beland, Darin Frey, and Frederick P. Rivara. 1997. "Effectiveness of a Violence Prevention Curriculum among Children in Elementary School: A Randomized Controlled Trial." *The Journal of the American Medical Association* 277(20), 1605–1612.

Groves, Robert M. and Mick P. Couper. 1998. *Nonresponse in Household Interview Surveys.* New York: Wiley.

Gruenewald, Paul J., Andrew J. Treno, Gail Taff, and Michael Klitzner. 1997. *Measuring Community Indicators: A Systems Approach to Drug and Alcohol Problems.* Thousand Oaks, CA: Sage.

Guba, Egon G. and Yvonna S. Lincoln. 1989. *Fourth Generation Evaluation.* Newbury Park, CA: Sage.

Guba, Egon G. and Yvonna S. Lincoln. 1994. "Competing Paradigms in Qualitative Research." In *Handbook of Qualitative Research,* edited by Norman K. Denzin and Yvonna S. Lincoln, 105–117. Thousand Oaks, CA: Sage.

Gubrium, Jaber F. and James A. Holstein. 1997. *The New Language of Qualitative Method.* New York: Oxford University Press.

Gubrium, Jaber F. and James A. Holstein. 2000. "Analyzing Interpretive Practice." In *The Handbook of Qualitative Research,* 2nd ed., edited by Norman Denzin and Yvonna S. Lincoln, 487–508. Thousand Oaks, CA: Sage.

Hafner, Katie. 2005. "In Challenge to Google, Yahoo Will Scan Books." *The New York Times,* October 3, pp. C1, C4.

Hagan, John. 1994. *Crime and Disrepute.* Thousand Oaks, CA: Pine Forge Press.

Hage, Jerald and Barbara Foley Meeker. 1988. *Social Causality.* Boston: Unwin Hyman.

Hagedorn, John. 1988. *People and Folks.* Chicago: Lake View Press.

Haney, C., C. Banks, and Philip G. Zimbardo. 1973. "International Dynamics in a Simulated Prison." *International Journal of Criminology and Penology* 1: 69–97.

Hantrais, Linda and Steen Mangen. 1996. "Method of Management of Cross-National Social Research." In *Cross-National Research Methods in the Social Sciences,* edited by Linda Hantrais and Steen Mangen, 1–12. New York: Pinter.

Harding, Sandra. 1989. "Value-Free Research is a Delusion." *The New York Times,* October 22, p. E24.

Hart, Chris. 1998. *Doing a Literature Review: Releasing the Social Science Research Imagination.* London: Sage.

Heckathorn, Douglas D. 1997. "Respondent-Driven Sampling: A New Approach to the Study of Hidden Populations." *Social Problems* 44: 174–199.

Heimer, Karen and Stacy De Coster. 1999. "The Gendering of Violent Delinquency." *Criminology* 37(2): 277–318.

Herek, Gregory. 1995. "Developing a Theoretical Framework and Rationale for a Research Proposal." In *How to Write a Successful Research Grant Application: A Guide for Social and Behavioral Scientists*, edited by Willo Pequegnat and Ellen Stover, 85–91. New York: Plenum Press.

Hirschel, J. David, Ira W. Hutchison III, and Charles W. Dean. 1992. "The Failure of Arrest to Deter Spouse Abuse." *Journal of Research in Crime and Delinquency* 29(1): 7–33.

Hock, Randolph. 2004. *The Extreme Searcher's Internet Handbook: A Guide for the Serious Searcher.* Medford, NJ: CyberAge.

Hoover, Kenneth R. 1980. *The Elements of Social Scientific Thinking*, 2nd ed. New York: St. Martin's Press.

Howell, J. C. 2003. *Preventing and Reducing Juvenile Delinquency: A Comprehensive Framework.* Thousand Oaks, CA: Sage.

Hoyle, Carolyn and Andrew Sanders. 2000. "Police Response to Domestic Violence: From Victim Choice to Victim Empowerment." *British Journal of Criminology* 40:14–26.

Huberman, A. Michael and Matthew B. Miles. 1994. "Data Management and Analysis Methods." In *Handbook of Qualitative Research*, edited by Norman K. Denzin and Yvonna S. Lincoln, 428–444. Thousand Oaks, CA: Sage.

Humphrey, Nicholas. 1992. *A History of the Mind: Evolution and the Birth of Consciousness.* New York: Simon & Schuster.

Humphreys, Laud. 1970. *Tearoom Trade: Impersonal Sex in Public Places.* Chicago: Aldine.

Hunt, Morton. 1985. *Profiles of Social Research: The Scientific Study of Human Interactions.* New York: Russell Sage Foundation.

Huston, P. and C. D. Naylor. 1996. Health Services Research: Reporting on Studies Using Secondary Data Sources. *Canadian Medical Association Journal 155:* 1697–1702.

James. T. S. and J. M. Granville. 1984. "Practical Issues in Vocational Education for Serious Juvenile Offenders." In *Violent Juvenile Offenders: An Anthology,* edited by R. Mathias, P. DeMuro, and R. Allison, 486–506. San Francisco: National Council on Crime and Delinquency.

Jervis, Robert. 1996. "Counterfactuals, Causation, and Complexity." In *Counterfactual Thought Experiments in World Politics: Logical, Methodological, and Psychological Perspectives*, edited by Philip E. Tetlock and Aaron Belkin, 309–316. Princeton, NJ: Princeton University Press.

Johnson, Dirk. 1997. "Party Animals in Fraternities Face the Threat of Extinction." *The New York Times*, May 15, pp. A1, A29.

Kandakai, Tina L., James H. Price, Susan K. Telljohann, and Carter A. Wilson. 1999. "Mothers' Perceptions of Factors Influencing Violence in Schools." *Journal of School Health* 69(5): 189–205.

Kaplan, Fred. 2002. "NY Continues to See Plunge in Number of Felonies." *The Boston Globe,* April 15, p. A3.

Kaufman, Sharon R. 1986. *The Ageless Self: Sources of Meaning in Late Life.* Madison: University of Wisconsin Press.

Kennedy, David M., Anne M. Piehl, and Anthony A. Braga. 1996. "Youth Violence in Boston: Gun Markets, Serious Youth Offenders, and a Use-Reduction Strategy." *Law and Contemporary Problems* 59:147–196.

Kincaid, Harold. 1996. *Philosophical Foundations of the Social Sciences: Analyzing Controversies in Social Research.* Cambridge, UK: Cambridge University Press.

King, Gary, Robert O. Keohane, and Sidney Verba. 1994. *Scientific Inference in Qualitative Research.* Princeton, NJ: Princeton University Press.

Kobelarcik, E. L., C. A. Alexander, R. P. Singh, and G. M. Shapiro. 1983. "Alternative Reference Periods for the National Crime Survey." In *Proceedings of the American Statistical Association: Section on Survey Methods.* Washington, DC: American Statistical Association.

Koegel, Paul. 1987. *Ethnographic Perspectives on Homeless and Homeless Mentally Ill Women.* Washington, DC: Alcohol, Drug Abuse, and Mental Health Administration, Public Health Service, U.S. Department of Health and Human Services.

Kohn, Melvin L. 1987. "Cross-National Research as an Analytic Strategy." *American Sociological Review* 52: 713–731.

Kvale, Steinar. 1996. *InterViews: An Introduction to Qualitative Research Interviewing.* Thousand Oaks, CA: Sage.

Labaw, Patricia. 1980. *Advanced Questionnaire Design.* Cambridge, MA: ABT Books.

Lamott, Anne. 1994. *Bird by Bird: Some Instructions on Writing and Life.* New York: Anchor Books.

Larson, Calvin J. 1993. *Pure and Applied Sociological Theory: Problems and Issues.* New York: Harcourt Brace Jovanovich.

Lavrakas, Paul J. 1987. *Telephone Survey Methods: Sampling, Selection, and Supervision.* Newbury Park, CA: Sage.

Lempert, Richard. 1989. "Humility Is a Virtue: On the Publicization of Policy-Relevant Research." *Law and Society Review* 23: 146–161.

Lempert, Richard and Joseph Sanders. 1986. *An Invitation to Law and Social Science: Desert, Disputes, and Distribution.* New York: Longman.

Levine, J. P. 1976. The Potential for Crime Overreporting in Criminal Victimization Surveys. *Criminology* 14: 307–330.

Lewin, Tamar. 2001. "Income Education Is Found to Lower Risk of New Arrest." *The New York Times,* November 16, p. A18.

Lichtblau, Eric. 2000. "Crime Dip Levels Off; Assault, Rape Up." *The New York Times,* December 19, p. A2.

Liptak, Adam. 2004. "Long Term in Drug Case Fuels Debate on Sentencing." *The New York Times,* September 12, p. 16.

Litwin, Mark S. 1995. *How to Measure Survey Reliability and Validity.* Thousand Oaks, CA: Sage.

Locke, Lawrence F., Stephen J. Silverman, and Waneen Wyrick Spirduso. 1998. *Reading and Understanding Research.* Thousand Oaks, CA: Sage.

Lofland, John and Lyn H. Lofland. 1984. *Analyzing Social Settings: A Guide to Qualitative Observation and Analysis,* 2nd ed. Belmont, CA: Wadsworth.

Lynch, Michael and David Bogen. 1997. "Sociology's Asociological 'Core': An Examination of Textbook Sociology in Light of the Sociology of Scientific Knowledge." *American Sociological Review* 62: 481–493.

MacKenzie, D. L. 1994. "Results of a Multisite Study of Boot Camp Prisons." *Federal Probation* 58(2): 60–66.

MacKenzie, D. L., R. Brame, D. McDowall, and C. Souryal. 1995. "Boot Camp, Prisons and Recidivism in Eight States." *Criminology* 33(3): 401–430.

MacKenzie, D. L. and C. Souryal. 1995. "Inmate Attitude Change During Incarceration: A Comparison of Boot Camp with Traditional Prison." *Justice Quarterly* 12(2): 125–150.

Mangione, Thomas W. 1995. *Mail Surveys: Improving the Quality.* Thousand Oaks, CA: Sage.

Margolis, Eric. 2004. "Looking at Discipline, Looking at Labour: Photographic Representations of Indian Boarding Schools." *Visual Studies* 19: 72–96.

Martin, Lawrence L. and Peter M. Kettner. 1996. *Measuring the Performance of Human Service Programs.* Thousand Oaks, CA: Sage.

Martin, Linda G. and Kevin Kinsella. 1995. "Research on the Demography of Aging in Developing Countries." In *Demography of Aging,* edited by Linda G. Martin and Samuel H. Preston, 356–403. Washington, DC: National Academy Press.

Maxwell, Joseph A. 1996. *Qualitative Research Design: An Interactive Approach.* Thousand Oaks, CA: Sage.

McLellan, A. Thomas, Lester Luborsky, John Cacciola, Jeffrey Griffith, Frederick Evans, Harriet L. Barr, and Charles P. O'Brien. 1985. "New Data from the Addiction Severity Index: Reliability and Validity in Three Centers." *The Journal of Nervous and Mental Disease* 173(7): 412–423.

Merton, Robert K. 1983. "Social Structure and Anomie." *American Sociological Review* 3: 672–682.

Messner, Steven F. and Richard Rosenfeld. 1994. *Crime and the American Dream*. Belmont, CA: Wadsworth.

Miethe, T. D., W. C. Regoeczi and K. A. Drass. 2004. *Rethinking Homicide: Exploring the Structure and Process Underlying Deadly Situations*. Cambridge, MA: Cambridge University Press.

Milgram, Stanley. 1965. "Some Conditions of Obedience and Disobedience to Authority." *Human Relations* 18: 57–75.

Mill, John Stuart. 1872. *A System of Logic: Ratiocinative and Inductive*, 8th ed., vol. 2. London: Longmans, Green, Reader, & Dyer.

Miller, Delbert C. 1991. *Handbook of Research Design and Social Measurement*, 5th ed. Newbury Park, CA: Sage.

Miller, Jody. 2000. *One of the Guys: Girls, Gangs, and Gender*. New York: Oxford University Press.

Miller, Susan. 1999. *Gender and Community Policing: Walking the Talk*. Boston: Northeastern University Press.

Mills, C. Wright. 1959. *The Sociological Imagination*. New York: Oxford University Press.

Mohr, Lawrence B. 1992. *Impact Analysis for Program Evaluation*. Newbury Park, CA: Sage.

Monkkonen, Eric H. 1994. "Introduction." In *Engaging the Past: The Uses of History Across the Social Sciences*, 1–8. Durham, NC: Duke University Press.

Moore, Joan W. 1978. *Homeboys: Gangs, Drugs, and Prison in the Barrios of Los Angeles*. Philadelphia: Temple University Press.

Moore, Joan W. 1991. *Going Down to the Barrio: Homeboys and Homegirls in Change*. Philadelphia: Temple University Press.

Morrill, Calvin, Christine Yalda, Madeleine Adelman, Michael Musheno, and Cindy Bejarano. 2000. "Telling Tales in School: Youth Culture and Conflict Narratives." *Law & Society Review* 34: 521–565.

Mosher, Clayton. J., Terance D. Miethe, and Dretha M. Phillips 2002. *The Mismeasure of Crime*. Thousand Oaks, CA: Sage.

Mullins, Carolyn J. 1977. *A Guide to Writing and Publishing in the Social and Behavioral Sciences*. New York: Wiley.

National Institute of Alcohol Abuse and Alcoholism. 1994. "Alcohol-Related Impairment." *Alcohol Alert* 25 (July): 1–5.

National Institute of Alcohol Abuse and Alcoholism. 1997. "Alcohol Metabolism." *Alcohol Alert* 35 (January): 1–4.

National Opinion Research Center (NORC). 1992. *The NORC General Social Survey: Questions and Answers*. Chicago: National Data Program for the Social Sciences. Mimeographed.

National Victim Center and the Crime Victims Research and Treatment Center. 1992. *Rape in America: A Report to the Nation*. Arlington, VA: Author.

Neuendorf, Kimberly A. 2002. *The Content Analysis Guidebook*. Thousand Oaks, CA: Sage.

Newbury, D. 2005. Editorial: The Challege of Visual Studies. *Visual Studies 20:* 1–3.

Newport, Frank. 2000. "Popular Vote in Presidential Race Too Close to Call." Princeton: The Gallup Organization, December 13. Retrieved from www.gallup.com/poll/releases/pr001107.asp.

Nie, Norman H. and Lutz Erbring. 2000. *Internet and Society: A Preliminary Report*. Palo Alto, CA: Stanford Institute for the Quantitative Study of Society.

Novak, David. 2003. "The Evolution of Internet Research: Shifting Allegiances." *Online* 27: 21.

O'Dochartaigh, Niall. 2002. *The Internet Research Handbook: A Practical Guide for Students and Researchers in the Social Sciences*. Thousand Oaks, CA: Sage.

Orcutt, James D. and J. Blake Turner. 1993. "Shocking Numbers and Graphic Accounts: Quantified Images of Drug Problems in the Print Media." *Social Problems* 49 (May): 190–206.

Padilla, Felix M. 1992. *The Gang as an American Enterprise.* New Brunswick, NJ: Rutgers University Press.

Papineau, David. 1978. *For Science in the Social Sciences.* London: Macmillan.

Parlett, Malcolm and David Hamilton. 1976. "Evaluation as Illumination: A New Approach to the Study of Innovative Programmes." Pp. 140–157 in *Evaluation Studies Review Annual,* Vol. 1, edited by G. Glass. Beverly Hills, CA: Sage.

Pate, Anthony M. and Edwin E. Hamilton. 1992. "Formal and Informal Deterrents to Domestic Violence: The Dade County Spouse Assault Experiment." *American Sociological Review* 57: 691–697.

Paternoster, Raymond, Robert Brame, Ronet Bachman, and Lawrence W. Sherman. 1997. "Do Fair Procedure Matter? The Effect of Procedural Justice on Spouse Assault." *Law & Society Review 31*(1): 163–204.

Patton, Michael Quinn 1997. *Utilization Focused Evaluation: The New Century Text,* 3rd ed. Thousand Oaks, CA: Sage.

Patton, Michael Quinn. 2002. *Qualitative Research & Evaluation Methods,* 3rd ed. Thousand Oaks, CA: Sage.

Pepinsky, Harold E. 1980. "A Sociological on Police Patrol." In *Fieldwork Experience: Qualitative Approaches to Social Research*, edited by William B. Shaffir, Robert A. Stebbins, and Allan Turowetz, 223–234. New York: St. Martin's Press.

Peterson, R. A. 2000. *Constructing Effective Questionnaires.* Thousand Oaks, CA: Sage.

Phoenix, Ann. 2003. "Neoliberalism and Masculinity: Racialization and the Contradictions of Schooling for 11- to 14-Year-Olds." *Youth & Society* 36: 227–246.

Posavac, E. J. and R. G. Carey. 1997. *Program Evaluation: Methods and Case Studies.* Upper Saddle River, NJ: Prentice Hall.

Powell, Kenneth E., Lois Muir-McClain, and Lakshmi Halasyamani. 1995. "A Review of Selected School-Based Conflict Resolution and Peer Mediation Projects." *Journal of School Health* 65(10): 426–432.

Presley, Cheryl A., Philip W. Meilman, and Rob Lyerla. 1994. "Development of the Core Alcohol and Drug Survey: Initial Findings and Future Directions." *Journal of American College Health* 42: 248–255.

Pyrczak, F. 2005. *Evaluating Research in Academic Journals: A Practical Guide to Realistic Evaluation,* 3rd Ed. Glendale, CA: Pyrczak Publishing.

Punch, Maurice. 1994. "Politics and Ethics in Qualitative Research." In *Handbook of Qualitative Research*, edited by Norman K. Denzin and Yvonna S. Lincoln, 83–97. Thousand Oaks, CA: Sage.

Ragin, Charles C. 1994. *Constructing Social Research.* Thousand Oaks, CA: Pine Forge Press.

Regoli, R. M. and J. D. Hewitt. 1994. *Delinquency in Society: A Child-Centered Approach.* New York: McGraw-Hill.

Reiss, Albert J. Jr. 1971. *The Police and the Public.* New Haven, CT: Yale University Press.

Reiss, Albert J. and Jeffrey A. Roth. 1993. *Understanding and Preventing Violence.* Washington, DC: National Academy Press.

Reynolds, Paul Davidson. 1979. *Ethical Dilemmas and Social Science Research.* San Francisco: Jossey-Bass.

Richards, Thomas J. and Lyn Richards. 1994. "Using Computers in Qualitative Research." In *Handbook of Qualitative Research*, edited by Norman K. Denzin and Yvonna S. Lincoln, 445–462. Thousand Oaks, CA: Sage.

Richardson, Laurel. 1995. "Narrative and Sociology." In *Representation in Ethnography*, edited by John Van Maanen, 198–221. Thousand Oaks, CA: Sage.

Riedel, Marc. 2000. *Research Strategies for Secondary Data: A Perspective for Criminology and Criminal Justice.* Thousand Oaks, CA: Sage.

Riessman, Catherine Kohler. 2002. "Narrative Analysis." Pp. 217–270 in *The Qualitative Researcher's Companion,* edited by A. Michael Huberman and Matthew B. Miles. Thousand Oaks, CA: Sage.

Ringwalt, Christopher L., Jody M. Greene, Susan T. Ennett, Ronaldo Iachan, Richard R. Clayton, and Carl G. Leukefeld. 1994. *Past and Future Directions of the D.A.R.E. Program: An Evaluation Review.* Research Triangle, NC: Research Triangle Institute.

Rise, Eric W. 1995. *The Martinsville Seven: Race, Rape, and Capital Punishment.* Charlottesville, VA: University Press of Virginia.

Rives, Norfleet W. Jr., and William J. Serow. 1988. *Introduction to Applied Demography: Data Sources and Estimation Techniques.* Sage University Paper Series on Quantitative Applications in the Social Sciences, series no. 07–039. Newbury Park, CA: Sage.

Rosen, Lawrence. 1995. "The Creation of the Uniform Crime Report: The Role of Social Science." *Social Science History* 19: 215–238.

Rosenberg, Morris. 1968. *The Logic of Survey Analysis.* New York: Basic Books.

Rosenfeld, Richard, Timothy M. Bray, and Arlen Egley. 1999. "Facilitating Violence: A Comparison of Gang-Motivated, Gang-Affiliated, and Nongang Youth Homicides." *Journal of Quantitative Criminology* 15(4): 496–516.

Rossi, P. H. and H. E. Freeman. 1989. *Evaluation: A Systematic Approach*, 4th ed. Newbury Park, CA: Sage.

Rubin, Herbert J. and Irene S. Rubin. 1995. *Qualitative Interviewing: The Art of Hearing Data.* Thousand Oaks, CA: Sage.

Rueschemeyer, Dietrich, Evelyne Huber Stephens, and John D. Stephens. 1992. *Capitalist Development and Democracy.* Chicago: University of Chicago Press.

Sacks, T., McKendrick, K., DeLeon, G., French, M. T., and McCollister, K. E. 2002. Benefit-Cost Analysis of a Modified Therapeutic Community for Mentally Ill Chemical Abusers. *Evaluation & Program Planning, 25,* 137–148.

Sampson, Robert J. and Janet L. Lauritsen. 1994. "Violent Victimization and Offending: Individual-, Situational-, and Community-Level Risk Factors." In *Understanding and Preventing Violence: Vol. 3, Social Influences*, edited by Albert J. Reiss, Jr. and Jeffrey A. Roth, 1–114. Washington, DC: National and Academy Press.

Sampson, Robert J. and Stephen W. Raudenbush. 1999. "Systematic Social Observation of Public Spaces: A New Look at Disorder in Urban Neighborhoods." *American Journal of Sociology* 105: 603–651.

Sampson, Robert J., Stephen W. Raudenbush, and Felton Earls. 1997. "Neighborhoods and Violent Crime: A Multilevel Study of Collective Efficacy." *Science* 277: 918–924.

Sanchez-Jankowski, Martin. 1991. *Islands in the Street.* Berkeley, CA: University of California Press.

Savelsberg, Joachim L., Ryan King, and Lara Cleveland. 2002. "Politicized Scholarship? Science on Crime and the State." *Social Problems* 49: 327–348.

Schuman, Howard and Stanley Presser. 1981. *Questions and Answers in Attitude Surveys: Experiments on Question Form, Wording, and Context.* New York: Academic Press.

Sechrest, Lee and Souraya Sidani. 1995. "Quantitative and Qualitative Methods: Is There an Alternative?" *Evaluation and Program Planning* 18: 77–87.

Seltzer, Richard A. 1996. *Mistakes That Social Scientists Make: Error and Redemption in the Research Process.* New York: St. Martin's Press.

Shadish, William R. 1995. "Philosophy of Science and the Quantitative-Qualitative Debates: Thirteen Common Errors." *Evaluation and Program Planning* 18: 63–75.

Shadish, William R., Thomas D. Cook, and Laura C. Leviton, eds. 1991. *Foundations of Program Evaluation: Theories of Practice.* Thousand Oaks, CA: Sage.

Shaw, Clifford, R. and Henry D. McKay. 1942. *Juvenile Delinquency and Urban Areas.* Chicago: University of Chicago Press.

Shepherd, Jane, David Hill, Joel Bristor, and Pat Montalvan. 1996. "Converting an Ongoing Health Study to CAPI: Findings from the National Health and Nutrition Study." In *Health Survey Research*

Methods Conference Proceedings, edited by Richard B. Warnecke, 159–164. Hyattsville, MD: U.S. Department of Health and Human Services.

Sherman, L. W. 1992. *Policing Domestic Violence: Experiments and Dilemmas*. New York: Free Press.

Sherman, L. W. and Richard A. Berk. 1984. "The Specific Deterrent Effects of Arrest for Domestic Assault." *American Sociological Review* 49: 261–272.

Sherman, L. W., P. Gartin, and M. Buerger. 1989. "Hot Spots of Predatory Crime: Routine Activities and the Criminology of Place." *Criminology* 27: 27–56.

Sherman, L. W., D. Gottfredson, D. MacKenzie, J. Eck, P. Reuter, and S. Bushway. 1997. "Preventing Crime: What Works, What Doesn't, What's Promising." Unpublished report by the Department of Criminology and Criminal Justice, University of Maryland.

Sherman, L. W., Douglas A. Smith, Janell D. Schmidt, and Dennis P. Rogan. 1992. "Crime, Punishment, and Stake in Conformity: Legal and Informal Control of Domestic Violence." *American Sociological Review* 57: 680–690.

Sjoberg, Gideon and Roger Nett. 1968. *A Methodology for Social Research*. New York: Harper & Row.

Skocpol, Theda. 1984. "Emerging Agendas and Recurrent Strategies in Historical Sociology." In *Vision and Method in Historical Sociology*, edited by Theda Skocpol, 356–391. New York: Cambridge University Press.

Smith, J. 1991. A Methodology for Twenty-First Century Sociology. *Social Forces* 70: 1–17.

Sosin, Michael R., Paul Colson, and Susan Grossman. 1988. *Homelessness in Chicago: Poverty and Pathology, Social Institutions and Social Change*. Chicago: Chicago Community Trust.

Stake, Robert E. 1995. *The Art of Case Study Research*. Thousand Oaks, CA: Sage.

Straus, M. 1979. "Measuring Intrafamily Conflict and Violence: The Conflict Tactics (TC) Scale." *Journal of Marriage and the Family* 41: 75–88.

Straus, Murray A. and Richard J. Gelles. 1990. *Physical Violence in American Families: Risk Factors and Adaptations to Violence in 8,145 Families*. New Brunswick, NJ: Transaction Publishers.

Strunk, William, Jr., and E. B. White. 1979. *The Elements of Style*, 3rd ed. New York: Macmillan.

Sudman, Seymour. 1976. *Applied Sampling*. New York: Academic Press.

Tannenbaum, F. 1938. *Crime and the Community*. New York: Columbia University Press.

Thorne. Barrie. 1993. *Gender Play: Girls and Boys in School*. New Brunswick, NJ: Rutgers University Press.

Thrasher, Frederic. 1927. *The Gang: A Study of 1,313 Gangs in Chicago*. Chicago: University of Chicago Press.

Tjaden, Patricia and Nancy Thoennes. 2000. "Extent, Nature, and Consequences of Intimate Partner Violence." In *Findings from the National Violence Against Women Survey*. Washington, DC: National Institute of Justice, U.S. Department of Justice.

Toby, Jackson. 1957. "Social Disorganization and Stake in Conformity: Complementary Factors in the Predatory Behavior of Hoodlums." *Journal of Criminal Law, Criminology and Police Science* 48: 12–17.

Tourangeau, R. and Smith, T. W. 1996. "Asking Sensitive Questions: The Impact of Data Collection Mode, Question Format, and Question Context." *Public Opinion Quarterly* 60: 275–301.

Turabian, Kate L. 1967. *A Manual for Writers of Term Papers, Theses, and Dissertations*, 3rd ed., rev. Chicago: University of Chicago Press.

Turner, Charles F. and Elizabeth Martin (Eds.). 1984. *Surveying Subjective Phenomena* (vols. I and II). New York: Russell Sage Foundation.

Tyler, T. 1990. *Why People Obey the Law*. New Haven, CT: Yale University Press.

van de Vijver, Fons and Kwok Leung. 1997. *Methods and Data Analysis for Cross-Cultural Research*. Thousand Oaks, CA: Sage.

Van Maanen, John. 1982. "Fieldwork on the Beat." In *Varieties of Qualitative Research*, edited by John Van Maanen, James M. Dabbs, Jr., and Robert R. Faulkner, 103–151. Beverley Hills: Sage.

Venkatesh, Sudhir Alladi. 1997. "The Social Organization of Street Gang Activity in an Urban Ghetto." *American Journal of Sociology* 103: 82–102.

Vidich, Arthur J. and Stanford M. Lyman. 1994. "Qualitative Methods: Their History in Sociology Anthropology." In *Handbook of Qualitative Research*, edited by Norman K. Denzin and Yvonna S. Lincoln, 23–59. Thousand Oaks, CA: Sage.

Vigil, James Diego. 1988. *Barrio Gangs*. Austin: University of Texas Press.

Wallace, Walter L. 1983. *Principles of Scientific Sociology*. New York: Aldine.

Walters, Pamela Barnhouse, David R. James, and Holly J. McCammon. 1997. "Citizenship and Public Schools: Accounting for Racial Inequality in Education for the Pre-and Post-Disfranchisement South." *American Sociological Review* 62: 34–52.

Watson, Roy E. L. 1986. "The Effectiveness of Increased Police Enforcement as a General Deterrent." *Law and Society Review* 20(2): 293–299.

Webb, Eugene, Donald T. Campbell, Richard D. Schwartz, and Lee Sechrest. 1966. *Unobtrusive Measures: Nonreactive Research in the Social Sciences*. Chicago: Rand McNally.

Weber, Max. 1949. *The Methodology of the Social Sciences*, translated and edited by Edward A. Shils and Henry Finch. New York: Free Press.

Weber, Robert Philip. 1985. *Basic Content Analysis*. Beverly Hills, CA: Sage.

Wechsler, Henry, Andrea, Davenport, George Dowdall, Barbara Moeykens, and Sonia Castillo. 1994. "Health and Behavioral Consequences of Binge Drinking in College: A National Survey of Students at 140 Campuses." *JAMA: The Journal of the American Medical Association* 272(21): 1672–1677.

Weisburd, D., L. Maher, and L. Sherman. 1992. "Contrasting Crime General and Crime Specific Theory: The Case of Hot Spots of Crime." *Advances in Criminological Theory* 4: 45–69.

Weisburd, David, Stanton Wheeler, Elin Waring, and Nancy Bode. 1991. *Crimes of the Middle Class: White-Collar Offenders in the Federal Courts*. New Haven, CT: Yale University Press.

Weiss, Carol H. 1993. "Where Politics and Evaluation Research Meet." *Evaluation Practice* 14: 93–106.

Whyte, William Foote. 1943. *Street Corner Society: The Social Structure of an Italian Slum*. Chicago: University of Chicago Press.

Whyte, William Foote. 1991. *Social Theory for Social Action: How Individuals and Organizations Learn to Change*. Newbury Park, CA: Sage.

Williams, Kirk R. and Richard Hawkins. 1986. "Perceptual Research on General Deterrence: A Critical Review." *Law and Society Review* 20: 545–572.

Wines, Michael. 2006. "To Fill Notebooks, and Then a Few Bellies." *The New York Times,* August 27, Week in Review.

Wolcott, Harry F. 1995. *The Art of Fieldwork*. Walnut Creek, CA: AltaMira Press.

Wolf, N., C. L. Blitz, J. Shi, R. Bachman, and J. Siegel. 2006. "Sexual Violence Inside Prisons: Rates of Victimization." *Journal of Urban Health* 83: 835–846.

Wolfgang, Marvin E. and F. Ferracuti. 1967. *The Subculture of Violence*. London: Tavistock.

Wright, Richard and Scott Decker. 1994. *Burglars on the Job: Streetlife and Residential Break-ins*. Boston: Northeastern University Press.

Zaret, David. 1996. "Petitions and the 'Invention' of Public Opinion in the English Revolution." *American Journal of Sociology* 101: 1497–1555.

Glossary/Index